HIGH COU[illegible] CASE SUMMARIES

CRIMINAL PROCEDURE

Keyed to Israel, Kamisar, LaFave and King's
Casebook on Criminal Procedure,
2007 Edition

Memory Graphics by Stu Rees (www.stus.com)

Mat #40702897

610 Opperman Drive
St. Paul, MN 55123
1-800-313-9378

Printed in the United States of America

ISBN: 978-0-314-19001-7

Table of Contents

*

Alphabetical Table of Cases

*

CHAPTER TWO

The Nature and Scope of Fourteenth Amendment Due Process; The Applicability of the Bill of Rights to the States

Palko v. Connecticut

Instant Facts: Following Palko's (D) conviction for second-degree murder, the state (P) appealed numerous trial errors and received a new trial; the second trial proceeded over Palko's (D) objections that it was prohibited as double jeopardy and ended with Palko's (D) conviction for first-degree murder.

Black Letter Rule: Only those provisions of the Bill of Rights that are *implicit in the concept of ordered liberty* are applicable to the states through the Fourteenth Amendment.

Adamson v. California

Instant Facts: Adamson (D) was convicted of murder after the judge and prosecutor pointed out to the jury that Adamson (D) had not testified at trial, making no effort to explain the case against him.

Black Letter Rule: The Fifth Amendment's protection against self-incrimination does not apply to defendants in state prosecutions through the Fourteenth Amendment's Equal Protection Clause.

Duncan v. Louisiana

Instant Facts: Duncan (D) was denied his request for a jury trial on an assault charge because the Louisiana Constitution provided a right to jury trial only in felony cases.

Black Letter Rule: Under the Sixth Amendment, all criminal defendants have a constitutional right to trial by jury.

Palko v. Connecticut

(*Convicted Murderer*) v. (*Prosecuting State*)
302 U.S. 319, 58 S. Ct. 149, 82 L. Ed. 288 (1937)

THE FIFTH AMENDMENT'S PROHIBITION ON DOUBLE JEOPARDY DOES NOT APPLY TO THE STATES THROUGH THE FOURTEENTH AMENDMENT

■ **INSTANT FACTS** Following Palko's (D) conviction for second-degree murder, the state (P) appealed numerous trial errors and received a new trial; the second trial proceeded over Palko's (D) objections that it was prohibited as double jeopardy and ended with Palko's (D) conviction for first-degree murder.

■ **BLACK LETTER RULE** Only those provisions of the Bill of Rights that are *implicit in the concept of ordered liberty* are applicable to the states through the Fourteenth Amendment.

■ PROCEDURAL BASIS

Certiorari to review the defendant's conviction.

■ FACTS

Palko (D) was indicted for murder. At the conclusion of his trial, he was found guilty of second-degree murder and sentenced to life in prison. The State (P) appealed, arguing that evidence had been improperly excluded and that the jury was improperly instructed on the difference between first-and second-degree murder. The Connecticut Supreme Court agreed and ordered a new trial. Palko (D) argued that the new trial violated the Fourteenth Amendment's guarantee against double jeopardy. The state trial court overruled Palko's (D) objection. In the second trial, Palko (D) was convicted of first-degree murder and sentenced to death. The Connecticut Supreme Court affirmed.

■ ISSUE

Does the Fifth Amendment's prohibition of double jeopardy apply to the states through the Fourteenth Amendment?

■ DECISION AND RATIONALE

(Cardozo, J.) No. Not all constitutional guarantees afforded federal criminal defendants apply to state defendants through the Fourteenth Amendment. In prior cases, the Fifth Amendment's requirement that a capital or other serious crime be based on an indictment has been held not to apply to the states, yet the Fifth Amendment prohibition against self-incrimination has at times been held to apply to the states. The Sixth and Seventh Amendment requirements of a trial by jury in criminal and civil cases have not been held to strictly apply to the states. But the Fourteenth Amendment prohibits a state from enacting legislation abridging freedom of speech, religion, or the press. From a reading of these earlier cases, it is clear that some but not all constitutional safeguards ensured by the Fifth Amendment to defendants in federal court apply to trials in the state courts.

While the Court does not deny that all protections afforded under the Constitution are important, when applying them to the states, not all of them rise to the level such that encroachment by the states on those rights results in the withholding of justice. Only those protections that are essential to "the concept of ordered liberty" will be held to apply to the states through the Fourteenth Amendment. Allowing a state the right to appeal when a defendant was convicted of a lesser offense due to a trial error did not violate a fundamental principle of justice. Affirmed.

Analysis:

Palko was overruled thirty-two years later in *Benton v. Maryland*, 395 U.S. 784 (1969). While the holding of this case is no longer good law, it does serve to explain the process followed by the Court in eventually reaching the decision that the federal prohibition on double jeopardy must also apply to the individual states. It also serves to show how far judicial reasoning has come in the years since this case was decided.

■ CASE VOCABULARY

DOUBLE JEOPARDY CLAUSE: The Fifth Amendment provision stating, "nor shall any person be subject for the same offence to be twice put in jeopardy of life or limb."

FOURTEENTH AMENDMENT: The constitutional amendment, ratified in 1868, whose primary provisions effectively apply the Bill of Rights to the states by forbidding states from denying due process and equal protection and from abridging the privileges and immunities of U.S. citizenship.

Adamson v. California

(*Convicted Murderer*) v. (*Prosecuting State*)
332 U.S. 46, 67 S. Ct. 1672, 91 L. Ed. 1903 (1947)

THE FOURTEENTH AMENDMENT DOES NOT REQUIRE THE SAME PROTECTIONS AGAINST SELF-INCRIMINATION AS THE FIFTH

■ **INSTANT FACTS** Adamson (D) was convicted of murder after the judge and prosecutor pointed out to the jury that Adamson (D) had not testified at trial, making no effort to explain the case against him.

■ **BLACK LETTER RULE** The Fifth Amendment's protection against self-incrimination does not apply to defendants in state prosecutions through the Fourteenth Amendment's Equal Protection Clause.

■ **PROCEDURAL BASIS**

On appeal to the U.S. Supreme Court seeking review of the California Supreme Court's decision affirming Adamson's (D) conviction.

■ **FACTS**

Adamson (D) challenged his conviction for murder in a California (P) court. At his trial, both the prosecutor and the judge pointed out to the jury that Adamson (D) had failed to take the stand and explain the evidence against him, as permitted by state statute. Adamson (D) argued that these comments violated his constitutional right against self-incrimination under the Fifth Amendment.

■ **ISSUE**

Does the Fourteenth Amendment require that the protections against self-incrimination afforded by the Fifth Amendment extend to actions based on state law?

■ **DECISION AND RATIONALE**

(Reed, J.) No. Simply because the comments made by the California judge and prosecutor would not be permitted in a federal court does not mean they are prohibited in state court. The prohibition against self-incrimination in the Fifth Amendment is not automatically applied to the states through the Fourteenth Amendment. Previous courts have not held that the right against self-incrimination is a "right of national citizenship" or "a personal privilege or immunity secured by the Federal Constitution." A person is at once a citizen of the United States and a citizen of his or her home state. No state can act to take away the federal rights of its citizens. But a state is free to act with respect to the state rights and privileges of its citizens so long as in so doing it does not abridge those rights inherent in national citizenship. Since the protection against self-incrimination is not a privilege or immunity of national citizenship, a state need not protect it. The right to a fair trial is indeed a right protected by the Fourteenth Amendment; however, under *Palko*, the right to a fair trial does not require enforcement of the protection against self-incrimination, since it is not "implicit in the concept of ordered liberty."

Under the statutory scheme at issue here, the right to comment on the defendant's failure to testify and deny the evidence against him is limited. It does not permit a presumption of guilt, but rather affords the opportunity to draw a reasonable inference of guilt. While a defendant may have valid reasons for refusing to testify on his own behalf, the impact of the defendant's silence is uniquely in the control of the state responsible for the efficient administration of its criminal justice system. The defendant has a choice to remain silent or confront the evidence against him. When he chooses not to testify, he does so at his own peril. Affirmed.

■ CONCURRENCE

(Frankfurter, J.) In the past seventy years, many judges have reviewed the impact of the Fourteenth Amendment on the remainder of the Constitution. That the Fourteenth Amendment was a shorthand method for imposing the Bill of Rights on the states has never been advanced, though many of the Courts' members have been champions of "safeguarding and promoting the interests of liberty and human dignity." Instead, when a conviction presents itself to the Supreme Court raising questions of due process, the investigation is not to determine whether one of the first eight amendments has been violated, but rather whether the defendant's trial deprived him or her of due process under the Constitution. The determination cannot be made with reference to a list, but the standards are not so abstract as to allow the judges to decide cases according to their subjective assessment of the importance of the right at stake.

■ DISSENT

(Black, J.) The history of the Fourteenth Amendment would appear to provide a basis for the position that no state may deprive its citizens of the privileges and protections afforded by the Bill of Rights. Between selectively incorporating provisions of the Bill of Rights and incorporating none, selective incorporation is the lesser of two evils. However, to permit judges to select those guarantees of the Bill of Rights that should be granted to the citizens of the individual states frustrates the purpose of the Constitution and calls for judicial interpretation not of constitutional protections, but of principles of natural law that find no mention within the Constitution.

■ DISSENT

(Murphy, J.) The Bill of Rights should be carried over in full to the Fourteenth Amendment. However, beyond the Bill of Rights, the courts should be able to look at a proceeding where all the requirements of the Bill of Rights have been met and still determine when due process was lacking.

Analysis:

Adamson is another of the early cases in which the Court was faced with deciding which of the Constitutional safeguards of the Bill of Rights applied to the states by virtue of the Fourteenth Amendment. When the Court finally overruled this case in *Malloy v. Hogan*, 84 S. Ct. 1489, 1495 (1964), Justice Brennan explained that "[i]t would be incongruous to have different standards determine the validity of a claim of privilege based on the same feared prosecution, depending on whether the claim was asserted in a state or federal court. Therefore, the same standards must determine whether an accused's silence in either a federal or state proceeding is justified."

■ CASE VOCABULARY

RIGHT AGAINST SELF-INCRIMINATION: A criminal defendant's or a witness's constitutional right—under the Fifth Amendment, but waivable under certain conditions—guaranteeing that a person cannot be compelled by the government to testify if the testimony might result in the person's being criminally prosecuted. Although this right is most often asserted during a criminal prosecution, a person can also "plead the Fifth" in a civil, legislative, administrative, or grand-jury proceeding.

SELF-INCRIMINATION: The act of indicating one's own involvement in a crime or exposing oneself to prosecution, especially by making a statement.

Duncan v. Louisiana

(Convicted Assailant) v. *(Prosecuting Government)*

391 U.S. 145, 88 S. Ct. 1444, 20 L. Ed. 2d 491 (1968)

THE FOURTEENTH AMENDMENT INCORPORATES THE SIXTH AMENDMENT RIGHT TO A JURY TRIAL

■ INSTANT FACTS Duncan (D) was denied his request for a jury trial on an assault charge because the Louisiana Constitution provided a right to jury trial only in felony cases.

■ BLACK LETTER RULE Under the Sixth Amendment, all criminal defendants have a constitutional right to trial by jury.

■ PROCEDURAL BASIS

Certiorari to review the defendant's conviction.

■ FACTS

Duncan (D) was charged with simple assault in Louisiana state court. Duncan (D) requested a jury trial, which was denied because the Louisiana Constitution provided for jury trials only in felony cases. Duncan (D) was convicted and sentenced to sixty days in a local prison and a fine.

■ ISSUE

Is the Sixth Amendment's right to trial by jury incorporated in the Fourteenth Amendment?

■ DECISION AND RATIONALE

(White, J.) Yes. The Sixth Amendment guarantees all criminal defendants the constitutional right to a jury trial. The right to a trial by jury has long been considered "fundamental to the American scheme of justice." In the years leading up to the drafting of the Constitution, trial by jury had been a prominent right in England and was carried forward to the state constitutions of the original thirteen colonies as a protection against oppression by the government. In light of this historical perspective, the right to trial by jury is afforded to all state court criminal defendants if such a right would be afforded in a federal court. Reversed.

■ CONCURRENCE

(Black, J.) Not only is the Sixth Amendment incorporated in the Fourteenth Amendment, but all provisions of the Bill of Rights are applicable to the states. The Fourteenth Amendment forbids a state from enacting or enforcing "any law which shall abridge the privileges and immunities of the citizens of the United States." The right to claim the protections afforded by the Bill of Rights is a fundamental privilege of American citizens. The dissent's view that the Due Process Clause provides no "permanent meaning" and is left to the subjective interpretation of the Court on a case-by-case basis strips the Fourteenth Amendment of the protections established to limit governmental power by empowering judges to selectively determine from time to time which protections remain implicit in the concept of ordered liberty.

■ CONCURRENCE

(Fortas, J.) While states are bound by the Sixth Amendment's right to a jury trial, the states need not follow federal procedures governing the operation of trial by jury. Federal notions of due process do not infringe upon the construction of that term by the states. Principles of federalism require that states be free to determine for themselves how due process can be achieved, because federal practices like unanimous verdicts and twelve-member juries, for example, should not be thrust upon the states as long as the states otherwise maintain practices furthering the fundamental fairness required by the Fourteenth Amendment.

■ DISSENT

(Harlan, J.) The majority's decision to incorporate the Sixth Amendment is without logical reason. If the goal of the Fourteenth Amendment is to achieve fundamental fairness in the judicial system, there is no justifiable reason to hold that the requirements of the Sixth Amendment are necessary in every case considered by a state court, as not every case presents such unfairness. The Court offers no reason to declare the rights afforded by the Sixth Amendment to be fundamental, while other rights in the Bill of Rights are not. While the Fourteenth Amendment was never intended to incorporate any of the rights afforded in the Bill of Rights, *total* incorporation would at least provide a logical reason to support the Court's conclusion. The concepts of due process and liberty are evolving principles, not confined to any specific rights or protections that may change through time as society progresses. The Due Process Clause requires only that criminal trials in the states be fundamentally fair, and trial by jury is not necessarily a requirement for fairness. Without evidence of unfairness in the trial below, due process has not been offended and the conviction should be sustained.

Analysis:

Justice Black's concurring opinion argues for "total incorporation" of the Bill of Rights by the Fourteenth Amendment. Under this approach, the Due Process Clause extends each right protected by the Bill of Rights to the states, but creates no other rights. Refusing to apply total incorporation, the majority employed "selective incorporation," the process of selecting those rights deemed fundamentally fair to the administration of justice. While the "total incorporation" approach never gained support in the Supreme Court, many of the rights espoused in the Bill of Rights have been selectively incorporated over time.

■ CASE VOCABULARY

INCORPORATION: The process of applying the provisions of the Bill of Rights to the states by interpreting the Fourteenth Amendment's Due Process Clause as encompassing those provisions.

CHAPTER THREE

Arrest, Search and Seizure

Wolf v. Colorado

Instant Facts: The excerpt includes no factual background for this case.

Black Letter Rule: The Fourteenth Amendment incorporates the Fourth Amendment, restraining states from unreasonable searches and seizures.

Mapp v. Ohio

Instant Facts: Mapp (D) was convicted of possession of obscene materials after police broke into her home and seized the materials without a warrant.

Black Letter Rule: All evidence obtained by unreasonable searches and seizures in violation of the Fourth Amendment is inadmissible in state court.

United States v. Leon

Instant Facts: The excerpt includes no factual background for this case.

Black Letter Rule: The exclusionary rule does not bar use by the prosecution in its case-in-chief of evidence seized by law enforcement acting in reasonable reliance on a search warrant issued by a detached and neutral magistrate, even if subsequently found to be unsupported by probable cause.

Hudson v. Michigan

Instant Facts: Police entered Hudson's (D) home just seconds after knocking and announcing their presence, and Hudson (D) moved to suppress the evidence discovered in the resulting search.

Black Letter Rule: The exclusionary rule does not apply to suppress evidence obtained through a violation of the knock-and-announce rule.

Katz v. United States

Instant Facts: Katz (D) was convicted of transmitting gaming information via telephone based on evidence obtained by FBI agents who had attached a listening device to a public telephone.

Black Letter Rule: The Fourth Amendment protects all communications that a person does not knowingly expose to the public.

California v. Greenwood

Instant Facts: Greenwood (D) was arrested and charged with drug trafficking after the police searched his garbage without a warrant.

Black Letter Rule: An unreasonable search and seizure requires that the defendant have a subjective expectation of privacy in the property searched that is objective by society's standards.

Florida v. Riley

Instant Facts: Police observed Riley's (D) greenhouse from a helicopter 400 feet above his home.

Black Letter Rule: Surveillance from the airspace above a residence does not constitute a search for which a warrant is required under the Fourth Amendment.

United States v. Karo

Instant Facts: A federal agent installed a beeper in a container to be shipped to Karo (D) in order to track drug smuggling activity.

Black Letter Rule: Seizure of property requires a meaningful interference with a possessory interest.

Kyllo v. United States

Instant Facts: Federal agents used a thermal-imaging device from the street outside Kyllo's (D) residence to determine that the amount of heat emanating from the house was consistent with the presence of high-temperature lamps used to cultivate marijuana.

Black Letter Rule: The use of a device not used by the general public to obtain evidence emanating from the interior of a residence that cannot otherwise be obtained without physical intrusion constitutes a search.

United States v. White

Instant Facts: White (D) was convicted of drug charges based on the testimony of government agents who overheard incriminating conversations between the defendant and an informant by way of a listening device carried by the informant.

Black Letter Rule: A person bears the risk that communications with another regarding criminal activities will be transmitted, electronically or otherwise, to government agents.

Zurcher v. Stanford Daily

Instant Facts: The Stanford Daily (P) sought declaratory relief after the police obtained a search warrant to search for evidence potentially related to others' criminal activity.

Black Letter Rule: A warrant may issue to search any property, regardless of whether the occupant is suspected of a crime.

Aguilar -

Spinelli v. United States

Instant Facts: Spinelli (D) was convicted of gambling offenses proscribed by Missouri law and challenged the constitutionality of the warrant authorizing the FBI search that uncovered the evidence supporting his conviction.

Black Letter Rule: In order for a search warrant based on an informant's tip to be valid, the informant must declare either that he himself saw or perceived the fact or facts asserted or that the underlying circumstances surrounding his information sufficiently demonstrate its reliability.

Illinois v. Gates

Instant Facts: Police searched the defendants' home and car after obtaining a warrant based in part on an anonymous handwritten tip.

Black Letter Rule: Probable cause for a warrant resulting from an anonymous informant's tip can be adduced under the totality of the circumstances.

Maryland v. Pringle

Instant Facts: Pringle (D) was arrested after cocaine was found in the rear seat of a vehicle in which Pringle (D) was a front-seat passenger.

Black Letter Rule: Probable cause generally requires a reasonably particularized ground for belief of a defendant's guilt.

Maryland v. Garrison

Instant Facts: Garrison's (D) apartment was searched as a result of a lack or awareness that his apartment was separate from the premises identified in a search warrant.

Black Letter Rule: Good faith factual mistakes do not invalidate an otherwise valid search warrant.

Richards v. Wisconsin

Instant Facts: Police forcibly entered a hotel room without knocking and announcing their presence and seized drugs on the premises.

Black Letter Rule: In order to dispense with the knock-and-announce requirement, police must demonstrate their reasonable suspicion that application of the rule would be dangerous or futile or would result in destruction of evidence of the crime.

United States v. Watson

Instant Facts: Watson (D) was arrested without a warrant by a federal postal inspector as authorized by federal statute.

Black Letter Rule: Felony arrests may be made solely on the basis of probable cause, without a warrant.

United States v. Robinson

Instant Facts: Robinson (D) was convicted of possession of a controlled substance after evidence obtained in a search incident to arrest was admitted at trial.

Black Letter Rule: No matter how insignificant an arrest, the police have the right to search the suspect's person for potential weapons or evidence.

Whren v. United States

Instant Facts: Whren (D) was charged with violating various federal drug laws after a traffic stop and challenged the admission of contraband evidence discovered pursuant to the stop

Black Letter Rule: The temporary detention of a motorist who the police have probable cause to believe has committed a civil traffic violation is consistent with the Fourth Amendment .

Atwater v. City of Lago Vista

Instant Facts: Atwater (P) was arrested without a warrant for minor traffic offenses, none of which was punishable by imprisonment.

Black Letter Rule: If a law enforcement officer has probable cause to believe that a person has committed even a very minor criminal offense in his or her presence, the officer may arrest that person without a warrant.

Tennessee v. Garner

Instant Facts: A police officer shot and killed Garner, who was known to be unarmed, when Garner attempted to flee the scene of a burglary.

Black Letter Rule: Under the Fourth Amendment, peace officers may not use deadly force to prevent the escape of a felony suspect unless the officers have probable cause to believe that the suspect presents a threat to the life or safety of the officers or others.

Payton v. New York

Instant Facts: In separate cases, New York police officers entered the private residences of two felony suspects without a warrant to make arrests.

Black Letter Rule: An arrest warrant is required to arrest a person in his or her home.

Chimel v. California

Instant Facts: Chimel (D) was charged with two counts of burglary and argued that items taken from his home and admitted into evidence against him had been unconstitutionally seized.

Black Letter Rule: Pursuant to a lawful arrest, the police may conduct a search of any area within the immediate reach of the accused criminal.

Vale v. Louisiana

Instant Facts: Vale (D) was convicted after police arrested him on his front steps and searched his house for narcotics.

Black Letter Rule: A search incident to a lawful arrest must be substantially contemporaneous with the arrest and confined to the immediate vicinity of the arrest.

California v. Carney

Instant Facts: Carney (D) was charged with possession of marijuana for sale after police seized drugs in his motor home during a warrantless search.

Black Letter Rule: Warrantless searches of readily movable vehicles are not unreasonable when probable cause supports the search.

Thornton v. United States

Instant Facts: A police officer searched Thornton's (D) vehicle although he was arrested for drug possession outside his vehicle.

Black Letter Rule: A police officer may search a vehicle incident to lawful arrest once probable cause exists to arrest a recent occupant of the vehicle who had access to the interior of the vehicle.

Knowles v. Iowa

Instant Facts: Knowles (D) was convicted of drug possession after his car was searched incident to a speeding citation.

Black Letter Rule: An officer may not search a vehicle incident to a citation.

California v. Acevedo

Instant Facts: Police seized marijuana from Acevedo's (D) car without a warrant after seeing him emerge from an apartment known to contain marijuana.

Black Letter Rule: The police may search an automobile and the containers within it if they have probable cause to believe contraband or evidence is contained therein.

Wyoming v. Houghton

Instant Facts: Houghton (D) was convicted when evidence recovered from her purse during a search of a vehicle in which she was a passenger was admitted against her at trial.

Black Letter Rule: Police officers with probable cause to search a car may inspect passengers' belongings found in the car that are capable of concealing the object of the search.

Colorado v. Bertine

Instant Facts: Evidence obtained from a closed backpack in Bertine's (D) van during an arrest was suppressed.

Black Letter Rule: A routine inventory search is not a criminal investigation and does not require a warrant or probable cause.

Terry v. Ohio

Instant Facts: Evidence of a gun found on Terry during a protective frisk by a police officer was admitted into evidence and resulted in his conviction.

Black Letter Rule: If the police have reasonable suspicion that a suspect has committed a crime or is about to commit a crime, they may stop the person, detain him briefly for questioning, and then frisk the suspect if they reasonably believe the suspect is carrying a dangerous weapon.

Florida v. J.L.

Instant Facts: Police received an anonymous tip that someone matching J.L.'s (D) description was carrying a gun, and J.L. (D) was stopped and frisked.

Black Letter Rule: An anonymous tip that does not bear any indicia of reliability does not justify a stop-and-frisk search.

Illinois v. Wardlow

Instant Facts: Wardlow (D) was arrested for possession of a handgun discovered after a protective police pat-down.

Black Letter Rule: Flight from police is not indicative of wrongdoing, but it is certainly suggestive of such.

Florida v. Royer

Instant Facts: Royer (D) was convicted of drug possession after his luggage was searched at an airport and marijuana was seized.

Black Letter Rule: When officers have reasonable suspicion that a person has committed a crime or is about to commit a crime, they may temporarily detain the individual for questioning no longer than necessary to serve the purposes of the stop.

United States v. Drayton

Instant Facts: Drayton (D) was a passenger on an intercity bus who was arrested after a search of his person during a police "sweep" of the bus showed that he was carrying illegal drugs.

Black Letter Rule: There is no seizure of a person if a police officer does not do anything to suggest to a reasonable person that he or she is not free to terminate the encounter.

Brendlin v. California

Instant Facts: Brendlin (D) claimed that drugs and drug paraphernalia were inadmissible against him because the traffic stop that resulted in the discovery of the evidence was illegal.

Black Letter Rule: A person is seized pursuant to the Fourth Amendment when an officer, by means of force or authority, intentionally terminates or restrains the person's freedom of movement.

United States v. Place

Instant Facts: Place (D) was indicted for possession of cocaine with intent to distribute based on narcotics found in one of Place's (D) suitcases, which the police seized without a warrant.

Black Letter Rule: When an officer's observations lead him reasonably to believe that a traveler is carrying luggage that contains narcotics, the officer may detain the luggage briefly to investigate the circumstances that aroused his suspicion, provided that the investigative detention is properly limited in scope.

Samson v. California

Instant Facts: A police officer searched Samson (D), a parolee, as he walked down the street, based simply on his parolee status, and Samson (D) moved to suppress the evidence seized during the search.

Black Letter Rule: The Fourth Amendment does not prohibit a police officer from conducting a suspicionless search of a parolee.

Schneckloth v. Bustamonte

Instant Facts: Bustamonte (D) was charged with theft after three stolen checks were discovered during a search of an automobile consented to by the vehicle owner's brother.

Black Letter Rule: An individual need not be informed that he has the right to refuse consent to a search before his consent to the search will be considered voluntary.

Georgia v. Randolph

Instant Facts: Randolph (D) was convicted of a drug offense based on evidence that resulted from a search of his home to which only his wife consented, over his objection.

Black Letter Rule: "[A] warrantless search of a shared dwelling for evidence over the express refusal of consent by a physically present resident cannot be justified as reasonable as to him on the basis of consent given to the police by another resident."

Wolf v. Colorado

(*Convicted Criminal*) v. (*Prosecuting Government*)
338 U.S. 25, 69 S. Ct. 1359, 93 L. Ed. 1782 (1949)

DUE PROCESS DOES NOT REQUIRE THE EXCLUSION OF *ALL* EVIDENCE OBTAINED BY AN UNREASONABLE SEARCH

■ **INSTANT FACTS** The excerpt includes no factual background for this case.

■ **BLACK LETTER RULE** The Fourteenth Amendment incorporates the Fourth Amendment, restraining states from unreasonable searches and seizures.

■ PROCEDURAL BASIS

Certiorari to review an undisclosed decision.

■ FACTS

The excerpt includes no factual background for this case.

■ ISSUE

Is a state court conviction based on evidence obtained under circumstances that would have rendered it inadmissible in federal court a violation of due process?

■ DECISION AND RATIONALE

(Frankfurter, J.) No. The Fourteenth Amendment incorporates the Fourth Amendment, thereby restraining states from unreasonable searches and seizures. While the Fourteenth Amendment does not totally incorporate the Bill of Rights, due process encompasses those rights "implicit in the concept of ordered liberty." These rights are not static, but rather progress through time as society progresses. "The security of one's privacy against arbitrary intrusion by the police—which is at the core of the Fourth Amendment—is basic to a free society." Accordingly, the right to be free from unreasonable search and seizure is enforceable against the states by the Fourteenth Amendment. However, states are free to establish through local community standards other means of protection that are consistent with due process. Due process does not require the exclusion of evidence obtained by an unreasonable search and seizure when local concerns require other equally effective methods for preserving due process.

■ CONCURRENCE

(Black, J.) The federal rule of exclusion is not a constitutional demand, but rather a rule of evidence that may be congressionally negated. As such, it is not binding on the states.

■ DISSENT

(Murphy, J.) The only alternative to the rule of exclusion is no sanction at all. By leaving enforcement of a rule that is effective by local standards to those by whom those standards are created, the Court requires nothing of the states, for their judgment of effectiveness will always preserve due process in their discretion.

■ DISSENT

(Douglas, J.) Without an exclusionary rule, there is no sanction for an unreasonable search and seizure.

Analysis:

Wolf generally provides that the Fourth Amendment right to be free from unreasonable searches and seizures is incorporated by the Fourteenth Amendment and applies to the states. A distinction must be drawn between a state's use of an unreasonable search and seizure to obtain evidence and the exclusion of such evidence at trial. Here the Court allowed the state to use the evidence obtained by the police to convict Wolf (D). The Court held that while the right to be free from unreasonable searches and seizures is fundamental to the concept of ordered liberty, the exclusion of relevant evidence obtained in violation of the Fourth Amendment "is not an essential ingredient of the right."

■ CASE VOCABULARY

DUE PROCESS: The conduct of legal proceedings according to established rules and principles for the protection and enforcement of private rights, including notice and the right to a fair hearing before a tribunal with the power to decide the case.

SEIZURE: The act or an instance of taking possession of a person or property by legal right or process; especially, in constitutional law, a confiscation or arrest that may interfere with a person's reasonable expectation of privacy.

UNREASONABLE SEARCH: A search conducted without probable cause or other considerations that would make it legally permissible.

Mapp v. Ohio

(*Obscenity Defendant*) v. (*Prosecuting Government*)
367 U.S. 643, 81 S. Ct. 1684, 6 L. Ed. 2d 1081 (1961)

THE SUPREME COURT OVERRULES *WOLF v. COLORADO*

■ **INSTANT FACTS** Mapp (D) was convicted of possession of obscene materials after police broke into her home and seized the materials without a warrant.

■ **BLACK LETTER RULE** All evidence obtained by unreasonable searches and seizures in violation of the Fourth Amendment is inadmissible in state court.

■ PROCEDURAL BASIS

Certiorari to review the defendant's conviction.

■ FACTS

Three state police officers approached Mapp's (D) apartment searching for a bombing suspect and illegal gambling paraphernalia. When the officers knocked, Mapp (D) refused to allow them into her home without a warrant. Three hours later, the officers again approached the home, broke through the door, and entered. When Mapp (D) demanded they produce their search warrant, one officer showed her a piece of paper, which Mapp (D) seized and concealed in her shirt. A struggle ensued in which the police physically recovered the paper from Mapp (D). After placing Mapp (D) in handcuffs, the police searched through her belongings, recovering four books alleged to contain obscene materials. No warrant was ever produced. Mapp (D) was convicted of possession of lewd and lascivious materials under state law.

■ ISSUE

Must evidence obtained as a result of an unreasonable search and seizure be excluded in a state proceeding?

■ DECISION AND RATIONALE

(Clark, J.) Yes. The evidence obtained through unreasonable searches and seizures that violate the Fourth Amendment is inadmissible in state court. In *Wolf v. Colorado*, the Court held that while the Fourth Amendment applies to the states through the Fourteenth Amendment, the exclusionary rule set forth in *Weeks v. United States* does not. The *Wolf* Court reasoned that the right to have relevant evidence excluded at trial is not an essential element of the right to be free from unreasonable searches and seizures. Without applying the *Weeks* exclusionary rule to state violations of the Fourth Amendment, *Wolf* leaves no remedy for the constitutional violation and states are free to violate the Fourth Amendment rights of their citizens without any meaningful consequences. *Wolf v. Colorado* is therefore overruled. Reversed and remanded.

■ CONCURRENCE

(Black, J.) Nothing in the Fourth Amendment specifically or implicitly requires that evidence obtained through unreasonable searches and seizures be excluded from trial. To reach that conclusion, the Fourth Amendment and Fifth Amendment must be read together. Reading these two amendments together, a state may not commit unreasonable searches and seizures under the Fourth Amendment, and the Fifth Amendment requires incriminating evidence obtained in violation of the Fourth Amendment to be excluded at trial.

■ CONCURRENCE

(Douglas, J.) "I believe that this is an appropriate case in which to put an end to the asymmetry which *Wolf* imported into the law."

■ DISSENT

(Harlan, J.) The Fourth Amendment does not require exclusion of relevant evidence against a defendant in a state proceeding. The Fourteenth Amendment, through which the majority enforces the Fourth Amendment, requires that all defendants receive due process of the law. The exclusionary rule, which is primarily procedural in nature, is but one means of ensuring due process. Federalism requires that the states be free to utilize any procedural mechanism that preserves their citizens' due process rights in state court proceedings.

Analysis:

While several justifications have been offered for application of the exclusionary rule in state court proceedings, the reasoning that has continued to gain judicial approval is the deterrence against future Fourth Amendment violations. As stated by the majority, there is little value in holding that the Constitution requires the states to refrain from unreasonable searches and seizures if evidence obtained by those constitutional violations may nonetheless be used as if no violation occurred. The deterrence rationale serves to prevent future constitutional violations rather than remedy those that have already occurred.

■ CASE VOCABULARY

STARE DECISIS: The doctrine of precedent, under which it is necessary for a court to follow earlier judicial decisions when the same points arise again in litigation.

United States v. Leon

(*Prosecuting Government*) v. (*Drug Offender*)
468 U.S. 897, 104 S. Ct. 3405, 82 L. Ed. 2d 677 (1984)

THE EXCLUSIONARY RULE IS LIMITED BY THE GOOD–FAITH EXCEPTION

■ **INSTANT FACTS** The excerpt includes no factual background for this case.

■ **BLACK LETTER RULE** The exclusionary rule does not bar use by the prosecution in its case-in-chief of evidence seized by law enforcement acting in reasonable reliance on a search warrant issued by a detached and neutral magistrate, even if subsequently found to be unsupported by probable cause.

■ **PROCEDURAL BASIS**

Certiorari to review an undisclosed decision.

■ **FACTS**

The excerpt includes no factual background for this case.

■ **ISSUE**

May the prosecution use in its case-in-chief evidence obtained by officers acting in reasonable reliance on a search warrant issued by a detached and neutral magistrate but ultimately found to be unsupported by probable cause?

■ **DECISION AND RATIONALE**

(White, J.) Yes. The exclusionary rule is designed to safeguard Fourth Amendment rights through its deterrent effect. Whether it should be applied in a particular case is determined by weighing the costs and benefits of excluding the evidence. The rule should be restricted to those cases in which its remedial objectives are most effectively served. In the instant case, suppression of the evidence seized pursuant to a warrant does not further the deterrent effect of the rule. First, exclusion of the evidence will not have a significant deterrent effect on the issuing judge or magistrate, who unlike members of law enforcement, are neutral judicial officers with no stake in the outcome of particular criminal prosecutions. Moreover, the exclusionary rule cannot deter offending officers who acted on the objectively reasonable belief that their conduct was lawful, because there is nothing to deter. But the officers' reliance on the magistrate's probable cause determination and on the technical sufficiency of the warrant must be objectively reasonable. Therefore, suppression remains an appropriate remedy if (1) the magistrate or judge issuing the warrant was misled by information in an affidavit that the affiant knew was false or would have known was false except for his reckless disregard of the truth; (2) the issuing magistrate wholly abandons his judicial role, such that no reasonably well-trained officer should rely on the warrant; (3) an affidavit is "so lacking in indicia of probable cause as to render official belief in its existence entirely unreasonable"; or (4) a warrant is so facially deficient, e.g., in failing to particularize the place to be searched or the items to be seized, that the executing officers cannot reasonably presume its validity.

In the case at bar, the officers' application for a warrant clearly was supported by much more than a "bare bones" affidavit. It related the results of an extensive investigation, and reviewing judges disagreed as to whether it was sufficient enough to give rise to probable cause. Under these circumstances, the officers' reliance on the magistrate's determination of probable cause was objectively reasonable, and the evidence should have been admitted. Reversed.

■ CONCURRENCE

(Blackmun, J.) The good-faith exception to the exclusionary rule must be tested in the real world of state and federal law enforcement. If its application materially changes police compliance with the Fourth Amendment, the Court will have to reconsider the exception.

■ DISSENT

(Brennan, J.) The Court's decision sanctions the use by the prosecution in its case in chief of illegally obtained evidence against the individual whose rights have been violated. *Mapp* put to rest what the Court revives today—that the exclusionary rule is merely a judicially created prophylactic rule designed to safeguard Fourth Amendment rights through its deterrent effect, rather than a personal constitutional right. However, the Fourth Amendment condemns not only the initial unconstitutional invasion of privacy, but also the subsequent use of any evidence so obtained. Its provisions are not directed solely at government agents who actually invade an individual's constitutionally protected privacy, but also to the courts, who are under a direct constitutional duty to exclude illegally obtained evidence. When a court admits illegally obtained evidence, the same constitutional concerns as apply to the initial seizure are implicated. The judiciary thereby becomes part of what is in fact "a single governmental action" prohibited by the terms of the Amendments.

Furthermore, as applied here, the deterrence theory is misguided and unworkable. It is not the exclusionary rule, but the Fourth Amendment itself that imposes the "cost" of excluding reliable evidence. In performing the cost/benefit analysis, the Court mistakenly weighs the aggregated costs of exclusion in *all* cases against the potential benefits associated with the narrow range of cases in which law enforcement has mistakenly, but reasonably, relied on a search warrant. Moreover, the deterrent effect of the exclusionary rule does operate in those situations that fall under the good-faith exception. The chief deterrent function of the rule is its tendency to promote institutional law enforcement compliance with the Fourth Amendment, not to "punish" individual officers who violate its strictures. As to situations that fall within the exception, the exclusionary rule has a long-term deterrent effect. If, for example, evidence is consistently excluded in such cases, police departments will instruct their officers to devote greater care and attention to providing sufficient information to establish probable cause in the warrant application, and to review attentively the form of the warrant issued rather than automatically assuming that whatever document the magistrate has signed will necessarily comport with Fourth Amendment requirements. Additionally, the Court's decision insulates the magistrate's decisions to issue warrants from subsequent judicial review. Because any mistakes made by a magistrate will have virtually no consequence, their standard of care in reviewing warrant applications will significantly decrease.

■ DISSENT

(Stevens, J.) Under normal Court procedure, the Court should have remanded the case for consideration under the standards established in *Illinois v. Gates* rather than employ a new rule based on its notions of wise social policy.

Analysis:

The government's burden of demonstrating that officers acted in objective good faith is not a difficult one. Therefore, in order to suppress evidence when a warrant is involved, one of the four situations enunciated in *Leon* must be shown to have existed. In most cases in which the good-faith exception is argued, successful counterarguments emphasize that the rule's deterrent purpose would not be furthered by the exception's application.

■ CASE VOCABULARY

EXCLUSIONARY RULE: A rule that excludes or suppresses evidence obtained in violation of an accused person's constitutional rights.

GOOD–FAITH EXCEPTION: An exception to the exclusionary rule whereby evidence obtained under a warrant later found to be invalid (especially because it is not supported by probable cause) is nonetheless admissible if the police reasonably relied on the notion that the warrant was valid.

MAGISTRATE: A judicial officer with strictly limited jurisdiction and authority, often on a local level and often restricted to criminal cases.

Hudson v. Michigan

(*Convicted Criminal*) v. (*Prosecuting State*)
___ U.S. ___, 126 S.Ct. 2159, 165 L.Ed.2d 56 (2006)

POLICE ANNOUNCING THEIR PRESENCE AT A HOME MUST WAIT AN APPROPRIATE AMOUNT OF TIME BEFORE ENTERING

■ **INSTANT FACTS** Police entered Hudson's (D) home just seconds after knocking and announcing their presence, and Hudson (D) moved to suppress the evidence discovered in the resulting search.

■ **BLACK LETTER RULE** The exclusionary rule does not apply to suppress evidence obtained through a violation of the knock-and-announce rule.

■ PROCEDURAL BASIS

Certiorari to review a state appellate court decision refusing to suppress the evidence.

■ FACTS

Police executing a search warrant at Hudson's (D) home waited only three to five seconds after knocking and announcing their presence before they entered. Hudson (D) moved to suppress the drugs and weapons found as a result of the search. The trial court held that the premature entry violated Hudson's (D) Fourth Amendment rights and that the evidence was inadmissible, but the appellate court reversed, holding that suppression is an inappropriate remedy when entry is made, pursuant to a warrant, after a "knock and announce."

■ ISSUE

If the police violate the knock-and-announce rule, must the evidence they obtain through the subsequent entry and search be excluded?

■ DECISION AND RATIONALE

(Scalia, J.) No. The exclusionary rule does not apply to suppress evidence obtained through a violation of the knock-and-announce rule. The knock-and-announce rule is ancient, and is also commanded by the Fourth Amendment. There are, however, exceptional circumstances when the rule does not apply. If the police have a reasonable suspicion that evidence may be destroyed, for instance, or if a threat of physical harm exists, officers do not need to knock and announce their presence. When the rule does apply, just how long must the officers wait? The reasonable wait time depends on how long it would take to destroy or conceal the evidence, but that question is not at issue here. In this case, the knock-and-announce rule was violated, as all the lower courts agreed. The question here is what sanction should be imposed for that violation.

The exclusionary rule has a high cost and should not be applied indiscriminately. Exclusion is not appropriate in every case in which the defendant's Fourth Amendment rights have been violated, because not all evidence resulting from an unconstitutional search is the "fruit of the poisonous tree," particularly where the causal connection is remote. The knock-and-announce rule is meant to protect various rights, including the protection of one's dwelling from forcible entry and one's person from possible harm, but it was not meant to prevent the government from taking evidence described in a warrant.

If an officer has to be concerned that too short a wait will result in the exclusion of seized evidence, he or she may err on the side of waiting too long, thereby potentially jeopardizing a case and subjecting the public to a risk of harm. And it cannot be assumed that exclusion of the evidence would even serve a deterrent function. Moreover, the victim of a knock-and-announce violation has the option of redressing his injury through a civil action. This potential civil liability of the violating officers, as well as the prospect of discipline within the police department itself, serves a sufficient deterrent function, without the need to exclude the evidence obtained.

For all of these reasons, when the knock-and-announce rule is violated, resort to suppressing evidence of guilt is unjustified. Affirmed.

■ CONCURRENCE

(Kennedy, J.) The majority's decision should not be read as stating that knock-and-announce violations are trivial, nor is application of the exclusionary rule in doubt. Rather, the holding here is simply that a violation of the knock-and-announce rule is not sufficiently related to the later discovery of evidence to justify suppression.

■ DISSENT

(Breyer, J.) The exclusionary rule *should* apply to knock-and-announce violations. The use of evidence secured through illegal, unconstitutional searches and seizures is barred at criminal trials, and the deterrent effect of that suppression cannot be ignored. What reason is there to think the police will be deterred by the threat of civil litigation? That threat was not held sufficient in the *Mapp* case, nor should it be here.

Prior to this decision, the Court has declined to apply the exclusionary rule only when it would not result in appreciable deterrence to do so, and when admissibility in contexts other than criminal trials was at issue. Neither of those exceptions exists here. Nor does the majority's "inevitable discovery" argument work. The government could not show in this case that the evidence sought to be suppressed would have inevitably been discovered through lawful means. In this case, had the illegal entry not occurred, the police simply would not have discovered the guns and drugs. And the fact that the officers had a warrant does not change that conclusion, because it was *not* a no-knock warrant. The inevitable discovery rule requires a showing that the evidence would have been discovered anyhow through legal means, such as in *Nix*, where a search party would have discovered the victim's body, irrespective of the defendant's unconstitutional admission as to where the body was, after he had invoked his right to counsel. In *Segura* and *Murray*, the evidence was independently obtained pursuant to a valid warrant, well after the initial, illegal search. Here, by contrast, without the unlawful entry, the police would not have discovered the incriminating evidence at all; the majority has wrongfully construed and applied the inevitable discovery rule.

The majority also argues that the exclusionary rule does not apply if the causal connection between the unlawful search and the evidence is attenuated, but then it goes on to give "attenuated" an entirely new meaning. The majority argues that attenuation occurs when the constitutional interest that has been violated would not be served by suppressing the evidence. But that argument ignores the fact that the knock-and-announce rule serves not only the interests listed by the majority, but also to protect the important privacy rights of the occupants. But even this is not really the point in this case. When evidence results from an unlawful search, it should be suppressed, despite what interests are served or violated. Moreover, the argument that compliance with the knock-and-announce rule may subject police officers to danger is an argument against the rule itself, not against the exclusion of evidence obtained by its violation.

The knock-and-announce rule is a subsidiary of the Fourth Amendment, and the majority could not, therefore, simply conclude that it is not important enough to warrant a suppression remedy. The knock-and-announce rule *is* important, as established precedent confirms. Common sense dictates that without suppression, there is little to deter violations of the knock-and-announce rule. The departures from Fourth Amendment principles in this case are simply not justified.

Analysis:

There is significant tension between the majority and dissenting opinions in this case, with the majority coming down on the side of the prosecution and the dissent favoring the protection of criminal defendants' constitutional rights. Lower courts had grappled with this conflict, with the Seventh Circuit Court of Appeals and the Michigan Supreme Court holding that the inevitable discovery doctrine creates a per se exception to the exclusionary rule for evidence seized after a Fourth Amendment knock-and-announce violation, and the Sixth and Eighth Circuits, the Arkansas Supreme Court, and the Maryland Court of Appeals holding that evidence is subject to suppression after such violations. The Supreme Court resolved that conflict in this case, and now all lower courts must follow suit.

■ CASE VOCABULARY

EXCLUSIONARY RULE: A rule that excludes or suppresses evidence obtained in violation of an accused person's constitutional rights.

FRUIT–OF–THE–POISONOUS–TREE DOCTRINE: The rule that evidence derived from an illegal search, arrest, or interrogation is inadmissible because the evidence (the "fruit") was tainted by the illegality (the "poisonous tree"). Under this doctrine, for example, a murder weapon is inadmissible if the map showing its location and used to find it was seized during an illegal search.

INEVITABLE DISCOVERY RULE: The rule providing—as an exception to the fruit-of-the-poisonous-tree doctrine—that evidence obtained by illegal means may nonetheless be admissible if the prosecution can show that the evidence would eventually have been legally obtained anyway.

KNOCK–AND–ANNOUNCE RULE: The requirement that the police knock at the door and announce their identity, authority, and purpose before entering a residence to execute an arrest or search warrant.

NO–KNOCK SEARCH WARRANT: A search warrant that authorizes the police to enter premises without knocking and announcing their presence and purpose before entry because a prior announcement would lead to the destruction of the objects searched for or would endanger the safety of the police or another person.

SEARCH WARRANT: A judge's written order authorizing a law-enforcement officer to conduct a search of a specified place and to seize evidence.

Katz v. United States

(*Gambler*) v. (*Prosecuting Government*)
389 U.S. 347, 88 S. Ct. 507, 19 L. Ed. 2d 576 (1967)

A WIRETAP IN A PUBLIC PHONE BOOTH VIOLATES THE FOURTH AMENDMENT

■ **INSTANT FACTS** Katz (D) was convicted of transmitting gaming information via telephone based on evidence obtained by FBI agents who had attached a listening device to a public telephone.

■ **BLACK LETTER RULE** The Fourth Amendment protects all communications that a person does not knowingly expose to the public.

■ PROCEDURAL BASIS

Certiorari to review a decision of a federal court of appeals sustaining the conviction.

■ FACTS

Katz (D) had been indicted for transmitting illegal wagering information over the telephone in violation of a federal statute. At trial, the prosecution introduced evidence of the defendant's conversations obtained by FBI agents through a listening device attached to a public telephone without a search warrant. Katz (D) objected to the use of the evidence as a violation of the Fourth Amendment. The trial court overruled the objection and the defendant was convicted. The court of appeals affirmed the conviction.

■ ISSUE

Does the use of a listening device to record conversations made in a public phone booth violate the Fourth Amendment?

■ DECISION AND RATIONALE

(Stewart, J.) Yes. The Fourth Amendment protects people—not places—against unreasonable searches and seizures. It affords protection to all communications that a person does not knowingly expose to the public. Because the defendant took precautions to ensure his conversations would not be overheard, he did not knowingly expose his conversations to the public. The fact that his conversations took place in a public place, as opposed to a home, office, or other private place, is constitutionally insignificant. An unreasonable search and seizure occurs even without any technical "trespass" into a space—public or private—in which a person has an expectation of privacy. Because the defendant had a reasonable expectation of privacy in the phone booth, it was a constitutionally protected area. Reversed.

■ CONCURRENCE

(Harlan, J.) A two-pronged analysis should determine what rights the Fourth Amendment affords. First, a person must have shown a subjective expectation of privacy. Second, that expectation must be objectively reasonable. Applied to the facts of this case, a telephone booth, isolated from the public at times of use, is a "temporarily private place" in which an expectation of privacy is reasonable. The Fourth Amendment protects such an expectation of privacy from unreasonable search and seizure.

■ DISSENT

(Black, J.) Recording a conversation by electronic means constitutes neither a search nor a seizure as the Fourth Amendment intended that those terms be applied. The plain language of the Fourth Amendment applies only to tangible objects and does not encompass conversations, which are capable of neither search nor seizure. Because eavesdropping existed at the time the Fourth Amendment was drafted, the framers' choice of language must be given effect and not applied to intangible objects.

Analysis:

Katz is widely accepted as the beginning of the "privacy approach" to Fourth Amendment analysis. As Justice Black's dissent highlights, the language of the Fourth Amendment applies literally only to tangible objects. Pre-*Katz* decisions held similarly by requiring a trespass to constitute a search and seizure. The majority departs from the trespass requirement, expanding the rights protected under the Fourth Amendment.

■ CASE VOCABULARY

RIGHT OF PRIVACY: The right to personal autonomy. The U.S. Constitution does not explicitly provide for a right of privacy, but the Supreme Court has repeatedly ruled that this right is implied in the "zones of privacy" created by specific constitutional guarantees.

California v. Greenwood

(*Prosecuting Government*) v. (*Drug Trafficker*)
486 U.S. 35, 108 S. Ct. 1625, 100 L. Ed. 2d 30 (1988)

THERE IS NO REASONABLE EXPECTATION OF PRIVACY IN TRASH PLACED ON THE CURB FOR REMOVAL

■ **INSTANT FACTS** Greenwood (D) was arrested and charged with drug trafficking after the police searched his garbage without a warrant.

■ **BLACK LETTER RULE** An unreasonable search and seizure requires that the defendant have a subjective expectation of privacy in the property searched that is objective by society's standards.

■ **PROCEDURAL BASIS**

Certiorari to review a decision of the California Court of Appeals affirming the dismissal of the charges against the defendant.

■ **FACTS**

After receiving information that Greenwood (D) could have been involved in illegal narcotics trafficking, a police investigator requested the trash collector to pick up the trash bags in front of Greenwood's (D) residence and turn them over to her without commingling them with other trash. When looking through Greenwood's (D) trash, the investigator found items indicative of narcotics trafficking. Recounting her findings in an affidavit, the investigator obtained a search warrant for Greenwood's (D) home. Upon finding narcotics in the home, Greenwood (D) was arrested and posted bail. Greenwood (D) was arrested a second time after officers again searched his trash in the same manner. The California Superior Court dismissed the charges against Greenwood (D) because the warrantless search of his trash violated the Fourth Amendment. The court of appeals affirmed.

■ **ISSUE**

Is a warrantless search of one's garbage an unreasonable search and seizure?

■ **DECISION AND RATIONALE**

(White, J.) No. An unreasonable search and seizure requires that the defendant have a subjective expectation of privacy in the property searched that is objective by society's standards. Here, the trash was placed on the curb in front of Greenwood's (D) house where others could easily access it. In fact, Greenwood (D) intended a third party to pick it up and carry it away. He could have no reasonable expectation of privacy in the trash after it was left in a public place and exposed to third parties. Reversed.

■ **DISSENT**

(Brennan, J.) A search of one's personal effects is no less a search than one of his home or person. A defendant's trash contains private information concerning his eating, reading, and recreational habits, as well as other intimate details of his life. When he places such information in an opaque plastic bag for trash removal, he has not made it open to all who wish to view it, but rather maintains a reasonable expectation of privacy in it. Certainly, if the trash were invaded by a nongovernment intruder and exposed to the eyes of the police, no expectation of privacy would exist. But the mere possibility that others may expose the defendant's private matters because he has discreetly placed it on his curb does not justify a warrantless police search of the trash.

Analysis:

The Court's decision seems to ignore *Katz v. United States*, 389 U.S. 347 (1967), wherein the defendant's telephone conversation occurred in a public place but was accompanied by a reasonable expectation of privacy from police investigation because he took sufficient measures, such as closing the door of the telephone booth, to ensure his privacy. Could one could consider placing one's trash on the curb for disposal in a secure container as a sufficient measure to ensure one's privacy despite its exposure to third persons?

■ CASE VOCABULARY

WARRANT: A writ directing or authorizing someone to do an act, especially one directing a law enforcer to make an arrest, a search, or a seizure.

WARRANTLESS SEARCH: A search conducted without obtaining a proper warrant. Warrantless searches are permissible under exigent circumstances or when conducted incident to an arrest.

Florida v. Riley

(*Prosecuting Government*) v. (*Greenhouse Operator*)

488 U.S. 445, 109 S. Ct. 693, 102 L. Ed. 2d 835 (1989)

THE FOURTH AMENDMENT DOES NOT APPLY TO OBSERVATION FROM THE AIRSPACE ABOVE A HOME

■ **INSTANT FACTS** Police observed Riley's (D) greenhouse from a helicopter 400 feet above his home.

■ **BLACK LETTER RULE** Surveillance from the airspace above a residence does not constitute a search for which a warrant is required under the Fourth Amendment.

■ PROCEDURAL BASIS

Certiorari to review a decision of the Florida Supreme Court on a certified question.

■ FACTS

A lower Florida court certified a question to the Florida Supreme Court, which concluded that surveillance of the interior of a partially covered greenhouse in a residential backyard from the vantage point of a helicopter located 400 feet above the greenhouse constitutes a search for which a warrant is required under the Fourth Amendment.

■ ISSUE

Does the surveillance of the interior of a partially covered greenhouse in a residential backyard from the vantage point of a helicopter located 400 feet above the greenhouse constitute a search for which a warrant is required under the Fourth Amendment?

■ DECISION AND RATIONALE

(White, J.) No. The Fourth Amendment protects against a search only where the individual maintains a subjective expectation of privacy that is reasonable by societal standards. While an individual may maintain an expectation of privacy from police observation from the airspace above, the expectation is not reasonable. As long as the police comply with all flight rules and regulations, view the premises with the naked eye, and act in a manner in which the general public may act, the Fourth Amendment is not violated.

■ CONCURRENCE

(O'Connor, J.) Because *Katz* requires that the helicopter be operated at an altitude and in a manner consistent with that of the general public, the focus of the inquiry should be whether the aerial observation complies with the general public use. While compliance with federal regulations may be instructive, there may be circumstances in which the government meets federal regulations but the public use is not sufficiently prevalent to destroy the individual's reasonable expectation of privacy.

■ DISSENT

(Brennan, J.) The lawfulness of the officer's act is not the measure of a Fourth Amendment violation. While the officer may have complied with all flight regulations, the crucial question is whether his view is one the general public enjoys. While it is possible for a member of the public to view the defendant's property from a helicopter from 400 feet above, it is quite difficult. The public use of the airspace using expensive, and high-tech equipment at that altitude is too rare to legitimize the lengths the government went to view the defendant's property.

■ DISSENT

(Blackmun, J.) The government should bear the burden of proof that the general public use of the airspace 400 feet above the defendant's property is common enough to justify the search. Because the government did not meet that burden, the Fourth Amendment was violated.

Analysis:

By focusing on the helicopter's compliance with federal flight regulations, the Court failed to conclude whether Riley's (D) expectation of privacy was objectively reasonable by society's standards. Instead, the court implies that when the police do not violate the law, any member of society could act similarly, eliminating the expectation of privacy. Yet, the Court did not determine whether, despite the lawful altitude, society would endorse Riley's (D) expectation of privacy. Societal standards, not FAA regulations, should determine reasonableness.

■ CASE VOCABULARY

CERTIFIED QUESTION: A point of law on which a federal appellate court seeks guidance from either the U.S. Supreme Court or the highest state court by the procedure of certification.

United States v. Karo

(*Prosecuting Government*) v. (*Drug Smuggler*)

468 U.S. 705, 104 S. Ct. 3296, 82 L. Ed. 2d 530 (1984)

INSTALLING A BEEPER IN A CONTAINER BEFORE POSSESSION IS NOT A SEIZURE

■ **INSTANT FACTS** A federal agent installed a beeper in a container to be shipped to Karo (D) in order to track drug smuggling activity.

■ **BLACK LETTER RULE** Seizure of property requires a meaningful interference with a possessory interest.

■ PROCEDURAL BASIS

Certiorari to review decision of the court of appeals reversing the defendant's conviction.

■ FACTS

A federal agent learned from an informant that Karo (D) had ordered a large quantity of ether. When the informant told the agent the ether was to be used to extract cocaine from imported clothing, the government obtained a court order to place a beeper inside a container to be included in the shipment. After agents obtained a search warrant based on information provided by the beeper, a search of the premises uncovered cocaine and laboratory equipment. The district court granted Karo's (D) motion to suppress the evidence because the initial warrant for the placement of the beeper was invalid. On appeal, the federal court of appeals affirmed, holding that a warrant was required for the initial placement of the beeper and the evidence seized was tainted by the invalid warrant.

■ ISSUE

Does the installation of a beeper in a container of chemicals with the consent of the original owner constitute a seizure under the Fourth Amendment when the container is delivered to a buyer with no knowledge of the presence of the beeper?

■ DECISION AND RATIONALE

(White, J.) No. A seizure occurs only when there is some meaningful interference with an individual's possessory interests in the subject property. While the container in which the beeper was placed in this case was the property of the government, the beeper could be placed therein without such interference. The government was also free to place the beeper in one of the informant's containers, since the agent had obtained the consent of the informant for placement of the beeper and the informant was free to do what he wanted with it prior to shipment. Upon transfer to the defendant, no seizure took place. Because the placement of the beeper did not infringe on the defendant's possessory interests in the container, no seizure occurred.

Continued monitoring of the beeper, however, presents a different issue. Once the container entered a private residence, its possessor maintained a reasonable expectation of privacy over it. Absent exigent circumstances, a valid warrant is required to infringe on that privacy interest. Just as the agents could not enter the house without a valid warrant, the electronic monitoring of information inside the house without a warrant is similarly prohibited. However, the warrant affidavit, after striking references to facts obtained through the monitoring of the beeper, demonstrates sufficient probable cause for the warrant to issue. The evidence should not have been suppressed. Reversed.

CONCURRENCE IN PART

(O'Connor, J.) A privacy interest in the premises is different than a privacy interest in a container brought into the premises. Before a defendant can establish a privacy interest protected by the Fourth Amendment, he must show that the beeper was monitored when visual tracking of the container was impossible and that his interest in the container itself enabled him to give consent to the search of the container. Without control over the container, he does not have a reasonable expectation of privacy.

DISSENT IN PART

(Stevens, J.) A possessory interest in the container includes the right to exclude unwanted items and the right to use it exclusively. By attaching a beeper to a container, the government converted the property for its use, thus constituting a seizure.

Analysis:

Many fear the Court's conclusion that the placement of a beeper in a can is not a search or seizure under the Fourth Amendment will result in expanded police observation over personal property. While there is a distinction between a beeper that tracks movements and a microphone that records incriminating conversations, the Court's decision could potentially lead to further erosion of Fourth Amendment protections.

Kyllo v. United States

(Drug Dealer) v. *(Prosecuting Government)*

533 U.S. 27, 121 S. Ct. 2038, 150 L. Ed. 2d 94 (2001)

USING THERMAL IMAGING TO OBTAIN EVIDENCE FROM A PRIVATE RESIDENCE CONSTITUTES A SEARCH

■ **INSTANT FACTS** Federal agents used a thermal-imaging device from the street outside Kyllo's (D) residence to determine that the amount of heat emanating from the house was consistent with the presence of high-temperature lamps used to cultivate marijuana.

■ **BLACK LETTER RULE** The use of a device not used by the general public to obtain evidence emanating from the interior of a residence that cannot otherwise be obtained without physical intrusion constitutes a search.

■ PROCEDURAL BASIS

Certiorari to review the defendant's conviction.

■ FACTS

A federal agent, suspecting Kyllo (D) was cultivating marijuana in his residence, used a thermal-imaging device to detect the relative amount of heat emanating from his residence as compared to those surrounding him. After reviewing the test results, the agent concluded that the heat disparity between Kyllo's (D) residence and those around him suggested the presence of high-temperature lamps used to grow marijuana. On the basis of the test results and other evidence, the agent obtained a warrant and seized over 100 marijuana plants. Kyllo (D) moved to suppress the evidence at trial, which motion was denied.

■ ISSUE

Does the use of a non-intrusive technological device to obtain evidence from inside a person's home constitute a search under the Fourth Amendment?

■ DECISION AND RATIONALE

(Scalia, J.) Yes. The expectation of privacy safeguarded by the Fourth Amendment protects one's actions within his own home. The use of technological devices not in use by the general public in order to obtain information regarding the interior of one's home, which could not otherwise be obtained without physical intrusion, thus constitutes a search. While technology has complicated questions concerning the Fourth Amendment, the privacy of one's home must be preserved to ensure that the Fourth Amendment maintains, at a minimum, the purpose for which it was adopted. Reversed and remanded.

■ DISSENT

(Stevens, J.) The information collected by the thermal-imaging device did not emanate from the interior of the house, but rather was only that exposed to the general public from the outside of the house. The device did not penetrate the walls into the house's interior, measuring only the heat disparity between that home's exterior walls as compared to its neighbors'. Heat differences can be determined from the exterior of the house by any member of the public using the senses. Once heat leaves the house, the occupant no longer maintains a subjective expectation of privacy. The Court's reliance on future advances in technology and the impact its decision will have on Fourth Amendment privacy rights is troubling. It is at once too broad and too narrow, in that it excepts technological advancements that come within the general use of the public and encompasses all "sense-enhancing technology," including dogs trained to sniff out narcotics, but it protects only the interior of a home, to the exclusion of other places where a reasonable expectation of privacy exists. Further, the Court's decision ignores the factual distinctions with *Katz*, in which the content of the communication was obtained through a listening device. Here, the device did not detect the source of the heat, but merely its presence outside the house.

Analysis:

Commentators suggest that the Court's decision will have only limited effect on Fourth Amendment cases. Generally siding with the dissent, they argue that the Court's holding leaves open to debate whether the device utilized in a given circumstance is generally used by the public. Even at the time of the decision in 2001, debate surfaced whether the device used by the officers in 1991 was in general use by the public.

United States v. White

(*Prosecuting Government*) v. (*Drug Dealer*)
401 U.S. 745, 91 S. Ct. 1122, 28 L. Ed. 2d 453 (1971)

ELECTRONIC SURVEILLANCE EVIDENCE OBTAINED WITH AN INFORMANT'S CONSENT IS ADMISSIBLE

■ **INSTANT FACTS** White (D) was convicted of drug charges based on the testimony of government agents who overheard incriminating conversations between the defendant and an informant by way of a listening device carried by the informant.

■ **BLACK LETTER RULE** A person bears the risk that communications with another regarding criminal activities will be transmitted, electronically or otherwise, to government agents.

■ PROCEDURAL BASIS

Certiorari to review a decision of the court of appeals setting aside the defendant's conviction.

■ FACTS

White (D) and a government informant discussed several illegal drug transactions in the informant's home and car and in public. Government agents, through a listening device placed on the informant's person with his permission, overheard the conversations. At trial, the informant was not produced, but the testimony of the government agents was introduced to support the charges. Over objections, the court allowed the agents' testimony. White (D) was convicted. The court of appeals reversed, finding that *Katz* rendered evidence obtained through electronic surveillance inadmissible against the defendant.

■ ISSUE

Does the Fourth Amendment bar testimony from government agents who overheard conversations between a defendant and a government informant who was wearing a listening device on his person?

■ DECISION AND RATIONALE

(White, J.) No. Criminal defendants bear the risk that communications with others will be transmitted, electronically or otherwise, to government agents. Although *Katz* protects individuals from search and seizure when they maintain a justifiable expectation of privacy, White (D) had no such justifiable expectation. One who discusses criminal activities with another can have no justifiable expectation that the conversations will not be reported to the police. The fact that the police may overhear the conversations through a listening device carried by an informant does not affect this expectation. Whether the individual speaks directly to an undercover agent, the informant later reveals the conversation to the police, or the informant relays the conversation through a listening device, a defendant bears the risk that his or her privacy will be breached. This expectation of privacy is not justifiable. Reversed.

■ CONCURRENCE

(Black, J.) "Justice Black ... concurs in the judgment of the Court for the reasons set forth in his dissent in *Katz v. United States*."

■ CONCURRENCE

(Brennan, J.) While current Fourth Amendment law requires a warrant in situations such as those presented, *Katz* does not apply retroactively to events occurring before the decision was rendered, such as those at issue here.

■ DISSENT

(Douglas, J.) Monitoring threatens to infringe on one's ability to freely speak and confine his message to a small group of trusted individuals. The "essence of the idea of privacy" contained in the First, Fourth, and Fifth Amendments demands some protection of free expression.

■ DISSENT

(Harlan, J.) The Court's holding affords law enforcement too much power and invades the fundamental protections of the Fourth Amendment. The admission of evidence obtained through electronic surveillance in every case overly burdens citizens' expectations of privacy under the Fourth Amendment. When, as here, the agents utilize a listening device solely with the consent of an informant, the free exchange of information underlying the liberties afforded by the Fourth Amendment is restricted. Courts should not rely exclusively on the self-restraint of law enforcement officers in deciding whether electronic surveillance will be used, but should first require a warrant so that the government must justify the need to employ such surveillance, rather than placing the risk on society.

■ DISSENT

(Marshall, J.) The protections provided by the requirement of a warrant become especially important in the area of electronic surveillance and must be strictly enforced in accordance with the Fourth Amendment.

Analysis:

The Court's opinion focuses on the defendant's risk that the person to whom he communicates is or may be betraying him to the government. In *Katz*, the government agents acted unilaterally in listening to the conversation, without assistance from the parties to the conversation. Here, however, the informant consented to the government's actions. While no warrant was obtained in either instance, the cooperation of one of the parties to the conversation relieves Fourth Amendment concerns. Note that the Court places some emphasis on the second prong of the analysis set forth in Justice Harlan's concurrence in *Katz*. While the defendant here had a subjective expectation of privacy, his expectation was considered objectively unreasonable.

■ CASE VOCABULARY

INFORMANT: One who informs against another; especially, one who confidentially supplies information to the police about a crime, sometimes in exchange for a reward or special treatment.

Zurcher v. Stanford Daily

(*Government Official*) v. (*Newspaper*)
436 U.S. 547, 98 S. Ct. 1970, 56 L. Ed. 2d 525 (1978)

THE PRESS IS NOT IMMUNE FROM A VALID SEARCH WARRANT

■ **INSTANT FACTS** The Stanford Daily (P) sought declaratory relief after the police obtained a search warrant to search for evidence potentially related to others' criminal activity.

■ **BLACK LETTER RULE** A warrant may issue to search any property, regardless of whether the occupant is suspected of a crime.

■ PROCEDURAL BASIS

Certiorari to review an undisclosed appellate decision.

■ FACTS

Nine police officers were injured by demonstrators at the Stanford University Hospital. Several days later, the Stanford Daily (P) published photos of the alleged assailants. A warrant was issued to search the Stanford Daily's (P) offices for information related to the demonstration, but no evidence was found. The Stanford Daily (P) then instituted a civil action seeking declaratory relief. The court held that the Fourth Amendment forbade a warrant to search the possessions of one not accused of a crime unless a subpoena duces tecum would be impracticable, and that the First Amendment bars the search of a newspaper's offices unless a clear showing is made that important materials would otherwise be destroyed or lost.

■ ISSUE

May the police obtain a search warrant to search the property of a newspaper company not suspected of a crime?

■ DECISION AND RATIONALE

(White, J.) Yes. The Fourth Amendment permits a valid warrant to search any property on which there is probable cause to believe that evidence of a crime will be found. It is immaterial whether the property is occupied by a third party. The State's interest in preventing crime remains the same regardless of the occupant's status. Similarly, the State's interest in preserving evidence early in an investigation often requires prompt action to collect evidence that may be lost or destroyed while a subpoena duces tecum issues and all challenges to its validity are resolved. A warrant does not become unconstitutional merely because the press is involved. When First Amendment interests may be implicated by a warrant, the court must employ exacting scrutiny to ensure that these interests are not unduly infringed, but need not decline to issue the warrant.

■ CONCURRENCE

(Powell, J.) "Even aside from the difficulties involved in deciding on a case-by-case basis whether a subpoena can serve as an adequate substitute, . . . there is no constitutional basis for such a reading."

■ DISSENT

(Stewart, J.) Police searches of newspaper offices disrupt the physical operations of the newspaper and burden the freedom of the press. Newsgathering, writing, editing, and publishing are interrupted while the police search places in which the press works. A subpoena, by contrast, enables the newspaper to retrieve and turn over the requested evidence without such a disruption. The more important burden, however, is the potential disclosure of confidential sources and material necessary to truthgathering and a free press. The mere threat of a police raid of the newspaper offices undermines the First Amendment.

■ DISSENT

(Stevens, J.) Countless citizens may have information in their possession that may relate to ongoing criminal investigations. Allowing the police to obtain a search warrant to locate such information places no limits on where the police may look and what other private matters they may find. A warrant necessarily requires a showing of probable cause for forcible entry, but without a showing that the custodian of evidence is a criminal, there is no probable cause to justify the force. Without probable cause, the search violates the Fourth Amendment.

Analysis:

In response to the *Zurcher* decision, the California legislature amended Cal. Penal Code § 1524 to bar search warrants that authorize the search of items protected by the newspaper privilege. The section was further amended to expand the applicable privileges to include the attorney-client privilege, the doctor-patient privilege, and others so long as the possessor of the items is not himself reasonably suspected of criminal activity to which the items relate.

■ CASE VOCABULARY

FREEDOM OF THE PRESS: The right to print and publish materials without government intervention, as guaranteed by the First Amendment.

Spinelli v. United States

(*Convicted Criminal*) v. (*Prosecuting Government*)
393 U.S. 410, 89 S. Ct. 584, 21 L. Ed. 2d 637 (1969)

AN INFORMANT MUST HAVE RELIABLE KNOWLEDGE OF THE SUBJECT MATTER OF HIS TIP

■ **INSTANT FACTS** Spinelli (D) was convicted of gambling offenses proscribed by Missouri law and challenged the constitutionality of the warrant authorizing the FBI search that uncovered the evidence supporting his conviction.

■ **BLACK LETTER RULE** In order for a search warrant based on an informant's tip to be valid, the informant must declare either that he himself saw or perceived the fact or facts asserted or that the underlying circumstances surrounding his information sufficiently demonstrate its reliability.

■ PROCEDURAL BASIS

Certiorari to review the Eighth Circuit Court of Appeals' decision affirming the federal district court's conviction of the defendant for interstate travel in aid of racketeering.

■ FACTS

Spinelli (D) was convicted of traveling to St. Louis, Missouri from Illinois with the intention of conducting gambling activities proscribed by Missouri law. The warrant police used to obtain the evidence necessary for Spinelli's (D) conviction was based on information from a confidential and reliable police informant. The informant indicated to police that Spinelli was accepting wagers and disseminating wagering information by means of two specific telephone numbers. The tip from the informant did not indicate whether the informant had personal knowledge of the alleged gambling activities.

■ ISSUE

Is a tip from an informant based on hearsay, even when part of it has been corroborated by independent police sources, as trustworthy as a tip from an informant who has seen or perceived the facts asserted, such that it supports the issuance of a search warrant?

■ DECISION AND RATIONALE

(Harlan, J.) No. An informant's report must first be measured against the standard set forth in *Aguilar v. Texas*, 378 U.S. 108 (1964), so that its probative value may be assessed. Under *Aguilar*, in order for a search warrant based on an informant's tip to be valid, the warrant application must present sufficient underlying circumstances necessary to enable the magistrate to independently determine probable cause and an assertion of the affiant that the informant was credible and his information reliable. Here, the affiant asserted that the informant was reliable, but gave no reason justifying his assertion. Moreover, the informant's tip does not contain underlying circumstances from which his contention that Spinelli (D) was engaging in illegal gambling activities can be supported, such as how the information was obtained or why his sources were reliable. It is crucial that the magistrate have particular details on the manner in which the informant obtained his information to corroborate its truthfulness and determine that probable cause exists. Reversed.

■ CONCURRENCE

(White, J.) Once the informant specifically identified two different telephone lines from which Spinelli (D) allegedly engaged in gambling activities, his gambling allegations became reliable enough to infer a business operation occurring in the apartment and, considering police awareness of his past criminal activities, to support probable cause.

Analysis:

This decision affirmed the importance of the standards set forth by the Court in *Aguilar*. It is important to determine whether an informant has personal knowledge or observation of the events or circumstances referenced in the tip to authorities. Without evidence of such knowledge, further substantiation of the reasons for the informant's conclusions is required.

■ CASE VOCABULARY

PROBABLE CAUSE: A reasonable ground to suspect that a person has committed or is committing a crime or that a place contains specific items connected with a crime.

Illinois v. Gates

(*Prosecuting Government*) v. (*Drug Offender*)
462 U.S. 213, 103 S. Ct. 2317, 76 L. Ed. 2d 527 (1983)

PROBABLE CAUSE IS NOT A MECHANICAL, TECHNICAL CONCEPT

■ **INSTANT FACTS** Police searched the defendants' home and car after obtaining a warrant based in part on an anonymous handwritten tip.

Black Letter Rule: Probable cause for a warrant resulting from an anonymous informant's tip can be adduced under the totality of the circumstances.

■ PROCEDURAL BASIS

Certiorari to review a decision of the Illinois Supreme Court affirming the trial court's decision to suppress evidence seized pursuant to a search warrant.

■ FACTS

Respondents Lance and Susan Gates (D) were indicted for violation of state drug laws after police officers, executing a search warrant, discovered marijuana and other contraband in their automobile and home. The search was executed based on an anonymous handwritten letter that detailed how the couple traveled separately to Florida to buy drugs, with Susan Gates (D) driving the family car down to Florida and Lance Gates (D) flying down to Florida to meet her several days later before the couple would drive their automobile back to Illinois. The police verified driver's license information and flight information. Agents then followed Lance's flight to Florida and followed him to a hotel room rented by his wife. They observed the couple drive off in a car with Illinois plates on a freeway used to travel to Illinois. The couple returned to Illinois only thirty-six hours after Lance originally flew out of Illinois. A judge issued a search warrant for their residence based on this information. The trial court suppressed the evidence seized from the Gates' home because of a lack of probable cause. The Illinois Appellate Court and Supreme Court each affirmed.

■ ISSUE

In order for a warrant based on an informant's anonymous tip to be valid, must the elements of "veracity," "reliability," and "basis of knowledge" exist separately and independently?

■ DECISION AND RATIONALE

(Rehnquist, J.) No. While an informant's veracity, reliability, and basis of knowledge are important considerations in evaluating the value of his information, they should be understood simply as closely intertwined issues that may usefully illuminate the common-sense, practical question whether there is "probable cause" to believe that contraband or evidence exists in a particular place. This totality of the circumstances test is far more consistent with the Court's prior treatment of probable cause than any rigid demand that specific tests be satisfied by every tip. By considering the overall effect of the three factors rather than mechanically applying each, an informant's history of consistently reliable information can compensate for times when the basis of his knowledge may be weaker than desired. Likewise, tips from an unreliable informant acting with a vindictive motive may nonetheless support probable cause if the basis of his knowledge is strong. Setting too high a high standard for probable cause may force magistrates to conduct full evidentiary hearings before issuing warrants, or may force police to conduct warrantless searches in the hopes they will get consent rather than face the threat that their good-faith affidavits supporting the warrant will be found defective. Reversed.

■ CONCURRENCE

(White, J.) While the anonymous tip standing alone did not establish probable cause for the warrant, the affidavit describing the police investigation corroborated it sufficiently to establish probable cause. The critical issue is not whether the activities observed by the police are innocent or suspicious, but rather whether the actions of the suspects, whatever their nature, give rise to an inference that the informant is credible and that he obtained his information in a reliable manner. By treating each factor independently, the Court reaches a curious conclusion that a tip from an anonymous informant known for his reliability may suffice to establish probable cause, yet an officer's affidavit that fails to profess a basis for his knowledge, but is known as reliable to the magistrate, could not possibly support a warrant. It was not necessary to overrule *Aguilar-Spinelli* to reach the correct result here.

■ DISSENT

(Brennan, J.) In *Spinelli*, the Court established that police corroboration of an anonymous informant's tip may satisfy *Aguilar*'s basis of knowledge and veracity prongs. By requiring police to provide certain crucial information to magistrates and by structuring magistrates' probable cause inquiries, *Aguilar* and *Spinelli* assure the magistrate's role as an independent arbiter of probable cause and greater accuracy in probable cause determinations. Under the Court's totality of the circumstances approach, however, neither magistrates nor the police are afforded any guidance in determining whether probable cause exists.

■ DISSENT

(Stevens, J.) The anonymous letter incorrectly indicated that Susan Gates (D) drove the car to Florida, left it, and flew back to Illinois. Instead, Susan Gates (D) drove to Florida, remained there until her husband joined her, and returned in the car with him. The incorrect prediction of the informant casts doubt on his reliability, and the true facts are less suspicious than alleged in the letter. Because of these discrepancies, the police were not able to corroborate the informant's tip sufficiently to establish probable cause.

Analysis:

This decision effectively overruled *Aguilar* and *Spinelli*. The former rule required tips from informants to meet separate tests for "veracity" and "basis of knowledge." The new rule applies a "totality of the circumstances" test in which a deficiency in one element may be compensated for by the other in determining the overall reliability of the tip.

■ CASE VOCABULARY

CORROBORATION: Confirmation or support by additional evidence or authority.

VERACITY: Truthfulness.

Maryland v. Pringle

(*Prosecuting Government*) v. (*Drug Possessor*)

540 U.S. 366, 124 S. Ct. 795, 157 L. Ed. 2d 769 (2003)

REASONABLE SUSPICION ESTABLISHES PROBABLE CAUSE

■ **INSTANT FACTS** Pringle (D) was arrested after cocaine was found in the rear seat of a vehicle in which Pringle (D) was a front-seat passenger.

■ **BLACK LETTER RULE** Probable cause generally requires a reasonably particularized ground for belief of a defendant's guilt.

■ PROCEDURAL BASIS

Certiorari to review a decision of the Court of Appeals of Maryland reversing the defendant's conviction.

■ FACTS

Pringle (D) was the front-seat passenger in a vehicle driven by a friend. Another passenger was in the rear seat. When the vehicle was stopped for speeding, the officer noticed a large roll of money in the glove compartment. The officer searched the vehicle with the driver's consent and found cocaine behind the rear-seat armrest, which was folded up against the back seat of the car. All three men were arrested after none of them claimed ownership of the drugs. At the police station, Pringle (D) confessed to ownership of the drugs and claimed the other occupants were unaware of their existence. At trial, however, Pringle (D) moved to suppress his confession as the fruit of an illegal arrest, arguing that the officer had no probable cause to arrest him. The motion was denied and Pringle (D) was convicted. On appeal, the Court of Appeals of Maryland reversed, finding that the officer had no probable cause to arrest Pringle (D) because there was no indication that Pringle (D) had knowledge and dominion or control over the drugs at the time of arrest.

■ ISSUE

Did the officer have probable cause to arrest the defendant based on contraband found in the backseat of a car in which he was a front-seat passenger?

■ DECISION AND RATIONALE

(Rehnquist, C.J.) Yes. Probable cause generally requires a reasonably particularized ground for belief of a defendant's guilt. Here, there was no doubt that a crime had been committed. The officer found a large amount of money rolled up in the vehicle's glove compartment and thereafter discovered illegal narcotics concealed in the small vehicle in which the three men were riding. As nobody claimed personal responsibility for the drugs, there was a reasonable inference that any or all of the men had knowledge, dominion, or control of the drugs. The officer had probable cause to arrest Pringle (D) and his confession should not have been suppressed. Reversed and remanded.

Analysis:

Although there was no evidence at the time of arrest that Pringle (D) had actual control over the drugs in the car, the Court held here that probable cause for his arrest existed nonetheless. Fourth

Amendment advocates have suggested that the Court's ruling gives law enforcement far too much power to arrest individuals under the mere suspicion of criminal activity. Because it was clear that a crime was committed, Pringle's (D) arrest without an individualized assessment of his involvement in the crime amounted to an arrest by association.

■ CASE VOCABULARY

LAWFUL ARREST: The taking of a person into legal custody either under a valid warrant or on probable cause that the person has committed a crime.

MOTION TO SUPPRESS: A request that the court prohibit the introduction of illegally obtained evidence at a criminal trial.

Maryland v. Garrison

(Prosecuting Government) v. *(Drug Possessor)*

480 U.S. 79, 107 S. Ct. 1013, 94 L. Ed. 2d 72 (1987)

POLICE OFFICERS HAVE LATITUDE IN EXECUTING VALID SEARCH WARRANTS

■ **INSTANT FACTS** Garrison's (D) apartment was searched as a result of a lack or awareness that his apartment was separate from the premises identified in a search warrant.

■ **BLACK LETTER RULE** Good faith factual mistakes do not invalidate an otherwise valid search warrant.

■ PROCEDURAL BASIS

Certiorari to review a decision of the Maryland Supreme Court reversing the defendant's conviction and remanding for a new trial.

■ FACTS

The police obtained a warrant to search the person of McWebb and the third floor apartment at a specified address, believing that the third floor contained only one apartment. Police executed the warrant by searching the third floor of the premises and discovered drugs and other contraband. After seizing the evidence, however, the police learned that the third floor contained two apartments, including the one leased to Garrison (D) where the contraband was discovered. The trial court denied Garrison's (D) motion to suppress the evidence, and he was convicted of violating the Maryland Controlled Substances Act. The court of special appeals affirmed, but the Maryland Supreme Court reversed and remanded.

■ ISSUE

Do good faith factual mistakes invalidate an otherwise valid search warrant or its execution?

■ DECISION AND RATIONALE

(Stevens, J.) No. To prevent general searches, the Fourth Amendment permits only warrants "particularly describing the place to be searched and the persons or things to be seized." This limitation restricts the scope of the search to those places and things for which probable cause supports the search. Here, the description of the place to be searched was broader than necessary because of the good faith factual mistake concerning the number of apartments on the third floor. Clearly, if the officers had known Garrison's (D) apartment was separate from McWebb's, they would have been obligated to exclude it from the warrant. However, from the information available to the police and presented to the magistrate, probable cause existed to support the issuance of the warrant, and it is not invalidated because of the mistake of fact.

Police are entitled to some latitude for honest mistakes in executing a valid search warrant. Clearly had the officers known at the time of the search that the third floor contained two apartments, they would not be justified executing the warrant on Garrison's (D) apartment. Likewise, upon discovering the error in the warrant, they were obligated to terminate the search, which they did. At all times, the officers' actions were objectively reasonable, suggesting that they neither knew nor should have known of the factual errors of the warrant. The execution of the warrant was valid. Reversed and remanded.

■ DISSENT

(Blackmun, J.) The warrant specifically authorized the search and seizure of drugs on McWebb's person and in his apartment only. It is illogical to read the "third floor apartment" language of the warrant as permitting the search of the entire third floor. The warrant supported the search of one apartment on the floor, and the search of Garrison's (D) apartment was therefore warrantless and unconstitutional. Furthermore, the police did not act reasonably in gathering information concerning the configuration of the apartment to excuse their actions as good faith. Had they even approached the building during their investigation, they would have learned that there were seven mailboxes in front, indicating seven separate apartments, and calling for more thorough investigation to particularly describe the place to be searched.

Likewise, police execution of the warrant was not reasonable. At the time of execution they should have noticed the seven mailboxes and further inquired as to McWebb's residence. At a minimum, when they entered the common area separating McWebb's apartment from Garrison's (D) apartment, it should have been readily apparent that the two apartments were separate. Most importantly, the officers conducted a preliminary security sweep of both apartments before executing the warrant. From this sweep, the officers certainly should have realized that the two apartments were separate.

Analysis:

Just as the exclusionary rule cannot cure a constitution violation that has already occurred, one may wonder why a good faith exception can justify a warrantless search that has already infringed upon Fourth Amendment rights. The exclusionary rule is judicially invoked not to remedy an unreasonable search or seizure, but rather to deter against such violations in the future. The Court appears to take a contrary approach in *Garrison*, for although the constitutional violation has occurred, the good faith exception does nothing to deter against future violations. Instead, the exception excuses them.

■ CASE VOCABULARY

GOOD FAITH: A state of mind consisting in (1) honesty in belief or purpose, (2) faithfulness to one's duty or obligation, (3) observance of reasonable commercial standards of fair dealing in a given trade or business, or (4) absence of intent to defraud or to seek unconscionable advantage.

Richards v. Wisconsin

(*Drug Offender*) v. (*Prosecuting Government*)
520 U.S. 385, 117 S. Ct. 1416, 137 L. Ed. 2d 615 (1997)

POLICE USUALLY MUST KNOCK AND ANNOUNCE THEIR PRESENCE PRIOR TO EXECUTING A WARRANT

■ **INSTANT FACTS** Police forcibly entered a hotel room without knocking and announcing their presence and seized drugs on the premises.

■ **BLACK LETTER RULE** In order to dispense with the knock-and-announce requirement, police must demonstrate their reasonable suspicion that application of the rule would be dangerous or futile or would result in destruction of evidence of the crime.

■ PROCEDURAL BASIS

Certiorari to review a decision of the Wisconsin Supreme Court affirming the defendant's conviction.

■ FACTS

Police went to the defendant's motel room and knocked on the door. One officer was dressed as a maintenance man, two were in plain clothes, and one was a uniformed officer. The suspect opened door with the chain attached and slammed it shut when he saw officers. The officers waited two to three seconds before breaking the door open, announcing that they were police officers as they did so. The officers seized cash and cocaine found in the room. Richards (D) moved to suppress the evidence because the officers failed to knock and announce their presence before forcibly entering the room. The court denied the motion because the officers could reasonably presume from the defendant's behavior that he knew they were police officers and that evidence may likely be destroyed. The Wisconsin Supreme Court affirmed his conviction, holding that an officer need not ever announce his presence in a felony drug case because his safety would likely be jeopardized.

■ ISSUE

Does the threat of physical violence or destruction of evidence during execution of a search warrant in felony drug cases justify dispensing with the knock-and-announce requirement in every case?

■ DECISION AND RATIONALE

(Stevens, J.) No. The fact that felony drug investigations may frequently present circumstances warranting a no-knock entry cannot remove from the neutral scrutiny of the reviewing court the reasonableness of the police decision not to knock and announce in a particular case. In each case it is the duty of the court confronted with the question to determine whether the facts and circumstances of the particular entry justified dispensing with the knock-and-announce requirement. Creating a blanket exception to the knock-and-announce rule for a general category of criminal behavior creates concerns of over-generalization and the possibility of the exception being applied to other categories of behavior that it was not intended to govern. Before dispensing with the knock-and-announce requirement, the police must have a reasonable suspicion that application of the rule would be dangerous or futile, or that it would inhibit effective law enforcement. Although the Wisconsin Supreme Court erred in creating a blanket exception for felony drug cases, the facts sufficiently demonstrate that the officers were justified in dispensing with the requirement here because a reasonable suspicion of destruction of evidence existed.

Analysis:

The Court here affirmed the principles set out in *Wilson v. Arkansas*, 514 U.S. 927 (1995), in which it recognized that the knock-and-announce requirement could give way "under circumstances presenting a threat of physical violence," or "where police officers have reason to believe that evidence would likely be destroyed if advance notice were given." The Court believed these considerations were insufficient to warrant a blanket exception for all felony drug cases, however, and held that each case should be reviewed on an individual basis.

■ CASE VOCABULARY

KNOCK–AND–ANNOUNCE RULE: The requirement that the police knock at the door and announce their identity, authority, and purpose before entering a residence to execute an arrest or search warrant.

United States v. Watson

(*Prosecuting Government*) v. (*Felon*)
423 U.S. 411, 96 S. Ct. 820, 46 L. Ed. 2d 598 (1976)

A STATUTE AUTHORIZING WARRANTLESS FELONY ARRESTS IS CONSTITUTIONAL.

■ **INSTANT FACTS** Watson (D) was arrested without a warrant by a federal postal inspector as authorized by federal statute.

■ **BLACK LETTER RULE** Felony arrests may be made solely on the basis of probable cause, without a warrant.

■ **PROCEDURAL BASIS**

Certiorari to review a decision of a federal court of appeals reversing the defendant's conviction.

■ **FACTS**

A reliable informant told a federal postal inspector that Watson (D) had provided him with a stolen credit card and agreed to provide more at a meeting to be held several days later. At the meeting, the informant signaled the inspector that Watson (D) had the cards, and Watson (D) was arrested without a warrant as authorized by federal statute. Watson (D) was convicted, but the court of appeals reversed, finding the warrantless arrest unconstitutional.

■ **ISSUE**

Is a federal statute authorizing a warrantless arrest based on probable cause unconstitutional?

■ **DECISION AND RATIONALE**

(White, J.) No. The federal statute authorizes a postal inspector to make a warrantless arrest based on probable cause. The Fourth Amendment does not require a warrant to make a felony arrest, but rather insists upon reasonable grounds for the making the arrest. At common law, federal marshals were authorized to make warrantless arrests to the same extent as state law enforcement officers. While it is judicially preferred that arrests be made on a valid warrant, there is no reason to invalidate the longstanding practice, both statutory and at common law, of permitting arrests solely on probable cause. The statute does not violate the Fourth Amendment. Reversed.

■ **CONCURRENCE**

(Powell, J.) Because the Fourth Amendment applies equally to searches and seizures, it would appear that the warrant requirement applicable to searches should properly apply to seizures of the person. Yet, warrantless arrests had gained considerable approval at the time of the adoption of the Fourth Amendment, justifying the result the Court reaches. A warrant requirement for felony arrests would severely hamper law-enforcement objectives, because a warrantless arrest would demand that the criminal be set free while a delayed arrest after obtaining a warrant may result in release due to the lapse of time.

■ **DISSENT**

(Marshall, J.) Watson's (D) arrest was justified under the exigent circumstances. The informant's signal that Watson (D) possessed the stolen credit cards immediately provided the inspector probable cause to believe that Watson (D) had committed a crime and was in possession of crucial evidence. Because a warrantless arrest is permitted under such exigent circumstances, the Court should not have considered whether a warrant was otherwise necessary. Because this case involves exigent circumstances, there is no need to explore the conditions in which a warrantless arrest is appropriate when such circumstances are not present. Furthermore, the Court's reliance on historical treatment of warrantless arrests is misguided, for at common law only the most serious offenses were felonies, justifying warrantless arrests. Today many crimes constitute felonies even though they were mere misdemeanors in the past. The rationale applicable to warrantless felony arrests thus simply does not extend to modern times. A warrant requirement will not unjustly interfere with law-enforcement objectives, for once probable cause exists, it will continue to exist until a warrant can issue. There is no risk that the police will be compelled to terminate their investigation to obtain a warrant nor that probable cause will become stale by any delay.

Analysis:

The Court's decision takes the determination of probable cause away from a magistrate and places it in the hands of law enforcement officers. Without a warrant application, a magistrate is not permitted to evaluate the facts presented to determine whether an arrest is justified. Instead, the law enforcement officer is charged with determining probable cause and making the arrest, perhaps putting too much authority and discretion in one basket.

■ CASE VOCABULARY

EXIGENT CIRCUMSTANCES: A situation in which a police officer must take immediate action to effectively make an arrest, search, or seizure for which probable cause exists, and thus may do so without first obtaining a warrant.

United States v. Robinson

(*Prosecuting Government*) v. (*Drug Offender*)
414 U.S. 218, 94 S. Ct. 467, 38 L. Ed. 2d 427 (1973)

POLICE MAY SEARCH ARRESTEES FOR EVIDENCE OR WEAPONS

■ **INSTANT FACTS** Robinson (D) was convicted of possession of a controlled substance after evidence obtained in a search incident to arrest was admitted at trial.

■ **BLACK LETTER RULE** No matter how insignificant an arrest, the police have the right to search the suspect's person for potential weapons or evidence.

■ PROCEDURAL BASIS

Certiorari to review the decision of the court of appeals reversing the judgment of conviction.

■ FACTS

The police stopped Robinson (D) and arrested him for driving without a license. The police performed a protective frisk of Robinson (D) during the arrest and felt and removed a hard object in his shirt pocket, knowing it was not a weapon. The object turned out to be a crumpled up cigarette pack that contained drugs. The officer conducting the frisk said the object felt like a cigarette pack, but did not feel like it contained cigarettes. The evidence was admitted at trial, and Robinson (D) was convicted. On appeal, the court of appeals reversed, holding that the evidence had been seized during an illegal search.

■ ISSUE

Do government agents have the authority to conduct a full search of a person pursuant to a lawful custodial arrest?

■ DECISION AND RATIONALE

(Rehnquist, J.) Yes. The fact of the lawful arrest establishes the authority to search. In the case of a lawful custodial arrest, a full search of the person is not only an exception to the warrant requirement of the Fourth Amendment, but is also a reasonable search under the Amendment without any independent justification for the search. It is the nature of the custodial arrest that endangers officers, not the severity of the crime for which the suspect is arrested. Police should not be required to make subjective decisions in each case as to whether the suspect may be armed or in possession of valuable evidence in danger of destruction. Reversed.

■ DISSENT

(Marshall, J.) The Fourth Amendment requires a case-by-case assessment of the reasonableness of a search incident to arrest. While the officer here was instructed to take Robinson (D) into custody, many traffic violations are punishable only by citation. Yet, under the Court's per se rule and officer has the authority to search the individual. Potentially, the police, not capable of establishing probable cause for a search warrant, may use a traffic stop as pretext to conduct a search.

Determining whether a search and seizure are unreasonable requires a court to consider whether the officer's action was justified at its inception and whether the scope of the search was reasonably related to the circumstances that justified it. Here, the officer was justified in conducting a limited patdown upon arrest to ensure that Robinson (D) was not carrying a weapon. However, the officer had no reason to believe that the object in Robinson's (D) pocket was a weapon. Because the search did not produce a weapon and could not have produced any evidence related to the traffic violation charged, the scope of the search exceeded the initial justification and was unreasonable. And even assuming the officer was justified in searching the person and removing the package from his pocket to ensure his safety, the search of the package itself raises different concerns, for the search expands beyond the person to his papers and effects. The package could not have contained a weapon. Even if it did, Robinson (D) could not have used it once the package was in the officer's hands.

Analysis:

The Court here rejected the idea that the reason for searching a person incident to a lawful arrest must be litigated in each case. The Court set forth a bright-line rule that an arrest is a triggering event that entitles government agents to conduct a full search of the person, regardless of whether the police have reason to believe the suspect is armed or carrying contraband.

■ CASE VOCABULARY

LAWFUL ARREST: The taking of a person into legal custody either under a valid warrant or on probable cause that the person has committed a crime.

PROTECTIVE SEARCH: A search of a detained suspect and the area within the suspect's immediate control, conducted to protect the arresting officer's safety and often to preserve evidence.

Whren v. United States

(*Drug Offender*) v. (*Prosecuting Government*)
517 U.S. 806, 116 S. Ct. 1769, 135 L. Ed. 2d 89 (1996)

POLICE STOPS NEED ONLY BE SUPPORTED BY PROBABLE CAUSE

■ **INSTANT FACTS** Whren (D) was charged with violating various federal drug laws after a traffic stop and challenged the admission of contraband evidence discovered pursuant to the stop.

■ **BLACK LETTER RULE** The temporary detention of a motorist who the police have probable cause to believe has committed a civil traffic violation is consistent with the Fourth Amendment.

■ PROCEDURAL BASIS

Certiorari to review a decision of a federal court of appeals affirming the defendants' convictions.

■ FACTS

Plainclothes officers saw a vehicle stopped in a suspicious manner in a high-crime area. When they turned to pull up next to the vehicle, the vehicle turned without signaling and sped off. The officers chased the vehicle and stopped it. When the officers went to the window of the vehicle, they saw bags of drugs lying on the defendant passenger's lap and arrested the defendants. At a pretrial suppression hearing, the defendants challenged the legality of the stop and subsequent seizure of the drugs. Specifically, the defendants contended that the stop was pretextual without suspicion of drug activity. The court denied the suppression motion and the defendants were convicted. The court of appeals affirmed the convictions, holding that the traffic stop was appropriate as long as a reasonable officer in the same position would have stopped the car.

■ ISSUE

Is the temporary detention of a motorist who the police have probable cause to believe has committed a civil traffic violation inconsistent with the Fourth Amendment's prohibition against unreasonable seizures?

■ DECISION AND RATIONALE

(Scalia, J.) No. A brief detention on a traffic violation is a seizure within the meaning of the Fourth Amendment and must be based on probable cause to believe that a traffic violation has occurred. Even when an office has ulterior motives for his stop, those motives will not make an otherwise appropriate seizure invalid if probable cause for the traffic stop existed. Thus, the temporary detention of a motorist who the police have probable cause to believe has committed a civil traffic violation is not inconsistent with the Fourth Amendment's prohibition against unreasonable seizures. Affirmed.

Analysis:

This decision has been criticized as overlooking an important issue regarding a pervasive law enforcement practice. Critics have alleged that pretextual traffic stops have increased markedly since the *Whren* decision. Critics also believe that the *Whren* decision has led to increased racial profiling in traffic stops.

■ CASE VOCABULARY

PRETEXT: A false or weak reason or motive advanced to hide the actual or strong reason or motive.

Atwater v. City of Lago Vista

(Parent) v. *(Arresting Government)*

532 U.S. 318, 121 S. Ct. 1536, 149 L. Ed. 2d 549 (2001)

WARRANTLESS ARRESTS ARE AUTHORIZED EVEN FOR OFFENSES PUNISHABLE BY ONLY A FINE

■ **INSTANT FACTS** Atwater (P) was arrested without a warrant for minor traffic offenses, none of which was punishable by imprisonment.

■ **BLACK LETTER RULE** If a law enforcement officer has probable cause to believe that a person has committed even a very minor criminal offense in his or her presence, the officer may arrest that person without a warrant.

■ PROCEDURAL BASIS

Appeal from a decision affirming the district court's order granting summary judgment for the City of Lago Vista (D).

■ FACTS

Atwater (P) was seen driving her pickup truck with her two children in the front seat. None of the three was wearing a seat belt. A police officer employed by the City of Lago Vista (D) stopped Atwater (P) and asked to see her driver's license and insurance information. Atwater (P) said she did not have her license or insurance papers because her purse had been stolen the day before. The officer then handcuffed Atwater (P) and took her to the police station where she was photographed, booked, and placed in a jail cell for approximately one hour. Atwater (P) was released on $310 bond and charged with driving without her seatbelt fastened, failing to secure her children in seatbelts, driving without a license, and failing to provide proof of insurance. She pleaded no contest to the seatbelt offenses and paid a fifty-dollar fine. Atwater (P) then brought a suit for civil rights violations pursuant to 42 U.S.C. § 1983, alleging that her arrest violated her Fourth Amendment right to be free from unreasonable seizure. The district court granted the City's (D) motion for summary judgment. A panel of the Fifth Circuit Court of Appeals reversed, but that decision was vacated by the full court sitting en banc.

■ ISSUE

Does the Fourth Amendment prohibit a warrantless arrest for a minor offense punishable only by a fine?

■ DECISION AND RATIONALE

(Souter, J.) No. If a law enforcement officer has probable cause to believe that a person has committed even a very minor criminal offense in his or her presence, the officer may arrest that person without a warrant. Historically, there has been an understanding that warrantless arrests for nonviolent misdemeanors are reasonable. Atwater (D) contends that the Court should fashion a rule prohibiting warrantless arrests for offenses that carry no jail time if the government shows no compelling need for immediate detention. Such a rule would be unworkable, however, and would not provide guidance for law enforcement officers faced with a need to make a quick decision. It is not always possible for an officer to determine immediately whether an offense may carry jail time. The imposition of jail time often depends upon facts that will not be readily apparent, such as prior offenses. Similarly, it is difficult to determine which offenders might pose a danger to the public upon being released.

In Fourth Amendment jurisprudence, there is a preference for a categorical rule that precludes the kind of individualized review that would be necessary under the rule proposed by Atwater (P). It does not appear that the problem is serious enough to merit the development of a new body of constitutional law. Accordingly, as with all criminal offenses, if an officer has probable cause to believe that an offense has been committed, he may arrest the offender without a warrant. Affirmed.

■ DISSENT

(O'Connor, J.) Probable cause alone is not sufficient to make a warrantless arrest for fine-only offenses. A custodial arrest is a serious matter, and more than probable cause should be required before a person is taken into custody for an offense that carries no jail time. If the State has decided that the offense lacks the severity to punish the offender with jail time, it has also determined that its interest in taking the offender into custody is minimal. The arresting officer should be able to point to specific, articulable facts that, along with the rational inferences drawn from those facts, reasonably warrant a full custodial arrest.

Analysis:

Most minor, fine-only crimes do not involve the kind of split-second analysis the Court seeks to avoid. In most cases, it is generally clear to the officer at the scene what the probable charge will be. It seems clear, too, that the majority doesn't view the issue here as a big problem, both in the sense that it is not widespread, and that the harm to the individual is minimal. Thus, in essence, the majority does not want to make a rule that restricts police conduct in cases not seen as posing a major issue.

■ CASE VOCABULARY

INFRACTION: A violation, usually of a rule or local ordinance and usually not punishable by incarceration.

MISDEMEANOR: A crime that is less serious than a felony and is usually punishable by fine, penalty, forfeiture, or confinement (usually for a brief term) in a place other than prison (such as a county jail).

Tennessee v. Garner

(*State Government*) v. (*Shooting Victim's Father*)
471 U.S. 1, 105 S. Ct. 1694, 85 L. Ed. 2d 1 (1985)

SHOOTING AN UNARMED BURGLARY SUSPECT WHO WAS ATTEMPTING TO FLEE VIOLATES THE FOURTH AMENDMENT

■ **INSTANT FACTS** A police officer shot and killed Garner, who was known to be unarmed, when Garner attempted to flee the scene of a burglary.

■ **BLACK LETTER RULE** Under the Fourth Amendment, peace officers may not use deadly force to prevent the escape of a felony suspect unless the officers have probable cause to believe that the suspect presents a threat to the life or safety of the officers or others.

■ PROCEDURAL BASIS

Certiorari to review a decision of the Sixth Circuit Court of Appeals reversing a trial court decision declaring a Tennessee statute constitutional.

■ FACTS

Memphis police officers were dispatched after receiving a call regarding a suspected burglary in progress. Upon arriving at the scene, the officers spoke with the caller, who claimed to have heard glass breaking next door. One officer went around to the back of the house, where he heard a door slam and saw Garner flee across the yard. When Garner stopped at the fence bordering the yard, the officer saw Garner's face and hands and noticed that Garner was not carrying a weapon. As the officer approached Garner and advised him not to move, Garner began to climb the fence to escape. In order to prevent Garner from escaping, the officer shot him in the back of the head. Garner died on the operating table. The shooting complied with police department policy and a Tennessee statute permitting the use of deadly force to stop a fleeing suspect. Garner's father (P) sued the officer and the police department under 42 U.S.C. § 1983, seeking damages for violations of his son's constitutional rights. The State of Tennessee (D) intervened to defend the constitutionality of its statute. The federal district court declared the statute and the officer's actions constitutional, but the Sixth Circuit Court of Appeals reversed. The State (D) sought certiorari in the United States Supreme Court.

■ ISSUE

Is the use of deadly force by an officer to prevent the escape of an unarmed felony suspect constitutional if the suspect does not pose a significant threat of death or bodily injury to the officer or others?

■ DECISION AND RATIONALE

(White, J.) No. A police officer's action that prevents a person from walking away constitutes a seizure under the Fourteenth Amendment. The reasonableness of his actions, therefore, comes into question. Because reasonableness relates not only to the need for a seizure, but also to the manner in which it is conducted, reasonableness governs both when and how the seizure is made. These factors must be weighed against the extent of the intrusion to determine whether a seizure is reasonable. This balancing approach indicates that while an officer may seize a person if probable cause that the person committed a crime exists, he may not always do so by killing the suspect. Deadly force is the most severe intrusion upon an individual's liberty and may not be used merely to advance the governmental objective of deterrence. A seizure by deadly force is both the beginning and the end of the criminal process. Any deterrent effect of deadly force, by encouraging the peaceful surrender of suspected felons, comes at too great a cost to the liberty interests of the individual. It would be better to have guilty suspects escape than to have innocent suspects die. That is not to say, however, that the use of deadly force is unconstitutional per se. When a police officer has probable cause to believe that a felony suspect is a threat to the life or safety of the officer or others, the officer may employ deadly force to prevent the suspect's escape. Accordingly, the Tennessee statute is not unconstitutional on its face, but only as applied to those situations in which probable cause is lacking. As the officer here could not have reasonably believed the unarmed suspect posed a threat to the officer or others, the use of deadly force violated the Fourth Amendment in this case. Affirmed.

■ DISSENT

(O'Connor, J.) Whether Garner's seizure violates the Fourth Amendment requires a balancing of the public interest in crime prevention with the individual's liberty interests. The public interest involved relates to preventing serious and dangerous crimes. Because of the probability that violence will result, burglary is a serious and dangerous felony, and the public interest in its prevention is compelling. While the individual's liberty interest in his life is obviously important, it does not encompass the right to flee the scene of a burglary when ordered to stop by a police officer. Weighing these two interests, there is an apparent clash between the public interest in preventing dangerous felonies and an individual's liberty interests.

Analysis:

One aspect not addressed by *Garner* is exactly when a nondangerous suspect becomes dangerous to others. When a fleeing suspect who appears not to be dangerous runs from police, the police are not justified in using deadly force, but they are justified in pursuing the suspect. If the suspect flees by vehicle and drives erratically, the question remains whether the suspect constitutes an imminent threat to the safety of others, though the danger results not from the initial felony, but from the police chase. High-speed police pursuits continue to be the subject of controversy and great public interest.

■ CASE VOCABULARY

DEADLY FORCE: Violent action known to create a substantial risk of causing death or serious bodily harm.

Payton v. New York

(*Accused Criminal*) v. (*Prosecuting Government*)
445 U.S. 573, 100 S. Ct. 1371, 63 L. Ed. 2d 639 (1980)

ARRESTS ARE SIMILAR TO SEARCHES FOR PURPOSES OF WARRANT REQUIREMENTS

■ **INSTANT FACTS** In separate cases, New York police officers entered the private residences of two felony suspects without a warrant to make arrests.

■ **BLACK LETTER RULE** An arrest warrant is required to arrest a person in his or her home.

■ PROCEDURAL BASIS

Certiorari to review a decision of the New York Court of Appeals affirming the defendants' convictions.

■ FACTS

Acting on information that Theodore Payton (D) had murdered a gas station attendant, police went to his apartment, without a warrant, with the intent to arrest Payton (D). Hearing music within the apartment, police knocked on the door but received no answer. Police then used crowbars to open the door to the apartment. No one was there, but police seized a shell casing that was found in plain view on the door opening. Payton (D) was indicted for murder and convicted after the shell casing was admitted into evidence.

In a separate case, police knocked on Riddick's (D) door after he was identified by the victims of two armed robberies that had occurred several years earlier. When his young son answered, the police could see Riddick (D) lying in a bed covered by a sheet. They entered the house without a warrant, searched it, and arrested him. Evidence of narcotics and drug paraphernalia was admitted against him at trial, which resulted in his conviction.

In a consolidated decision, the New York Court of Appeals affirmed both convictions.

■ ISSUE

Can police enter a private residence without a warrant to make a routine felony arrest?

■ DECISION AND RATIONALE

(Stevens, J.) No. Searches and seizures inside a home without a warrant are presumptively unreasonable. Just as with a warrantless entry to recover weapons or other evidence reasonably believed to be in a private dwelling, the constitutional protection afforded to an individual's interest in privacy in is own home precludes a warrantless entry for the purpose of arresting a resident of the house, for it is inherent in such an entry that a search for the suspect may be required before he can be apprehended. In other words, both an entry to seize property and an entry to make an arrest intrude upon the privacy of one's home. Reversed and remanded.

■ DISSENT

(White, J.) The Fourth Amendment is concerned with protecting people, not places, but here talismanic significance is given to the fact that an arrest occurs in the home rather than elsewhere. The requirements that police officers knock and announce their presence for a felony arrest, do so only during daytime hours, and have reasonable grounds to believe that the arrestee has committed a crime and is in fact present in the home should be sufficient protections of an individual's privacy interest in the home. It should not be necessary for the police to have an arrest warrant if it is guaranteed that the person's privacy interests in the home can be protected by a means less stringent to police.

Analysis:

The Court emphasized here that "the Fourth Amendment has drawn a firm line at the entrance to the house." The home has always been considered a sacred place. Requiring the police to obtain a warrant to arrest people in their homes does not place a significant burden on law enforcement. Police may, for instance, arrest the suspects when they leave their homes, or, if they know they are going to stay there, they can obtain a warrant.

Chimel v. California

(*Burglary Suspect*) v. (*Prosecuting State*)
395 U.S. 752, 89 S. Ct. 2034, 23 L. Ed. 2d 685 (1969)

IMMEDIATE–REACH SEARCHES ARE ALLOWED WHEN AN ARREST IS MADE

■ **INSTANT FACTS** Chimel (D) was charged with two counts of burglary and argued that items taken from his home and admitted into evidence against him had been unconstitutionally seized.

■ **BLACK LETTER RULE** Pursuant to a lawful arrest, the police may conduct a search of any area within the immediate reach of the accused criminal.

■ PROCEDURAL BASIS

Certiorari to review a decision of a state appellate court affirming the defendant's conviction.

■ FACTS

Police arrived at Chimel's (D) home with a warrant to arrest him for burglary. The officers knocked on the door and announced themselves to Chimel's (D) wife, who then let them into the home to wait for Chimel (D) to arrive. Chimel (D) arrived about fifteen minutes later and the police gave him the arrest warrant and asked for permission to search the house. Chimel (D) refused, but the police told him they were going to search the house incident to a lawful arrest. The police searched the entire house, including the attic and garage. The police also had Chimel's (D) wife open several drawers in the sewing room and move things aside so they could see clearly. Several items were seized, including coins, medals, tokens, and other objects. At trial, Chimel (D) was convicted after the admission of the evidence. The conviction was affirmed on appeal.

■ ISSUE

Can the police search an accused criminal's entire home incident to a lawful arrest?

■ DECISION AND RATIONALE

(Stewart, J.) No. Pursuant to a lawful arrest, the police may conduct a search of any area within the immediate reach of the accused criminal. The purpose of this exception to the warrant requirement is to allow searches for weapons or anything the accused may use to harm police or conduct an escape. The search must be contained to any area where the police reasonably believe a weapon may be hidden and to which the defendant may readily obtain access. Additionally, the police may search the accused's person and seize any evidence discovered to avoid its destruction.

There is no comparable justification for routinely searching any room other than that in which an arrest occurs. Any such search may only be conducted pursuant to a valid search warrant or upon the existence of exigent circumstances. Here, the search extended considerably beyond the area within Chimel's (D) immediate control and within which he may have concealed a weapon that threatened police safety. Because the search was unreasonable, the conviction cannot stand. Reversed.

■ CONCURRENCE

(Harlan, J.) The Court's decision will have significant implications on local law enforcement systems throughout the country. The Court should consider such implications to better understand the problems its warrant requirement will cause.

■ DISSENT

(White, J.) When the existence of probable cause is independently established and would justify a warrant for a broader search for evidence, a search of the entire house should be permitted without a warrant since the fact of arrest supplies an exigent circumstance justifying police action before evidence can be removed and alerts the suspect to the search, so that he can immediately seek judicial determination of probable cause.

Analysis:

The Court applied the "principle of particular justification," which provides that the police must, whenever practicable, obtain advance judicial approval of searches and seizures through the warrant procedure, and that the scope of a search must be strictly tied to and justified by the circumstances that rendered the initiation of the search permissible. In reaching this decision the Court overruled *Rabinowitz* and *Harris*, which permitted searches of an office and a four-room apartment incident to a lawful arrest. The Court believed that if police were allowed to search the entire dwelling where a suspect was arrested, the Fourth Amendment protection in this area would approach the evaporation point.

Vale v. Louisiana

(Drug Dealer) v. *(Prosecuting Government)*
399 U.S. 30, 90 S. Ct. 1969, 26 L. Ed. 2d 409 (1970)

THE SEARCH OF A HOUSE IS NOT INCIDENT TO ARREST WHEN THE ARREST OCCURRED OUTSIDE THE HOUSE

■ **INSTANT FACTS** Vale (D) was convicted after police arrested him on his front steps and searched his house for narcotics.

■ **BLACK LETTER RULE** A search incident to a lawful arrest must be substantially contemporaneous with the arrest and confined to the immediate vicinity of the arrest.

■ PROCEDURAL BASIS

Certiorari to review a decision of the Louisiana Supreme Court affirming the defendant's conviction.

■ FACTS

With two warrants for Vale's (D) arrest, officers set up surveillance at his home in an unmarked car. The officers watched as Vale (D) left the house, approached a car, and returned back inside. A few minutes later, Vale (D) returned and leaned through the passenger window after looking up and down the street. When the officers drove toward Vale (D), he looked up and abruptly turned to return inside while the driver of the car attempted to drive away. The officers got out of their car and instructed Vale (D) to stop and that he was under arrest. The driver of the car was seen quickly placing something in his mouth and was also arrested. The police then searched Vale's (D) house and found nobody else present, but narcotics were located. The Louisiana Supreme Court upheld the search because it was within the vicinity of the arrest and "substantially contemporaneous therewith."

■ ISSUE

Is a search of a house incident to arrest lawful when the arrest occurs on the front steps?

■ DECISION AND RATIONALE

(Stewart, J.) No. A search incident to a lawful arrest must be "substantially contemporaneous with the arrest and . . . confined to the *immediate* vicinity of the arrest." For a search of a house to be incident to arrest, the arrest must be made inside the house. Without consent, an officer may not search a house without a warrant unless exceptional circumstances exist. The State (P) has not demonstrated any such circumstances. An arrest on the street, by itself, cannot establish its own exigent circumstance. Reversed and remanded.

■ DISSENT

(Black, J.) The arrest occurred outside the house, but only after the police witnessed Vale (D) move back and forth between the house and the car in an apparent drug transaction. The police did not know whether anybody else was in the house and the risk that others could destroy evidence was substantial. Had the police abandoned their search after Vale's (D) family was informed of his arrest, any delay in obtaining a warrant would have given them time to destroy any evidence necessary for his conviction. Quite aside from the arrest, the police had probable cause to believe that narcotics were present in the house. Such exigent circumstances justify a warrantless search whether an arrest had been made or not.

Analysis:

The Court again acknowledges the heightened expectation of privacy of one's home. Note that while the police may not search a recently occupied home when an arrest is made nearby, the police may search a recently occupied automobile incident to arrest although the driver was not arrested in the vehicle. Automobiles do not enjoy the same level of privacy expectations as one's home.

California v. Carney

(Prosecuting Government) v. *(Accused Criminal)*
471 U.S. 386, 105 S. Ct. 2066, 85 L. Ed. 2d 406 (1985)

THE AUTOMOBILE EXCEPTION TO THE WARRANT REQUIREMENT APPLIES TO LIVE–IN VEHICLES

■ **INSTANT FACTS** Carney (D) was charged with possession of marijuana for sale after police seized drugs in his motor home during a warrantless search.

■ **BLACK LETTER RULE** Warrantless searches of readily movable vehicles are not unreasonable when probable cause supports the search.

■ PROCEDURAL BASIS

Certiorari to review a decision of the California Supreme Court reversing the defendant's conviction.

■ FACTS

Police received information that a motor home occupied by Carney (D) was being used to exchange marijuana for sex. Government agents accompanied a youth to the motor home and the youth entered the motor home and remained inside for one and one-quarter hours. When the youth emerged from the motor home, he informed a drug enforcement agent that he had received marijuana in exchange for allowing Carney (D) to engage in sexual contact with him. The agent then accompanied the youth to the motor home, where the youth knocked on the door. When Carney (D) stepped out, the agents identified themselves as law enforcement officers and entered the motor home without a warrant or consent. Inside the motor home, the agents observed marijuana, plastic bags, and a scale of the kind used to measure drugs. Carney was taken into custody and the agents took possession of the motor home. During a later search of the motor home, they discovered additional marijuana in the cupboards and refrigerator. The evidence was used against Carney (D) to gain a conviction, but the California Supreme Court reversed, ruling the search unreasonable because no warrant was obtained.

■ ISSUE

Does the automobile exception to the warrant requirement apply to vehicles such as a motor home, which individuals may be using as their home?

■ DECISION AND RATIONALE

(Burger, C.J.) Yes. If a vehicle is being used on the highways or if it is readily capable of such use and is found stationary in a place not regularly used for residential purposes, temporary or otherwise, two justifications for the vehicle exception come into play. First, when a vehicle is readily mobile, there is a lesser expectation of privacy than with regard to a permanent residence because of the heavy government regulation over the operation and registration of motor vehicles. Second, because a vehicle can be quickly moved, it is often impracticable to obtain a warrant before a search. In these circumstances, the overriding societal interests in effective law enforcement justify an immediate search before the vehicle and its occupants become unavailable. While a vehicle may have many of the characteristics of a home, its mobility requires the application of the motor-vehicle exception. The search was not unreasonable. Reversed.

■ DISSENT

(Stevens, J.) Motor homes, by their common use and construction, afford their owners a substantial and legitimate expectancy of privacy when they dwell within. When a motor home is parked in a location that is removed from the public highway, society should be prepared to recognize that the expectations of privacy within are not unlike the expectations one has in a fixed dwelling. Warrantless searches of living quarters in a motor home should be presumptively unreasonable absent exigent circumstances.

Analysis:

Critics have argued the decision in this case goes too far. The Court's decision was based partly on the fact that automobiles are subject to a variety of government regulations. The critics have questioned whether it opened the door for warrantless searches of individual dwellings that are subject to building, health, and safety codes.

Thornton v. United States

(*Drug Possessor*) v. (*Prosecuting Government*)
541 U.S. 615, 124 S. Ct. 2127, 158 L. Ed. 2d 905 (2004)

POLICE OFFICERS MAY SEARCH A RECENTLY OCCUPIED VEHICLE INCIDENT TO A LAWFUL ARREST

■ **INSTANT FACTS** A police officer searched Thornton's (D) vehicle although he was arrested for drug possession outside his vehicle.

■ **BLACK LETTER RULE** A police officer may search a vehicle incident to lawful arrest once probable cause exists to arrest a recent occupant of the vehicle who had access to the interior of the vehicle.

■ PROCEDURAL BASIS

Certiorari to review the defendant's conviction.

■ FACTS

When a police officer discovered that the license tags on Thornton's (D) vehicle had been issued to another vehicle, the officer stopped Thornton (D). Thornton (D) parked and exited the vehicle. The officer approached him, informed him of the license violation, and asked if he had any illegal drugs on him. Thornton (D) produced some marijuana and crack cocaine and was placed in the police car. A search of the vehicle produced a handgun under the driver's seat. Thornton (D) was convicted of drug possession and possession of a firearm.

■ ISSUE

May a police officer search a vehicle incident to an arrest when the arrest occurs outside the vehicle?

■ DECISION AND RATIONALE

(Rehnquist, C.J.) Yes. In *New York v. Belton*, 453 U.S. 454 (1981), the Supreme Court established that a police officer may search the passenger compartment of a vehicle incident to a lawful arrest of the occupant because the occupant had access to and control over the interior of the vehicle. When the suspect has left the vehicle, the officer's right to search the vehicle is no different, for the immediate access to and control over the interior of the vehicle exists no less when the occupant has recently exited the vehicle than when he remains seated in the driver's seat. As a bright-line approach, "[o]nce an officer determines that there is probable cause to make an arrest, it is reasonable to allow officers to ensure their safety and to preserve evidence by searching the entire passenger compartment."

■ CONCURRENCE

(O'Connor, J.) While the Court's decision is a logical extension of *Belton*, the law in this area is unsettled and requires further definition. Justice Scalia's position appears the better approach, but should not apply in this case where neither party had an opportunity to comment upon its merits.

■ CONCURRENCE

(Scalia, J.) The type of search at issue can be reasonably justified as necessary to prevent the concealment or destruction of evidence of the commission of the crime for which the suspect has been arrested. Searches for this purpose find support in Court precedent as a narrow exception to the broad goal of collecting and preserving evidence. The Court's decision here moves away from the narrow purpose of avoiding the destruction of evidence toward the broader goal of collecting evidence, which risks violating a motorist's reasonable expectation of privacy in his vehicle, given the wide array of arrests that may occur. To balance this danger, the search of one's vehicle incident to an arrest must be limited to those cases in which the officer reasonably believes evidence relevant to the crime of arrest might be found.

■ DISSENT

(Stevens, J.) When a pedestrian is arrested for a crime, his constitutional interest in privacy should overcome the state's need to search his vehicle for any potentially valuable evidence. The law clearly provides that an officer may not search a pedestrian's home incident to arrest when the suspect is not in the home. There should be no distinction between a person's home and his vehicle when he is present in neither. Further, the bright-line test established by the Court permits the police to search a vehicle in which an arrested suspect has been a "recent occupant," but fails to determine or define how recent is "recent." Without resolving such important issues, the Court's bright-line test threatens the unjustified expansion of searches of vehicles incident to arrest.

Analysis:

Once Thornton (D) was lawfully arrested for drug possession, one may wonder why the warrantless search of the vehicle was necessary. If Thornton (D) no longer had access to the vehicle to retrieve the handgun or any other contents, the threat to the officer's safety and the risk of destruction of evidence appear minimal. On the facts of this case, sufficient time appears to have been available to obtain a proper warrant to search the vehicle.

■ CASE VOCABULARY

SEARCH: An examination of a person's body, property, or other area that the person would reasonably be expected to consider as private, conducted by a law-enforcement officer for the purpose of finding evidence of a crime.

Knowles v. Iowa

(Speeder) v. *(Prosecuting Government)*
525 U.S. 113, 119 S. Ct. 484, 142 L. Ed. 2d 492 (1998)

POLICE MAY NOT SEARCH A VEHICLE FOLLOWING A TRAFFIC CITATION

■ **INSTANT FACTS** Knowles (D) was convicted of drug possession after his car was searched incident to a speeding citation.

■ **BLACK LETTER RULE** An officer may not search a vehicle incident to a citation.

■ PROCEDURAL BASIS

Certiorari to review a decision of the Iowa Supreme Court affirming the defendant's conviction.

■ FACTS

Knowles (D) was stopped for speeding and was issued a citation. The officer then searched the car and discovered marijuana and drug paraphernalia. Knowles (D) was arrested for drug possession. At trial, the court denied Knowles's (D) request to suppress the evidence because Iowa law had established that an officer may conduct a full search of a car stopped for a traffic violation. Knowles (D) was convicted. On appeal, the Iowa Supreme Court affirmed the conviction and reaffirmed the officer's right to search the vehicle incident to a citation, finding that an actual custodial arrest is not necessary.

■ ISSUE

May a police officer conduct a full search of a car driven by a person stopped for speeding and issued a citation?

■ DECISION AND RATIONALE

(Rehnquist, C.J.) No. A warrantless search incident to arrest is permissible because of the need to disarm a suspect in order to take him into custody and to preserve evidence for trial. When there is no custodial arrest, the danger to the officer is significantly lessened due to the brief encounter between the officer and the suspect. The degree of danger in such situations does not justify a full search of the vehicle. Likewise, when a speeding citation is issued, all evidence needed to support the citation has been collected. The officer will find no evidence demonstrating the suspect's excessive speed from a search of the vehicle. An officer may not search a vehicle incident to a citation. Reversed and remanded.

Analysis:

The Court's decision may actually place a greater burden on traffic offenders than it relieves. Under state law, an arresting officer had the option of issuing a citation and making a custodial arrest for the traffic violation. As a result of this case, any officer wishing to search the vehicle for weapons or other evidence appears to be able to do so only by invoking his option to arrest the suspect. That result places a far greater burden on the otherwise innocent traffic offender than would a search of his vehicle incident to citation.

California v. Acevedo

(Prosecuting Authority) v. *(Drug Offender)*
500 U.S. 565, 111 S. Ct. 1982, 114 L. Ed. 2d 619 (1991)

POLICE MAY SEARCH A SEALED CONTAINER IN AN AUTOMOBILE WHEN PROBABLE CAUSE EXISTS

■ **INSTANT FACTS** Police seized marijuana from Acevedo's (D) car without a warrant after seeing him emerge from an apartment known to contain marijuana.

■ **BLACK LETTER RULE** The policy may search an automobile and the containers within it if they have probable cause to believe contraband or evidence is contained therein.

■ PROCEDURAL BASIS

Certiorari to review the decision of the California Court of Appeals affirming the defendant's conviction.

■ FACTS

Monitoring Daza's apartment because they had observed him take a package known to contain marijuana into his home, police saw Acevedo (D) enter Daza's apartment and emerge carrying a brown paper bag the size of the marijuana package. Acevedo (D) placed the bag in the trunk of his car and drove away. Police stopped his car without a warrant, opened the trunk, and found the bag of marijuana, which they then opened. The California Court of Appeals held that the evidence should have been suppressed.

■ ISSUE

Does the Fourth Amendment require police to obtain a warrant to open a container placed in an automobile, which they have probable cause to believe contains contraband, simply because they lack probable cause to search the entire car?

■ DECISION AND RATIONALE

(Blackmun, J.) No. A warrantless search of an automobile may include a search of a container or package found inside the vehicle when such a search is supported by probable cause. Different rules applicable to the search of an automobile as opposed to a private container placed in an automobile lead to confusion for law-enforcement officers about the proper boundaries of a search. The rule should not rely on whether a search of an automobile coincidentally uncovers a container or whether a search of a container coincidentally occurs in an automobile. "The policy may search an automobile and the containers within it where they have probable cause to believe contraband or evidence is contained." Reversed.

■ CONCURRENCE

(Scalia, J.) The standard for automobile searches should be the "reasonableness" requirement of the Fourth Amendment, which affords the same protection the common law afforded. The judgment in the present case should be reversed not because a closed container carried inside a car becomes subject to the "automobile" exception to the general warrant requirement, but because the search of a closed container, outside a privately owned building, with probable cause to believe that the container contains contraband, and when it does in fact contain contraband, is not one of those searches whose Fourth Amendment reasonableness depends upon a warrant.

■ DISSENT

(White, J.) "Agreeing as I do with most of Justice Stevens' opinion and with the result he reaches, I dissent and would affirm the judgment below."

■ DISSENT

(Stevens, J.) A person carrying a bag or a briefcase down the street may not be subject to a warrantless search, yet here the Court has decided that once that same container is placed in a car, those protections disappear. One's privacy interest in one's personal belongings can certainly not be diminished by one's removing them from a public thoroughfare and placing them, out of sight, in a privately owned vehicle. Nor is the danger that evidence will escape increased if the personal belongings are placed in a car rather than on the street. In either location, if the police have probable cause, they are authorized to seize the property and detain it until they obtain judicial approval for a search. Any line demarking an exception to the warrant requirement will appear blurred at the edges, but the Court has certainly erred if it believes that, by erasing one line and drawing another, it has drawn a clearer boundary.

Analysis:

The law applicable to a closed container in an automobile has troubled courts and law enforcement since it was first considered in *Chadwick*. The Court here attempted to set out a bright-line rule that would govern all searches of automobiles, including any containers contained within an automobile. Many have criticized the decision as merely muddying the confusion surrounding the "automobile" exception to the general warrant requirement even more.

■ CASE VOCABULARY

STARE DECISIS: The doctrine of precedent, under which it is necessary for a court to follow earlier judicial decisions when the same points arise again in litigation.

Wyoming v. Houghton

(Prosecuting Government) v. *(Drug Possessor)*
526 U.S. 295, 119 S. Ct. 1297, 143 L. Ed. 2d 408 (1999)

PASSENGERS HAVE A LIMITED EXPECTATION OF PRIVACY IN A VEHICLE

■ **INSTANT FACTS** Houghton (D) was convicted when evidence recovered from her purse during a search of a vehicle in which she was a passenger was admitted against her at trial.

■ **BLACK LETTER RULE** Police officers with probable cause to search a car may inspect passengers' belongings found in the car that are capable of concealing the object of the search.

■ PROCEDURAL BASIS

Certiorari to review a decision of the Wyoming Supreme Court reversing the defendant's conviction.

■ FACTS

Police stopped a vehicle driven by Young for speeding and a faulty taillight. In the front seat with Young were his girlfriend and Houghton (D). While questioning Young, police noticed a hypodermic syringe in his pocket and asked him to exit the vehicle. Young admitted using the needle to inject drugs. Houghton (D) and the girlfriend were asked to exit the vehicle and provide identification. Houghton (D) provided a false name without producing identification. The police then searched the vehicle and discovered a purse claimed by Houghton (D) in the back seat. Upon searching the purse, police found identification contradicting her earlier statement. Also in the purse was a brown pouch and a black container, but Houghton (D) denied ownership and claimed not to know how they got in her purse. Drug paraphernalia were also discovered, of which Houghton (D) admitted ownership. Houghton (D) was arrested for drug possession. At trial, the court denied a motion to suppress the evidence seized, finding that the officer had probable cause to search the car and its contents. Houghton (D) was convicted. On appeal, the Wyoming Supreme Court reversed, holding that the officers had no reason to believe that the purse belonged to the female passenger.

■ ISSUE

May police officers with probable cause to search a car inspect passengers' belongings found in the car that are capable of concealing the object of the search?

■ DECISION AND RATIONALE

(Scalia, J.) Yes. To determine whether a Fourth Amendment violation occurred, a court must first consider whether such a search was forbidden under the common law at the time the Amendment was adopted. Historical evidence and Court precedent support a general rule that when an officer has probable cause to believe that a vehicle contains contraband, he is justified in searching the entire vehicle, including its contents, without a warrant. It is not the ownership of the property searched that is important, but rather whether the property searched is reasonably believed to contain contraband.

Moreover, a balancing of the interests involved demonstrates the reasonableness of the search. Passengers possess a reduced expectation of privacy in the property they carry into a vehicle and transport on a public highway highly regulated by the government. Law enforcement, on the other hand, would be substantially hampered if police were prohibited from searching containers belonging to a passenger when probable cause exists to suspect the vehicle contains contraband. Individuals involved in a criminal enterprise could easily evade police detection by placing such items in passengers' containers rather that those belonging to the driver. Police officers with probable cause to search a car may inspect passengers' belongings found in the car that are capable of concealing the object of the search. Reversed.

■ CONCURRENCE

(Breyer, J.) It is far too much to expect a police officer with probable cause to establish the ownership of a container within a vehicle before a search. Such a rule, however, is limited only to automobile searches and not to searches of the person. While a passenger has a limited expectation of privacy in her belongings in an automobile, the expectation of her personal privacy is not so limited. If the purse were attached to her person, the police may not have been justified in searching it, just as if it were outer clothing.

■ DISSENT

(Stevens, J.) The search of a passenger's purse or briefcase involves a substantial intrusion on her privacy. Before such a search can occur, probable cause should be more precise than a belief that the vehicle contained contraband. There should be probable cause that the purse or briefcase, specifically, contains contraband.

Analysis:

Critics point to the *Houghton* decision as an unjustified expansion of the automobile exception, eroding the expectation of privacy in an automobile to virtually nothing. Had the police searched Houghton's (D) purse while she was sitting in a public place rather than in an automobile, the Fourth Amendment would surely be violated. However, the Court effectively holds that one who chooses to ride in an automobile consents to a search of her belongings when probable cause to search the car exists.

Colorado v. Bertine

(Prosecuting Government) v. *(Arrested Motorist)*
479 U.S. 367, 107 S. Ct. 738, 93 L. Ed. 2d 739 (1987)

POLICE DO NOT NEED A WARRANT TO SEARCH A CLOSED CONTAINER IN A VEHICLE PURSUANT TO AN INVENTORY SEARCH

You're under arrest for drunk driving.
Now we'll conduct an invasive "inventory" of the contents of your van for your own protection. No need to thank me.

■ **INSTANT FACTS** Evidence obtained from a closed backpack in Bertine's (D) van during an arrest was suppressed.

■ **BLACK LETTER RULE** A routine inventory search is not a criminal investigation and does not require a warrant or probable cause.

■ PROCEDURAL BASIS

Certiorari to review a decision of the Colorado Supreme Court affirming a trial court decision to suppress evidence.

■ FACTS

Bertine (D) was arrested for driving his van under the influence of alcohol. After he was taken into custody but before his van was towed, another officer inventoried the van's contents. In doing so, he opened a closed backpack to find narcotics and drug paraphernalia. At trial on the drug charges, the evidence was suppressed because although the court held the search did not violate the Fourth Amendment, it did violate the Colorado Constitution. The Colorado Supreme Court affirmed, but concluded that a Fourth Amendment violation did occur.

■ ISSUE

Does a warrantless inventory search of a vehicle incident to arrest not based on probable cause violate the Fourth Amendment?

■ DECISION AND RATIONALE

(Rehnquist, C.J.) No. "The standard of probable cause is peculiarly related to criminal investigations, not routine, noncriminal procedures." A routine inventory search is not a criminal investigation and does not require a warrant or probable cause. Instead, inventory searches protect a person's belongings while they are in police custody to prevent lost, damaged, or stolen property and protect the police from danger. Here, the police did not act in bad faith or for an investigatory purpose. Their sole purpose was to determine the property to be taken into custody to protect against unauthorized interference. The Fourth Amendment does not require that the police make available to the defendant other means of securing his belongings, but rather requires that the police act reasonably in doing so. The police inventoried and towed Bertine's (D) vehicle in good faith, satisfying the Fourth Amendment. Reversed.

■ CONCURRENCE

(Blackmun, J.) Inventories are important, but must be narrowly tailored to standardized police procedures. Only when such procedures mandate the opening of closed containers in an impounded vehicle should such actions be permitted.

■ DISSENT

(Marshall, J.) The officer's discretion in taking an inventory of the vehicle was not limited by any standardized police regulation. Department policy indicates that an officer may allow a third-person to take custody of the vehicle, take it to a public facility, lock it, and take the keys or impound and inventory the vehicle. Only the third option permits a search of the contents of the vehicle to prepare an inventory. When the vehicle itself is not evidence of a crime, the officer should be given guidance as to what sort if items to inventory rather than relying on his own suspicions. Inventory searches are not to be justified as an extension of a police investigation and should not be legitimized because they occur in good faith. The government has little interest in conducting inventory searches unrelated to the crime charged, but the invasion of the defendant's expectation of privacy is substantial.

Analysis:

The Court gives considerable deference to police motives during an inventory search. Permitting an inventory search and allowing any evidence coincidentally found in the process to be admitted at trial relieves the police of any need for good faith. And they need not affirmatively search for incriminating evidence, since they will gain the benefit of any found in the process of their inventory search.

■ CASE VOCABULARY

INVENTORY SEARCH: A complete search of an arrestee's person before that person is booked into jail; the search of an arrestee's impounded vehicle for the purpose of listing everything it contains. All possessions are typically held in police custody.

Terry v. Ohio

(*Weapons Violator*) v. (*Prosecuting Government*)
392 U.S. 1, 88 S. Ct. 1868, 20 L. Ed. 2d 889 (1968)

POLICE MAY STOP AND FRISK SOMEONE REASONABLY BELIEVED TO HAVE COMMITTED A CRIME

■ **INSTANT FACTS** Evidence of a gun found on Terry during a protective frisk by a police officer was admitted into evidence and resulted in his conviction.

■ **BLACK LETTER RULE** If the police have reasonable suspicion that a suspect has committed a crime or is about to commit a crime, they may stop the person, detain him briefly for questioning, and then frisk the suspect if they reasonably believe the suspect is carrying a dangerous weapon.

■ PROCEDURAL BASIS

Certiorari to review a state appellate decision affirming the defendant's conviction.

■ FACTS

A police officer observed two men standing on a corner for a long time. They then walked down the street, peered into a store window, and turned around to walk back to the corner again. This series of events happened several times. At one point, another man approached the two men and spoke with them and then walked in the other direction. He then came back and they followed him. The officer suspected the men were casing the store before committing a robbery. He stopped them to ask for their names. When the men failed to answer audibly, the officer spun Terry (D) around and patted down the outside of his overcoat for a weapon. Upon feeling a gun, the officer ordered the men into a store, where he removed Terry's (D) overcoat and retrieved the gun. After finding a gun on another man, the men were arrested. The trial court denied Terry's (D) motion to suppress the evidence and the Ohio Court of Appeals affirmed.

■ ISSUE

If the police have reason to believe a suspect has committed a crime or is about to commit a crime, may they conduct a stop on less than probable cause?

■ DECISION AND RATIONALE

(Warren, C.J.) Yes. If the police have reasonable suspicion that a suspect has committed a crime or is about to commit a crime, they may stop the person and detain him briefly for questioning, on less than probable cause. An officer may then frisk the suspect if the officer reasonably believes the suspect is carrying a dangerous weapon. In order for crime prevention and detection to be effective, an officer must be able to, in appropriate circumstances and in an appropriate manner, approach a person for purposes of investigating possible criminal behavior even though there is no probable cause to make an arrest. Law enforcement officers must be able to protect themselves and other prospective victims of violence in situations in which they are investigating suspicious behavior of suspected criminals at close range. Affirmed.

■ CONCURRENCE

(Harlan, J.) In order for a frisk to be justified, the officer must first have constitutional grounds to insist on an encounter and make a forcible stop. When the reason for the stop is an articulable suspicion of a crime of violence, however, the right to frisk must be immediate and automatic.

■ CONCURRENCE

(White, J.) Nothing in the Constitution prevents a police officer from questioning one he suspects of criminal behavior, but that suspect is generally free to walk away. Under appropriate circumstances, however, an officer is justified in briefly detaining a suspect while he questions him, although the suspect may not be compelled to answer the questions.

■ DISSENT

(Douglas, J.) By holding that a police officer may stop a person based only upon reasonable suspicion that a crime has been committed, the Court gives the police greater authority to make a seizure and conduct a search than a judge has to authorize such actions. Any seizure must be considered unreasonable unless supported by probable cause.

Analysis:

The result of the *Terry* decision has been a significant diminution in the role of the Warrant Clause in Fourth Amendment jurisprudence. *Terry* provided the impetus for the Supreme Court to move away from the proposition that warrantless searches are per se unreasonable, to the competing view that the appropriate test of police conduct is not whether it was reasonable for police to have secured a search warrant, but whether the search was reasonable. After *Terry*, warrantless searches became much more justifiable. Also, the Court now takes into consideration the level of intrusiveness of each search, instead of treating all searches and seizures alike.

■ CASE VOCABULARY

FRISK: A pat-down search to discover a concealed weapon.

REASONABLE SUSPICION: A particularized and objective basis, supported by specific and articulable facts, for suspecting a person of criminal activity.

Florida v. J.L.

(*Prosecuting Government*) v. (*Juvenile*)

529 U.S. 266, 120 S. Ct. 1375, 146 L. Ed. 2d 254 (2000)

ANONYMOUS TIPS DO NOT ORDINARILY JUSTIFY A STOP AND FRISK

■ **INSTANT FACTS** Police received an anonymous tip that someone matching J.L.'s (D) description was carrying a gun, and J.L. (D) was stopped and frisked.

■ **BLACK LETTER RULE** An anonymous tip that does not bear any indicia of reliability does not justify a stop-and-frisk search.

■ PROCEDURAL BASIS

Appeal from an order of the Florida Supreme Court holding that a search was invalid.

■ FACTS

An anonymous caller informed police that a young black male standing at a particular bus stop and wearing a plaid shirt was carrying a gun. Police officers were sent to the bus stop and saw J.L. (D), who was wearing a plaid shirt, standing at the bus stop with two other males. J.L. (D) was not brandishing a gun and no threatening conduct was observed. Acting solely on the anonymous tip, the officers frisked J.L. (D) and found a gun. He was charged with carrying a concealed firearm without a license and possessing a firearm while under the age of eighteen. The trial court granted J.L.'s (D) motion to suppress the evidence of the gun, but the intermediate appellate court reversed. The Florida Supreme Court reversed the appellate court, holding that the search was invalid.

■ ISSUE

Is an anonymous tip that a person is carrying a gun sufficient justification for a stop-and-frisk search?

■ DECISION AND RATIONALE

(Ginsburg, J.) No. An anonymous tip that does not bear any indicia of reliability does not justify a stop-and-frisk search when it alleges the illegal possession of a firearm. Anonymous tips, standing alone, seldom are sufficiently reliable to justify a search. In some cases, however, the tip may show sufficient reliability to provide reasonable suspicion for an investigatory stop. The anonymous tip here did not contain any such indicia of reliability, so the police had no means to test its accuracy. Although the tip accurately described J.L. (D), it did not show that the informant knew he was involved in criminal activity. It does not matter that a gun was found; the reliability of the tip must be justified on the basis of what was known before the search was conducted.

There is no "firearm exception" to the requirement of reasonable suspicion for a stop-and-frisk search. An automatic exception whenever firearms are involved would go too far and would enable harassment by anyone who wanted to set in motion an embarrassing search of another. Furthermore, it would be difficult to confine the search to firearms. Since drug traffickers often carry guns, an unreliable anonymous tip about drug possession could be used to justify a search for firearms. The rule in this case does not mean that police may not search a person who is the subject of a lawful stop. The decision in this case relates only to the initial stop of a person based on an anonymous tip. Affirmed.

■ CONCURRENCE

(Kennedy, J.) The majority's opinion is correct, on the basis of the record. There may, however, be situations in which an anonymous tip bears indicia of reliability not yet raised by cases before the Court. An anonymous tip may include facts that support reliability or that narrow the likely class of informants, which could provide a lawful basis for police action.

Analysis:

Anonymity is regarded with some suspicion because it does not provide any basis for holding a tipster accountable or for evaluating the tipster's reliability. The concurrence seems to focus more on the anonymity of the tip than on the "bare bones" nature of the information that was provided. A point not raised here is that the tip, as related by the majority, did not even allege criminal activity. The informant apparently did not say that the young black male in a plaid shirt did not have a permit, or that he was a juvenile in possession of a gun, and there is no clear reason given to assume that the young black male did not have the right to carry a gun.

■ CASE VOCABULARY

STOP AND FRISK: A police officer's brief detention, questioning, and search of a person for a concealed weapon when the officer reasonably suspects that the person has committed or is about to commit a crime. The stop and frisk, which can be conducted without a warrant or probable cause, was held constitutional by the Supreme Court in *Terry v. Ohio,* 392 U.S. 1 (1968).

Illinois v. Wardlow

(*Prosecuting State*) v. (*Weapons Violator*)
528 U.S. 119, 120 S. Ct. 673, 145 L. Ed. 2d 570 (2000)

FLIGHT ALONE IS NOT INDICATIVE OF WRONGDOING

■ **INSTANT FACTS** Wardlow (D) was arrested for possession of a handgun discovered after a protective police pat-down.

■ **BLACK LETTER RULE** Flight from police is not indicative of wrongdoing, but it is certainly suggestive of such.

■ PROCEDURAL BASIS

Certiorari to review the decision of the Illinois Supreme Court reversing the defendant's conviction for unlawful use of a weapon by a felon.

■ FACTS

Police were patrolling an area known for heavy narcotics trafficking when officers observed Wardlow (D) flee after he spotted them. Two police officers pursued Wardlow (D), stopped him, and conducted a protective pat-down to look for weapons, squeezing the bag he was carrying. The officer opened the bag to find a concealed loaded handgun.

■ ISSUE

Is the police pat-down of a fleeing individual in a high-crime area unconstitutional?

■ DECISION AND RATIONALE

(Rehnquist, C.J.) No. First, flight from police is not indicative of wrongdoing, although it is certainly suggestive of such. And an individual's presence in an area of expected criminal activity, standing alone, is not enough to support a reasonable, particularized suspicion that the person is committing a crime. But, on the other hand, officers are not required to ignore the relevant characteristics of a location in determining whether the circumstances are sufficiently suspicious to warrant further investigation. Nervous, evasive behavior and unprovoked flight are pertinent factors to create a reasonable suspicion of criminal wrongdoing. Reversed and remanded.

CONCURRENCE IN PART

(Stevens, J.) The Court was right to reject the per se rules proferred by the parties. A pedestrian may break into a run for a variety of reasons, many of them innocent and having no relation to flight from police. There are unquestionably circumstances in which a person's flight is suspicious, and undeniably instances in which a person runs for entirely different reasons. Given the diversity of possible motivations for flight, it would be profoundly unwise to adopt a per se rule that flight alone gives rise to reasonable suspicion.

Analysis:

The Court has held in previous cases that nervous, evasive behavior is a pertinent factor in determining reasonable suspicion. Although the Court stated here that flight is the consummate act of evasion, it declined to adopt a bright-line rule that flight equals reasonable suspicion. There is concern that if such a bright-line rule were adopted, it could be subject to police abuse, particularly in high-crime areas.

Florida v. Royer

(Prosecuting Government) v. *(Drug Possessor)*
460 U.S. 491, 103 S. Ct. 1319, 75 L. Ed. 2d 229 (1983)

A PERSON MAY NOT VOLUNTARILY CONSENT TO A SEARCH OF HIS PROPERTY WHILE HIS IS ILLEGALLY DETAINED

■ **INSTANT FACTS** Royer (D) was convicted of drug possession after his luggage was searched at an airport and marijuana was seized.

■ **BLACK LETTER RULE** When officers have reasonable suspicion that a person has committed a crime or is about to commit a crime, they may temporarily detain the individual for questioning no longer than necessary to serve the purposes of the stop.

■ PROCEDURAL BASIS

Certiorari to review a decision of a Florida appellate court reversing the defendant's conviction.

■ FACTS

After he booked a one-way flight under an assumed name, two detectives approached Royer (D), suspecting him of acting as a drug courier. Royer (D) produced his airline ticket and driver's license and explained that a friend had booked his reservation under the assumed name. Without returning his ticket or driver's license, the detectives asked Royer (D) to accompany them to a small room. When Royer's (D) luggage was retrieved from the airline without his consent, Royer (D) produced a key and unlocked the luggage, in which marijuana was found. The police pried open another suitcase when Royer (D) could not remember the combination and found more marijuana. Royer (D) was arrested and convicted of drug possession after the trial court refused to suppress the evidence found in his luggage. On appeal, the Florida District Court of Appeal reversed, finding that the police had no probable cause to search the luggage and that Royer's (D) detention exceeded the limited restraint authorized to stop and frisk him.

■ ISSUE

Was Royer (D) illegally detained at the time of his consent to the search of his luggage such that the evidence obtained from the search was inadmissible?

■ DECISION AND RATIONALE

(White, J.) Yes. While law enforcement officers may approach an individual for questioning without a warrant, the individual is free to not answer any questions and go on his way. However, when the officers have reasonable suspicion that the person has committed a crime or is about to commit a crime, they may temporarily detain the individual for questioning, but no longer than necessary to serve the purposes of the stop. Even while investigating the individual, the police may not carry out a full search of his belongings without the individual's consent.

Here, when the officers obtained Royer's (D) ticket and driver's license and asked him to accompany them into the room, he was effectively seized, because "a reasonable person would have believed that he was not free to leave." While the seizure and resulting investigative search were justified by the officers' reasonable suspicion that he was carrying drugs and Royer's (D) consent was voluntary, his detention was more serious than can be justified by mere suspicion of criminal activity. By the time the police searched Royer's (D) luggage, he had consented to go to the police room, but his consent cannot extend further. The police had isolated him in the room, retained his ticket and driver's information, and seized his luggage without informing him that he was free to leave at any time. He had been effectively arrested, and any consent had evaporated. Furthermore, the officers' actions were more intrusive that necessary to conduct an investigation. While safety may require that the investigation be transferred to a confined area, there was no showing here of such a need. The relocation thus appears to be a police effort to coerce Royer's (D) consent. Likewise, Royer's (D) luggage could have been searched by less intrusive means, such as trained dogs, without detaining him at all. Affirmed.

■ CONCURRENCE

(Brennan, J.) There is no reason to endorse the legality of the officers' initial stop in this case because whether it was legal or not, their subsequent actions exceeded the proper scope of that stop. *Terry* stops are extremely limited and justify only the briefest detentions. The initial stop was not legal because Royer (D) could not have reasonably believed he was free to go at any time.

■ DISSENT

(Blackmun, J.) The stop at issue was minimally intrusive and the government's need to prevent drug trafficking permits the detention of individuals upon reasonable suspicion. Royer (D) was not formally arrested and cannot be said to have been effectively arrested. Royer (D) had no greater expectation of privacy in a public airport than he would have had if he had been approached in an automobile. Because the detention was lawful, Royer's (D) consent to accompany the police to the room was voluntary.

■ DISSENT

(Rehnquist, J.) While the officers could have chosen different methods of investigating Royer (D), their chosen methods were not unreasonable under the conditions of a crowded airport. Royer was legally approached in the airport and consented to go to the police room. But it does not follow that his consent had evaporated and that he was "arrested" when entering the room.

Analysis:

It is curious that the Court approved the initial confrontation and found Royer's (D) initial consent to accompany the officers voluntary, but refused to sanction the police actions while in the room. What does the Court expect was going to happen in the police room? While certainly the police could have employed trained dogs to discover the drugs, how is that less intrusive than obtaining the key from Royer (D) to look in the luggage? Royer (D) was informed he was under suspicion of drug possession and chose to allow access to the incriminating evidence.

■ CASE VOCABULARY

CONSENT: Agreement, approval, or permission as to some act or purpose, especially if given voluntarily by a competent person.

VOLUNTARY: Done by design or intention.

United States v. Drayton

(*Prosecuting Government*) v. (*Bus Passenger*)

536 U.S. 194, 122 S. Ct. 2105, 153 L. Ed. 2d 242 (2002)

A PERSON IS NOT "SEIZED" IF HE OR SHE IS FREE TO LEAVE

■ **INSTANT FACTS** Drayton (D) was a passenger on an intercity bus who was arrested after a search of his person during a police "sweep" of the bus showed that he was carrying illegal drugs.

■ **BLACK LETTER RULE** There is no seizure of a person if a police officer does not do anything to suggest to a reasonable person that he or she is not free to terminate the encounter.

■ PROCEDURAL BASIS

Certiorari to review a decision of the Eleventh Circuit Court of Appeals reversing the defendant's conviction.

■ FACTS

Drayton (D) and Brown were passengers on an intercity bus. The bus made a scheduled stop and, during the stop, three police officers got on the bus as a part of a routine drug and weapons interdiction effort. The three officers were wearing plain clothes, but their badges were visible. They carried concealed weapons. One officer stayed at the front of the bus but did not block the exit or the aisle. A second officer went to the back of the bus and stayed there, while the third officer spoke with individual passengers. That officer asked passengers about their travel plans and whether they were carrying any luggage. The questioning officer testified that a passenger who did not want to cooperate or who wanted to leave the bus would have been allowed to do so. The officer did not, however, inform passengers of their right to refuse to cooperate.

The officer approached Brown and Drayton (D), identified himself as a police officer, and asked if Brown and Drayton (D) were carrying any luggage. He spoke only as loudly as was necessary for him to be heard, and his face was twelve to eighteen inches from Drayton's (D) when he spoke. Both men pointed at a suitcase in the overhead rack, and the officer asked if he could check it. Brown agreed and the bag was searched. No contraband was found. The officer then noted that Brown and Drayton (D) were wearing heavy jackets and baggy pants, even though the weather was warm. The officer asked Brown if he could "check [his] person." Brown agreed, and the officer found hard objects similar to drug packages. Brown was placed under arrest. The officer then asked Drayton (D) if he could check him, and Drayton (D) lifted his hands from his legs. The officer patted Drayton's (D) thighs and found hard objects similar to those on Brown. Drayton (D) was arrested. The objects found on both men contained cocaine. The trial court denied motions to suppress the evidence, but the Eleventh Circuit Court of Appeals reversed.

■ ISSUE

Did the questioning and pat down of the passengers on the bus pursuant to a routine sweep constitute a seizure?

■ DECISION AND RATIONALE

(Kennedy, J.) No. There is no seizure of a person if a police officer does not do anything to suggest to a reasonable person that he or she is not free to terminate the encounter. Although the police officers did not inform passengers that they were not required to cooperate, or that they were free to leave, they did not brandish their weapons or block the exit of the bus. They did not use force, act in an intimidating manner, or use an authoritative tone of voice. Brown's arrest does not change the analysis with regard to Drayton (D), because the arrest of one person does not become a seizure of everyone around that person. If anything, Drayton (D) should have been put on notice of the probable consequences of continued cooperation. There is no question that the encounter would have been constitutional if it had taken place on the street, and the nature of the encounter is not changed because it takes place on a bus rather than a street. Reversed and remanded.

■ DISSENT

(Souter, J.) The majority's statement that passengers consent to the type of search conducted here to enhance their safety and the safety of other passengers has an air of unreality to it. The reasonable inference from the words used by the officers is that they were conducting an "interdiction," that it would be carried out no matter what the circumstances were, and that although consent was preferred, the "interdiction" would be carried out with or without consent. It is hard to imagine that Drayton (D) would have refused consent in these circumstances. The facts required more from the officers than a polite tone; a police officer who is certain to get his way has no need to shout.

Analysis:

The majority's analysis assumes that the average person knows that he or she is generally under no obligation to speak to a police officer, or to consent to a search. Although the officers in this case noted that passengers in other searches had refused to cooperate, and that it was not unusual for passengers to leave the bus during a search, the officers also testified that they had informed passengers in other searches of their right not to cooperate. Justice Kennedy's statement that Brown's arrest should have put Drayton (D) on notice of the consequences of further cooperation ignores the counterpoint that Drayton (D) may have deduced the probable consequences of his *not* cooperating.

Brendlin v. California

(*Criminal Defendant*) v. (*Prosecuting State*)
___ U.S. ___, 127 S.Ct. 2400, 168 L.Ed.2d 132 (2007)

PASSENGERS IN VEHICLES SUBJECTED TO A TRAFFIC STOP ARE "SEIZED"

■ **INSTANT FACTS** Brendlin (D) claimed that drugs and drug paraphernalia were inadmissible against him because the traffic stop that resulted in the discovery of the evidence was illegal.

■ **BLACK LETTER RULE** A person is seized pursuant to the Fourth Amendment when an officer, by means of force or authority, intentionally terminates or restrains the person's freedom of movement.

■ PROCEDURAL BASIS

Supreme Court review of a state court decision against the defendant.

■ FACTS

Following a traffic stop that was concededly illegal due to lack of reasonable suspicion, Brendlin (D), a passenger in the stopped vehicle, was found to have an outstanding arrest warrant. The police arrested him and found drugs and paraphernalia on his person and near him in the vehicle during searches incident to his arrest. Brendlin (D) claimed that the evidence was the fruit of his illegal seizure, which arose from the illegal stop of the car in which he was riding. The California Supreme Court rejected that argument, because Brendlin (D) was a mere passenger and had not been "seized." Brendlin (D) appealed.

■ ISSUE

Was the drug evidence discovered in the searches incident to Brendlin's (D) arrest on an outstanding warrant the fruit of the illegal traffic stop?

■ DECISION AND RATIONALE

(Souter, J.) Yes. A person is seized pursuant to the Fourth Amendment when an officer, by means of force or authority, intentionally terminates or restrains the person's freedom of movement. An unintended person may be the object of the detention, as long as the detention is willful and not simply the consequence of an unknowing act. There is, however, no seizure without actual submission; otherwise, there is at most an attempted seizure as far as the Fourth Amendment is concerned.

When it seems that someone has passively acquiesced to a show of authority, the test for whether a seizure occurred is if, in view of all the circumstances surrounding the incident, a reasonable person would have believed that he was not free to leave. When a person has no desire to leave for reasons unrelated to police conduct, the coercive effect of the encounter is measured by asking whether a reasonable person would feel free to decline the officers' requests or otherwise terminate the encounter.

A traffic stop clearly entails a seizure of the driver, even thought the purpose of the stop is limited and the detention quite brief. Although the Court has not yet held that a passenger in the stopped car is also seized, we have indicated in dicta on numerous occasions that, during a traffic stop, an officer seizes *everyone* in the vehicle. The question can be resolved by asking, in this case, would a reasonable person in Brendlin's (D) position have believed himself free to terminate the encounter with the police after they stopped the car in which he was riding? We think that, under these circumstances, no reasonable person would have thought himself free to depart without police permission.

We reject the California Supreme Court's reasoning. Holding that a passenger in a private car is not seized in a traffic stop would invite police officers to stop cars with passengers, regardless of probable cause or reasonable suspicion of anything illegal. The fact that evidence uncovered as a result of an arbitrary stop would be admissible would be a powerful incentive to run "roving" patrols that would violate the driver's Fourth Amendment rights. Reversed.

Analysis:

Probable cause is not established simply by showing that the officer who made the arrest or search subjectively believed he or she had grounds for the action. As the Court emphasized in *Beck v. Ohio*, 379 U.S. 89 (1964), "If subjective good faith alone were the test, the protection of the Fourth Amendment would evaporate, and the people would be 'secure in their persons, houses, papers, and effects' only in the discretion of the police." The probable cause test is thus an objective one: in order for there to be probable cause, the facts must be such that they warrant a belief by a reasonable person under the circumstances.

■ CASE VOCABULARY

PROBABLE CAUSE: Reasonable ground to suspect that a person has committed or is committing a crime or that a place contains specific items connected with a crime. Under the Fourth Amendment, probable cause—which amounts to more than a bare suspicion but less than evidence that would justify a conviction—must be shown before an arrest warrant or search warrant may be issued.

REASONABLE SUSPICION: A particularized and objective basis, supported by specific and articulable facts, for suspecting a person of criminal activity. A police officer must have a reasonable suspicion to stop a person in a public place.

SEIZE: To forcibly take possession (of a person or property); to place (someone) in possession; to be in possession (of property).

SEIZURE: The act or an instance of taking possession of a person or property by legal right or process; especially, in constitutional law, a confiscation or arrest that may interfere with a person's reasonable expectation of privacy.

United States v. Place

(*Prosecuting Government*) v. (*Drug Offender*)
462 U.S. 696, 103 S. Ct. 2637, 77 L. Ed. 2d 110 (1983)

NINETY–MINUTE INVESTIGATIVE DETENTIONS OF PERSONAL PROPERTY ARE UNREASONABLE

■ **INSTANT FACTS** Place (D) was indicted for possession of cocaine with intent to distribute based on narcotics found in one of Place's (D) suitcases, which the police seized without a warrant.

■ **BLACK LETTER RULE** When an officer's observations lead him reasonably to believe that a traveler is carrying luggage that contains narcotics, the officer may detain the luggage briefly to investigate the circumstances that aroused his suspicion, provided that the investigative detention is properly limited in scope.

■ PROCEDURAL BASIS

Certiorari to review the decision of the Second Circuit Court of Appeals reversing the defendant's conviction.

■ FACTS

While in Miami International Airport, police grew suspicious of Place (D) as he waited in line to purchase a ticket to New York. When Place (D) approached his gate, the officers requested his ticket and identification, seeking permission to search the two bags he had checked. Because his flight was leaving, the bags were not searched, but the police checked the address tags and telephone number given to the airline. Noting some discrepancies, the officers notified the Drug Enforcement Administration to relay the information to New York. Upon arriving in New York, Place (D) claimed his bags and was approached by two DEA agents. Place (D) refused to consent to a search of his bags, and the agents seized his luggage to obtain a search warrant. Ninety minutes later at a different airport, the police exposed the bags to a dog trained to detect narcotics. The dog reacted positively to one of the bags. A search warrant was issued to search the bag, which uncovered cocaine. Place (D) was indicted for possession of cocaine with intent to distribute. The trial court denied a motion to suppress the evidence as a product of a warrantless search, and Place (D) was convicted. On appeal, the Second Circuit Court of Appeals reversed.

■ ISSUE

May police temporarily seize luggage without a warrant based on a reasonable suspicion that they contain illegal contraband or evidence of a crime?

■ DECISION AND RATIONALE

(O'Connor, J.) Yes. Police may temporarily seize personal property without a warrant based on an objectively reasonable suspicion that it contains illegal contraband or evidence of a crime. Under *Terry v. Ohio*, a court must balance the governmental interest in seizing the property against the nature of the intrusion to determine the reasonableness of Fourth Amendment seizures. When the government maintains reasonable suspicion that personal property contains illegal contraband or evidence of a crime, the government's interest in seizing the property is substantial. On the other hand, many temporary seizures of personal property for limited investigative purposes have minimal intrusive effect. "[W]hen an officer's observations lead him reasonably to believe that a traveler is carrying luggage that contains narcotics, . . . the officer [may] detain the luggage briefly to investigate the circumstances that aroused his suspicion, provided that the investigative detention is properly limited in scope."

Here, the scope of the seizure was not sufficiently reasonable to withstand the Fourth Amendment. A seizure of luggage infringes upon a person's interest in his property and his liberty interests to carry on with his itinerary. It must therefore be reasonably limited to that time necessary to effect an appropriate investigative search. The New York agents were informed of Place's (D) arrival time and could have arranged for their investigation to occur upon arrival to minimize the intrusion. The ninety-minute detention was unreasonable under the circumstances, especially given that the agents failed to inform Place (D) of the location where his luggage would be taken, the time for which his bags would be detained, and arrangements for their retrieval in the event no evidence was found. The scope of the detention was not properly limited. Affirmed.

■ CONCURRENCE

(Brennan, J.) Place's (D) detention and the detention of his luggage implicate two separate Fourth Amendment concerns. The seizure of Place's (D) luggage, independent of his personal detention, requires probable cause, not merely reasonable suspicion, of criminal activity. *Terry* does not permit the seizure of personal property independent of the seizure of the person.

■ CONCURRENCE

(Blackmun, J.) While the Court sets out to establish guidelines for *Terry* seizures, it does so at the risk of establishing a general statement that warrantless seizures must only be reasonable, when in fact *Terry* applies only to exceptional circumstances in which swift action is necessary.

Analysis:

In the ordinary case, the Court has viewed seizure of personal property as per se unreasonable within the meaning of the Fourth Amendment unless it is accomplished pursuant to a judicial warrant issued upon probable cause and particularly describing the items to be seized. Here, the Court chooses to apply the exception set out in *Terry* to seizures of personal property, as well as to seizures of persons. However, the Court also decided to apply the time limitation for such searches set out in *Terry*. In *Place,* the Court determined that ninety minutes was too long to detain a person's luggage in a *Terry* stop.

■ CASE VOCABULARY

CONTRABAND: Illegal or prohibited trade.

Samson v. California

(*Convicted Criminal*) v. (*Prosecuting State*)
___ U.S. ___, 126 S.Ct. 2193, 165 L.Ed.2d 250 (2006)

EVIDENCE SEIZED IN A SUSPICIONLESS SEARCH OF A PAROLEE IS ADMISSIBLE

■ **INSTANT FACTS** A police officer searched Samson (D), a parolee, as he walked down the street, based simply on his parolee status, and Samson (D) moved to suppress the evidence seized during the search.

■ **BLACK LETTER RULE** The Fourth Amendment does not prohibit a police officer from conducting a suspicionless search of a parolee.

■ PROCEDURAL BASIS

Certiorari to review a decision of the California Court of Appeal upholding the defendant's conviction.

■ FACTS

Samson (D) was on parole after being convicted of being a felon in possession of a firearm. A police officer observed Samson (D) walking down the street and stopped him for questioning. Pursuant to California law, an officer has the authority, and a parolee must submit to, a warrantless search and seizure simply by virtue of the parolee status. The officer searched Samson (D) and found methamphetamine on his person. At his possession trial, Samson (D) moved to suppress the evidence seized as a result of the search of his person, but his motion was denied and he was convicted. He appealed to the California Court of Appeal, which held that a search is reasonable under the Fourth Amendment as long as it is not arbitrary, capricious, or harassing, and that this search was none of those. The Supreme Court granted certiorari.

■ ISSUE

Can a condition of release so diminish a released prisoner's expectation of privacy that a suspicionless search does not offend the Fourth Amendment?

■ DECISION AND RATIONALE

(Thomas, J.) Yes. The Fourth Amendment does not prohibit a police officer from conducting a suspicionless search of a parolee. Whether a search is reasonable depends on the degree to which it intrudes on an individual's privacy and the degree to which it is needed to promote legitimate governmental interests. We recently addressed a similar issue in *U.S. v. Knights*, in which, pursuant to California law, a probationer was subject to suspicionless searches. We noted that probationers are not entitled to the same liberties to which the average citizen is entitled, and that the terms of Knights's probation clearly set out the condition of his consent to search and seizure. Under these circumstances, Knights's expectation of privacy was significantly diminished. Moreover, the state has no obligation to ignore statistics on recidivism; it clearly has a strong interest in keeping close tabs on probationers, such as by searching Knights's apartment in that case. Weighing the competing interests at stake, we held that because the officers had a reasonable suspicion of Knights's continuing criminal activity, the warrantless search of his apartment did not run afoul of the Fourth Amendment. But because reasonable suspicion existed in that case, we did not have to decide whether the same conclusion would be reached if the search were based entirely on the terms of probation. That is the question before the Court in this case, albeit in the context of parolees.

Parolees, like probationers, have a diminished expectation of privacy, perhaps even more so than probationers, because parole is more like prison than probation is. While on parole, the parolee is still in the legal custody of the department of corrections and must adhere to stringent requirements lest parole be revoked. As in *Knights*, the defendant here was clearly advised of the consent-to-search condition of his parole. Accordingly, he did not have a legitimate expectation of privacy with regard to the search of his person. By contrast, the state has an overwhelming interest in supervising parolees. Empirical evidence of recidivism establishes the need for close supervision of those who have already been convicted of criminal offenses. And it does not matter here that other states may require reasonable suspicion before similar searches can be conducted; what is at issue here is whether California's system is drawn to meet that state's needs, in view of the parolees' diminished expectations of privacy. California's system is not without limits, given the prohibition on arbitrary, capricious, and harassing searches. Accordingly, the decision of the California appellate court is affirmed.

■ DISSENT

(Stevens, J.) Although we previously held in *Knights* that a probationer has a diminished expectation of privacy, and in *Griffin v. Wisconsin* that probation or parole officers have discretion to determine how closely their charges must be supervised, we have never held that the police have unbridled discretion to perform suspicionless searches of parolees or probationers. The Court here sanctions an unprecedented curtailment of liberty, reasoning that parolees have no greater expectation of privacy than prisoners. The Fourth Amendment simply does not support the conclusion that a suspicionless search of a parolee is reasonable. Although special needs may justify a search of a parolee, the Court does not rely on a special-needs analysis in this case. At least a special-needs analysis assures some evenhandedness, but here there are no protective measures in place, no procedural safeguards required, and no suspicion justifying the search.

There is simply no basis for the majority's conclusion that a parolee has no legitimate expectation of privacy. A parolee is not a prisoner, and even notice of the consent to search is not enough to put parolees and prisoners on equal par. The Court seems to think that deprivation of Fourth Amendment rights is part and parcel of being a convicted criminal. But this assumption loses focus on the actual question that must be asked in each case: does the balance between the legitimate expectation of privacy of the person being searched and the government's interest in conducting the search justify dispensing with the traditional Fourth Amendment safeguards of warrants and probable cause? The answer is not the same for parolees as it is for prisoners.

The situation may be different if only parole officers were authorized to perform suspicionless searches, or if only certain parolees were subject to the consent requirement. But where there are no programmatic procedural protections in place, the risk of Fourth Amendment violations is too great. The prohibition on arbitrary and capricious searches is not enough to safeguard parolees from the indignity that results from suspicionless searches and the affect they may have on reintegration into productive society. The requirement of individualized suspicion is the shield the Framers selected to guard against arbitrary, capricious, and harassing searches. Doing away with that shield is paying lip service to the end while withdrawing the means.

Analysis:

The California Supreme Court denied Samson's petition for certiorari in this case, but the United States Supreme Court agreed to hear the case without costs. The outcome hinged largely on the Court's interpretation of the earlier *Knights case*, which addressed the diminished privacy rights of probationers, not parolees. Although the majority discusses the continuum of possible punishments, and seems to acknowledge that prison, parole, and probation fall at different points on that continuum, it also seems, unlike the dissent, to equate the reasonable expectations of privacy applicable to all three.

■ CASE VOCABULARY

PAROLE: The release of a prisoner from imprisonment before the full sentence has been served. Although not available under some sentences, parole is usually granted for good behavior on the condition that the parolee regularly report to a supervising officer for a specified period.

Schneckloth v. Bustamonte

(*Prison Official*) v. (*Thief*)

412 U.S. 218, 93 S. Ct. 2041, 36 L. Ed. 2d 854 (1973)

CONSENT TO A SEARCH IS VALID EVEN IF THE CONSENTER DID NOT KNOW HE COULD REFUSE

■ **INSTANT FACTS** Bustamonte (D) was charged with theft after three stolen checks were discovered during a search of an automobile consented to by the vehicle owner's brother.

■ **BLACK LETTER RULE** An individual need not be informed that he has the right to refuse consent to a search before his consent to the search will be considered voluntary.

■ PROCEDURAL BASIS

Certiorari to review the decision of the Ninth Circuit Court of Appeals vacating the judgment of the lower court.

■ FACTS

A police officer stopped a car because one of its headlights and the car's license plate light were burned out. When the driver of the car could not produce a license, the officer obtained consent from Alcala, who claimed his brother owned the car, to a search of the vehicle. Alcala actually opened the trunk and the glove compartment for the officer. The search uncovered three stolen checks that were later linked to Bustamonte (D). After Bustamonte's (D) conviction, the California Court of Appeals affirmed. Bustamonte (D) then petitioned for a writ of habeas corpus, which was denied, but the denial was reversed on appeal to the Ninth Circuit Court of Appeals.

■ ISSUE

In order for consent to a search to be considered voluntary, must the individual consenting be informed that he has the right to refuse consent?

■ DECISION AND RATIONALE

(Stewart, J.) No. An individual need not be informed that he has the right to refuse consent to a search before his consent to such a search will be considered voluntary. Whether consent to a search was in fact "voluntary" and not the product of duress or coercion is a question of fact to be determined from the totality of the circumstances. The problem of reconciling the recognized legitimacy of consent searches with the requirement that they be free from any aspect of official coercion cannot be resolved by any infallible touchstone. In examining all the surrounding circumstances to determine if in fact consent to the search was coerced, account must be taken of subtly coercive police questions, as well as the possibly vulnerable subjective state of the person who consents. Neither Court precedent nor the traditional definition of "voluntariness" requires proof of knowledge of a right to refuse as the *sine qua non* of an effective consent to a search. "[W]hen the subject of a search is not in custody and the State attempts to justify a search on the basis of his consent, the Fourth and Fourteenth Amendments require that it demonstrate that the consent was in fact voluntarily given, and not the result of duress or coercion, express or implied." Reversed.

■ DISSENT

(Marshall, J.) Voluntary consent and voluntary confessions are two different constitutional issues. Freedom from coercion in confessions is a substantive right protected by the Fifth Amendment. Consent, however, is a "mechanism by which substantive rights are avoided." Consent should be viewed as a relinquishment of Fourth Amendment rights and should be taken literally to require a "knowing" choice. If consent to search means that a person has chosen to forgo his right to exclude the police from the place they seek to search, it follows that his consent cannot be considered a meaningful choice unless he knew that he could in fact exclude the police.

Analysis:

In situations in which the police have some evidence of illicit activity, but lack probable cause to arrest or search, a search authorized by a valid consent may be the only means of obtaining important and reliable evidence. Even in those cases in which there is probable cause to arrest or search, but the police lack a warrant, a consent search may still be valuable. If the search is conducted and proves fruitless, that in itself may convince police that an arrest with its possible stigma and embarrassment is unnecessary, or that a far more extensive search pursuant to a warrant is not justified. A search pursuant to consent may result in significantly less inconvenience for the subject of the search, and, properly conducted, is a constitutionally permissible and wholly legitimate aspect of effective police activity.

■ CASE VOCABULARY

SINE QUA NON: An indispensable condition or thing; something on which something else necessarily depends.

Georgia v. Randolph

(Prosecuting State) v. *(Convicted Criminal)*

547 U.S. 103, 126 S.Ct. 1515, 164 L.Ed.2d 208 (2006)

POLICE MAY NOT SEARCH A DWELLING IF ONE CO–OCCUPANT REFUSES TO CONSENT

■ **INSTANT FACTS** Randolph (D) was convicted of a drug offense based on evidence that resulted from a search of his home to which only his wife consented, over his objection.

■ **BLACK LETTER RULE** "[A] warrantless search of a shared dwelling for evidence over the express refusal of consent by a physically present resident cannot be justified as reasonable as to him on the basis of consent given to the police by another resident."

■ PROCEDURAL BASIS

Certiorari to review a state court decision on the admissibility of evidence.

■ FACTS

When the police responded to a domestic disturbance, the wife told the officers that there were items of drug evidence in the house, but Randolph (D), the husband, refused to let the officers search. They turned back to the wife for consent, which she readily granted, leading the officers to the evidence. When one of the officers went outside to get an evidence bag, he called the district attorney's office and was advised to get a warrant. Then, when the officer re-entered the house, the wife withdrew her consent. Nonetheless, the officers took what evidence they already had, along with the Randolphs (D), to the police station; they later returned to the house, pursuant to a search warrant, to gather more evidence. Randolph (D) was indicted for possession of cocaine, and at his trial he moved to suppress the evidence obtained at his home as the fruit of a warrantless search. He argued that his wife could not consent to the search over his refusal. The trial court disagreed, ruling that Randolph's (D) wife had common authority to consent, and Randolph (D) was convicted. He appealed, and the court of appeals reversed, holding that the evidence was not admissible. The Supreme Court granted certiorari to resolve a split of authority on the issue of co-occupant consent to searches.

■ ISSUE

Can one co-occupant of a dwelling consent to a search of the premises over the other co-occupant's refusal?

■ DECISION AND RATIONALE

(Souter, J.) No. Although a fellow occupant who shares common authority over a premises may consent to a search of that premises in the absence of the suspect, the same is not true if the suspect is present and refuses. "[A] warrantless search of a shared dwelling for evidence over the express refusal of consent by a physically present resident cannot be justified as reasonable as to him on the basis of consent given to the police by another resident." It is true that one co-tenant may have an interest in bringing his or her criminal co-tenant to justice, but this result can be accomplished by means other than allowing a warrantless search of the home in the presence of the suspect's outright refusal.

Based on common-sense concepts of co-tenants' rights and ordinary principles of joint residency, it follows that the police may assume that one who jointly resides in a home may consent to its search if the other tenant is not present. But customary social understanding does not accord the consenting tenant authority powerful enough to prevail over a physically present co-tenant's objections. In the *Matlock* case, the suspect was not available to consent, although he was nearby in a squad car; and in the *Rodriguez* case, the suspect was unavailable, although asleep in the apartment. This is admittedly a very fine line, but it is the one the Court chooses to draw. If the co-tenant is at the door refusing entry, a search cannot be conducted even if a co-tenant consents. Affirmed.

■ CONCURRENCE

(Stevens, J.) Even the most dedicated adherent to a constitutional-interpretation approach that relies primarily on a search for original understanding would recognize the relevance of societal changes.

■ CONCURRENCE

(Breyer, J.) This decision will not adversely affect law enforcement practices, because the fact of an abuse victim's invitation of police officers into the home may itself provide the proof sought.

■ DISSENT

(Roberts, J.) The majority's analogy to the social situation of declining to enter a home if one of the occupants shouts "stay out" does not support its conclusion, because there are many situations in which a social caller would enter despite such hostility from one co-tenant. Moreover, according to the majority's random rule, a co-tenant is not present for purposes of refusing to consent to a search if he or she is merely in the backyard, or listening to music through headphones so that he doesn't hear the police at the door. This rule could have particularly adverse consequences in domestic abuse situations, such as this case. The majority's decision would apparently prevent the police from entering the victim's home in a domestic disturbance call if the abuser stands at the door telling them they cannot come inside. The majority attempts to brush this concern aside by saying the police can respond differently in exigent circumstances, but why craft such a rule in the first place?

■ DISSENT

(Scalia, J.) This is not just a case about property rights, but even if it were, we must be cognizant of recent alterations in property rights in regard to married women, without altering the Fourth Amendment itself.

■ DISSENT

(Thomas, J.) The *Coolidge* case should govern the outcome here. The principle applied in that case was that "[i]t is an act of responsible citizenship for individuals to give whatever information they may have to aid in law enforcement." Randolph's (D) wife should have been allowed to consent to the search.

Analysis:

The Court admits to drawing a fine line here, but as Justice Roberts's dissenting opinion points out, that line could result in random law-enforcement application. The majority opinion suggests that the only time a co-tenant's refusal to consent bars a search is when he or she is physically present, virtually in the doorway, and proactively asserts the refusal. In other words, the police do not need to seek out the occupant and ask for permission to search, even if he or she is a short distance away, or even within view but asleep or listening to his iPod. It is apparent why the dissenting Justices had concerns with the majority's viewpoint in this case.

■ CASE VOCABULARY

CONSENT: Agreement, approval, or permission as to some act or purpose, especially given voluntarily by a competent person; legally effective assent.

CHAPTER FOUR

Police "Encouragement" and the Defense of Entrapment

United States v. Russell

Instant Facts: Russell (D) was convicted of the unlawful manufacture and sale of methamphetamine after an undercover narcotics agent provided him with the necessary chemicals.

Black Letter Rule: The entrapment defense prohibits law enforcement officers from instigating a criminal act by persons otherwise innocent in order to lure them to its commission and punish them.

Jacobson v. United States

Instant Facts: Jacobson (D) was convicted of receiving child pornography through the mails after a two-and-a-half-year sting operation by the government.

Black Letter Rule: Predisposition to a broad range of conduct does not demonstrate a predisposition to commit specific acts falling within that range.

United States v. Russell

(*Prosecuting Government*) v. (*Drug Dealer*)
411 U.S. 423, 93 S. Ct. 1637, 36 L. Ed. 2d 366 (1973)

WHETHER A DEFENDANT IS PREDISPOSED TO COMMIT A CRIME IS DETERMINED SUBJECTIVELY

■ **INSTANT FACTS** Russell (D) was convicted of the unlawful manufacture and sale of methamphetamine after an undercover narcotics agent provided him with the necessary chemicals.

■ **BLACK LETTER RULE** The entrapment defense prohibits law enforcement officers from instigating a criminal act by persons otherwise innocent in order to lure them to its commission and punish them.

■ PROCEDURAL BASIS

Certiorari to review a decision of the Ninth Circuit Court of Appeals reversing the defendant's conviction.

■ FACTS

Shapiro, an undercover federal narcotics agent, went to Russell's (D) home to meet with Russell (D) and two other men to locate an illegal methamphetamine laboratory. Shapiro told the defendants that he represented an organization interested in controlling the production and distribution of methamphetamine, offering to supply the defendants with chemicals necessary to manufacture the drug in exchange for one-half of all methamphetamine produced. During the conversation, one of the defendants, Connelly (D), informed Shapiro that he had been producing methamphetamine for several months and gave Shapiro a small bag of the drug. Shapiro and Connelly (D) then left for Connelly's (D) house, where Shapiro observed Connelly's (D) meth lab. Several months later, Shapiro returned to Connelly's (D) house with chemicals and observed Connelly (D) and Russell (D) manufacture two batches of methamphetamine. After Shapiro took his one-half share, he purchased the rest from the defendants. Several days later, Shapiro returned to the house with a search warrant and confiscated chemical containers not provided by him. The defendants were charged with and convicted of the unlawful manufacture and illegal sale of a controlled substance. Russell (D) appealed his conviction to the Ninth Circuit Court of Appeals, alleging that although the jury could have found him predisposed to commit the offenses, the facts presented constituted entrapment as a matter of law. The Ninth Circuit agreed, reversing Russell's (D) conviction because Shapiro's act of providing the chemicals necessary to manufacture the drug, which were difficult to obtain, constituted unreasonable governmental involvement in the crime.

■ ISSUE

Is the nature and extent of government involvement in a criminal enterprise dispositive of the entrapment defense issue?

■ DECISION AND RATIONALE

(Rehnquist, J.) No. "[T]he entrapment defense prohibits law enforcement officers from instigating a criminal act by persons otherwise innocent in order to lure them to its commission and to punish them." The entrapment defense thus focuses on the defendant's predisposition to commit the crime, to distinguish between a defendant who would not have committed the crime without the government's involvement and a defendant who would. Here, the evidence was sufficient for the jury to conclude that Russell (D) was predisposed to commit the crime. Although the chemicals supplied by Shapiro were difficult to obtain, it would not have been impossible to get them. The defendants admitted producing the drug both before and after Shapiro provided the chemicals, and the defendants' criminal enterprise existed before Shapiro's actions. The Government's (P) use of undercover narcotics agents to infiltrate drug rings in an effort to curb the supply of drugs across the country does not violate "fundamental fairness," even when the agent provides the chemicals necessary to manufacture the chemicals. The essential element of the entrapment defense is the defendant's predisposition to commit the crime, and not the nature and extent of the government's involvement in the criminal enterprise. Because Russell (D) was involved in the criminal enterprise before Shapiro's involvement, the evidence supports the jury's conclusion of his predisposition. Reversed.

■ DISSENT

(Stewart, J.) The defense of entrapment should be based not on the subjective intent or predisposition of the defendant, but rather on the objective conduct of government agents, whether the defendant is predisposed to the crime or not. To view the defense otherwise leads to the illogical conclusion that one who commits a crime, although not predisposed to its commission, is somehow "innocent" and blameless. Even though the government may have initiated the criminal plan, the defendant's subsequent involvement suggests a predisposition to the crime nonetheless. Because the defense cannot be viewed as relieving one who has committed a crime from liability, the only legitimate question remains whether the government's actions fall outside the limits of judicial toleration. Here, although the chemicals were obtainable by sources other than Shapiro, the fact remains that the conduct on which Russell's (D) conviction was based resulted from his manufacture of methamphetamine from the precise chemicals Shapiro provided. Russell (D) manufactured methamphetamine at the Government's (P) request, from the materials the Government (P) provided, and sold it back to the Government (P). It is the Government's (P) duty to prevent crime, not create it for the purpose of punishment. Under the objective approach, the Government's (P) conduct entrapped Russell (D).

Analysis:

Both the subjective and objective approaches present problems. Under the subjective approach, governmental conduct that may be appropriate under one set of circumstances may not be so under another. Under the objective test, the requirement of a static police procedure threatens to hamper law enforcement by limiting appropriate investigatory tactics and sting operations.

■ CASE VOCABULARY

ENTRAPMENT: A law-enforcement officer's or government agent's inducement of a person to commit a crime, by means of fraud or undue persuasion, in an attempt to later bring a criminal prosecution against that person.

PREDISPOSITION: A person's inclination to engage in a particular activity, especially an inclination that vitiates a criminal defendant's claim of entrapment.

Jacobson v. United States

(*Pornography Defendant*) v. (*Prosecuting Government*)
503 U.S. 540, 112 S. Ct. 1535, 118 L. Ed. 2d 174 (1992)

PRIOR INTEREST IN CHILD PORNOGRAPHY DOES NOT INDICATE A PREDISPOSITION TO RECEIVE CHILD PORNOGRAPHY

■ **INSTANT FACTS** Jacobson (D) was convicted of receiving child pornography through the mails after a two-and-a-half-year sting operation by the government.

■ **BLACK LETTER RULE** Predisposition to a broad range of conduct does not demonstrate a predisposition to commit specific acts falling within that range.

■ PROCEDURAL BASIS

Certiorari to review the defendant's conviction.

■ FACTS

Jacobson (D) ordered and received through the mail two magazines depicting child pornography involving preteen and teenage boys, which was legal under applicable federal law. Three months later, federal child pornography law was amended to criminalize the receipt by mail of sexually explicit materials involving children. That month, postal inspectors obtained Jacobson's (D) contact information from the distributor of the pornographic magazines and began to mail him a series of letters and brochures from fictitious organizations advertising child pornography. While the defendant responded to various questionnaires, he received no materials. Two years later, the Customs Service sent additional material through the mail from another fictitious organization advertising similar materials. Again Jacobson (D) received no materials. The Postal Service then sent Jacobson (D) another letter from yet another fictitious organization, questioning the infringement of his rights by the pornography laws and offering a catalog. Jacobson (D) ordered and received a magazine depicting minor boys engaging in sexual activities. He was arrested and convicted under federal child pornography laws, despite raising an entrapment defense.

■ ISSUE

Must a conviction be overturned when the government induces the crime and fails to prove beyond a reasonable doubt that the defendant had a predisposition to commit the crime?

■ DECISION AND RATIONALE

(White, J.) Yes. A defendant's predisposition to a broad range of conduct does not demonstrate a predisposition to commit specific acts falling within that range. To rebut an entrapment defense beyond a reasonable doubt, the government must prove that a defendant's predisposition to commit the crime encompasses more than a broad range of conduct, some of which is illegal. Here, the government offered evidence that the defendant had received magazines depicting child pornography in the past. Such receipt, however, occurred prior to the federal law criminalizing such conduct, and there was no proof that the defendant had prior knowledge of the content of the magazines before receipt. The government also offered evidence that the defendant expressed an interest in preteen and teen pornography, but failed to prove that the defendant was inclined to violate the law in order to further those interests. The crime was committed after two and a half years of inducement, primarily under the guise of promoting his individual rights through lobbying efforts. Reversed.

■ DISSENT

(O'Connor, J.) The majority improperly removed the question of predisposition from the jury. Sufficient evidence exists to sustain the jury's conviction, and the majority improperly redefined the meaning of predisposition. Rather than showing a predisposition at the earliest opportunity to commit a crime, the majority requires proof of predisposition at the time a government investigation begins—at the time of its first contact with the defendant. The defendant had no opportunity to commit a crime until the first offer to purchase magazines was extended, at which time he placed an order. He again placed an order when a second offer was extended. Because the defendant had no opportunity to commit the crime until these offers were made, predisposition could be formed only at that time.

The majority also requires not only that the Government (P) must prove that the defendant was predisposed to engage in illegal conduct, but that he was predisposed to knowingly break the law as well. By doing so, the majority creates a specific intent element for the crime when Congress established no such requirement. In the process, the majority requires more to prove predisposition than the statute requires to support a conviction. While the majority may be correct that the Government (P) went too far in its actions, the question was one for the jury's determination.

Analysis:

The majority's holding in this case demonstrates the difficulties in separating the subjective test from the objective test. While the Court claimed to apply the subjective test to determine the defendant's predisposition, it placed considerable emphasis on the government's actions in inducing the crime—a reflection of the objective test. "[T]he strong arguable inference is that, by waving the banner of individual rights and disparaging the legitimacy and constitutionality of efforts to restrict the availability of sexually explicit materials, the Government not only excited [Jacobson's] interest in sexually explicit materials banned by law but also exerted substantial pressure on [Jacobson] to obtain and read such material as part of a fight against censorship and the infringement of individual rights."

Betts v. Brady

(*Convicted Robber*) v. (*Prosecuting Authority*)
316 U.S. 455, 62 S. Ct. 1252, 86 L. Ed. 1595 (1942)

THE REFUSAL TO APPOINT COUNSEL DOES NOT ALWAYS VIOLATE DUE PROCESS

■ INSTANT FACTS Betts (D), indicted for robbery in state court, was denied his request to have counsel appointed to represent him.

■ BLACK LETTER RULE The Fourteenth Amendment does not command a state court to appoint counsel to represent a criminal defendant in every case.

■ PROCEDURAL BASIS

Certiorari to review the defendant's conviction.

■ FACTS

Betts (D) was indicted for robbery in state court. Unable to afford counsel, he requested that the trial judge appoint counsel to represent him. The court denied the defendant's request because state practice allowed appointment of counsel only for charges of murder and rape. Without waiving an objection to his right to counsel, the defendant pleaded not guilty and represented himself at trial. The defendant was convicted and sentenced to eight years in prison.

■ ISSUE

Does a court's refusal to appoint counsel upon the defendant's request in a state felony case deprive the defendant of his Fourteenth Amendment rights?

■ DECISION AND RATIONALE

(Roberts, J.) No. The Fourteenth Amendment does not require a state court to appoint counsel to represent a criminal defendant in *every* case. The Sixth Amendment ensures a defendant's right to counsel in *federal* courts. The Fourteenth Amendment does not incorporate the Sixth Amendment and does not require a right to counsel in state criminal cases. Under certain circumstances, however, the denial of counsel to state criminal defendants may be so fundamental to a fair trial that due process under the Fourteenth Amendment requires the appointment of counsel. Whether a defendant's due process rights have been violated is determined by the totality of the facts presented. When a defendant is not prejudiced by lack of representation such that it is not offensive to "the fundamental ideas of fairness and right," a defendant has no right to have counsel appointed to him. Here, Betts (D), a man of ordinary intelligence with prior experience in the Maryland court system, adequately presented an alibi defense to rebut the State's evidence supporting conviction. The only issue presented was the credibility of the evidence. As the defendant was afforded an adequate opportunity to present his defense, he was not disadvantaged by the lack of counsel and due process was not offended. Affirmed.

■ DISSENT

(Black, J.) Not only does the Fourteenth Amendment incorporate the Sixth Amendment and apply it to state courts, even the rule set forth by the majority requires reversal of the defendant's conviction. "[F]undamental ideas of fairness and right" require appointment of counsel to every criminal defendant when he cannot afford one of his choosing. Refusal to appoint counsel to indigent defendants "subjects innocent men to increased dangers of conviction merely because of their poverty." Additionally, the Court has previously enunciated that due process is denied if the manner in which trial is conducted is "shocking to the universal sense of justice." Denial of the right to counsel to those who are unable to afford counsel of their own meets this standard in every case. Even under the standards recognized by the majority, however, denial of the right to counsel to indigent defendants violates the Fourteenth Amendment. The defendant's examination of the witnesses at trial demonstrates that he was a man of little education and that he required the assistance of counsel to present a persuasive defense.

Analysis:

Betts has been criticized as too speculative and subjective to guide courts in determining whether a refusal to appoint counsel violates the Fourteenth Amendment. The majority emphasized the merits of the case in determining that Betts (D) was not prejudiced by lack of representation because "there was no question of the commission of the robbery." In many cases, however, a defendant without representation is incapable of presenting the evidence in such a way as to prove his innocence. Confined to the record on appeal, which will most likely tend to show the commission of the offense charged, an appellate court would be hard pressed to find prejudice under such circumstances.

■ CASE VOCABULARY

DUE PROCESS: The conduct of legal proceedings according to established rules and principles for the protection and enforcement of private rights, including notice and the right to a fair hearing before a tribunal with the power to decide the case.

INCORPORATION: The process of applying the provisions of the Bill of Rights to the states by interpreting the Fourteenth Amendment's Due Process Clause as encompassing those provisions.

SIXTH AMENDMENT: The constitutional amendment, ratified with the Bill of Rights of 1791, guaranteeing in criminal cases the right to a speedy and public trial, the right to be informed of the nature of the accusation, the right to confront witnesses, the right to counsel, and the right to compulsory process for obtaining favorable witnesses.

Gideon v. Wainwright

(*Accused Criminal*) v. (*State Official*)
372 U.S. 335, 83 S. Ct. 792, 9 L. Ed. 2d 799 (1963)

STATE COURT FELONY DEFENDANTS ARE ENTITLED TO COUNSEL

■ **INSTANT FACTS** Gideon (D) was charged with a felony offense in Florida and asked the trial judge to appoint counsel; the judge refused, stating that Florida law only allowed for appointed counsel in capital cases.

■ **BLACK LETTER RULE** Indigent defendants charged with felonies in state court proceedings have the right to have counsel appointed for them.

■ **PROCEDURAL BASIS**

Certiorari to review the defendant's conviction.

■ **FACTS**

Gideon (D) was charged with breaking and entering with intent to commit a misdemeanor, which is a felony offense in Florida. Gideon (D) asked the trial judge to appoint counsel for him. The trial judge refused, stating that Florida law allowed for appointed counsel only in capital cases. Gideon's (D) case went to trial before a jury, and Gideon (D) conducted his own defense as best he could. Gideon (D) was convicted and sentenced to five years in prison.

■ **ISSUE**

Does an indigent criminal defendant charged with a felony in state court have a Sixth Amendment right to have counsel appointed to represent him?

■ **DECISION AND RATIONALE**

(Black, J.) Yes. Indigent criminal defendants charged with felonies in state courts have the right to have counsel appointed for them because the Sixth Amendment to the Constitution applies to the states via the Fourteenth Amendment. A provision in the Bill of Rights that is essential to a fair trial is made applicable to the states by the due process provisions of the Fourteenth Amendment. The appointment of counsel is a fundamental right because lawyers in criminal courts are "necessities, not luxuries." Because the government is able to hire a lawyer to prosecute a case, a criminal defendant who cannot afford to do the same is at a disadvantage. Thus, to ensure that all criminal defendants receive a fair trial, indigent defendants must be entitled to have counsel appointed to represent them. The Supreme Court's earlier ruling in *Betts v. Brady*, 316 U.S. 455 (1942), which held that the failure to appoint counsel did not necessarily violate a defendant's due process rights, is overruled. Reversed.

■ **CONCURRENCE**

(Clark, J.) The Sixth Amendment does not distinguish between capital and non-capital offenses. Similarly, due process under the Fourteenth Amendment cannot recognize that a defendant's liberty is less protected because the punishment he faces is less severe than in other cases. Counsel should be appointed in all criminal cases.

■ CONCURRENCE

(Harlan, J.) Although *Betts v. Brady* should be overruled, its holding was not as aberrational as the majority opinion suggests. The holding in *Betts* simply extended to non-capital cases the decision in *Powell v. Alabama*, 287 U.S. 45 (1932), which held that defendants in capital cases were entitled to appointed counsel. Moreover, it has long been recognized that the Sixth Amendment right to appointed counsel is broader in federal prosecutions; at the time *Betts* was decided, it would have been a break in precedent to extend this broad right to the states. Since *Betts*, however, special circumstances are no longer required for the appointment of counsel in capital cases, and the time has come to dispose of the requirement in non-capital cases as well.

Analysis:

A defendant's right to the assistance of counsel and to have counsel appointed has been incorporated into Fed. R. Crim. P. 44. Earlier, attorneys who were appointed to represent indigent defendants were not paid for their services. Congress recognized the unfairness in this situation and enacted the Criminal Justice Act of 1964, which required federal courts to adopt plans that included limited compensation for appointed attorneys.

■ CASE VOCABULARY

INDIGENT DEFENDANT: A person who is too poor to hire a lawyer and who, upon indictment, becomes eligible to receive aid from a court-appointed attorney and a waiver of court costs.

RIGHT TO COUNSEL: A criminal defendant's constitutional right, guaranteed by the Sixth Amendment, to representation by a court-appointed lawyer if the defendant cannot afford to hire one.

Alabama v. Shelton

(*Prosecuting Authority*) v. (*Indigent Defendant*)

535 U.S. 654, 122 S. Ct. 1764, 152 L. Ed. 2d 888 (2002)

COURTS MAY NOT CIRCUMVENT THE SIXTH AMENDMENT BY REVOKING PROBATION AND ENFORCING A PRISON SENTENCE

■ **INSTANT FACTS** The trial court suspended Shelton's (D) jail term and placed him on probation; Shelton (D) was not provided appointed counsel at his criminal trial.

■ **BLACK LETTER RULE** An indigent misdemeanor defendant is entitled to appointed counsel at a criminal trial when a suspended sentence of imprisonment may later be enforced upon revocation of probation.

■ PROCEDURAL BASIS

Certiorari to review a decision of the Supreme Court of Alabama reversing the defendant's sentence and revoking a term of probation.

■ FACTS

After being convicted of third-degree assault, a misdemeanor, Shelton (D), an indigent defendant who had not been afforded counsel, was sentenced to a jail term of thirty days, which sentence the trial court immediately suspended. Shelton (D) was then placed on two years unsupervised probation. On appeal, the Alabama Supreme Court affirmed the conviction, but reversed the sentence and vacated the term of probation because Shelton (D) had not been afforded counsel.

■ ISSUE

May a trial court impose a suspended or probationary prison sentence upon an indigent misdemeanor defendant who has not been provided counsel?

■ DECISION AND RATIONALE

(Ginsburg, J.) No. In *Argersinger v. Hamlin*, 407 U.S. 25 (1972) and *Scott v. Illinois*, 440 U.S. 367 (1979), it was well established that an indigent defendant standing trial for misdemeanor crimes is constitutionally entitled to appointed counsel when the defendant is sentenced to actual imprisonment upon conviction. However, those cases did not address whether an unassisted sentence of imprisonment that is later suspended in lieu of probation, such that the defendant suffers no actual imprisonment unless probation is revoked, violates the Sixth Amendment's right to counsel. But when a sentence is suspended in lieu of probation, a probationary violation results in incarceration for the original conviction, not for violation of the terms of probation. As a result, the defendant suffers a denial of his liberty without the assistance of counsel as required by the Sixth Amendment.

In Alabama, a hearing for revocation of probation is informal, with no right to counsel and without strict rules of evidence. It does not compensate for the absence of counsel at the initial trial and does not even consider whether the underlying conviction was correct. While there may be hearing procedures that could conceivably protect the defendant in such circumstances, the facts of Alabama's procedure do not compensate for the failure to appoint counsel at the defendant's trial. This decision does not prohibit states from imposing probation as a legitimate sentence. However, states may not impose probation upon a suspended sentence when counsel has not been afforded to the indigent defendant. Should states not wish to incur the expense of state-appointed counsel for misdemeanor defendants, they may continue to offer pretrial probation, available in many states, by which probation is agreed upon before an adjudication of guilt. Should probation be later revoked, a formal adjudication of guilt and proper sentence would follow.

Because Shelton (D) faced imprisonment for the underlying conviction upon revocation of his probation, he was entitled under the Sixth Amendment to appointed counsel at the criminal trial. Affirmed.

■ DISSENT

(Scalia, J.) The majority invalidates the defendant's prison sentence although he has suffered no denial of his liberty interests. The defendant has not been imprisoned and will not be imprisoned as long as he abides by the terms of his probation. The majority endeavors to speculate as to how the Alabama Supreme Court would decide should the suspended sentence actually be imposed, although that issue has not been brought before the Court. The question presented is merely whether the imposition of a suspended sentence without the assistance of counsel is unconstitutional. The answer is no. While a sentence is suspended, there is merely the threat of imprisonment, and the Sixth Amendment right to counsel does not attach. By requiring appointed counsel in all cases in which the court may consider probation, which is for the defendant's benefit, the Court now effectively imposes difficult obligations on the states, regardless of the strain on state resources.

Analysis:

As Justice Scalia suggests in his dissent, the majority's speculative decision effectively requires appointed counsel in every misdemeanor case in which the threat of future imprisonment exists after an adjudication of guilt. While the denial of counsel in the underlying trial is not necessarily unconstitutional, it limits the appropriate sentence to a monetary fine. In fact, even if the imposition of a suspended sentence was upheld by the Court, a failure to appoint counsel would likely restrict a court's enforcement of the terms of probation, for any later imprisonment would likely face a Sixth Amendment challenge.

■ CASE VOCABULARY

MISDEMEANOR: A crime that is less serious than a felony and is usually punishable by fine, penalty, forfeiture, or confinement (usually for a brief term) in a place other than prison (such as a county jail).

PROBATION: A court-imposed criminal sentence that, subject to stated conditions, releases a convicted person into the community instead of sending the criminal to jail or prison.

SUSPENDED SENTENCE: A sentence postponed so that the defendant is not required to serve time unless he or she commits another crime or violates some other court-imposed condition.

Douglas v. California

(Convicted Felon) v. *(Prosecution)*
372 U.S. 353, 83 S. Ct. 814, 9 L. Ed. 2d 811 (1963)

INDIGENT DEFENDANTS ARE ENTITLED TO COUNSEL FOR THE FIRST APPEAL AS OF RIGHT

■ **INSTANT FACTS** Douglas (D) was convicted in California on thirteen felony charges and appealed as of right, but his request for appointed counsel to assist with the appeal was denied.

■ **BLACK LETTER RULE** A criminal defendant has a constitutional right to appointed counsel to assist him or her in pursuing an appeal of a conviction.

■ PROCEDURAL BASIS

Certiorari to review the California Supreme Court's decision affirming the lower courts' decisions to uphold Douglas's (D) convictions.

■ FACTS

On appeal of his conviction to the California District Court of Appeal, Douglas (D) requested, but was denied, appointed appellate counsel. Pursuant to California law, the California District Court of Appeal reviewed the record and determined that appointing counsel would assist neither Douglas (D) nor the court.

■ ISSUE

Does an indigent defendant have a constitutional right to appointed counsel on the first appeal of right?

■ DECISION AND RATIONALE

(Douglas, J.) Yes. Indigent defendants are entitled to appointed counsel for their first appeal as of right because the denial of counsel amounts to discrimination against those who cannot afford to retain appellate counsel. The kind of appeal a defendant pursues should not depend on whether he or she can pay for counsel. Under California's procedure, if a defendant can pay for counsel, the court of appeals passes on the merits of the case with the benefit of written briefs and oral argument. If a defendant cannot afford counsel, then the court of appeals prejudges the merits of the case without the benefit of briefs or argument. This result is unfair, because wealthy defendants can require the court to listen to arguments before deciding the merits, but a poor defendant cannot. Poor defendants who are denied counsel and opt to pursue an appeal are further burdened with a preliminary determination that their cases lack merit. Vacated and remanded.

■ DISSENT

(Clark, J.) It is well known that the majority of in forma pauperis appeals are frivolous. The California procedure merely requires the appellate court to make a preliminary review of the record to determine whether that appeal has merit and thereafter appoint counsel to those that do. The Fourteenth Amendment requires no more. To require appointed counsel in every appeal brought by an indigent appellant would waste the State's resources without serving any meaningful purpose.

■ DISSENT

(Harlan, J.) The majority improperly decided the case using an equal-protection analysis; rather, the majority should have focused solely on whether California's procedure is consistent with due process. The California procedure is not unconstitutional because it does not actually deny indigent defendants the right to an appeal. Although the majority characterizes California's procedure as discriminating in favor of the wealthy, there is nothing in the Constitution that requires the states to equalize economic imbalances that inevitably result from certain uniform laws. The law treats all individuals, rich or poor, alike, for counsel is not appointed to wealthy appellants any more than to indigent ones. California's procedure does not violate due process because, even if counsel is not appointed, a defendant receives an appraisal of the merits of his case based on the trial record, as well as full consideration of his appeal.

Analysis:

While nothing in the Constitution requires convicted defendants to be given the right to appeal in state or federal prosecutions, if a jurisdiction provides an appellate procedure, it must be equally accessible to all. Although a defendant may pursue an appeal without the benefit of counsel, having counsel is beneficial for both the defendant and the courts. Lawyers can distinguish good claims from bad, prepare concise pleadings that focus only on promising arguments, and dissuade prisoners from bogging down the court system with voluminous pleadings containing frivolous arguments.

■ CASE VOCABULARY

APPEAL AS OF RIGHT: An appeal to a higher court from which permission need not be first obtained. Also termed "appeal by right."

EX PARTE: Done or made at the instance and for the benefit of one party only, and without notice to, or argument by, any person adversely interested.

IN FORMA PAUPERIS: In the manner of an indigent who is permitted to disregard the filing fees and court costs.

Ross v. Moffitt

(*State Official*) v. (*Convicted Felon*)

417 U.S. 600, 94 S. Ct. 2437, 41 L. Ed. 2d 341 (1974)

INDIGENT DEFENDANTS ARE NOT ENTITLED TO APPOINTED COUNSEL FOR DISCRETIONARY APPEALS

■ **INSTANT FACTS** Moffitt (D) was denied appointed counsel to assist with his petition for discretionary review of his conviction to the North Carolina Supreme Court.

■ **BLACK LETTER RULE** A criminal defendant does not have a constitutional right to appointed counsel to assist in pursuing a discretionary appeal in a state court or a petition for certiorari in the Supreme Court of the United States.

■ PROCEDURAL BASIS

Certiorari to review a decision of the Fourth Circuit Court of Appeals overturning Moffitt's (D) conviction.

■ FACTS

Moffitt (D) was tried and convicted in Mecklenberg County, North Carolina. The State provided Moffitt (D) with counsel for his trial and for his first appeal as of right. However, Moffitt (D) was denied counsel for purposes of pursuing a discretionary appeal in the North Carolina Supreme Court. On a writ of habeas corpus, the Ninth Circuit Court of Appeals determined that *Douglas v. California* required that counsel be appointed.

■ ISSUE

Does an indigent defendant have a constitutional right to appointed counsel for purposes of pursuing a discretionary appeal in state court or an application for review by the Supreme Court of the United States?

■ DECISION AND RATIONALE

(Rehnquist, J.) No. The decision in *Douglas v. California*, 372 U.S. 353 (1963), should not be extended because neither the Due Process Clause nor the Equal Protection Clause requires that a defendant be provided with counsel for discretionary appeals. Denying a defendant counsel is not manifestly unfair because, in appellate proceedings, a defendant does not need an attorney as a shield as in trial proceedings, but rather seeks to use counsel as a sword to overturn a conviction. The right to appeal is not fundamental and may be entirely denied by a state should it so choose. And the refusal to appoint counsel for discretionary appeals does not discriminate against indigent defendants on the basis of their poverty. The Fourteenth Amendment does not require absolute equality of rights or that we "equalize economic conditions." Although poor defendants do not have the same advantages as rich defendants, the relative disparity in this context is far less than in the context of a first appeal as of right. The materials prepared by appointed counsel on the first appeal, along with a defendant's own filings, are enough to give a state supreme court an adequate basis for deciding whether to grant review.

In addition, the purpose of discretionary review, unlike an appeal as of right, is not to decide whether the finding of guilt was correct, but rather whether the case has significant public interest to warrant further review, and the court need not grant discretionary review even when it believes that the conviction appears to be incorrect. This conclusion applies to discretionary review in the state court system as well as the decision to grant certiorari in the United States Supreme Court. States may *choose* to grant the right of counsel at all appellate stages, but the Fourteenth Amendment does not require them to do so.

■ DISSENT

(Douglas, J.) The majority should have affirmed the lower courts' decisions because, as the appellate judge found, there is no logical basis for differentiating between appeals as of right and discretionary appeals. The decision in *Douglas* should be extended to the discretionary review context because that decision was grounded on fairness and equality. These same concepts require counsel in subsequent discretionary appeals, for indigent appellants are equally disadvantaged in presenting their arguments on discretionary review as they are in an initial appeal.

Analysis:

The opinion in *Ross* does not address whether a defendant is entitled to appointed counsel if discretionary review is granted and the defendant is required to present a brief and oral argument. However, as a matter of practice, state high courts and the United States Supreme Court routinely appoint counsel once review has been granted. In addition, the decisions in *Douglas* and *Ross* left open the question of whether a defendant is entitled to appointed counsel for a second appeal as of right.

■ CASE VOCABULARY

DISCRETIONARY REVIEW: The form of appellate review that is not a matter of right but that occurs only with the appellate court's permission.

CHAPTER SIX

Police Interrogation and Confessions

Ashcraft v. Tennessee

Instant Facts: Ashcraft (D) was questioned in relays by police investigators for thirty-six continuous hours without rest, in order for the police to obtain a confession.

Black Letter Rule: The Constitution does not permit a conviction based on a coerced confession.

Watts v. Indiana

Instant Facts: Watts (D) made incriminating statements while in custody after days of persistent police questioning.

Black Letter Rule: Relentless, systematic police questioning producing a confession violates the Due Process Clause.

Massiah v. United States

Instant Facts: Massiah (D) was convicted of drug violations on the basis of incriminating statements overheard on a listening device by federal agents after Massiah was (D) indicted.

Black Letter Rule: The Sixth Amendment prohibits government interrogation of a defendant after indictment outside the presence of counsel.

Escobedo v. Illinois

Instant Facts: Escobedo (D) was convicted of murder based in part on incriminating statements he made after being denied an opportunity to consult with counsel.

Black Letter Rule: When a police investigation is no longer a general inquiry into an unsolved crime but begins to focus on a particular suspect and the suspect has been taken into police custody, if the police carry out a process of interrogations that lends itself to eliciting incriminating statements and the suspect has requested and been denied an opportunity to consult with his lawyer, and the police have not effectively warned him of his absolute constitutional right to remain silent, the accused has been denied his right to counsel.

Miranda v. Arizona (No. 759)

Instant Facts: While in custody, four separate defendants were convicted of crimes, although the evidence did not prove that they had been advised of their right to remain silent or the right to counsel.

Black Letter Rule: No statements obtained during a custodial interrogation, whether exculpatory or inculpatory, may be used against the defendant at trial unless the prosecution proves that the accused was advised of the right to remain silent, that any statements made can and will be used against the accused at trial, and that the accused has the right to an attorney prior to and during questioning.

Yarborough v. Alvarado

Instant Facts: Alvarado (D), a minor, confessed to committing murder and attempted robbery during pre-custody questioning.

Black Letter Rule: Whether a suspect is "in custody" under *Miranda* is determined objectively by how a reasonable person in the suspect's situation would understand his ability to terminate questioning and leave.

Rhode Island v. Innis

Instant Facts: After invoking his *Miranda* right to consult with a lawyer, Innis (D) volunteered incriminating statements in response to a conversation between police while riding in the back of the patrol vehicle.

Black Letter Rule: For purposes of *Miranda*, an "interrogation" occurs when police either expressly question a suspect in custody or engage in any actions or dialogue that the police should know is reasonably likely to elicit an incriminating response from the suspect.

Illinois v. Perkins

Instant Facts: While incarcerated for an unrelated crime, Perkins (D) confessed to killing a man to an undercover police officer.

Black Letter Rule: *Miranda* warnings are not required when the suspect is unaware that he is speaking to a law enforcement officer and gives a voluntary statement.

Minnick v. Mississippi

Instant Facts: After initially consulting with counsel, Minnick (D) confessed to murder in the absence of counsel.

Black Letter Rule: When counsel is requested, interrogation must cease, and officials may not reinitiate interrogation without counsel present, whether or not the accused has consulted with his attorney.

New York v. Quarles

Instant Facts: Quarles (D) was arrested in a supermarket where he had discarded a gun allegedly used to commit a recent crime, and he responded to police questions regarding the location of the weapon without being advised of his *Miranda* rights.

Black Letter Rule: *Miranda* warnings are not required before police question a suspect in custody about imminent matters related to public safety.

United States v. Patane

Instant Facts: Patane (D) was convicted of possession of a firearm as a felon after he voluntarily admitted possession without being read his *Miranda* rights.

Black Letter Rule: Nontestimonial evidence obtained as a result of a defendant's voluntary statement given without the benefit of *Miranda* warnings need not be excluded at the defendant's trial.

Missouri v. Seibert

Instant Facts: After Seibert (D) made an incriminating statement without a *Miranda* warning, she was read her *Miranda* rights and repeated the statement.

Black Letter Rule: Incriminating statements initially made before *Miranda* warnings are given are not admissible simply because they are repeated after proper warnings are given.

Moran v. Burbine

Instant Facts: After waiving his right to counsel, Burbine (D) confessed to murder without knowing that counsel had been retained for him.

Black Letter Rule: Absent coercion, a defendant's waiver made with a full understanding of his rights is valid as a matter of law.

Dickerson v. United States

Instant Facts: Dickerson (D) was convicted based on statements admitted against him pursuant to a federal statute under which, contrary to the *Miranda* decision, admissibility was based on voluntariness.

Black Letter Rule: Congress may not legislatively supersede Court decisions interpreting and applying the Constitution.

Chavez v. Martinez

Instant Facts: After being shot in a police altercation, Martinez (P) requested that Chavez (D), a patrol officer, cease interrogation until he could receive medical treatment.

Black Letter Rule: The Fifth Amendment right against self-incrimination does not attach until criminal proceedings have been initiated.

Brewer v. Williams (Williams I)

Instant Facts: During a long car trip with a police officer, Williams (D) confessed to murder after the officer persuaded him to reveal the location of the victim's body outside the presence of Williams's (D) attorney.

Black Letter Rule: The right to the assistance of counsel can be waived only by the knowing relinquishment of that right.

Kuhlmann v. Wilson

Instant Facts: Wilson (D) was convicted of murder after incriminating statements made to a cellmate were admitted against him.

Black Letter Rule: When police take no direct action to solicit incriminating statements, but merely listen to voluntary statements made by an accused, the right to counsel is not violated.

Ashcraft v. Tennessee

(*Murder Suspect*) v. (*Prosecuting Authority*)
322 U.S. 143, 64 S. Ct. 921, 88 L. Ed. 1192 (1944)

A CONFESSION FOLLOWING LENGTHY, CONTINUOUS INTERROGATION IS NOT VOLUNTARY

■ **INSTANT FACTS** Ashcraft (D) was questioned in relays by police investigators for thirty-six continuous hours without rest, in order for the police to obtain a confession.

■ **BLACK LETTER RULE** The Constitution does not permit a conviction based on a coerced confession.

■ PROCEDURAL BASIS

Certiorari to review the defendant's conviction.

■ FACTS

Nine days after Ashcraft's (D) wife had been murdered, police came to his house and took him into custody. Ashcraft (D) was taken into a room at the county jailhouse, where he was questioned "in relays" for approximately thirty-six consecutive hours. The officers testified that they questioned him in relays because they grew too tired to do so continuously. Ashcraft (D) contended that during his questioning, he became physically and mentally exhausted from continual police threats and abuse. Ashcraft (D) denied confessing or implicating another suspect in the murder, but the police claimed to have obtained a confession from the other suspect stating that Ashcraft (D) had hired him to kill his wife. The police further contended that Ashcraft (D) corroborated the suspect's account, but he refused to sign the transcript of the questioning.

■ ISSUE

If Ashcraft (D) confessed to the murder after thirty-six hours of continuous police interrogation, was his confession knowing and voluntary?

■ DECISION AND RATIONALE

(Black, J.) No. Setting aside the factual disputes surrounding Ashcraft's (D) confession, even if he did confess, it was not voluntary. By secluding Ashcraft (D) in a room for thirty-six hours without rest, the coercive force of the questioning was inherent. Due process would not permit the prosecution to cross-examine a witness at trial in relays for such a duration without rest. Surely the Constitution cannot permit such conduct behind closed doors and away from the eyes of the jury. And the Constitution does not permit a conviction based on a coerced confession.

■ DISSENT

(Jackson, J.) In setting aside Ashcraft's (D) conviction, the Court fashions a new irrebuttable presumption regarding coercion that precludes consideration of other evidence supporting the voluntariness of a confession. In the process, the Court casts doubt on the State's (P) inherent duty to protect its citizens without regard to the results of its law enforcement efforts. While the effects on a suspect stemming from actual or threatened physical force are too certain to question, a confession resulting from mere interrogation is not per se violent. Questioning is required in the pursuit of justice and is itself "inherently coercive." It does not, however, possess the coercive effects of physical force that always render a confession involuntary.

The time under which a suspect endures police questioning will have varying effects on different suspects. For some, questioning of only a short duration may solicit a confession, but others may withstand many hours before ultimately issuing incriminating statements. It is the mental state of the suspect at the time of the confession that determines whether a confession was voluntary, not the duration of the questioning. The facts here indicate that at the time of his confession, Ashcraft (D) made an intelligent, knowing, and voluntary confession. Rather than establishing a per se due process violation, these facts must be considered.

Analysis:

While the Court in this case establishes a rule that excessively long questioning violates the Constitution, the parameters of the rule are not entirely clear. Nowhere does the Court establish a specified point after which questioning necessarily becomes coercive. And if Ashcraft (D) was not questioned in relays, but rather by an officer of sufficient endurance and stamina to continuously question him for thirty-six hours, would the questioning here have been unconstitutional?

■ CASE VOCABULARY

COERCED CONFESSION: A confession that is obtained by threats or force.

COERCION: Compulsion by physical force or threat of physical force.

CONFESSION: A criminal suspect's acknowledgement of guilt, usually in writing and often including details about the crime.

Watts v. Indiana

(*Murder Suspect*) v. (*Prosecuting Authority*)
338 U.S. 49, 69 S. Ct. 1347, 93 L. Ed. 1801 (1949)

A CONFESSION FOLLOWING DAYS OF PERSISTENT POLICE QUESTIONING IS NOT VOLUNTARY

■ **INSTANT FACTS** Watts (D) made incriminating statements while in custody after days of persistent police questioning.

■ **BLACK LETTER RULE** Relentless, systematic police questioning producing a confession violates the Due Process Clause.

■ PROCEDURAL BASIS

Certiorari to review the defendant's conviction.

■ FACTS

Watts (D) was arrested on suspicion of attempted criminal assault. Later that day, a woman was found murdered near the scene of the alleged assault, and the police suspected Watts's (D) involvement. Watts (D) was transferred from the county jail to State Police Headquarters, where he was questioned in relays from 11:30 p.m. until approximately 3:00 a.m. The following day, he was again questioned in relays from 5:30 p.m. until around 3:00 a.m. This pattern of questioning continued for four of the next five days. At 3:00 a.m. on the final day, Watts (D) stated that he possessed the murder weapon on the night of the murder. Not satisfied with the statement, the prosecutor took Watts (D) to an experienced interrogator to obtain a more incriminating statement. Throughout his questioning, Watts (D) was kept in solitary confinement and driven around town for hours in order for the police to obtain additional statements. Watts (D) was not advised of his constitutional rights nor permitted to consult with counsel, and he was not granted a timely preliminary hearing. Based on his confession, Watts (D) was convicted.

■ ISSUE

Does relentless, systematic police questioning producing a confession violate the Due Process Clause?

■ DECISION AND RATIONALE

(Frankfurter, J.) Yes. To support a conviction, a confession must be a product of the suspect's free choice. Sustained police questioning deprives a suspect of free choice, for succumbing to unrelenting police pressure is a natural product of the human condition. Relentless pressure ultimately creates the impression that the police will continue questioning the suspect until he waives his constitutional rights and confesses to the crime. But permitting such conduct when it would be constitutionally impermissible in open court violates the essence of due process.

The criminal justice system requires the prosecution to prove the defendant's guilt beyond a reasonable doubt and affords the defendant the right to remain silent and refrain from self-incrimination. The prosecution's burden must be met not through individual confessions, but by evidence collected through skillful investigation. The constitutional rights to which the defendant is entitled all underlie this accusatorial system. Due process requires that police follow appropriate accusatorial procedures before a liberty interest is denied. The fruits of impermissible interrogation cannot form the basis for a defendant's conviction. Reversed.

■ CONCURRENCE

(Douglas, J.) Watts (D) was held and questioned until he broke. Only then was he arraigned and formally afforded his constitutional rights. When a suspect is detained without arraignment, confessions obtained are necessarily coerced and must not be allowed.

■ CONCURRENCE

(Jackson, J.) In a criminal case, the State has a legitimate interest in obtaining sufficient evidence to solve the case and bring the offender to justice. At the same time, the suspect has constitutional interests in his right to counsel, right against self-incrimination, and other rights. The effect of these constitutional rights is that justice often depends not on the facts of what occurred, but rather on the facts that the defendant has not successfully shielded from the State. While confessions obtained through physical violence are unquestionably unreliable and inappropriate, if a confession obtained free of violence is corroborated by other evidence, such as the discovery of the murder weapon, the confession can be presumed to be genuine and truthful. This is no less true because the interrogation spans several hours or several days. If the State is to have any right to examine the suspect at all, it must be permitted to employ those techniques that are reasonably necessary under the facts of the case. State trial judges and appellate judges, then, are bound by the Fourteenth Amendment to determine whether the police techniques employed in a given case violate the defendant's rights. The Court should not lightly disturb those state decisions.

Analysis:

Does the Court give too much deference to the human condition by assuming that sustained police questioning will eventually cause even an innocent defendant to provide the answer the police are seeking? If a defendant initially lies, why is his revelation of the truth after further, even constant, questioning undesirable? And if a defendant tells the truth initially, how likely is he to recant the truth in the face of further questioning, assuming the police refrain from torture or the threat of violence?

■ CASE VOCABULARY

DUE PROCESS: The conduct of legal proceedings according to established rules and principles for the protection of private rights, including notice and a fair hearing before a tribunal with the power to decide the case.

INQUISITION: A persistent, grueling examination conducted without regard to the examinee's dignity or civil rights.

Massiah v. United States

(*Drug Dealer*) v. (*Prosecuting Government*)
377 U.S. 201, 84 S. Ct. 1199, 12 L. Ed. 2d 246 (1964)

POST–INDICTMENT INCRIMINATING STATEMENTS MADE TO A CO–DEFENDANT ARE INADMISSIBLE

■ **INSTANT FACTS** Massiah (D) was convicted of drug violations on the basis of incriminating statements overheard on a listening device by federal agents after Massiah was (D) indicted.

■ **BLACK LETTER RULE** The Sixth Amendment prohibits government interrogation of a defendant after indictment outside the presence of counsel.

■ PROCEDURAL BASIS

Certiorari to review a decision of the Second Circuit Court of Appeals affirming the defendant's conviction.

■ FACTS

Massiah (D) was indicted on drug charges. After retaining counsel and pleading not guilty, he was released on bail. Several days later, a co-defendant, Colson, agreed to cooperate with government agents, who installed a listening device in Colson's car. Through the listening device, an agent overheard Massiah (D) make incriminating statements concerning the crimes with which he was charged. Over the objection of defense counsel, the statements were offered to the jury, which convicted Massiah (D) on the drug charges. The Second Circuit Court of Appeals affirmed.

■ ISSUE

Is the Sixth Amendment violated when the government deliberately elicits incriminating statements from an accused after indictment, outside the presence of counsel?

■ DECISION AND RATIONALE

(Stewart, J.) Yes. After indictment, a criminal defendant in a federal proceeding has a right to counsel under the Sixth Amendment. This right is undermined when the government, outside the presence of counsel, deliberately elicits a confession or other incriminating statements and those statements are offered into evidence against the defendant. The violation is especially clear when, as here, the defendant is unaware that he is being interrogated by government agents through a cooperative co-defendant. While the government's actions may be an appropriate exercise of its duty to further investigate the matter, the incriminating statements may not be used as evidence to convict the defendant.

■ DISSENT

(White, J.) The exclusion of the defendant's incriminating statements, which are highly relevant, reliable, and probative, threatens the pursuit of truth and justice in that crucial evidence of the commission of the crime will not be considered. Unlike the exclusion of evidence obtained through an illegal search, in which the evidence seized violates the Fourth Amendment, the incriminating statements elicited from Massiah (D) do not require the same constitutional protection. The defendant had retained counsel and was free to consult with him as often as needed. The agent did not interfere with this right nor the defendant's ability to properly prepare for trial. Similarly, the statements were not made in the coercive environment of a police station or under intimidation of federal agents. The defendant voluntarily chose to make the incriminating statements outside the presence of counsel and has not been compelled to testify against himself. The fact that the statements were deliberately elicited through Colson should not require their exclusion when the statements would be otherwise admissible had Colson agreed to cooperate with the agents only after the statements were made. Massiah (D) assumed the risk that his statements would be passed along to the agents. Like a voluntary confession, the statements should be admissible.

Analysis:

Massiah demonstrates the scope of the right to counsel under the Sixth Amendment. Once a person is indicted, his status changes from merely a "suspect" to an "accused," resulting in the commencement of an adversary proceeding. Once an adversary proceeding is commenced, the Sixth Amendment right to counsel attaches and police interrogation outside the presence of counsel is prohibited, unless counsel is waived.

■ CASE VOCABULARY

INDICTMENT: The formal written accusation of a crime, made by a grand jury and presented to a court for prosecution against the accused person.

SIXTH AMENDMENT: The constitutional amendment guaranteeing in criminal cases the right to a speedy and public trial by jury, the right to be informed of the nature of the accusation, the right to confront witnesses, the right to counsel, and the right to compulsory process for obtaining favorable witnesses.

Escobedo v. Illinois

(*Murder Suspect*) v. (*Prosecuting Authority*)

378 U.S. 478, 84 S. Ct. 1758, 12 L. Ed. 2d 977 (1964)

WHEN POLICE INVESTIGATIONS SHIFT FROM INVESTIGATORY TO ACCUSATORY, THE RIGHT TO COUNSEL ATTACHES

■ **INSTANT FACTS** Escobedo (D) was convicted of murder based in part on incriminating statements he made after being denied an opportunity to consult with counsel.

■ **BLACK LETTER RULE** When a police investigation is no longer a general inquiry into an unsolved crime but begins to focus on a particular suspect and the suspect has been taken into police custody, if the police carry out a process of interrogations that lends itself to eliciting incriminating statements and the suspect has requested and been denied an opportunity to consult with his lawyer, and the police have not effectively warned him of his absolute constitutional right to remain silent, the accused has been denied his right to counsel.

■ PROCEDURAL BASIS

Certiorari to review a decision of the Illinois Supreme Court affirming the defendant's conviction.

■ FACTS

Following the shooting of Escobedo's (D) brother-in-law, Escobedo (D) was taken into police custody for questioning. He made no statement and was released on a writ of habeas corpus the next afternoon. Two weeks later, another suspect in police custody stated that Escobedo (D) fired the shots that killed his brother-in-law. Escobedo (D) was again arrested and taken to police headquarters. Along the way, Escobedo (D) was informed that he was implicated in the shooting by the other suspect, but he still refused to respond. Instead, Escobedo (D) asked to speak with his lawyer. His attorney arrived at police headquarters shortly after Escobedo (D), but was told he could not see his client. Escobedo's (D) repeated requests to consult with his attorney were denied. Instead, the police arranged a confrontation between Escobedo (D) and the other suspect. During the confrontation, Escobedo (D) stated, "I didn't shoot Manuel, you did." As a result, Escobedo (D) implicated himself in the murder. An assistant prosecutor then took Escobedo's (D) statement, which was later admitted into evidence. Escobedo (D) was convicted of murder. The Supreme Court of Illinois affirmed.

■ ISSUE

Does the refusal to honor an accused's request to consult with his lawyer during interrogation violate the accused's right to counsel under the Sixth Amendment, thereby rendering any incriminating statements elicited inadmissible in his criminal trial?

■ DECISION AND RATIONALE

(Goldberg, J.) Yes. Although Escobedo (D) had not been indicted for murder, his right to counsel had attached nonetheless. When the police denied him the opportunity to consult with counsel before interrogation, he became the "accused" from whom the interrogation was designed to elicit a confession. Escobedo (D) is a layperson who cannot be expected to know that admission of complicity in the murder is legally as damaging as firing the shots himself. The advice of counsel would have informed him of this fact and enabled him to exercise his right to remain silent.

The period between arrest and indictment is a critical point in the criminal proceeding. It is the point when many convictions are obtained by confession. Although the right to counsel at this stage may hamper law enforcement and prosecution of criminal offenses, the importance of this stage must balance in favor of the accused's constitutional rights. When "the investigation is no longer a general inquiry into an unsolved crime but has begun to focus on a particular suspect, the suspect has been taken into police custody, the police carry out a process of interrogations that lends itself to eliciting incriminating statements, the suspect has requested and been denied an opportunity to consult with his lawyer, and the police have not effectively warned him of his absolute constitutional right to remain silent, the accused has been denied" his right to counsel. Any statements obtained under such circumstances are inadmissible against him at trial. Reversed and remanded.

■ DISSENT

(Harlan, J.) "[T]he rule announced today is most ill-conceived and . . . seriously and unjustifiably fetters perfectly legitimate methods of criminal law enforcement."

■ DISSENT

(Stewart, J.) Until indictment, police questioning "does not involve the deliberate interrogation of a defendant after initiation of judicial proceedings against him." The initiation of judicial proceedings is important, for it marks the end of criminal investigations and the beginning of adversary proceedings under which constitutional guarantees attach. By extending constitutional rights beyond adversary proceedings, the Court has "pervert[ed] those precious constitutional guarantees, and frustrate[d] the vital interests of society in preserving the legitimate and proper function of honest and purposeful police investigation."

■ DISSENT

(White, J.) By affording the right to counsel not when a suspect has been indicted, but rather when the police begin to "focus" on the suspect, the Court in effect requires *Miranda* warnings for every person the police question and precludes the admission of any confession unless the right to counsel has been waived. The Court is unconcerned with whether the confession was voluntary or involuntary, and instead endeavors to preclude convictions based on any confession at all. In essence, by requiring the right to counsel whenever the aid of counsel would be helpful, police officers are prohibited from questioning any person outside the presence of counsel for fear that such statements will later be inadmissible. The right against self-incrimination applies only to protect individuals from compelled confessions and cannot be amended or superseded by the Sixth Amendment right to counsel. Because Escobedo's (D) confession was not coerced, the Court fashions a Sixth Amendment violation where no Fifth Amendment violation occurred.

Analysis:

It is difficult to determine at what point a police investigation changes from an unsolved crime to one focused on a suspect. Whenever the police suspect or even speculate regarding a person's involvement in a crime, isn't the investigation focused on that individual? More alarming, however, is the pressure placed on police to draw the line between an unsolved crime and a focused investigation at the time of the interrogation, since pursuant to this decision, the risk of reversal of a conviction is substantial.

■ CASE VOCABULARY

ACCUSED: A person who has been blamed for wrongdoing; especially, a person who has been arrested and brought before a magistrate or who has been formally charged with a crime (as by indictment or information).

RIGHT TO COUNSEL: A criminal defendant's constitutional rights, guaranteed by the Sixth Amendment, to representation by a court-appointed lawyer if the defendant cannot afford to hire one.

SUSPECT: A person believed to have committed a crime or offense.

Miranda v. Arizona (No. 759)

(*Convicted Rapist and Kidnapper*) v. (*Prosecuting State*)
384 U.S. 436, 86 S. Ct. 1602, 16 L. Ed. 2d 694 (1966)

DEFENDANTS MUST BE INFORMED OF THEIR RIGHTS PRIOR TO INTERROGATION

■ **INSTANT FACTS** While in custody, four separate defendants were convicted of crimes, although the evidence did not prove that they had been advised of their right to remain silent or the right to counsel.

■ **BLACK LETTER RULE** No statements obtained during a custodial interrogation, whether exculpatory or inculpatory, may be used against the defendant at trial unless the prosecution proves that the accused was advised of the right to remain silent, that any statements made can and will be used against the accused at trial, and that the accused has the right to an attorney prior to and during questioning.

■ PROCEDURAL BASIS

Certiorari to review appellate decisions on the defendants' convictions.

■ FACTS

Miranda (D) was arrested in Arizona and taken into police custody. After the complaining witness identified him, Miranda (D) was taken into an interrogation room and questioned by two police officers. The officers did not advise Miranda (D) that he had the right to have an attorney present during questioning. After two hours, the police secured a written confession signed by Miranda (D). The confession, which included a paragraph to the effect that the confession was made voluntarily, without threats or promises of immunity, and "with full knowledge of my legal rights, understanding that any statement I may make may be used against me," was admitted as evidence against Miranda (D) at trial. Miranda (D) was convicted of rape and kidnapping. Emphasizing that Miranda (D) did not specifically request counsel, the Supreme Court of Arizona affirmed the conviction, finding that police did not obtain the confession in violation of Miranda's (D) constitutional rights.

Vignera (D) was arrested in New York in connection with a robbery and taken to police headquarters, where he was questioned, orally admitted to committing the robbery, and was identified by witnesses. He was thereafter taken to a different precinct, where he was questioned by an assistant district attorney before a hearing reporter. At trial, no evidence was presented to demonstrate that Vignera (D) had been advised of his rights. He was convicted of robbery.

Westover (D) was arrested in Kansas City as a suspect in two robberies and a California felony. He was taken to the police station and booked on the robbery charges. Under interrogation by the Kansas City Police, Westover (D) denied any criminal involvement. The next day, however, he confessed to committing two earlier robberies in California. At trial, an FBI agent testified that he advised Westover (D) of his right to remain silent and his right to counsel. Westover (D) was convicted of the California robberies.

After a series of robberies resulting in one death, Stewart (D) was identified as the endorser of a dividend check taken in one of the robberies. He was arrested and consented to a search of his house, which uncovered various items stolen in the robberies. After five days of interrogation, Stewart (D) confessed to the robbery of the deceased victim. A jury convicted him of robbery and first-degree murder, but no evidence established that he had been advised of his rights. The California Supreme Court reversed, holding that the lack of proof that Stewart (D) had been advised of his rights prevented conviction.

■ ISSUE

In order for the defendant's statements to be admissible at trial, must a defendant subject to custodial interrogation be advised of his Fifth Amendment privilege against self-incrimination prior to questioning?

■ DECISION AND RATIONALE

(Warren, C.J.) Yes. Police interrogations occur in the confines of secret rooms in which only the suspect and the interrogators are present, leaving little record of the actual events that transpire. Because of this secrecy, police manuals highlighting effective interrogation practices serve as the best illustration of the tactics employed to elicit confessions and other incriminating statements. These manuals demonstrate that interrogators proceed with confidence in the suspect's guilt to obtain corroborating details, and they direct blame for the crime away from the suspect to psychologically direct the suspect to admit his guilt. Other times, the use of hostility and trickery is suggested to influence the suspect's confession. When the suspect remains silent, interrogators are trained to employ patience and perseverance, pointing to the silence as a suggestion of guilt. The entire interrogation procedure is designed to isolate the suspect from others to pressure the suspect into implicating himself in the commission of the crime. While confessions given in such an environment are not involuntary in the strict sense of the word, the failure to employ appropriate procedural safeguards against involuntary confessions frustrates the spirit of the Fifth Amendment.

The Self–Incrimination Clause strikes a balance between effective law enforcement and respect for the "dignity and integrity of citizens." It is effective only when a person's right to remain silent is preserved. Custodial interrogations in a psychologically hostile environment threaten this right unless adequate assurances are given that the suspect's rights will not be violated. Therefore, before an individual in custody may be interrogated, states must ensure that the accused is first informed in clear and unequivocal terms that he or she has the right to remain silent, that the accused understands that anything said can and will be used against him or her in court, and that the accused is clearly informed that he or she has the right to consult with a lawyer prior to questioning and to have the lawyer present during interrogation, and, in the case of indigent defendants, that a lawyer will be appointed to represent him or her. Once these warnings have been provided, the government bears the burden of proving that the suspect knowingly and intelligently waived these rights, and no waiver will be presumed absent such proof. In order to be valid, the waiver must precede any statement made under interrogation, for the likelihood that a pre-waiver statement is a product of inappropriate police coercion is high.

These requirements will undoubtedly cast a heavy burden on law enforcement seeking to obtain the truth surrounding a crime, but they do not prevent the police from carrying out their traditional investigatory functions. Police may continue to question individuals in non-custodial settings and may gather pertinent evidence as required. But when a suspect has been taken into custody, the police must pay respect to the individual rights conferred by the Fifth Amendment

Here, Miranda (D) was not advised in any way that he had the right to consult with an attorney and to have an attorney present during questioning, and because his right against self-incrimination was not otherwise protected, the statements were inadmissible. Moreover, the signed statement that included the paragraph asserting that Miranda (D) had "full knowledge" of his "legal rights" did not constitute a knowing and intelligent waiver of his constitutional rights. Reversed.

Likewise, Vignera (D) was questioned by both the police and the assistant district attorney without a warning of his constitutional rights, leaving his statements inadmissible at trial. Reversed.

Westover (D), too, did not receive warnings of his constitutional rights to remain silent and to speak with an attorney before making his statements to the FBI agent. His interrogation on the robberies in Kansas City spanned many hours immediately before the FBI questioned him about the California crimes. There is no evidence that the warnings were given before his waiver or that he voluntarily waived his rights before discussing the California offenses. Because the FBI interrogation immediately followed the local interrogation without a full explanation that different crimes were at issue, any general warnings given at that point were insufficient to inform Westover (D) that his rights were available. The FBI received the benefit of the psychological pressures exerted by the local authorities, jeopardizing the defendant's rights. Reversed.

Finally, Stewart's (D) conviction was reversed because of the failure to afford him the warnings necessary to protect his rights. Because the record does not reflect that any warnings were given such that a voluntary waiver could be made, the government failed to carry its burden. Affirmed.

■ DISSENT IN PART

(Clark, J.) The police manuals relied upon by the Court to demonstrate police interrogation practices are not official guidelines universally used in crime detection. Rather than impose strict Fifth Amendment requirements that will hamper law enforcement, traditional notions of due process provide adequate protection against unnecessary police coercion resulting in involuntary confessions.

■ DISSENT

(Harlan, J.) The Court's new rules do not guard against police brutality or other egregious forms of coercion, but rather negate all pressures and ultimately discourage any confession at all. There is no justifiable reason to extend the Fifth Amendment to police investigations. The rationale underlying the Court's decision actually invokes principles protected by the Sixth Amendment, which has no application to police interrogation. Although pretrial stages may be critical to a defendant's defense, the Sixth Amendment right to counsel does not apply to all extra-trial stages, including grand jury indictments, petitions for certiorari, and the illegal purchase of narcotics from an undercover agent. The minor pressures of police interrogation do not warrant an extension of Sixth Amendment protections. The right to counsel at all interrogations "simply invites the end of the interrogation" and seriously threatens legitimate law enforcement designed to punish criminals.

■ DISSENT

(White, J.) The privilege against self-incrimination has historically been applied to prevent compelled judicial interrogations, not police interrogations. There is no adequate factual basis for the conclusion that all confessions obtained during custodial interrogation are the product of compulsion. It is illogical to distinguish between a spontaneous product of the coercion (e.g., a blurted out confession), which the Court's decision views as "voluntary" despite the absence of warnings or knowledge of the rights, and the answer to an express question posed by law enforcement, which is "compelled" even if the accused has been clearly warned of his right to remain silent. In the latter instance, the response may be "involuntary" in the sense that it was provoked by an inquiry, but it is "patently unsound" to assert that the response was compelled. Even assuming the existence of a factual basis for the aforementioned conclusion, the *Miranda* rule is "irrational" because it is only if the accused is also warned of the right to counsel, and waives both that right and the right against self-incrimination, that the inherent compulsiveness of the interrogation disappears. It is impossible to foreclose questioning without the necessary warnings yet at the same time permit the accused to waive his right to consult with an attorney, for in the latter instance, would not the answer also be compelled? The Court's decision undermines the most basic governmental function to provide for the security of the individual and his property.

Analysis:

Perhaps no Supreme Court decision has had as great an impact on American criminal jurisprudence than *Miranda*. The rights recognized by *Miranda* have spawned a seemingly infinite number of legal challenges and substantial debate over the wisdom of the Court's decision. Yet, the legacy of *Miranda* remains strong, and few laypersons are unaware of their *Miranda* rights.

■ CASE VOCABULARY

CUSTODIAL INTERROGATION: Police questioning of a detained person about the crime that he or she is suspected of having committed.

DURESS: Strictly, the physical confinement of a person or the detention of a contracting party's property.

EXCULPATORY EVIDENCE: Evidence tending to establish a criminal defendant's innocence.

INCULPATORY EVIDENCE: Evidence showing or tending to show one's involvement in a crime or wrong.

MIRANDA RULE: The doctrine that a criminal suspect in police custody must be informed of certain constitutional rights before being interrogated. The suspect must be advised of the right to remain silent, the right to have an attorney present during questioning, and the right to have an attorney appointed if the suspect cannot afford one. If the suspect is not advised of these rights and does not validly waive them, any evidence obtained during the interrogation cannot be used against the suspect at trial (except for impeachment purposes).

RIGHT AGAINST SELF–INCRIMINATION: A criminal defendant's or a witness's constitutional right—under the Fifth Amendment, but waivable under certain conditions—guaranteeing that a person cannot be compelled by the government to testify if the testimony might result in the person's being criminally prosecuted. Although this right is most often asserted during a criminal prosecution, a person can also "plead the Fifth" in a civil, legislative, administrative, or grand-jury proceeding.

SELF–INCRIMINATION: The act of indicating one's own involvement in a crime or exposing oneself to prosecution, especially by making a statement.

Yarborough v. Alvarado

(*Prison Warden*) v. (*Convicted Murderer*)
541 U.S. 652, 124 S. Ct. 2140, 158 L. Ed. 2d 938 (2004)

A SUSPECT'S AGE AND EXPERIENCE DO NOT AFFECT A *MIRANDA* INQUIRY

■ **INSTANT FACTS** Alvarado (D), a minor, confessed to committing murder and attempted robbery during pre-custody questioning.

■ **BLACK LETTER RULE** Whether a suspect is "in custody" under *Miranda* is determined objectively by how a reasonable person in the suspect's situation would understand his ability to terminate questioning and leave.

■ PROCEDURAL BASIS

Certiorari to review a decision of the Ninth Circuit Court of Appeals reversing the defendant's conviction on a writ of habeas corpus.

■ FACTS

Alvarado (D), a minor, assisted another person in attempting to steal a truck, leading to the shooting of the truck's owner. The investigating officer notified Alvarado's (D) parents that she wanted to speak with Alvarado (D). Alvarado's (D) parents brought him to the police station, where they remained in the lobby while the officer interrogated Alvarado (D) in a solitary room without giving him *Miranda* warnings. After first denying his involvement, Alvarado (D) later admitted to helping the other person attempt to steal the truck and hide the murder weapon. At the conclusion of questioning, Alvarado (D) was returned to his parents. Alvarado (D) was charged with murder and attempted robbery.

The trial court denied Alvarado's (D) request to suppress the incriminating statements because he was not in custody during questioning, so no *Miranda* warnings were required. On appeal, the California District Court of Appeal agreed. Alvarado (D) filed a petition for a writ of habeas corpus with the federal district court, which denied the writ. The Ninth Circuit Court of Appeals reversed, however, holding that because of his youth and inexperience, Alvarado (D) could not have reasonably appreciated his right to leave during questioning. The Ninth Circuit further concluded that Alvarado's (D) juvenile status was relevant to habeas relief under the federal Antiterrorism and Effective Death Penalty Act of 1996, because his status "resulted in a decision [that] involved an unreasonable application [of] clearly established Federal law."

■ ISSUE

Is a suspect's age and experience with the judicial system relevant to a determination of his "in-custody" status during pre-arrest questioning?

■ DECISION AND RATIONALE

(Kennedy, J.) No. Under clearly established Court precedent, custody is determined by how a reasonable person in the suspect's situation would perceive his circumstances. If a reasonable person in the suspect's position would appreciate his ability to freely leave, the suspect is not in custody. Here, Alvarado (D) was not brought to the station by the police, he was never placed under arrest or threatened with arrest, the questioning focused on another person's conduct rather than his own, and his parents remained in the lobby. Under these objective facts, a reasonable person would feel free to terminate the questioning and leave at any time.

On the other hand, Alvarado (D) was questioned at the police station, he arrived at the initiative of his legal guardians rather than of his own volition, and his parents were not permitted to participate in the questioning. From these facts, a reasonable person may feel in custody. Because of the differing perspectives, the state court's application of federal law was reasonable, for this Court cannot second-guess whether the state court was correct in fact. The *Miranda* custody inquiry is an objective one and does not hinge on subjective elements such as the suspect's age and experience with the judicial system. The proper standard is that of a reasonable person, not a reasonable person of the suspect's age and experience. Because the state court properly considered the correct factors, its decision was reasonable.

■ CONCURRENCE

(O'Connor, J.) While a suspect's age may be relevant in some circumstances, the suspect here was so close to the age of majority that the police should not be required to recognize that the suspect was a juvenile. In other situations, however, a suspect's *obvious* minority may be relevant.

■ DISSENT

(Breyer, J.) No reasonable person in Alvarado's (D) position would have felt free to terminate the police questioning. Alvarado (D) was told by his parents that he needed to submit to police questioning, and his parents took him to the police station. He was separated from his parents, after they were denied participation, and taken to a small interrogation room. For two hours, the officers questioned Alvarado (D) concerning evidence they had against him and gave him an opportunity to tell the truth and "take care of himself." No reasonable person in his position would feel free to leave at any time.

The majority sees a reasonable difference of opinion as to whether Alvarado (D) was in custody, but points only to things the police *did not* do. A focus on what *did* happen, however, demonstrates he acted as a reasonable person would. And his age is not a *subjective* component of the standard, for a person of advanced age would not feel the pressure Alvarado (D) did when faced with his parents' role in the questioning. The reasonable person standard must account for personal characteristics, such as age, that ensure that a suspect's beliefs are properly compared to the expected beliefs of those similarly situated.

Analysis:

The Court's conclusion that age and inexperience are subjective factors that are unknowable by the police at the time of interrogation is questionable. With today's intricate police network, background checks on suspects are easily obtained and reviewed by police before an interrogation commences. While a suspect may lie about such facts, objective data within an officer's possession can easily satisfy the knowledge requirement of the objective standard.

■ CASE VOCABULARY

CUSTODY: The care and control of a thing or person for inspection, preservation, or security.

Rhode Island v. Innis

(*Prosecuting State*) v. (*Convicted Murderer*)

446 U.S. 291, 100 S. Ct. 1682, 64 L. Ed. 2d 297 (1980)

"INTERROGATION" INCLUDES THE "FUNCTIONAL EQUIVALENT" OF EXPRESS QUESTIONING

■ **INSTANT FACTS** After invoking his *Miranda* right to consult with a lawyer, Innis (D) volunteered incriminating statements in response to a conversation between police while riding in the back of the patrol vehicle.

■ **BLACK LETTER RULE** For purposes of *Miranda*, an "interrogation" occurs when police either expressly question a suspect in custody or engage in any actions or dialogue that the police should know is reasonably likely to elicit an incriminating response from the suspect.

■ PROCEDURAL BASIS

Certiorari to review a decision of the Rhode Island Supreme Court reversing the defendant's conviction.

■ FACTS

Innis (D) was arrested for murdering a taxicab driver with a sawed-off shotgun. At the time of his arrest, Innis (D) was unarmed. The police read Innis (D) his *Miranda* rights on three separate occasions, and Innis (D) stated that he understood those rights and wanted to speak with an attorney. On the way to the stationhouse, the officers spoke between themselves, indicating that a school for handicapped children was in the vicinity where Innis (D) was arrested, and that it would be unfortunate if an innocent handicapped child found the missing weapon and hurt herself with it. Innis (D) interrupted the conversation from the backseat of the car, telling the officers to return to the arrest scene so that he could show them where the gun was located. When they arrived back at the scene, Innis (D) was again given *Miranda* warnings. Innis (D) once more indicated that he understood those rights, but that he "wanted to get the gun out of the way because of the kids in the area in the school." Innis (D) then showed the officers where the gun was located. He was later convicted of murder. The Rhode Island Supreme Court reversed the conviction, concluding that the officers interrogated Innis (D) outside the presence of counsel.

■ ISSUE

Was the police officers' conversation in the defendant's presence, which elicited a response from him, an "interrogation" that violated the defendant's right to remain silent until he had consulted with a lawyer?

■ DECISION AND RATIONALE

(Stewart, J.) No. For purposes of *Miranda*, "interrogation" means express questioning or its functional equivalent, i.e., "any words or actions on the part of police officers that they *should have known* were reasonably likely to elicit an incriminating response." Here, the conversation was not the "functional equivalent" of questioning. The record does not reflect that the officers knew that the defendant was susceptible to an appeal to conscience concerning the safety of handicapped children, and nothing showed him to be unusually disoriented or upset at the time of arrest.

■ CONCURRENCE

(Burger, C.J.) The meaning of *Miranda* is clear, and law enforcement has adjusted to it; there is no need to overrule, disparage, or extend *Miranda*. Police officers are generally ill-equipped to determine the susceptibility of a suspect at the time of arrest.

■ DISSENT

(Marshall, J.) Applying an objective inquiry into the likely effect of police conduct on a typical individual (taking into account any special susceptibility of the suspect to certain kinds of pressure of which the police know or have reason to know), the facts of this case warrant the conclusion that an interrogation occurred. There is a strong appeal to *any* suspect that if a weapon is not found, an innocent individual (especially a handicapped child) will be hurt or killed. It is constitutionally immaterial whether the appeal was made directly to Innis (D), or merely within earshot such that he would necessarily overhear.

■ DISSENT

(Stevens, J.) There is a vast difference between a "faithful adherence" to *Miranda* and the "stinted test" enunciated in *Innis*, under which the form of the question is critical. The new test requires that any express question be labeled an "interrogation," whether or not the police have reason to believe that the defendant was susceptible to a particular appeal. Correspondingly, statements not in the form of a question but that are just as likely to elicit a response are not considered "interrogation." Police now have an incentive to ignore a suspect's invocation of his right in order to make incessant attempts at extracting information from him. A suspect who does not appear susceptible to a particular psychological pressure is an easy target to police who "are apparently free to exert that pressure on him despite [his] request for counsel, so long as they are careful not to punctuate their statements with question marks."

Analysis:

Innis suggests that an "interrogation" might occur other than by police-initiated questioning in situations such as (1) a line-up in which a coached witness picks the defendant as the perpetrator, which is designed to establish the fact of the defendant's guilt as a predicate for further interrogation; (2) the "reverse line-up," in which a defendant is identified by coached witnesses as having committed a fictitious crime to induce him to confess to the actual crime of which he was suspected; and (3) the use of psychological play, such as to "posi[t]" "the guilt of the subject," to "minimize the moral seriousness of the offense," and "to cast blame on the victim or on society." Such techniques of persuasion, in a custodial setting, may amount to interrogation. Note that if police carry on a lengthy "harangue" in the presence of the suspect, or if their comments are particularly "evocative," an interrogation may have occurred.

■ CASE VOCABULARY

INTERROGATION: The formal or systematic questioning of a person; especially intensive questioning by the police, usually of a person arrested for or suspected of committing a crime. The Supreme Court has held that, for purposes of the Fifth Amendment right against self-incrimination, interrogation includes not only express questioning but also words or actions that the police should know are reasonably likely to elicit an incriminating response.

Illinois v. Perkins

(*Prosecuting Authority*) v. (*Incarcerated Suspect*)

496 U.S. 292, 110 S. Ct. 2394, 110 L. Ed. 2d 243 (1990)

INCRIMINATING STATEMENTS MADE TO AN UNDERCOVER AGENT WHILE IN CUSTODY ARE ADMISSIBLE

■ **INSTANT FACTS** While incarcerated for an unrelated crime, Perkins (D) confessed to killing a man to an undercover police officer.

■ **BLACK LETTER RULE** *Miranda* warnings are not required when the suspect is unaware that he is speaking to a law enforcement officer and gives a voluntary statement.

■ PROCEDURAL BASIS

Certiorari to review an appellate decision to suppress incriminating statements.

■ FACTS

While Perkins (D) was incarcerated, he made incriminating statements concerning an unrelated murder to a fellow inmate, who informed police. Following up on this information, the police placed the inmate and an undercover agent in the cellblock with Perkins (D), with instructions to engage in casual conversation and report any information obtained. After meeting Perkins (D), the agent suggested the three attempt to escape, and casually asked whether Perkins (D) had ever killed anybody. Perkins (D) responded with details of the murder. At the murder trial, the trial court suppressed the statements, and the Appellate Court of Illinois affirmed, reasoning that *Miranda* prohibited all government contact with incarcerated suspects that is likely to elicit incriminating statements.

■ ISSUE

Are *Miranda* warnings required when the suspect is unaware that he is speaking to a law enforcement officer and gives a voluntary statement?

■ DECISION AND RATIONALE

(Kennedy, J.) No. *Miranda* seeks to avoid coerced confessions brought on by a "police-dominated atmosphere" and compulsion. When an incarcerated prisoner makes incriminating statements to an agent he believes to be a fellow inmate, there is no reason to assume that the statements are a product of police compulsion or fear of reprisal for remaining silent. Although Perkins (D) was in police custody at the time of the statements, his incarceration did not affect his ability to make reliable, voluntary statements when he was unaware that he was speaking to an undercover police officer. Absent coercion, the Fifth Amendment right against self-incrimination is not violated. Likewise, because Perkins (D) had not been charged with murder, the Sixth Amendment right to counsel had not attached and is inapplicable.

■ CONCURRENCE

(Brennan, J.) When a suspect makes statements to someone he does not know is an undercover police officer, the questioning cannot be considered interrogation within the meaning of *Miranda*. However, the Due Process Clause calls for a closer examination of the method of questioning. Although custody itself does not present the dangers sought to be remedied by *Miranda*, an incarcerated suspect feels pressure to confide in fellow inmates and engage in "jailhouse bravado" that calls the truth of his statements into question. When the suspect is in custody, the State controls the environment of the questioning and can take the necessary steps to ensure the suspect confesses. Because these due process concerns were not addressed in the court below, the case should be remanded for further consideration.

■ DISSENT

(Marshall, J.) Because Perkins (D) was interrogated while in custody, *Miranda* requires that he be apprised of his rights. *Miranda* was not concerned solely with police coercion. Instead, the purpose of *Miranda* warnings is to protect a suspect from any police tactics that may operate to compel a suspect to make incriminating statements without being informed of his rights. By using an undercover officer in a jailhouse to elicit incriminating statements, the police engaged in custodial interrogation in violation of *Miranda*. The police preyed on Perkins's (D) psychological mindset by questioning him in an environment in which the threat of physical violence from other inmates requires him to "demonstrate his toughness." This is no less compulsion than if Perkins (D) had been directly interrogated by the police.

Analysis:

What atmosphere is more "police-dominated" than a state prison? Clearly, the police control with whom the suspect speaks, since access in and out of the prison is restricted. Yet, an incarcerated suspect is not compelled by police coercion to speak with anybody, although practical events often dictate prisoners' actions. If the human condition necessarily compels an involuntary confession from constant questioning, as in *United States v. Watts*, it would seem that jailhouse confessions would likewise be decried.

■ CASE VOCABULARY

INCRIMINATING STATEMENT: A statement that tends to establish the guilt of an accused.

Minnick v. Mississippi

(*Accused Murderer*) v. (*Prosecuting Authority*)
498 U.S. 146, 111 S. Ct. 486, 112 L. Ed. 2d 489 (1990)

AFTER AN ACCUSED MEETS WITH COUNSEL, COUNSEL MUST BE PRESENT AT EVERY SUBSEQUENT INTERROGATION

■ **INSTANT FACTS** After initially consulting with counsel, Minnick (D) confessed to murder in the absence of counsel.

■ **BLACK LETTER RULE** When counsel is requested, interrogation must cease, and officials may not reinitiate interrogation without counsel present, whether or not the accused has consulted with his attorney.

■ PROCEDURAL BASIS

Certiorari to review a decision of the Mississippi Supreme Court affirming the defendant's conviction.

■ FACTS

Minnick (D) and another inmate escaped from a Mississippi prison, murdered two people, and fled to Mexico. After returning to California four months later, Minnick (D) was arrested and jailed. Minnick (D) was read his *Miranda* rights and acknowledged understanding them, but refused to sign a waiver form. Minnick (D) told the FBI that the other inmate killed one person and forced him to kill another, but did not go into further detail. After Minnick (D) was reminded of his right to counsel, Minnick (D) requested counsel before a more complete statement was given. Counsel was appointed and met with Minnick (D) on two or three occasions. Two days later, a Mississippi deputy sheriff arrived in California to question Minnick (D). He reminded Minnick (D) of his rights. Although Minnick (D) again refused to sign a waiver form, he made incriminating statements to the deputy, which were admitted against him over his objections in a Mississippi murder trial. Minnick (D) was convicted and sentenced to death. The Mississippi Supreme Court affirmed the conviction.

■ ISSUE

May police reinitiate questioning of an accused in the absence of counsel after he has consulted with an attorney?

■ DECISION AND RATIONALE

(Kennedy, J.) No. Under *Edwards v. Arizona*, 451 U.S. 477, once an accused requests counsel, questioning must cease until counsel has been made available to him. This rule provides clear instruction to law enforcement that any statements made after counsel has been requested will be presumed to be involuntary and produced by coercive pressure. A single consultation with counsel, however, does not relieve the coercive pressures of custody and police interrogation. An accused may not fully understand his counsel's advice, and the presence of counsel will ensure that the accused's rights are preserved. Here, for example, Minnick (D) may have made the statements under the misapprehension that they were inadmissible because he refused to sign the waiver form. Had counsel been present at the questioning, he could have corrected Minnick's (D) belief and advised him accordingly. Permitting police questioning following isolated consultation would undermine the purposes of *Miranda* and *Edwards* and remove the clarity of police interrogation techniques *Edwards* established. "[W]hen counsel is requested, interrogation must cease, and officials may not reinitiate interrogation without counsel present, whether or not the accused has consulted with his attorney."

■ DISSENT

(Scalia, J.) The Court's decision creates an irrebuttable presumption that an accused cannot waive his right to counsel after actually consulting with an attorney. Although the Court has acknowledged in the past that *Miranda* rights may be knowingly and voluntarily waived under appropriate circumstances, it has departed from those well-grounded principles here. In order to ensure effective law enforcement, *Edwards* should not be extended beyond its facts, and traditional principles of constitutional waivers should be enforced with a view toward the voluntariness of the waiver. When an accused has requested counsel and been denied, the likelihood that a confession is coerced is high. Once an accused has met with his attorney, however, those risks diminish significantly. The accused is more aware that counsel is available to him and that his right to remain silent permits him to cease police questioning in the absence of counsel. When the accused confesses to police nonetheless, there is no basis for concluding that the confession is involuntary merely because counsel was not available at that time.

Analysis:

When the right to counsel has been invoked and the police must include counsel in all interrogation sessions, may the police question the suspect on an unrelated crime? Suppose a suspect is held on burglary charges and the police later find that a murder occurred in the same vicinity. Does *Minnick* afford the suspect the right to counsel because of the burglary charges although the suspect has not been charged with murder? Much may depend on the fruits of the interrogation, for if the police uncover incriminating information relating to the burglary, the right to counsel will undoubtedly be violated.

■ CASE VOCABULARY

ACCUSED: A person who has been blamed for wrongdoing; especially, a person who has been arrested and brought before a magistrate or who has been formally charged with a crime (as by indictment or information).

New York v. Quarles

(*Prosecuting Authority*) v. (*Convicted Criminal*)
467 U.S. 649, 104 S. Ct. 2626, 81 L. Ed. 2d 550 (1984)

PUBLIC EXIGENCIES OUTWEIGH *MIRANDA* REQUIREMENTS

■ **INSTANT FACTS**: Quarles (D) was arrested in a supermarket where he had discarded a gun allegedly used to commit a recent crime, and he responded to police questions regarding the location of the weapon without being advised of his *Miranda* rights.

■ **BLACK LETTER RULE** *Miranda* warnings are not required before police question a suspect in custody about imminent matters related to public safety.

■ PROCEDURAL BASIS

Certiorari to review a decision of the New York Court of Appeals affirming the trial court's suppression of evidence.

■ FACTS

A woman notified the police that she had been raped by a man who had just entered a supermarket located nearby and was carrying a gun. Quarles (D), who fit the exact description given by the woman, was quickly spotted by an officer who entered the supermarket. Upon seeing the officer, Quarles (D) turned and ran toward the rear of the store. The officer pursued Quarles (D) with his gun drawn and ordered Quarles (D) to stop and put his hands over his head. Three other officers arrived at the scene. The officer who had given pursuit frisked Quarles (D) and found that Quarles (D) was wearing an empty shoulder holster. The officer handcuffed Quarles (D) and asked him where the gun was. Quarles (D) nodded in the direction of some empty cartons and replied, "[T]he gun is over there." The officer retrieved a loaded revolver from one of the cartons, formally placed Quarles (D) under arrest, and read him his *Miranda* rights. Quarles (D) waived his rights. Quarles (D) then admitted that the gun was his and that it was purchased in Miami, Florida. In the defendant's trial for possession of a handgun, the trial court excluded the statement "the gun is over there" because it was obtained in violation of *Miranda*. The other statements were likewise excluded as "evidence tainted by the prior *Miranda* violation."

■ ISSUE

When public safety is at risk, may law enforcement officials lawfully interrogate an individual in custody without first administering the *Miranda* warnings?

■ DECISION AND RATIONALE

(Rehnquist, J.) Yes. The concern for public safety takes precedence over adherence to the literal language of the "prophylactic rules" enunciated in *Miranda*. Contrary to the lower court's holding, the availability of this "public safety" exception does not depend on the subjective motivation of the officers involved. Here, the officers had every reason to believe that the suspect was armed and had discarded the weapon in a public place. In this locale, the weapon posed several dangers to the public safety, e.g., it could be used by an accomplice or found by a customer or employee. If, under circumstances like these, police are required to administer *Miranda* warnings before posing questions geared toward securing public safety, the suspect might be deterred from responding. The cost of deterrence in public safety situations would far exceed the mere failure of obtaining evidence useful in convicting the suspect. The *Miranda* warnings are "not themselves rights protected by the Constitution but [are] instead measures to insure that the right against compulsory self-incrimination [is] protected." Here, the defendant does not claim that his statements were the product of police compulsion. Rather, the issue is whether the officer justifiably withheld procedural safeguards associated with the Fifth Amendment privilege. The court of appeals erred in excluding the statement regarding the gun, the gun itself, and the subsequent statements as illegal fruits of a *Miranda* violation.

■ DISSENT IN PART

(O'Connor, J.) There is no need to depart from the clear strictures of *Miranda*, which has never prohibited police from interrogating suspects about matters of public safety. The critical question is whether the State or the suspect should bear the cost of securing public safety when questions are asked and answered in violation of the suspect's Fifth Amendment rights. *Miranda* correctly holds that the State bears the burden. Moreover, the creation of a "public safety" exception unnecessarily blurs *Miranda* and makes it more difficult to understand. What one court views as a particularly exigent circumstance, another clearly will not. "The end result will be a finespun new doctrine on public safety exigencies incident to custodial interrogation, complete with the hair-splitting distinctions that currently plague our Fourth Amendment jurisprudence."

■ DISSENT

(Marshall, J.) There is no factual basis to conclude that public safety was in danger; no customers or employees were wandering about the store at the time of the occurrence, and although the store was open to the public, the defendant's arrest took place during the middle of the night when the store was apparently deserted except for the clerks at the checkout counter. The police, aware that the gun was discarded somewhere near the scene of the arrest, could easily have cordoned off the store and searched for the missing weapon. The rationale of the decision is based on a "serious misunderstanding" of *Miranda* and the Fifth Amendment. *Miranda* never adopted a cost-benefit analysis on the issue of public safety versus individual rights against compelled self-incrimination, because the first factor was never part of the problem. Rather, *Miranda* was concerned with whether, under the Fifth Amendment, government officials could prosecute individuals based on statements made during custodial interrogations, which were presumed to be compelled. The public safety exception makes no reference to this problem. There is no basis for the determination that questioning a suspect in custody about public safety matters is any less coercive than interrogations into other matters. Moreover, the reasoning that *Miranda* warnings will deter responses from suspects in like circumstances is unpersuasive and clearly at odds with *Miranda*, which, unlike the case today, prohibits police officers from coercing criminal defendants into making involuntary statements. As a result of the opinion, the Government is now free to use coerced statements in its case-in-chief in violation of the Fifth Amendment privilege against self-incrimination. The Government may always question suspects without administering *Miranda* warnings. It simply may not use those statements against the accused in a court of law.

Analysis:

In addition to situations like *Quarles*, several lower courts have recognized the public safety exception when questions concern the location and condition of a kidnap victim and when questions are asked to protect the health of the accused. Note that the Court's repeated reference to the *Miranda* warnings as "prophylactic rules" becomes extremely relevant in the case of *Dickerson v. United States*, 530 U.S. 428, 120 S. Ct. 2326, 147 L. Ed. 2d 405 (2000).

■ CASE VOCABULARY

EXIGENCY: A state of urgency; a situation requiring immediate action.

United States v. Patane

(*Prosecuting Authority*) v. (*Convicted Felon*)

542 U.S. 630, 124 S. Ct. 2620, 159 L. Ed. 2d 667 (2004)

THE FAILURE TO GIVE *MIRANDA* WARNINGS IS NOT A CONSTITUTIONAL VIOLATION

■ **INSTANT FACTS** Patane (D) was convicted of possession of a firearm as a felon after he voluntarily admitted possession without being read his *Miranda* rights.

■ **BLACK LETTER RULE** Nontestimonial evidence obtained as a result of a defendant's voluntary statement given without the benefit of *Miranda* warnings need not be excluded at the defendant's trial.

■ PROCEDURAL BASIS

Certiorari to review a decision of the Tenth Circuit Court of Appeals reversing the defendant's conviction.

■ FACTS

Patane (D), a convicted felon, was handcuffed and arrested by a federal agent outside his home for possession of a handgun. As the agent began reading Patane (D) his *Miranda* rights, Patane (D) interrupted him, claiming to know his rights. No further *Miranda* warnings were given. Patane (D) then told the agent that the handgun was in his bedroom. The agent searched the home, found the handgun, and seized it. Patane (D) was convicted of possession of a firearm by a felon. Reviewing his conviction, the Tenth Circuit Court of Appeals held that the handgun and the statement of its location were inadmissible.

■ ISSUE

Is nontestimonial evidence obtained following a suspect's voluntary statement, made without being read his *Miranda* rights, inadmissible at trial?

■ DECISION AND RATIONALE

(Thomas, J.) No. Although the failure to continue with a reading of Patane's (D) rights is a violation of *Miranda* rules, those rules serve to protect the right against self-incrimination. The Self-Incrimination Clause protects a defendant's right not to testify against himself at trial, but does not affect the admission of nontestimonial evidence obtained as a result of a voluntary statement. The Self-Incrimination Clause does not rely upon the *Miranda* exclusionary rule, for it contains its own exclusionary rule. "No person [shall] be compelled in any criminal case to be a witness against himself." Since the Clause contains its own exclusionary principles, the Court may not expand the textual scope to include the *Miranda* rule.

Police failure to give *Miranda* warnings is not a constitutional violation. "Potential violations occur, if at all, only upon the admission of unwarned statements into evidence at trial." The Self-Incrimination Clause, however, applies only to testimonial evidence presented at trial, and the policy of protecting the defendant's right not to testify against himself is not furthered by excluding nontestimonial evidence obtained through a voluntary statement.

■ **DISSENT**

(Kennedy, J.) Because there is no constitutional violation under these facts, the Court need not have determined whether the agent's actions in this case violated the *Miranda* rule. It suffices to hold that no constitutional violation exists.

■ **DISSENT**

(Souter, J.) The Court's decision gives police an evidentiary advantage to introduce physical evidence obtained without providing a defendant his *Miranda* warnings. When a *Miranda* violation occurs, a presumption of police coercion exists, and the defendant's right against self-incrimination requires the exclusion of all derivative evidence under the fruit-of-the-poisonous-tree doctrine.

■ **DISSENT**

(Breyer, J.) Under the fruit-of-the-poisonous-tree approach, the Court should exclude all physical evidence obtained from unwarned questioning unless the *Miranda* violation was in good faith. Because the lower court made no such determination, the case should be remanded for further consideration.

Analysis:

From a practical standpoint, the exclusion of evidence obtained through voluntary statements made before *Miranda* warnings are given could cripple effective law enforcement. In fact, a suspect could voluntarily interrupt his *Miranda* warning, confess to the crime, disclose the existence and location of all incriminating evidence, and thereby virtually ensure the later exclusion of the evidence such that the prosecution has no meaningful way to convict the defendant.

■ **CASE VOCABULARY**

FRUIT–OF–THE–POISONOUS–TREE DOCTRINE: The rule that evidence derived from an illegal search, arrest, or interrogation is inadmissible because the evidence (the "fruit") was tainted by the illegality (the "poisonous tree"). Under this doctrine, for example, a murder weapon is inadmissible if the map showing its location and used to find it was seized during an illegal search.

Missouri v. Seibert

(*Prosecuting Authority*) v. (*Murder Defendant*)
542 U.S. 600, 124 S. Ct. 2601, 159 L. Ed. 2d 643 (2004)

"QUESTION–FIRST TACTICS" FRUSTRATE THE PURPOSES UNDERLYING *MIRANDA* WARNINGS

■ **INSTANT FACTS** After Seibert (D) made an incriminating statement without a *Miranda* warning, she was read her *Miranda* rights and repeated the statement.

■ **BLACK LETTER RULE** Incriminating statements initially made before *Miranda* warnings are given are not admissible simply because they are repeated after proper warnings are given.

■ PROCEDURAL BASIS

Certiorari to review a decision of the Missouri Supreme Court reversing the defendant's conviction.

■ FACTS

When Seibert (D), a murder suspect, was arrested, the arresting officer received specific instructions not to read her *Miranda* rights. Seibert (D) was questioned, made an incriminating statement, and was left alone. Thereafter, the interrogating officer read Siebert (D) her *Miranda* rights, which she waived. Seibert (D) then repeated the incriminating statement. At trial, the court excluded only the first statement made without the *Miranda* warning, but allowed the second statement. The Missouri Supreme Court reversed, holding that the second statement must be suppressed as well.

■ ISSUE

Is a confession given by a suspect who has not been read her *Miranda* warnings admissible if it is later repeated after *Miranda* warnings are given?

■ DECISION AND RATIONALE

(Souter, J.) No. Under *Miranda*, a custodial confession is admissible only if the suspect is informed of her rights. When the suspect has been read her *Miranda* rights, the admissibility of a confession is generally unquestionable. The practice of questioning a suspect first and providing warnings only after a confession challenges the purpose of the *Miranda* warnings. When the warnings are given only after an incriminating statement is made, the suspect's ability to effectively choose between invoking her rights and waiving them is limited. Telling a suspect that "anything you say can and will be used against you" suggests that the previous incriminating statement will be used as evidence, so there is little to gain by remaining silent. Especially when the successive questioning occurs in the same environment as the initial questioning, the suspect is left with the impression that the successive questioning is a continuation of the earlier questioning and no reasonable expectation that her initial statements would not be used against her. Because the "question-first tactic" frustrates the purpose of *Miranda* warnings, any successive statements are inadmissible at trial.

■ CONCURRENCE

(Breyer, J.) "Courts should exclude the 'fruits' of the initial unwarned questioning unless the failure to warn is in good faith." This approach comports with prosecutors' and judges' understanding of well-known evidentiary principles by limiting evidence collected as a product of illegal government conduct.

■ CONCURRENCE

(Kennedy, J.) While not every violation of the *Miranda* rule requires the suppression of evidence, evidence is inadmissible when it frustrates the purpose of *Miranda*. Here, the pre-warning statement was deliberately used to obtain the post-warning confession, and both statements should be excluded because no countervailing interests outweigh *Miranda*'s central purpose. The Court, however, uses an objective test to determine whether such is the case by viewing the situation from that of a reasonable suspect in Seibert's (D) position. *Miranda*'s strength is in its clarity, and the objective approach threatens to create a per se rule of inadmissibility when question-first tactics are employed. If such tactics are used deliberately to circumvent *Miranda*, the Court's approach reaches the correct result. However, there may be occasions when two-step questioning does not result in a substantial *Miranda* violation. When the police take curative measures to ensure that the suspect understands her rights and the consequences of her earlier statements, a subsequent confession may not offend *Miranda*'s purposes.

■ DISSENT

(O'Connor, J.) A suspect's confession should not be suppressed because she "let the cat out of the bag." To do so immunizes a suspect from the effects of incriminating statements made after receiving her *Miranda* warnings, considerably hampering law enforcement investigations. The important consideration when determining the admissibility of a suspect's statement is the voluntariness with which the statement was made. If the first statement was made without *Miranda* warnings, it cannot be voluntary and must be suppressed. When the statement is reiterated with the full benefit of *Miranda* warnings, however, the issue concerns whether the later statement was made voluntarily to permit its use against the defendant at trial.

Analysis:

Much debate among the Justices revolves around whether a *Miranda* violation should turn on the bad-faith intent of the interrogating officers. While the concurring opinions of Justices Breyer and Kennedy embrace an intent-based inquiry, the Court relies instead on objective principles to determine a *Miranda* violation, noting the impact the question-first technique has on the overall effectiveness of the *Miranda* warning.

Moran v. Burbine

(*Prison Official*) v. (*Convicted Murderer*)
475 U.S. 412, 106 S. Ct. 1135, 89 L. Ed. 2d 410 (1986)

EVENTS OCCURRING OUTSIDE AN ACCUSED'S PRESENCE DO NOT AFFECT THE VALIDITY OF HIS WAIVER

■ **INSTANT FACTS** After waiving his right to counsel, Burbine (D) confessed to murder without knowing that counsel had been retained for him.

■ **BLACK LETTER RULE** Absent coercion, a defendant's waiver made with a full understanding of his rights is valid as a matter of law.

■ PROCEDURAL BASIS

Certiorari to review a decision of the First Circuit Court of Appeals reversing the defendant's conviction.

■ FACTS

After waiving his *Miranda* rights and without requesting an attorney, Burbine (D) confessed to murder. While he was in custody, however, his sister attempted to retain counsel for Burbine (D). The attorney called the police station and was assured that all questioning would cease until Burbine (D) was allowed to consult with counsel. Nonetheless, the interrogation continued and resulted in the confession. At no time did Burbine (D) know counsel had been retained to represent him. Before trial, Burbine (D) moved to suppress the confession, but his motion was denied because the waiver was knowing and voluntary. Burbine (D) was convicted of murder. The Rhode Island Supreme Court affirmed, finding that the right to counsel belongs to the defendant and cannot be invoked by his retained counsel. In a federal habeas corpus proceeding, the First Circuit Court of Appeals held that the failure to inform the accused that counsel had been retained deprived Burbine (D) of crucial information needed to make an informed, voluntary waiver.

■ ISSUE

Must a pre-arraignment confession preceded by an otherwise valid waiver be suppressed because the police misinformed an attorney secured without the suspect's knowledge about their interrogation plans and failed to inform the suspect of the attorney's efforts to reach him?

■ DECISION AND RATIONALE

(O'Connor, J.) No. To be valid, a constitutional waiver must be voluntarily given free of police intimidation, coercion, and pressure, as well as made with full awareness of the right relinquished and the consequences of the waiver. Under this standard, events occurring outside the presence of the suspect have no bearing on whether a waiver is voluntary. Whether counsel was attempting to reach him or not, he was made aware of the charges against him, advised of his right to counsel, and chose to speak without counsel present. While he may have chosen to accept counsel's assistance had he known of the call, the Constitution does not "require that police supply a suspect with a flow of information to help him calibrate his self interest in deciding whether to speak or stand by his rights." Absent coercion, a waiver made with a full understanding of the maker's rights is valid as a matter of law. Whether or not the police officers intended to deprive Burbine (D) access to counsel by refusing to inform him of the calls, they did not deprive him of the knowledge needed to make a voluntary waiver. And while the police conduct in this case should not be condoned, *Miranda* does not apply to police deception of an attorney, for *Miranda* sought to balance proper criminal confessions against improper police coercion to protect the suspect's rights. In so doing, *Miranda* gave the suspect the power to control the flow of information by invoking the right to remain silent and consult with counsel, but did not require the presence of counsel during all custodial interrogations without the insistence of the accused. Reversed.

■ DISSENT

(Stevens, J.) Police interference with attorney-client communications has long been viewed as egregious conduct that cannot be condoned. Yet, the Court departs from this principle by justifying the police actions here because the defendant did not know counsel had been retained and his waiver was voluntary. Unless Burbine (D) knew that counsel had been retained to represent him, his waiver cannot be a product of his free will, for he was denied access to all information relevant to making such a choice. Deceit by omission offends the Constitution as much as deceit by action. If the assistance of counsel is to mean anything in American society, it must require at a minimum that when counsel has been retained to aid a defendant in the understanding of his rights, the defendant be given the opportunity to confer with his lawyer before custodial interrogation.

Analysis:

Critics claim that the Court endorsed intentional police interference with an accused's access to counsel by failing to inform Burbine (D) that counsel had been retained for him. Yet, none of the police actions in this case deprived Burbine (D) of his right to request counsel on his own behalf. He had been informed of his right and voluntarily waived that right. Had Burbine (D) requested counsel, the police would have been compelled to cease questioning because *he*, not the attorney assigned to represent him, invoked that constitutional right.

■ CASE VOCABULARY

WAIVER: The voluntary relinquishment or abandonment—express or implied—of a legal right or advantage.

Dickerson v. United States

(*Convicted Bank Robber*) v. (*Prosecuting Government*)
530 U.S. 428, 120 S. Ct. 2326, 147 L. Ed. 2d 405 (2000)

MIRANDA CANNOT BE SUPERSEDED BY ACTS OF CONGRESS

■ **INSTANT FACTS** Dickerson (D) was convicted based on statements admitted against him pursuant to a federal statute under which, contrary to the *Miranda* decision, admissibility was based on voluntariness.

■ **BLACK LETTER RULE** Congress may not legislatively supersede Court decisions interpreting and applying the Constitution.

■ PROCEDURAL BASIS

Certiorari to review reversal by the Fourth Circuit Court of Appeals of a suppression order entered by district court.

■ FACTS

After *Miranda* was decided, Congress enacted 18 U.S.C. § 3501, which made statements obtained during a custodial interrogation admissible against the accused if the statements were voluntarily made. Dickerson (D), who never received the *Miranda* warnings prior to interrogation, was convicted on evidence admitted under the statute. The Fourth Circuit Court of Appeals held that the decision in *Miranda* was not a constitutional holding and that, therefore, Congress could by statute have the final say on the question of admissibility.

■ ISSUE

Is *Miranda* a constitutional holding that cannot be effectively overruled by an act of Congress?

■ DECISION AND RATIONALE

(Rehnquist, C.J.) Yes. Prior to *Miranda*, the admissibility of a defendant's confession was determined largely on its voluntariness under principles mandated by the Fifth Amendment's Self–Incrimination Clause and the Fourteenth Amendment's Due Process Clause. Enforcing these provisions, *Miranda* changed the focus of the inquiry to evaluate the level of police coercion associated with the confession. In the process, the Court did not depart from its due process concerns of voluntariness.

Although there are several exceptions to *Miranda's* warning requirements and *Miranda* has repeatedly been referred to as "prophylactic," the protections announced in *Miranda* are constitutionally required. The following factors establish *Miranda* as a constitutional holding: (1) it has been consistently applied in state courts over which the Court has power only concerning constitutional issues, (2) certiorari was granted "to give concrete constitutional guidelines for law enforcement and agencies to follow," and (3) it invites legislative bodies to create procedures to protect the constitutional right against coerced self-incrimination. That Congress intended to overrule *Miranda* by enactment of § 3501 is clear from the following: (1) the statute expressly designates voluntariness as the foundation of admissibility, (2) the statute omits any warning requirement, and (3) the trial court is instructed to consider a nonexclusive list of factors relevant to the circumstances of a confession (a test previously found to risk overlooking involuntary custodial confessions and, therefore, not a legislative alternative to *Miranda* "equally effective in preventing coerced confessions"). But only the court may overrule a constitutional decision. Therefore, following the rue of *stare decisis*, which weighs heavily against overruling a decision whose "doctrinal underpinnings" remain strong, *Miranda* and its progeny will continue to govern the admissibility of statements made during custodial interrogation in both state and federal courts. Reversed.

■ DISSENT

(Scalia, J.) Section 3501 is not unconstitutional; it forbids the same use of the evidence that is forbidden by the Constitution—a compelled confession. By disregarding a statute that is constitutional but contradictory to a decision that "announced a constitutional rule," the Court not only applies the Constitution (a valid power), but *expands* it by imposing upon Congress and the states what are, in the Court's view, useful "prophylactic" restrictions. "That is an immense and frightening antidemocratic power, and it does not exist. By denying effect to this Act of Congress, the Court acts in plain violation of the Constitution."

Moreover, the *Miranda* decision is "preposterous" if read in terms of what the Constitution requires. There is no basis for concluding that a suspect, aware of all the rights described in *Miranda,* who responds to police questioning, is acting anyway but volitional. And why is the right to counsel included among the *Miranda* rights, if not for any reason other than to prevent a suspect from incriminating himself *foolishly* rather than simply from incriminating himself? The former is not required by the Constitution. The Court here establishes that a decision is "constitutional" if the Constitution "requires the result that the decision announces and the statute ignores."

Analysis:

Commentators, while agreeing with most of the "prophylactic rules," criticize their use, because the Court has failed to adequately explain its authority to prescribe such rules. The most often-noted criticisms are (1) the Court's failure to fully explain any difference between prophylactic and administratively based per se rules, (2) the Court's failure to provide clear guidelines as to when use of a prophylactic rule is justified, (3) the Court's inconsistency in using the "prophylactic" characterization to describe functionally similar standards, and (4) the Court's failure to establish any significant guidelines for determining when legislative safeguards are sufficient to replace prophylactic standards.

■ CASE VOCABULARY

PROPHYLACTIC: Formulated to prevent something.

STARE DECISIS: The doctrine of precedent, under which it is necessary for a court to follow earlier judicial decisions when the same points arise again in litigation.

Chavez v. Martinez

(*Patrol Officer*) v. (*Injured Criminal Suspect*)
538 U.S. 760, 123 S. Ct. 1994, 155 L. Ed. 2d 984 (2003)

POLICE MAY QUESTION A MATERIAL WITNESS DURING MEDICAL TREATMENT

■ **INSTANT FACTS** After being shot in a police altercation, Martinez (P) requested that Chavez (D), a patrol officer, cease interrogation until he could receive medical treatment.

■ **BLACK LETTER RULE** The Fifth Amendment right against self-incrimination does not attach until criminal proceedings have been initiated.

■ PROCEDURAL BASIS

Certiorari to review a decision of the Ninth Circuit Court of Appeals in favor of the plaintiff.

■ FACTS

Martinez (P) was shot several times in an altercation with police, resulting in partial blindness and paralysis. Chavez (D), a patrol officer on the scene, accompanied Martinez (P) to the hospital, where he questioned Martinez (P) while Martinez (P) received medical treatment. Martinez (P) was never given *Miranda* warnings. Initially, Martinez's (P) responses to Chavez's (D) questions included mainly complaints of pain. Later, Martinez (P) admitted drawing the officer's pistol from his holster and aiming it at him. Despite answering questions, Martinez (P) continued to complain of pain and request medical treatment. Martinez (P) was never charged with a crime, but he filed a civil suit against Chavez (D) under 42 U.S.C. § 1983 for violations of his Fifth Amendment right against self-incrimination and Fourteenth Amendment due process rights. The court concluded that Martinez's (P) constitutional rights were firmly established and that Chavez (D) "would have known that persistent interrogation" violated Martinez's (P) Fifth and Fourteenth Amendment rights.

■ ISSUE

Does continued police questioning of a material witness or criminal suspect after the suspect asks to terminate the questioning violate the Fifth Amendment right against self-incrimination?

■ DECISION AND RATIONALE

(Thomas, J.) No. Even before determining whether a police officer is entitled to qualified immunity in this case, it must be determined whether a constitutional violation occurred. If not, there is no need to consider whether the plaintiff's rights are "clearly established." The Fifth Amendment requires that "[n]o person . . . shall be compelled *in any criminal case* to be a *witness* against himself." But a criminal case requires the initiation of legal proceedings and is not so broad as to include police interrogation. Until a criminal case is initiated and a defendant's statements may be introduced against him, the Fifth Amendment right against self-incrimination does not attach.

Here, no charges were ever brought against Martinez (P) and he was never compelled to be a witness against himself. At most, Chavez's (D) actions violated various prophylactic rules established to protect Fifth Amendment rights in noncriminal cases. In such cases, a person may invoke an evidentiary privilege before giving incriminating testimony, to exclude the testimony in a future criminal trial against the person. Violations of these protective rules do not, however, extend the scope of the constitutional right itself and cannot support a § 1983 claim.

Similarly, Chavez's (D) questioning did not deprive Martinez (P) of a liberty interest within the meaning of the Due Process Clause. Martinez (P) was not denied medical treatment during the questioning and his injuries were not exacerbated by the questioning. Chavez (D) merely investigated the matter to determine whether there was any police misconduct that required additional investigation. Had Martinez (P) died, such evidence would have been lost forever.

■ CONCURRENCE IN PART

(Souter, J.) If police questioning that results in incriminating statements before charges are brought can support a constitutional violation in this case, all police questioning resulting in admissions or confessions constitutes a constitutional violation. Moreover, beyond evidentiary issues in a criminal case, police interrogation would effectively be eliminated by the threat of civil liability for the constitutional violation.

■ CONCURRENCE IN PART

(Scalia, J.) Section 1983 liability requires proof of a constitutional violation, not a violation of the prophylactic evidentiary rules judicially established to protect the constitutional right. Without proof of a constitutional violation, no civil liability exists.

■ DISSENT IN PART

(Stevens, J.) The defendant's questioning amounts to police action to obtain a confession by tortuous methods. The record demonstrates that Martinez (P) was in severe pain and mental anguish. Under such circumstances, continuing police questioning violated his protected liberty interest.

■ DISSENT IN PART

(Kennedy, J.) While a constitutional violation does not arise by the simple failure to give *Miranda* warnings before interrogation ensues, the Fifth Amendment is violated as soon as a police officer uses torture or coercive conduct in the course of interrogation. The violation depends upon the conduct displayed, not the future use of the fruits of the conduct, if any. While interrogation of a suspect in pain or anguish is not necessarily unconstitutional, there are police actions that amount to inappropriate coercion. When an officer inflicts pain or threatens to prolong pain or anguish, the officer should be civilly liable to the suspect for his actions. Here, the record shows that Martinez (P) thought that medical attention would be withheld and his pain increased until he responded to Chavez's (D) questioning. This evidence sustains the § 1983 action.

■ DISSENT IN PART

(Ginsburg, J.) The right against self-incrimination applies not only at the initiation of criminal proceedings, but also whenever a suspect is subjected to coercive measures to solicit a statement. Regardless of any benign intent, Chavez (D) should have reasonably known that his conduct was constitutionally impermissible.

Analysis:

While *Chavez* turned on the issue of a Fifth Amendment violation, the availability of § 1983 liability for a substantive due process violation in this case was reserved for remand. On remand, the Ninth Circuit Court of Appeals held that, if the evidence supported the allegations, Chavez's (D) conduct "shock[ed] the conscience" and "interfere[d] with rights implicit in the concept of ordered liberty." Thus, although Martinez's (P) Fifth Amendment rights were not violated, substantive due process violations established the requisite unconstitutional acts in the § 1983 suit.

Brewer v. Williams (Williams I)

(*Warden*) v. (*Convicted Murderer*)

430 U.S. 387, 97 S. Ct. 1232, 51 L. Ed. 2d 424 (1977)

ABSENT WAIVER, A CONFESSION CANNOT BE OBTAINED OUTSIDE COUNSEL'S PRESENCE AFTER COUNSEL IS SECURED

■ **INSTANT FACTS** During a long car trip with a police officer, Williams (D) confessed to murder after the officer persuaded him to reveal the location of the victim's body outside the presence of Williams's (D) attorney.

■ **BLACK LETTER RULE** The right to the assistance of counsel can be waived only by the knowing relinquishment of that right.

■ PROCEDURAL BASIS

Certiorari to review a decision of the Eighth Circuit Court of Appeals affirming in part a federal district court decision reversing the defendant's conviction on a petition for a writ of habeas corpus.

■ FACTS

On Christmas Eve, ten-year-old Pamela Powers went with her family to the YMCA in Des Moines and disappeared. That same day, Robert Williams (D), a YMCA resident who had recently escaped from a mental hospital, was seen carrying a large bundle wrapped in a blanket. A teenage boy assisting Williams (D) with the door to his vehicle saw two white legs extending from the blanket as it was placed in the car. Williams (D) drove away before he could be questioned. After his abandoned vehicle was found 160 miles away in Davenport, Iowa, a warrant was issued for his arrest on abduction charges. The day after Christmas, a Des Moines lawyer, McKnight, received a call from Williams (D), who wished to surrender. Williams (D) surrendered to the Davenport police and was booked. McKnight requested that Williams (D) be returned to Des Moines, and he asked the police officers to cease their questioning of Williams (D) until he had an opportunity to consult with McKnight. After agreeing not to interrogate Williams (D), a Des Moines police officer, Leaming, drove to Davenport to transport Williams (D) back to Des Moines.

In the meantime, Williams (D) was arraigned in Davenport and represented by a Davenport attorney, Kelly. Kelly advised Williams (D) not to speak with Leaming during the trip to Des Moines. Kelly similarly advised Leaming that he was not to interrogate Williams (D) until he had an opportunity to meet with McKnight in Des Moines. During the ride, and knowing that Williams (D) was a former mental patient and deeply religious man, Leaming broached the subject of religion. Leaming played on Williams's (D) religious beliefs by requesting that he inform them where Powers was located, as her body would be lost under the snow and she would not receive a proper Christian burial. Leaming also told Williams (D) that they knew where the body was located, though he in fact had no such knowledge. Leaming asked for no answer, but requested that Williams (D) think about his statements. Williams (D) then volunteered the location of the victim's shoes and the blanket, though neither was recovered. As the car approached the location of Powers's body, Williams (D) took Leaming to the scene, and the body was recovered.

At trial, the defense moved to suppress all evidence relating to the statements made during the car ride. While acknowledging the validity of the agreement between McKnight and Leaming not to interrogate Williams (D) in the absence of counsel, as the ride represented a critical stage of the litigation, the judge denied the motion because Williams (D) had waived his right to an attorney by giving the information. The defendant was convicted, and the Iowa Supreme Court affirmed. The federal district court granted a petition for a writ of habeas corpus and reversed the conviction, finding that the evidence was improperly admitted and that Williams (D) did not waive his right to counsel. The Eighth Circuit Court of Appeals affirmed in part.

■ ISSUE

Was the defendant denied his right to the assistance of counsel when he was persuaded by police to confess outside the presence of his attorney after arraignment?

■ DECISION AND RATIONALE

(Stewart, J.) Yes. While the scope of the Sixth Amendment right to counsel may be debated, at a minimum it provides a defendant the right to the assistance of counsel during interrogation after judicial proceedings have begun. Judicial proceedings were clearly instituted here as a warrant had been issued for Williams's (D) arrest and he was arraigned in Davenport on that warrant. Leaming clearly sought to deliberately elicit incriminating information without the presence of counsel, though he knew the defendant was represented and wished to confer with counsel prior to questioning.

Though the trial court conceded that Williams's (D) Sixth Amendment rights were violated, its conclusion that Williams (D) waived these rights under the totality of the circumstances by failing to expressly invoke his right to counsel at the time the statements were made conflicts with federal law. Under federal law, which governs the issue of waiver, the State must prove an intentional relinquishment or abandonment of a known right or privilege, and all reasonable presumptions must be indulged against waiver. Applying these standards, it is clear that Williams (D) had invoked his right to counsel by consulting with both Kelly and McKnight before the trip and securing an agreement from Leaming not to engage in questioning outside the presence of counsel. Nonetheless, Leaming proceeded with his questioning without first reminding the defendant of his right to counsel and securing a voluntary waiver of that right. While the need for swift, energetic law enforcement is recognized, such a clear violation of the defendant's Sixth Amendment rights cannot support his conviction. Affirmed.

■ CONCURRENCE

(Marshall, J.) There can be no doubt that Leaming set out to knowingly violate the defendant's Fifth and Sixth Amendment rights by isolating him from counsel and intentionally persuading the defendant to provide incriminating statements. If the defendant is to be freed, it is not because he deserves to be free, but because Leaming knowingly risked reversal when he chose to violate the defendant's constitutional rights. Good police work requires not only that the crime be solved, but that a defendant's constitutional rights be upheld in the process.

■ CONCURRENCE

(Powell, J.) The law permits a waiver of the right to counsel without notice to counsel and may be obtained through a confession free of coercion and interrogation. The defendant's actions in this case may be sufficient in other settings to constitute a valid waiver, but Leaming's coercive conduct here leads to the conclusion that no such a waiver was made.

■ DISSENT

(Burger, C.J.) The Court's decision punishes society for the wrongdoing of one individual officer by excluding relevant and reliable evidence of the defendant's guilt and setting a guilty defendant free. Williams (D) had been informed of his right to counsel on five different occasions and chose to confess to Leaming voluntarily, free from any coercion or threats. The Court's decision stretches the exclusionary rule too far by depriving a jury of the circumstances under which police found a murder victim's body, resulting in a game of "hide and seek" that threatens our criminal justice system. The evidence establishes that Williams (D) waived his Sixth Amendment right to counsel. He had been fully advised of his rights and it was not suggested that he failed to understand their import. The elements of voluntary waiver are established. However, a defendant who has initially asserted the right to counsel need not be permitted to consult with counsel before voluntarily waiving that right, for constitutional rights are personal and a suspect cannot be legally presumed incompetent to change his mind unless an attorney is present.

■ DISSENT

(White, J.) The majority fashions no new law respecting the waiver of one's constitutional rights, relying instead on well-founded principles contained in prior cases and holding merely that no waiver was proved in this case. A waiver requires the intentional relinquishment or abandonment of a known right or privilege. That the defendant knew of his right is unquestioned, as he had been informed of this right on numerous occasions by the police and two attorneys representing him. Similarly, the defendant's choice to reveal where he had hidden the evidence resulted from his own free will as the car approached each location without prodding or questioning from Leaming. Even if Leaming's earlier statements influenced Williams's (D) disclosures, those statements were not coercive or threatening and, in fact, were accompanied by a request not to respond. The defendant was not compelled to answer without the presence of counsel, but he chose to do so nonetheless. His waiver was knowing and intentional. The fact that Williams (D) had previously asserted his right to counsel does not make the waiver unintentional, but rather strengthens the grounds for finding it intentional as he was better informed of the rights he possessed. Waiver need not be express, but can arise out of events that demonstrate the defendant knew of his rights and chose to relinquish them. Furthermore, the right to counsel protects an accused from giving incriminating answers, not from being asked questions pertinent to the case. When no evidence of coercion exists, such as here, a rule requiring waiver at the time of the answer, rather than on the advice of counsel, adequately serves these purposes.

■ DISSENT

(Blackmun, J.) Even if Leaming "purposely sought during Williams'[s] (D) isolation from his lawyer to obtain as much incriminating information as possible," the Constitution is not necessarily offended. The isolation was not deliberately caused by the police, for it was necessary during his transport back to Des Moines. Likewise, Leaming did not solely seek incriminating information, but also whether Powers was alive and in need of assistance. Finally, Leaming's questioning did not amount to interrogation, for Williams (D) was counseled by his attorneys and the Davenport judge not to talk with Leaming during the trip, yet initiated travel conversations with Leaming. His statements were voluntary and not in response to unjustified police interrogation.

Analysis:

While the Court held that Williams (D) did not waive his Sixth Amendment right to counsel, it did not hold that such a waiver is impossible in the absence of counsel, as emphasized by Justice Powell's concurrence. Pointing to Williams's (D) express assertion of his Sixth Amendment rights both before the long trip and during his conversation with Leaming, the Court held that no voluntary waiver was given. If, however, the facts indicated otherwise, even in the absence of counsel a waiver may be valid.

■ CASE VOCABULARY

EXPRESS WAIVER: A voluntary and intentional waiver.

HABEAS CORPUS: A writ employed to bring a person before a court, most frequently to ensure that the party's imprisonment or detention is not illegal.

IMPLIED WAIVER: A waiver evidenced by a party's decisive, unequivocal conduct reasonably inferring the intent to waive.

Kuhlmann v. Wilson

(*Warden*) v. (*Convicted Murderer*)
477 U.S. 436, 106 S. Ct. 2616, 91 L. Ed. 2d 364 (1986)

USING POLICE INFORMANTS TO OBTAIN VOLUNTARY STATEMENTS FROM IS NOT UNCONSTITUTIONAL INTERROGATION

■ **INSTANT FACTS** Wilson (D) was convicted of murder after incriminating statements made to a cellmate were admitted against him.

■ **BLACK LETTER RULE** When police take no direct action to solicit incriminating statements, but merely listen to voluntary statements made by an accused, the right to counsel is not violated.

■ PROCEDURAL BASIS

Certiorari to review a decision of a federal court of appeals affirming the denial of a writ of habeas corpus.

■ FACTS

Wilson (D) and two other men robbed a garage and killed the dispatcher. Four days later, Wilson (D) surrendered to the police, claiming to have no involvement in the robbery. He gave descriptions of the robbers, but denied knowing them. Wilson (D) was arraigned for the murder and placed in a cell with a man named Lee, who had agreed to become a police informant. Lee was placed in the cell to deliberately solicit the identities of the other robbers. Lee was instructed not to ask Wilson (D) about the robbery, but to listen for any information identifying the robbers. Initially, Wilson (D) told Lee the same story he told police. Several days later, however, Wilson (D) changed his story and admitted that he had planned and carried out the robbery and killed the dispatcher. At Wilson's (D) trial, the judge denied his motion to suppress the statements because Lee had obeyed police instructions to only listen to Wilson (D). Wilson (D) was convicted, and the court of appeals affirmed. Wilson (D) sought a writ of habeas corpus, which was denied because the police did not interrogate Wilson (D). The federal court of appeals affirmed.

■ ISSUE

Is the right to counsel violated when police use a confidential informant to obtain voluntary incriminating statements from an accused outside the presence of counsel?

■ DECISION AND RATIONALE

(Powell, J.) No. When a government informant develops a relationship of trust with an accused and engages in conversation to obtain incriminating information, the police have engaged in inappropriate interrogation. However, when the police take no direct action to solicit such statements, but merely listen to voluntary statements made to the informant, the right to counsel is not violated. Here, Lee was instructed not to directly solicit information from Wilson (D). Instead, he was to merely listen to any statements Wilson (D) made to learn the identities of the others involved in the robbery and murder. Although Lee engaged in dialogue with Wilson (D), such interactions are insufficient to establish a Sixth Amendment violation.

■ DISSENT

(Brennan, J.) Although Lee did not directly solicit information from Wilson (D), more subtle means of eliciting incriminating statements can rise to the level of a constitutional violation. The government deliberately placed Lee in a situation where the pressures of the jailhouse made Wilson (D) more susceptible to general conversation and gave Lee an incentive to obtain the information sought through special treatment. The government intentionally created a situation in which it was foreseeable that Wilson (D) would provide any incriminating information he had. Whether Lee deliberately solicited the information or not, the government's actions constituted deliberate elicitation of the information, which cannot be used to support Wilson's (D) conviction.

Analysis:

If a statement obtained by a passive government informant listening to a suspect's incriminating statements is admissible, would the same statement be admissible if the police secretly recorded a jailhouse conversation? Under the *Kuhlmann* reasoning, the passive listening and relaying of incriminating statements would arguably be allowed. However, privacy and due process concerns would likely be implicated.

■ CASE VOCABULARY

INFORMANT: One who informs against another; especially, one who confidentially supplies information to the police about a crime, sometimes in exchange for a reward or special treatment.

United States v. Wade

(*Prosecuting Government*) v. (*Bank Robber*)
388 U.S. 218, 87 S. Ct. 1926, 18 L. Ed. 2d 1149 (1967)

DEFENSE COUNSEL SHOULD BE PRESENT AT LINEUPS

■ **INSTANT FACTS** Wade (D) was identified in a lineup as a bank robber, without notice to counsel providing an opportunity to participate.

■ **BLACK LETTER RULE** An in-court identification of a defendant by a witness must be excluded from evidence if it is based solely on a pretrial identification that was obtained without notice to and participation by defense counsel.

■ PROCEDURAL BASIS

Certiorari to review a decision of the Fifth Circuit Court of Appeals ordering a new trial.

■ FACTS

Wade (D) and others were indicted for bank robbery and conspiracy to commit bank robbery. Wade (D) was arrested and counsel was appointed to represent him twenty-four days later. Thereafter, without notice to counsel, an FBI agent placed Wade (D) in a lineup in the courtroom, where two bank employees identified the defendant as the robber through visual and voice recognition. At trial, the bank employees again identified the defendant as the robber on direct examination. After a witness testified to the prior lineup identification on cross-examination, the defense moved to strike the in-court identification because the lineup violated the Fifth and Sixth Amendments, since counsel was not given notice and an opportunity to participate. The motion was denied and Wade (D) was convicted. On appeal, the Fifth Circuit Court of Appeals ordered a new trial because the lineup violated Wade's (D) Sixth Amendment right to have counsel present.

■ ISSUE

Must courtroom identifications of a criminal defendant be excluded from evidence when the defendant was presented to the witness before trial at a post-indictment lineup conducted for identification purposes, without the presence of the defendant's counsel, if no independent basis exists for the identification?

■ DECISION AND RATIONALE

(Brennan, J.) Yes. Under the Sixth Amendment, notice to counsel must be given before exposing a defendant to a lineup to preserve the defendant's rights to assistance of counsel and a fair trial. A pretrial identification is not akin to other pretrial preparatory steps, such as the analysis of a defendant's fingerprints, blood samples, or clothing, which do not require the assistance of counsel at the early stages because adequate scientific challenges are available to such tactics through cross-examination. Instead, the dangers of mistaken identification through suggestive practices by the government, whether by intentional design or the inherent risks of misidentification, threaten a defendant's right to a fair trial. Once a lineup is completed, a defendant is without practical means of recreating the manner in which it was conducted to demonstrate any prejudices against him. Because a jury is left to consider the propriety of the lineup only by weighing the credibility of the police officers who orchestrated the lineup against that of the indicted defendant, a defendant often cannot later demonstrate any improper influence created by the police. A defendant under the observation of a witness or victim often is overcome with stress and emotion and unable to detect any improper influence so as to raise his objections. The assistance of counsel during the pretrial identification, when such influence can be corrected, is essential to relieve any prejudice against the defendant to allow him a fair trial.

The right to counsel at a pretrial identification does not, however, necessarily require exclusion of a subsequent in-court identification by the witness. When the government proves through clear and convincing evidence that an in-court identification arises independently of the pretrial identification, exclusion is not required. If it appears to the court that the witness maintains an independent basis for identifying the defendant in court, exclusion is not required. Relevant factors for consideration include any prior opportunity to observe the alleged criminal act, the existence of any discrepancy between any pre-lineup description and the defendant's actual description, any identification prior to lineup of another person, the identification by picture of the defendant prior to the lineup, failure to identify the defendant on a prior occasion, and the lapse of time between the alleged act and the lineup identification. Here, the record is insufficient to determine, on the basis of these factors, whether the in-court identification carried an independent basis, and such determination must therefore be left for the trial court's determination. Vacated and remanded.

■ CONCURRENCE IN PART

(White, J.) Requiring the government to bear the near-impossible burden of proving that an in-court identification arises independently of an identical pretrial identification threatens the use of relevant and reliable evidence against a defendant merely because counsel was not present at the pretrial identification. The rule excludes an in-court identification regardless of how long the witness has known the defendant, whether others have also identified the defendant, and whether other corroborative evidence identifying the defendant exists. Even when such circumstances demonstrate the reliability of the in-court identification, the majority requires that it be excluded if counsel for the defendant was not present at the lineup.

The states maintain a strong governmental interest in utilizing prompt tactics to ensure a proper investigation into the accuracy of the charges brought. Requiring counsel at all stages of pretrial identification threatens to delay an investigation and hinders witness participation, resulting in less reliable evidence. Moreover, the Court's holding ignores the government's duty to pursue the truth in every criminal case. While defense counsel must advocate for their clients' interests regardless of guilt or innocence, the government bears the burden of proving the defendant's guilt through accurate, reliable evidence. At a pretrial identification, defense counsel may permissibly obstruct the government's investigative function by instructing their clients to remain silent, refuse requested movements, or even refuse to appear in the lineup. The result will not be more reliable evidence for trial, as sought by the rule set forth by the Court, but rather the complete frustration of the adversary system.

Analysis:

Wade involved the exclusion of an in-court identification based on the absence of counsel at the pretrial identification stage. A companion case, *Gilbert v. California*, involved the exclusion of the pretrial identification itself. Together, the two cases have become known as the *Wade-Gilbert* doctrine, which requires exclusion of all pretrial identifications obtained outside the presence of counsel and those in-court identifications made without an independent basis.

■ CASE VOCABULARY

EXCLUSIONARY RULE: A rule that excludes or suppresses evidence obtained in violation of an accused person's constitutional rights.

LINEUP: A police identification procedure in which a criminal suspect and other physically similar persons are shown to the victim or a witness to determine whether the suspect can be identified as the perpetrator of the crime.

Kirby v. Illinois

(Robbery Defendant) v. *(Prosecuting Authority)*
406 U.S. 682, 92 S. Ct. 1877, 32 L. Ed. 2d 411 (1972)

THE SIXTH AMENDMENT CANNOT BE USED TO HAMPER REASONABLE POLICE INVESTIGATIONS

■ **INSTANT FACTS** Kirby (D) was convicted of robbery based in part on an out-of-court statement made at the police station outside the presence of counsel.

■ **BLACK LETTER RULE** The right to counsel does not attach until the initiation of formal judicial proceedings.

■ PROCEDURAL BASIS

Certiorari to review the defendant's conviction.

■ FACTS

Shard reported to the police that he had been robbed by two men, who stole his wallet containing three travelers' checks and a Social Security card. The next day, police stopped Kirby (D) and another man on the street while investigating an unrelated crime. When asked for identification, Kirby (D) produced a wallet with three travelers' checks and Shard's Social Security card. Kirby (D) and the other man were arrested, although the officer was unaware of the Shard robbery. Shard was brought to the police station, where he immediately identified the two defendants as the robbers. No counsel was present and Kirby (D) had not been informed of his right to counsel. After Shard testified to his initial identification of the defendants and made a subsequent in-court identification at trial, Kirby (D) was convicted of robbery.

■ ISSUE

Does the exclusionary rule apply to an out-of-court identification made outside the presence of counsel before formal judiciary proceedings are initiated?

■ DECISION AND RATIONALE

(Stewart, J.) No. The Sixth Amendment right to counsel "attaches only at or after the time that adversary judicial proceedings have been initiated . . . whether by formal charge, preliminary hearing, indictment, information, or arraignment." The initiation of formal judicial proceedings triggers the adversary criminal justice system and a defendant's right to counsel, for it is at that point that the Government has committed itself to the defendant's prosecution. A routine police investigation before charges are brought does not amount to a formal judicial proceeding, and evidence obtained during this time without counsel present is not excluded per se. While police identification may violate the Constitution, such as when a lineup is unnecessarily suggestive or conducive to mistaken identity, a positive identification made outside the presence of counsel does not fall within the exclusionary rule. Affirmed.

■ DISSENT

(Brennan, J.) The threat to a defendant's constitutional rights is the same whether an identification occurs after arrest or after the initiation of formal proceedings. An arrest is not merely a routine part of police investigation, but rather constitutes a critical confrontation between the defendant and the government in which the defendant's rights may be considerably deprived. This is especially true given the potential for mistake in the identification in this case. Shard identified the defendants after arriving in a room containing only the two defendants and a number of police officers. His in-court identification of the defendants as the men he identified at the police station does nothing to repair the potential mistaken identity under the circumstances.

■ DISSENT

(White, J.) The *Wade-Gilbert* exclusionary rule applies to this case and mandates reversal of Kirby's (D) conviction.

Analysis:

While Justice Brennan's point about the impact of pre-charge comments and police conduct on the defendant's rights is well taken, there must be a point at which the defendant's rights yield to legitimate law enforcement techniques. Surely a police officer would not need to refrain from questioning a suspect until counsel arrives to determine whether he should be arrested. Instead, the initiation-of-formal-proceedings standard protects individual rights while permitting effective police investigations.

■ CASE VOCABULARY

SHOWUP: A pretrial identification procedure in which a suspect is confronted with a witness to or the victim of a crime. Unlike a lineup, a showup is a one-on-one confrontation.

Manson v. Brathwaite

(*Representative of State Government*) v. (*Suspected Drug Dealer*)
432 U.S. 98, 97 S. Ct. 2243, 53 L. Ed. 2d 140 (1977)

A PHOTOGRAPH ID IS RELIABLE TWO DAYS AFTER A FACE–TO–FACE CONFRONTATION

■ **INSTANT FACTS** Brathwaite (D) was identified through a photograph as a drug dealer, two days after confrontation with an undercover narcotics agent.

■ **BLACK LETTER RULE** An unnecessarily suggestive pretrial identification of the defendant need not be excluded if, under the totality of the circumstances, it is sufficiently reliable.

■ PROCEDURAL BASIS

Certiorari to review a decision of the Second Circuit Court of Appeals granting a writ of habeas corpus and reversing the defendant's conviction.

■ FACTS

Glover, an undercover narcotics agent, and Brown, an informant, approached an apartment believed to be the residence of a known drug dealer to purchase drugs. After knocking on the door, an unknown man answered. Glover and Brown identified themselves and purchased $10 worth of drugs. Glover studied the man's appearance from nearby and described him to a fellow agent. Based on the description, the agent retrieved a file photograph of Brathwaite (D) and left it in Glover's office. When he returned to the office two days later, Glover identified Brathwaite (D) as the man in the apartment. Brathwaite (D) was charged with the possession and sale of illegal drugs. At trial eight months later, Glover testified that Brathwaite (D) was the man who sold him the drugs, providing a positive in-court identification. Brathwaite (D) was convicted. The Connecticut Supreme Court affirmed the conviction, and Brathwaite (D) sought a writ of habeas corpus. The Second Circuit Court of Appeals granted the relief, finding that the photograph was unnecessarily suggestive and should have been excluded from evidence.

■ ISSUE

Does the Due Process Clause of the Fourteenth Amendment compel the exclusion, in a state criminal trial, of pretrial identification evidence obtained by a police procedure that was suggestive and unnecessary?

■ DECISION AND RATIONALE

(Blackmun, J.) No. It is conceded that the use of one photograph is "suggestive" and that the identification was "unnecessary" because no emergent situation existed. Under such circumstances, two tests for admissibility have arisen in the courts. The court of appeals below applied a *per se* rule of exclusion because the out-of-court identification was unnecessarily suggestive, without regard to its reliability. This approach has been justified based on the elimination of unreliable evidence, deterrence of police conduct, and the fear of misidentification. Other courts rely on the totality of the circumstances to allow such evidence if it appears sufficiently reliable.

In determining which approach best makes for sound policy, several state interests must be weighed. First, while both tests alleviate concerns over the dangers of eyewitness identification, the *per se* rule goes too far by automatically excluding relevant and reliable evidence without consideration of alleviating factors. Similarly, both approaches have a deterrent effect on police conduct. Though to a lesser extent than a *per se* exclusion, the totality approach also threatens police with exclusion of evidence obtained through unnecessarily suggestive procedures. Finally, the *per se* rule denies courts reliable evidence necessary to the administration of justice. Accordingly, the admissibility of pretrial identification testimony must be determined according to various factors supporting its reliability, including the opportunity of the witness to view the criminal at the time of the crime, the witness's degree of attention, the accuracy of his or her prior description of the criminal, the level of certainty demonstrated at the confrontation, and the time between the crime and the confrontation. These factors are to be weighed against the corrupting effect of the suggestive identification.

Here, Glover stood several feet away from Brathwaite (D) for two to three minutes, with ample light to study his features. Glover was not a passerby catching a glimpse of the defendant, but a police officer trained in the details of eyewitness identification. His description was relayed to agents within minutes of his confrontation and he provided detailed information concerning the defendant's race, height, build, and facial features. Likewise, Glover provided positive assurance that the man in the apartment was Brathwaite (D). Finally, the photographic identification of the defendant occurred within two days, not weeks or months later. Under the totality of the circumstances, Glover's ability to make a positive identification is not outweighed by any corrupting effect, such as pressure to make an identification under coercion. The identification is sufficiently reliable for admission into evidence, despite its unnecessarily suggestive nature. Reversed.

■ DISSENT

(Marshall, J.) The Court overemphasizes the strength of the three factors to determine the reliability of out-of-court identifications under the totality of the circumstances approach. First, the *per se* rule provides a much stronger deterrent effect against police misconduct, as any unnecessarily suggestive procedure will always result in exclusion. Second, the dangers of mistaken identification present far too great a threat to permit the admission of evidence obtained through an unnecessarily suggestive identification in any case. Finally, the Court fails to credit the impact the *per se* rule has on the administration of justice. An unnecessarily suggestive out-of-court identification is not forever lost to the prosecution, because an in-court identification based on a reliable independent basis can be resurrected and offered against the defendant, or a second lineup can be arranged under less suggestive circumstances. Also, the purpose of the exclusionary rule at issue is to eliminate evidence that is both unreliable and irrelevant to the issue of guilt. The practice of unnecessarily suggestive identification procedures poses a greater societal threat than illegal searches or the denial of counsel, since such identifications may be erroneously used against innocent defendants and a guilty person may be set free. The *per se* rule better serves the administration of justice.

Even applying the totality of the circumstances approach, however, the identification here should be excluded. The evidence indicates that Glover's confrontation with Brathwaite (D) occurred not in a matter of minutes, but seconds. During that time, Glover's attention was not exclusively on Brathwaite's (D) features, for he provided details of the door, the interior of the apartment, and the transaction that took place. Further, his training in positive identification does not lead to the conclusion that he is incapable of mistaken identity. Next, while the fact that the identification occurred within two days after the confrontation enhances its reliability, "the greatest memory loss occurs within hours after an event." Finally, Glover's description provided only general details of Brathwaite's (D) physical characteristics, providing immaterial details of the clothing he was wearing and omitting more crucial details. Seen against the corrupting effect of using a single, static photograph for identification, these factors do not justify admission of the evidence.

Analysis:

The factors set forth by the Court to consider the reliability of an out-of-court identification also bear directly upon the question of whether a defendant's due process rights have been violated. While a due process challenge places the burden of proof upon the defendant to prove the violation of his rights, courts have tended to place the burden of proof on the prosecution, reasoning that the government gave rise to the issue by implementing an unnecessarily suggestive identification procedure.

CHAPTER EIGHT

Investigation by Subpoena

Boyd v. United States

Instant Facts: Boyd (D) was subject to forfeiture of imported merchandise after the court ordered disclosure of invoices relating to its purchase.

Black Letter Rule: The compulsory production of private books and papers subject to forfeiture compels the owner to be a witness against himself and is equivalent to an unreasonable search and seizure.

United States v. Dionisio

Instant Facts: Dionisio (D) was held in civil contempt after refusing to provide voice samples as required by a grand jury subpoena.

Black Letter Rule: The Fourth Amendment protects individuals from unreasonable search and seizure of all evidence in which they have a reasonable expectation of privacy.

United States v. Mandujano

Instant Facts: Mandujano's (D) false grand jury testimony was suppressed in his trial for attempting to sell heroin and knowingly making a false statement before a grand jury.

Black Letter Rule: *Miranda* warnings do not apply to grand jury investigations.

Kastigar v. United States

Instant Facts: Kastigar (D) was ordered to testify before a grand jury under statutory immunity.

Black Letter Rule: The Government may compel a witness's testimony under statutory immunity against the use of his testimony and all derivative evidence against him in a criminal case.

Fisher v. United States

Instant Facts: Taxpayers' attorneys were served with a summons to disclose tax documents prepared by the taxpayers' accountants that were provided to the attorneys to receive legal advice.

Black Letter Rule: The Fifth Amendment does not prevent compelled disclosure of client materials disclosed to an attorney where the materials would not be privileged in the hands of the client.

United States v. Hubbell

Instant Facts: Hubbell (D) was ordered to produce documents pursuant to a plea agreement and a grant of immunity, and the Government (P) brought tax charges against him based on information in the documents he produced.

Black Letter Rule: The privilege against self-incrimination protects against being compelled to provide information to a grand jury about the existence of sources of potentially incriminating evidence.

Boyd v. United States

(*Importer*) v. (*Prosecuting Authority*)

116 U.S. 616, 6 S. Ct. 524, 29 L. Ed. 746 (1886)

THE FOURTH AND FIFTH AMENDMENTS WORK TOGETHER

■ **INSTANT FACTS** Boyd (D) was subject to forfeiture of imported merchandise after the court ordered disclosure of invoices relating to its purchase.

■ **BLACK LETTER RULE** The compulsory production of private books and papers subject to forfeiture compels the owner to be a witness against himself and is equivalent to an unreasonable search and seizure.

■ PROCEDURAL BASIS

Certiorari to review the defendant's conviction and forfeiture order.

■ FACTS

Customs officials seized cases of imported glass and instituted a forfeiture proceeding under a statute authorizing a fine, incarceration, and the forfeiture of imported merchandise against any importer who defrauded the government by avoiding the payment of customs revenue. Boyd (D) was served with a court notice to produce an invoice for the cases on the prosecutor's motion describing the particular document and alleging its contents. By statute, failure to produce the notice acted as a confession of the prosecutor's assessment of its contents. Boyd (D) produced the notice, but objected to the validity of the confession and the notice's admission into evidence. Boyd (D) was convicted and a forfeiture order was issued.

■ ISSUE

Is a court order compelling the production of a document under penalty of confession in a forfeiture proceeding an unreasonable search and seizure?

■ DECISION AND RATIONALE

(Bradley, J.) Yes. While the court order merely demands the production of Boyd's (D) documents, it does so under penalty of confession of their alleged contents if the order is not followed. There is no physical intrusion upon the defendant's property or effects, but the order accomplishes the seizure nonetheless by forcing the defendant to disclose evidence against himself or risk the forfeiture of his property. Therefore, the court order constitutes a search and seizure within the meaning of the Fourth Amendment.

The individual security and privacy interests embedded in the Fourth Amendment parallel the Fifth Amendment's right against self-incrimination. When a search and seizure is used to obtain one's personal property for the purpose of collecting evidence of his criminal acts, the government action compels him to be a witness against himself. Accordingly, "a compulsory production of the private books and papers of the owner of goods sought to be forfeited . . . is compelling him to be a witness against himself, within the meaning of the Fifth Amendment to the Constitution, and is the equivalent of a search and seizure—and an unreasonable search and seizure—within the meaning of the Fourth Amendment."

■ CONCURRENCE

(Miller, J.) While the Court's decision correctly holds that the compulsion of Boyd's (D) property under penalty of a criminal confession violates his right against self-incrimination, there is no Fourth Amendment violation. The statute does not authorize a search of his house or property nor a seizure of any of his belongings. At most, the statute authorizes the service of notice.

Analysis:

Boyd is widely considered the Supreme Court's first important Fifth Amendment decision. Likely because of the unsettled state of Fifth Amendment jurisprudence at the time, however, many commentators question the rationale for the decision. As noted by Justice Miller's concurrence, there seems to be an illogical bridge between the Fourth Amendment unreasonable search and seizure and the Fifth Amendment right against self-incrimination. After all, if the order compelled Boyd (D) to incriminate himself, why would it matter whether the search and seizure constitutionally occurred or whether it was unreasonable?

■ CASE VOCABULARY

FOURTH AMENDMENT: The constitutional amendment, ratified with the Bill of Rights in 1791, prohibiting unreasonable searches and seizures and the issuance of warrants without probable cause.

RIGHT AGAINST SELF–INCRIMINATION: A criminal defendant's or a witness's constitutional right—under the Fifth Amendment, but waivable under certain conditions—guaranteeing that a person cannot be compelled by the government to testify if the testimony might result in the person's being criminally prosecuted. Although this right is most often asserted during a criminal prosecution, a person can also "plead the Fifth" in a civil, legislative, administrative, or grand-jury proceeding

SEARCH: An examination of a person's body, property, or other area that the person would reasonably be expected to consider as private, conducted by a law-enforcement officer for the purpose of finding evidence of a crime. Because the Fourth Amendment prohibits unreasonable searches (as well as seizures), a search cannot ordinarily be conducted without probable cause.

SEIZURE: The act or instance of taking possession of a person or property by legal right or process; especially, in constitutional law, a confiscation or arrest that may interfere with a person's reasonable expectation of privacy.

United States v. Dionisio

(*Prosecuting Authority*) v. (*Grand Jury Witness*)
410 U.S. 1, 93 S. Ct. 764, 35 L. Ed. 2d 67 (1973)

A PERSON HAS NO REASONABLE EXPECTATION OF PRIVACY IN THE SOUND OF HIS OR HER OWN VOICE

■ **INSTANT FACTS** Dionisio (D) was held in civil contempt after refusing to provide voice samples as required by a grand jury subpoena.

■ **BLACK LETTER RULE** The Fourth Amendment protects individuals from unreasonable search and seizure of all evidence in which they have a reasonable expectation of privacy.

■ PROCEDURAL BASIS

Certiorari to review a decision of the Seventh Circuit Court of Appeals reversing the defendant's detention.

■ FACTS

As part of a gambling investigation, a special grand jury subpoenaed Dionisio (D) and others to obtain voice samples for comparison purposes. Each witness was informed that he was a possible defendant, that he had the right to counsel, and that he would review a transcript of the material to be recorded and then read it back into a recording device. When Dionisio (D) refused to comply, the Government (P) petitioned a federal district court for an order compelling his participation. The court denied Dionisio's (D) constitutional challenges and ordered his compliance. When he refused, the court held him in civil contempt and ordered him taken into custody. The Seventh Circuit Court of Appeals reversed, holding that the Fourth Amendment applied to grand jury proceedings and that the taking of voice samples constitutes an unreasonable seizure.

■ ISSUE

Does a person have a Fourth Amendment right to conceal the sound of his voice from a grand jury?

■ DECISION AND RATIONALE

(Stewart, J.) No. The obtaining of physical evidence implicates the Fourth Amendment upon the initial seizure of the person by taking him into police custody and subsequently searching for and seizing evidence. But a subpoena to appear before a grand jury is not a seizure for Fourth Amendment purposes. Grand jury proceedings do not involve the social stigma of an arrest or an investigative stop made by force or threat of force. While the Fourth Amendment applies to protect a witness from compulsory self-incrimination or production of incriminating private books and records, it does not protect a witness from compulsory attendance at the proceedings as an unreasonable seizure.

Similarly, once compelled to appear, the Fourth Amendment does not afford the right to remain entirely silent without regard to the content of the testimony. The Fourth Amendment does not protect those things openly available to the public outside one's home, and the sound of one's voice, as opposed to the content of the message, is not within a reasonable expectation of privacy. The Fifth Amendment requires that every criminal prosecution be presented on indictment by the grand jury. Accordingly, the grand jury possesses broad investigative powers to consider all material evidence not otherwise constitutionally protected, in furtherance of its duty. Reversed.

■ DISSENT

(Marshall, J.) Just as when police effect investigatory seizures, the compulsion to appear before a grand jury constitutes an official investigatory seizure interfering with personal liberty. The Fourth Amendment clearly would not permit the compelled disclosure of private papers, and "persons" are entitled to the same protection. While a person must appear on subpoena to provide testimonial evidence sought, the sound of one's voice is physical, not testimonial, evidence. Furthermore, the stigma associated with testimony compelled by a grand jury formed to investigate illegal gambling operations is equal to that accompanying arrests and police investigatory stops. In its ordinary course, the grand jury serves to protect individuals from governmental pressure to provide a neutral, unbiased perspective on the crimes charged. When confined to testimonial evidence, the grand jury appropriately serves this function. But when the grand jury's authority exceeds testimonial review and delves into the collection of physical evidence of the crime, it becomes an extension of the police and endangers the witness's rights. Unless the Fourth Amendment applies to protect the witnesses, the grand jury is permitted to do indirectly what law enforcement cannot do directly. The grand jury subpoena power should be limited to testimonial evidence.

Analysis:

The investigative grand jury is a powerful law-enforcement tool. Had the police sought to investigate the audio recordings without a grand jury in this case, they would not have been able to constitutionally compel the witnesses to provide the voice samples. To do so, the police could question Dionisio (D), but without an arrest, he would be free to terminate questioning at any time without uttering a word. Likewise, if an arrest were made, *Miranda* requires the right to remain silent. Without the grand jury, police efforts to collect a voice exemplar would be severely hampered.

■ CASE VOCABULARY

CIVIL CONTEMPT: The failure to obey a court order that was issued for another party's benefit. A civil-contempt proceeding is coercive and remedial in nature. The usual sanction is to confine the contemner until he or she complies with the court order.

GRAND JURY: A body of (often 23) people who are chosen to sit permanently for at least a month—and sometimes a year—and who, in ex parte proceedings, decide whether to issue indictments.

INVESTIGATIVE GRAND JURY: A grand jury whose primary function is to examine possible crimes and develop evidence not currently available to the prosecution.

United States v. Mandujano

(*Prosecuting Authority*) v. (*Drug Dealer*)
425 U.S. 564, 96 S. Ct. 1768, 48 L. Ed. 2d 212 (1976)

A GRAND JURY WITNESS MAY NOT COMMIT PERJURY TO AVOID SELF–INCRIMINATION

■ **INSTANT FACTS** Mandujano's (D) false grand jury testimony was suppressed in his trial for attempting to sell heroin and knowingly making a false statement before a grand jury.

■ **BLACK LETTER RULE** *Miranda* warnings do not apply to grand jury investigations.

■ PROCEDURAL BASIS

Certiorari to review a decision of a federal court of appeals affirming the suppression of the defendant's grand jury testimony.

■ FACTS

Acting on information that Mandujano (D) was dealing in narcotics, an undercover agent met with Mandujano (D) to purchase heroin. The agent paid for the heroin, but Mandujano (D) refunded the money that night without making the delivery. The agent closed his file and reported the incident to federal prosecutors. Six weeks later, Mandujano (D) was subpoenaed to testify before a special grand jury investigating local drug trafficking. He was advised of his duty to answer truthfully, his right not to answer any incriminating questions, and his right to have counsel outside the room. Mandujano (D) had no counsel because he stated he was unable to afford one. During questioning, Mandujano (D) admitted purchasing heroin within the preceding five months but denied attempting to sell heroin any time within the preceding year. Mandujano (D) was subsequently indicted for attempting to distribute heroin and knowingly making a false statement before a grand jury. At trial, Mandujano (D) objected to the admission of his grand jury testimony because he was not given his *Miranda* warnings. The trial court suppressed the testimony, and a federal court of appeals affirmed.

■ ISSUE

Must *Miranda* warnings be given to a grand jury witness who is called to testify about criminal activities in which he may have been personally involved?

■ DECISION AND RATIONALE

(Burger, C.J.) No. Because the function of the grand jury is to uncover criminal activity, it is unrealistic to assume that those called to testify will be entirely free of criminal involvement. Accordingly, while a witness may be compelled to testify, he must have the assurances of his right not to respond to incriminating statements if he chooses. However, a witness may not knowingly commit perjury to avoid answering incriminating questions. The witness must either answer every question truthfully or invoke his constitutional protections. *Miranda* warnings do not alter these options. *Miranda*'s central concern was the prevention of compulsory self-incrimination in custodial interrogations by police, not grand juries. Grand jury investigations do not occur in the same coercive environment as police interrogations. They are conducted in a controlled atmosphere under the supervision of a presiding judge. An extension of the *Miranda* warnings to grand jury testimony would require that the witness have the absolute right to remain silent, which frustrates the entire function of the grand jury. The general warnings given by the prosecutor were a correct statement of applicable law, and sufficiently informed Mandujano (D) of his rights. He may not remain entirely silent, and he has no Sixth Amendment right to counsel at the grand jury stage. Reversed.

■ CONCURRENCE

(Brennan, J.) While the Fifth Amendment allows means to avoid self-incrimination, lying is not one of them. However, the Court's rationale threatens to undermine the Fifth Amendment right against self-incrimination and the Sixth Amendment right to counsel. When the government compels testimony from a grand jury witness that may tend to incriminate him, such testimony should not be admissible against him at trial absent a knowing and voluntary waiver of his rights. To permit otherwise would relieve the government of its burden of proving the defendant's guilt from evidence gathered in its investigative capacity, by supplanting such evidence with self-incriminating testimony. The Fifth Amendment cannot sanction such a result. Likewise, when a defendant is called before a grand jury investigating criminal activity, the government has initiated criminal proceedings against the witness. Because of the strong possibility of self-incrimination that may be used against the witness in a later trial, the right to counsel is particularly important. While the presence of counsel in the courtroom may not be required, the witness must be afforded the opportunity to consult with counsel before the proceedings and have an attorney appointed if he is unable to afford one.

■ CONCURRENCE

(Stewart, J.) The Fifth Amendment does not protect a witness from perjury. Because Mandujano's (D) statements were offered only in his perjury trial, it is sufficient to reverse the court of appeals' decision to suppress the testimony without consideration of the other issues presented.

Analysis:

The Court's decision comes in a unique case. Because Mandujano (D) committed perjury before the grand jury, the admission of his testimony was needed in the pursuit of justice. Yet, at its core, the Court's holding merely requires that a witness must appear before a grand jury when under subpoena, where he may invoke his Fifth Amendment privilege and say nothing. If the presiding judge denies the privilege, however, because it is perceived as an attempt to elude all questioning, the witness must answer in a manner that does not incriminate him. But the witness may never knowingly give false testimony to avoid testifying.

■ CASE VOCABULARY

PERJURY: The act or an instance of a person's deliberately making material false or misleading statements while under oath.

RIGHT AGAINST SELF-INCRIMINATION: A criminal defendant's or a witness's constitutional right—under the Fifth Amendment, but waivable under certain conditions—guaranteeing that a person cannot be compelled by the government to testify if the testimony might result in the person's being criminally prosecuted. Although this right is most often asserted during a criminal prosecution, a person can also "plead the Fifth" in a civil, legislative, administrative, or grand-jury proceeding.

Kastigar v. United States

(*Grand Jury Witness*) v. (*Prosecuting Government*)
406 U.S. 441, 92 S. Ct. 1653, 32 L. Ed. 2d 212 (1972)

STATUTORY IMMUNITY IS COEXTENSIVE WITH THE PRIVILEGE AGAINST SELF-INCRIMINATION

■ **INSTANT FACTS** Kastigar (D) was ordered to testify before a grand jury under statutory immunity.

■ **BLACK LETTER RULE** The Government may compel a witness's testimony under statutory immunity against the use of his testimony and all derivative evidence against him in a criminal case.

■ PROCEDURAL BASIS

Certiorari to review an undisclosed decision.

■ FACTS

Kastigar (D) was subpoenaed to testify before a federal grand jury. Believing that he would invoke his Fifth Amendment privilege against self-incrimination, the Government (P) sought a court order directing him to answer questions and produce evidence under immunity pursuant to 18 U.S.C. §§ 6002–6003. Kastigar (D) opposed the order, arguing that the statutory immunity was not sufficient to overcome his Fifth Amendment rights and compel his testimony. The court ordered Kastigar (D) to testify under the grant of immunity.

■ ISSUE

May the Government compel testimony from an unwilling witness who invokes the Fifth Amendment privilege against compulsory self-incrimination by conferring on the witness immunity from use of the compelled testimony in subsequent criminal proceedings, as well as immunity from use of evidence derived from the testimony?

■ DECISION AND RATIONALE

(Powell, J.) Yes. The government's authority to compel the testimony of witnesses before a grand jury and otherwise is well established. Yet, this authority must be balanced against the witness's Fifth Amendment privilege against compulsory self-incrimination. In striking this balance, immunity statutes further the values protected by the Fifth Amendment. They accommodate legitimate law enforcement investigatory needs while ensuring that the witness will not be punished by his own incriminating statements.

Section 6002 provides that no witness may refuse to comply with a court order directing his testimony, and that any such testimony or evidence derived therefrom cannot be admitted against him in any criminal case, other than one for perjury. The statutory immunity prohibiting the use of the witness's testimony and all evidence derived from his testimony is coextensive with the protections of the Fifth Amendment and is sufficient to compel the witness's testimony. Statutory immunity need not, however, afford full transactional immunity such that the witness may not be prosecuted for criminal offenses related to his compelled testimony. The Fifth Amendment protects against self-incrimination, but is not a grant of immunity against prosecution based on evidence independent of his compelled testimony. The immunity is sufficiently coextensive with the Fifth Amendment privilege, for both the federal and state governments are prohibited from using immunized testimony against the witness in any criminal case.

■ DISSENT

(Douglas, J.) If the privilege against self-incrimination is to mean anything, it must mean that a witness maintains the right to refuse to testify so long as there remains any possibility of criminal prosecution related to the testimony. By refusing to include transactional immunity in the Court's holding, the Court seriously contracts the Fifth Amendment privilege.

■ DISSENT

(Marshall, J.) As long as a witness may be prosecuted on evidence derived from an independent source, any immunity from prosecution based on his compelled testimony does not adequately protect his Fifth Amendment privilege. Placing the burden of establishing an independent source on the government does not rectify this problem, for the defendant is in no position to question and establish whether the government's asserted source is made in bad faith. Even when acting in good faith, complex criminal matters carry great potential to taint apparently independent evidence through subtle references to the witness's compelled testimony. Unlike an exclusionary rule that seeks to remedy police misconduct, immunity statutes encourage interrogation and evidence gathering that the Fifth Amendment would otherwise prohibit by offering a reliable source from which the investigation may draw valuable evidence. When offering immunity, the Government is thus obliged to remove all threat of self-incrimination. Likewise, because immunity precedes the interrogation, the Government must make a reasoned decision whether the benefits of the testimony outweigh its desire to punish any criminal act. When it so elects, it must ensure that the witness will not suffer from his own incriminating statements.

Analysis:

Without transactional immunity, the permissible uses of evidence against an immunized defendant can be difficult to determine. Suppose the prosecution has a list of individuals suspected of having valuable information concerning a crime. If an immunized defendant's testimony somehow corroborates one of the suspect's knowledge of certain facts, is evidence obtained from that suspect admissible against the defendant even if the defendant had no personal knowledge of the evidence himself?

■ CASE VOCABULARY

IMMUNITY: Freedom from prosecution granted by the government in exchange for the person's testimony. By granting immunity, the government can compel testimony—despite the Fifth Amendment right against self-incrimination—because that testimony can no longer incriminate the witness.

TRANSACTIONAL IMMUNITY: Immunity from prosecution for any event or transaction described in the compelled testimony. This is the broadest form of immunity.

USE IMMUNITY: Immunity from the use of the compelled testimony (or any information derived from that testimony) in a future prosecution against the witness. After granting use immunity, the government can still prosecute if it shows its evidence comes from a legitimate independent source.

Fisher v. United States

(*Taxpayer*) v. (*Prosecuting Government*)
425 U.S. 391, 96 S. Ct. 1569, 48 L. Ed. 2d 39 (1976)

THE FIFTH AMENDMENT DOES NOT PROTECT PAPERS IN A PERSON'S POSSESSION WHEN NO TESTIMONIAL COMPULSION EXISTS

■ **INSTANT FACTS** Taxpayers' attorneys were served with a summons to disclose tax documents prepared by the taxpayers' accountants that were provided to the attorneys to receive legal advice.

■ **BLACK LETTER RULE** The Fifth Amendment does not prevent compelled disclosure of client materials disclosed to an attorney where the materials would not be privileged in the hands of the client.

■ PROCEDURAL BASIS

Certiorari to review a decision of a federal court of appeals quashing a summons.

■ FACTS

In two separate cases, Internal Revenue agents interviewed the defendants concerning possible civil or criminal income tax liability. After the interviews, the defendants retrieved documents from their respective accountants relating to the preparation of their tax returns and provided them to their attorneys assisting with the investigations. The IRS issued summonses to the attorneys, directing them to turn over the documents. The attorneys refused to do so and the Government (P) initiated enforcement proceedings. At the appellate level, the court of appeals suggested that because the defendants had a reasonable expectation of privacy concerning the documents while in their hands, the privilege against self-incrimination was not lost by their transfer of the documents to obtain legal advice.

■ ISSUE

Is a summons directing an attorney to produce documents delivered to him by his client in connection with their attorney-client relationship enforceable?

■ DECISION AND RATIONALE

(White, J.) Yes. The Fifth Amendment provides that no person shall be compelled in any criminal case to be a witness against himself. By requiring an attorney to produce documents provided by his or her client, the client is not compelled to do anything, much less be a witness against himself. It is immaterial whether the attorney is the taxpayer's agent, for it is compulsion of the taxpayer that the Fifth Amendment protects, not compulsion of his agent. Not every invasion of privacy frustrates the Fifth Amendment, and when an invasion occurs without compelling the defendant himself to act, the evidence is within the Government's (P) reach. Likewise, the taxpayers may not rely on the attorney-client privilege to resist disclosure because pre-existing documents are not exempt from discovery merely by transferring them to an attorney unless they would be privileged from discovery in the taxpayer's hands. The only privilege asserted in these cases is derived from the Fifth Amendment. A subpoena served on the defendants to obtain documents prepared by an accountant does not compel oral testimony prohibited by the Fifth Amendment.

Yet, the act of disclosure carries some communicative aspects, such as an admission of the existence of the documents and the taxpayer's possession thereof. Whether these communications are testimonial and fall within the scope of the Fifth Amendment requires a review of the circumstances. Here, the documents sought are those normally prepared by an accountant when preparing tax returns. Communications supporting their existence and possession add very little to the content of the documents themselves. Moreover, any testimonial value of the communications is not incriminating, for there is nothing illegal about retaining an accountant to prepare one's tax return. Because the documents themselves are not the taxpayers' private papers, their disclosure does not communicate incriminating testimony within the meaning of the Fifth Amendment.

■ CONCURRENCE

(Brennan, J.) Because the accountants had prior access to the papers and because the papers are business rather than personal documents, the privilege against self-incrimination is not violated. However, the majority's decision threatens to undermine the privilege's central purpose of protecting personal privacy. The majority's literal reading of the Fifth Amendment ignores the more fundamental privacy protections the Amendment affords. Written papers are often a reflection of the individual's inner thoughts and contain as much expression as the spoken word. The Fifth Amendment cannot compel disclosure of the former when it clearly would not sanction the latter. It is the zone of privacy that determines the existence of the privilege, not the form in which the evidence exists. When the holder of the papers has sufficiently sought to maintain the papers in private, without third-party disclosure, the Fifth Amendment protects against compelled disclosure.

■ CONCURRENCE

(Marshall, J.) The proper focus of the Fifth Amendment privilege should be on the content of the documents at issue, for private documents carry the same import as private thoughts, and are equally incriminating under most circumstances.

Analysis:

The Court's decision has sparked considerable debate over the authority to compel disclosure of one's private papers. The Court does not resolve this issue, concluding only that the tax records at issue were not private papers subject to Fifth Amendment protection. Yet, the Court does not define what private papers are, leaving that question open to further debate.

■ CASE VOCABULARY

ATTORNEY–CLIENT PRIVILEGE: The client's right to refuse to disclose and to prevent any other person from disclosing confidential communications between the client and the attorney.

United States v. Hubbell

(*Prosecuting Authority*) v. (*Possessor of Documents*)
530 U.S. 27, 120 S. Ct. 2037, 147 L. Ed. 2d 24 (2000)

THE COMPELLED PRODUCTION OF DOCUMENTS VIOLATES THE FIFTH AMENDMENT

■ **INSTANT FACTS** Hubbell (D) was ordered to produce documents pursuant to a plea agreement and a grant of immunity, and the Government (P) brought tax charges against him based on information in the documents he produced.

■ **BLACK LETTER RULE** The privilege against self-incrimination protects against being compelled to provide information to a grand jury about the existence of sources of potentially incriminating evidence.

■ PROCEDURAL BASIS

Appeal from an order of the court of appeals vacating a judgment that dismissed an indictment.

■ FACTS

Hubbell (D) was prosecuted for violations of federal laws in connection with the Whitewater Development Corporation. As part of his plea agreement, he promised to provide the Independent Counsel who investigated his case with full and complete information about the case. While Hubbell was incarcerated, the Independent Counsel served him with a subpoena *duces tecum* asking for the production of documents before a grand jury. Hubbell (D) appeared before the grand jury and invoked his Fifth Amendment privilege against self-incrimination. The prosecutor provided Hubbell (D) with a court order that required him to testify and that granted him immunity "to the extent allowed by law." Hubbell (D) then produced 13,120 pages of documents.

The Independent Counsel obtained an indictment against Hubbell (D) for tax-related crimes, mail fraud, and wire fraud, based entirely on information obtained from the documents Hubbell (D) produced. The district court dismissed the indictment, because all of the evidence against Hubbell (D) came from Hubbell's (D) immunized act of producing the documents. The district court found that Hubbell (D) was not being investigated for tax issues when the subpoena was issued, and that the subpoena was "the quintessential fishing expedition." The court of appeals vacated the district court's decision and remanded for a determination of the extent of the government's independent knowledge of the documents and of Hubbell's (D) possession and control of them. The Independent Counsel acknowledged that he could not satisfy the independent knowledge requirement. Hubbell (D) and the Counsel entered into a conditional plea agreement, in which the Counsel agreed to dismiss the indictment unless the Supreme Court made a ruling that the grant of immunity would not pose a significant bar to prosecution.

■ ISSUE

Did the use of the information in the compelled documents violate Hubbell's (D) privilege against self-incrimination?

■ DECISION AND RATIONALE

(Stevens, J.) Yes. The privilege against self-incrimination protects against being compelled to provide information to a grand jury about the existence of sources of potentially incriminating evidence.

Producing the documents is not a testimonial act, except insofar as the testimony relates to the existence, authenticity, or custody of the documents. But using the documents to obtain a grand jury indictment is a use of the immunized testimony.

It was necessary for Hubbell (D) to make use of the contents of his own mind in identifying the documents that would be responsive to the request. Preparing the response to the document request was the functional equivalent of answering a detailed written interrogatory. That answer, in this case, provided the Counsel with a link in the chain of evidence needed to prosecute. The documents were produced during an investigation into whether Hubbell (D) had violated his first plea agreement, and the indictment obtained had nothing to do with that agreement. The Government (P) did not know of any reason to prosecute before it obtained the documents from Hubbell (D). The indictment must be dismissed and the court of appeals affirmed.

■ CONCURRENCE

(Thomas, J.) Although the Court correctly applies the act-of-production doctrine to protect persons compelled to turn over incriminating evidence that contains a testimonial feature, the Fifth Amendment properly applies to the production of all evidence, whether testimonial or not. A "witness," for purposes of the Fifth Amendment, includes a person who is required to produce evidence, not just testimony.

Analysis:

The majority focuses on the thought necessary to produce the documents. Under the reasoning of the majority, it would not be self-incrimination to obtain physical evidence (e.g., a blood or hair sample) from a defendant, because that would not require the defendant who supplies the sample to think about what he or she was giving up. The concurrence would go further. The concurrence focuses on the witness as a source of evidence and regards providing any kind of evidence as a form of testimony.

■ CASE VOCABULARY

INDEPENDENT COUNSEL: An attorney hired to provide an unbiased opinion about a case or to conduct an impartial investigation; especially, an attorney appointed by a governmental branch or agency to investigate alleged misconduct within that branch or agency.

SUBPOENA AD TESTIFICANDUM: A subpoena ordering a witness to appear and give testimony.

SUBPOENA DUCES TECUM: A subpoena ordering the witness to appear and to bring specified documents or records.

Stack v. Boyle

(*Communist Party Member*) v. (*Representative of the Federal Government*)
342 U.S. 1, 72 S. Ct. 1, 96 L. Ed. 3 (1951)

UNREASONABLE BAIL VIOLATES THE EIGHTH AMENDMENT

■ **INSTANT FACTS** Twelve defendants indicted for advocating the overthrow of the federal government were denied a request for reduction of bail.

■ **BLACK LETTER RULE** Under the Eighth Amendment, bail must be reasonably fixed to ensure a defendant will appear at trial based on the specific facts of the crime charged and not the character of the crime.

■ PROCEDURAL BASIS

Certiorari to review a decision of the Ninth Circuit Court of Appeals affirming a denial of a petition for a writ of habeas corpus.

■ FACTS

Twelve members of the Communist Party, including Stack (D), were arrested in California on charges of violating the Smith Act, a federal statute prohibiting the advocacy of the overthrow of the federal government. Bail was set for the defendants at various amounts, ranging from $2500 to $100,000. One defendant, arrested in New York, successfully sought reduction of his bail to $50,000 before removal to California. The government then successfully moved to fix bail at $50,000 for all defendants in California. The defendants subsequently moved for reduction, arguing that in light of their financial means, health, family relationships, and other information, the bail violated the Eighth Amendment as excessive. The government responded with evidence that other defendants charged under the statute have forfeited bail in the past, making defendants a flight risk. The court denied the defendants' motion. Stack (D) filed a petition for a writ of habeas corpus with the California federal court, which was denied. The Ninth Circuit Court of Appeals affirmed.

■ ISSUE

Is bail fixed at $50,000 based on the character of the offense and forfeiture of bail by other defendants in separate proceedings excessive in light of the crime charged?

■ DECISION AND RATIONALE

(Vinson, C.J.) Yes. The right to bail before trial in federal court is required to preserve the presumption of innocence and allow the defendant to prepare a defense against the charges. This right, however, requires adequate assurance that the defendant will appear to stand trial on those charges. Bail set above an amount reasonably likely to further these purposes is excessive in violation of the Eighth Amendment. The amount of bail is to be determined on a case-by-case basis under the specific facts of the case and not by the character of the offense charged. Here, the government failed to show any justification for bail far exceeding the maximum sentence of five years and a $10,000 fine for a Smith Act violation. The fact that other similarly situated defendants have chosen to forfeit lower bail amounts is insufficient justification for the increased bail. Remanded.

Analysis:

While the Eighth Amendment prohibits federal courts from imposing excessive bail, the Supreme Court has not applied that protection to state courts. Most states, however, have similar constitutional or statutory provisions to protect against excessive bail. The calculation of bail in state courts generally follows the same individualized approach discussed by the *Stack* Court.

■ CASE VOCABULARY

BAIL: A security such as cash or a bond, especially security required by a court for the release of a prisoner who must appear at a future time.

EXCESSIVE BAIL: Bail that is unreasonably high considering both the offense with which the accused is charged and the risk that the accused will not appear for trial.

HABEAS CORPUS: A writ employed to bring a person before a court, most frequently to ensure that the party's imprisonment or detention is not illegal.

United States v. Salerno

(*Federal Government*) v. (*Mob Boss*)

481 U.S. 739, 107 S. Ct. 2095, 95 L. Ed. 2d 697 (1987)

THE BAIL REFORM ACT IS NOT FACIALLY UNCONSTITUTIONAL

■ **INSTANT FACTS** Organized crime defendants were ordered detained pending trial upon a showing of a threat to the safety of others if released.

■ **BLACK LETTER RULE** Preventative detention of a criminal defendant after indictment does not violate substantive due process under the Fifth Amendment nor constitute excessive bail under the Eighth Amendment when the government has demonstrated through clear and convincing evidence that the defendant presents a threat to the safety of the community.

■ PROCEDURAL BASIS

Certiorari to review a decision of the Second Circuit Court of Appeals declaring a provision of the Bail Reform Act of 1984 unconstitutional.

■ FACTS

Salerno (D) and a co-defendant, Cafaro, were charged with various RICO violations, mail and wire fraud offenses, extortion, and gambling violations. At their arraignment, the Government (P) moved for preventative detention of the defendants under the Bail Reform Act of 1984. The Bail Reform Act permits a federal judge to order the pretrial detention of indicted defendants if, after a hearing, the Government proves through clear and convincing evidence that "no condition or combination of conditions will reasonably assure the appearance of the person as required and the safety of any other person and the community." The Government (P) offered evidence showing that Salerno (D) was the boss of a large organized crime family and that Cafaro was a captain. Witnesses testified that Salerno (D) was personally involved in two murder conspiracies. The trial court found that the Government (P) showed through clear and convincing evidence that the defendants' release would jeopardize the safety of the community. On appeal, the defendants argued that the Bail Reform Act is facially unconstitutional because it violates the Due Process Clause of the Fifth Amendment and constitutes excessive bail in violation of the Eighth Amendment. The Second Circuit Court of Appeals reversed the trial court's decision, holding that the Bail Reform Act facially violated substantive due process in that it allowed for the preventative detention of those who may commit future crimes, though not accused of a crime at that time.

■ ISSUE

Does the provision of the Bail Reform Act of 1984 allowing for preventative detention of individuals upon a clear and convincing showing of a threat to the safety of others facially violate substantive due process?

■ DECISION AND RATIONALE

(Rehnquist, C.J.) No. The preventative detention of criminal defendants after indictment does not violate substantive due process under the Fifth Amendment nor constitute excessive bail under the Eighth

Amendment when the government has demonstrated through clear and convincing evidence that the defendants present a threat to the safety of others. The defendants in this case failed to meet their burden of showing that no set of circumstances exists in which the statute could operate constitutionally. First, to establish that the statute violates substantive due process guarantees under the Fifth Amendment, defendants must show that government conduct interferes with a defendant's life, liberty, or property rights. To fall within this category, the Bail Reform Act must serve to punish, rather than regulate, defendants' conduct.

The court must review the legislative history of the statute to determine whether it sets forth a valid regulatory purpose and is rationally related to achieving that purpose. The legislative history of the Bail Reform Act demonstrates that Congress enacted the statute not to punish those who have committed a crime, but to regulate conduct that is likely to endanger the safety of others. The Act carefully sets forth the conduct to which detention is to apply, imposes upon the government a heightened burden of proof, and affords a defendant numerous procedural safeguards through which he or she can contest detention, including a hearing and an opportunity to present witnesses on his or her behalf. The Act is regulatory in nature and is reasonably tailored to achieve its purpose. Congress's interest in regulating the safety of all citizens need not yield to an individual's liberty interests. In times of war and ordinary police activity, for example, legitimate governmental interests in crime prevention can justify the detention of individuals deemed dangerous even before a criminal trial. In light of these legitimate interests, the carefully tailored language of the statute indicates that it may be constitutionally applied to at least some defendants, thus defeating the facial challenge.

Next, the defendants here argue that the Act facially violates the Eighth Amendment's prohibition against excessive bail, which requires bail to be set solely on the risk of flight in the interest of furthering the integrity of the judicial process. The Eight Amendment does not, however, restrict the government's pursuit of other compelling interests through the regulation of pretrial release. The risk of flight is just one of many factors that may be considered in determining whether the bail set is excessive under the Eighth Amendment. The only limit placed upon the court by the Eighth Amendment is that the bail must not be excessive in light of the governmental interest asserted. If preventative detention sufficiently meets the reasonable objectives sought by the court, the detention is not excessive. The Bail Reform Act of 1984 is not facially unconstitutional under the Fifth or Eighth Amendments. Reversed.

■ DISSENT

(Marshall, J.) The importance of the Eighth Amendment and the Fifth Amendment cannot be viewed separately to determine that the Bail Reform Act is facially constitutional. There is no meaningful distinction between the imposition of excessive bail and the total denial of bail. Whether bail is excessive or bail is denied, the defendant remains in jail just the same. It is illogical to assume that the Eighth Amendment prohibits one without the other. If such a distinction does exist, the Bail Reform Act serves no purpose, as courts would have unrestricted constitutional power to do that which the statute allows. Similarly, substantive due process under the Fifth Amendment protects much more than a person's right to be free of punishment before conviction. Fundamental to substantive due process is the presumption of innocence every defendant enjoys until proven guilty. This presumption arises at the time of the initial charge and carries through conviction. A defendant acquitted at trial, of course, cannot be detained because his innocence is established. The result should be no different for an indicted defendant enjoying the presumption of innocence. He is as innocent upon indictment as he is upon acquittal. The Bail Reform Act, however, permits the conclusion that one who is presumed innocent may be detained after he has been indicted.

The consideration of potential future criminal activity to permit preventative detention transforms an indictment into evidence against the defendant to refute the presumption of innocence. It bears no relation to the governmental function of ensuring that defendants stand trial, as does detention for a risk of flight, but rather presents a governmental interest that exceeds those to be analyzed to determine whether bail is excessive under the Eighth Amendment. The protections of the Eighth Amendment help secure a defendant's substantive due process by prohibiting excessive bail and unjustified detentions, because all defendants are presumed innocent until proven otherwise.

■ DISSENT

(Stevens, J.) While pretrial detention may promote a governmental interest in protecting the safety and welfare of the community in some circumstances, the defendant's past acts cannot support detention. If fear for the safety of others is sufficient to justify such detention, it should be immaterial whether the defendant has been charged, indicted, or convicted of a past crime. The appropriateness of preventative detention should be viewed in light of the evidence of the threat to the safety of the community whenever it exists, not merely after an indictment is brought.

Analysis:

Preventative detention, like that addressed in the Bail Reform Act, has been the subject of considerable criticism. While the criminal justice system traditionally requires proof of the commission of a crime to justify imprisonment, *Salerno* upholds detentions based not on conduct committed, but on conduct that potentially could be committed if the defendant were given the opportunity. Additionally, while conviction of a crime requires proof beyond a reasonable doubt, preventative detention requires only clear and convincing proof of the potential for future crime.

■ CASE VOCABULARY

PREVENTATIVE DETENTION: Confinement imposed usually on a criminal defendant who has threatened to escape, poses a risk of harm, or has otherwise violated the law while awaiting trial, or on a mentally ill person who may cause harm.

FACIAL CHALLENGE: A claim that a statute is unconstitutional on its face—that is, that it always operates unconstitutionally.

SUBSTANTIVE DUE PROCESS: The doctrine that the Due Process Clauses of the Fifth and Fourteenth Amendments require legislation to be fair and reasonable in content and to further a legitimate governmental objective.

CHAPTER TEN

Decision Whether to Prosecute

United States v. Armstrong

Instant Facts: Armstrong (D) and others were indicted on several charges involving possession and intent to distribute crack cocaine, as well as using a firearm. Armstrong (D) moved for discovery to show that he was singled out for prosecution because of his race.

Black Letter Rule: To go forward on a claim of selective prosecution based on race, the claimant must produce evidence that similarly situated offenders of a different race could have been prosecuted but were not.

United States v. Batchelder

Instant Facts: After Batchelder (D) was convicted and sentenced for receiving a firearm in violation of a federal statute, the court of appeals remanded the case for resentencing.

Black Letter Rule: Identical substantive criminal statutes do not offend due process by establishing different sentencing provisions available upon conviction.

United States v. Goodwin

Instant Facts: After Goodwin (D) invoked his right to a jury trial on misdemeanor charges against him, the charges were changed to felonies and he was convicted.

Black Letter Rule: Due process does not prohibit a prosecutor from adding more severe or additional charges against a defendant after the defendant requests a trial by jury.

United States v. Armstrong

(*Prosecuting Government*) v. (*Accused Crack Dealer*)

517 U.S. 456, 116 S. Ct. 1480, 134 L. Ed. 2d 687 (1996)

RACE-BASED PROSECUTION CLAIMS MUST DEMONSTRATE THAT SIMILAR OFFENDERS OF DIFFERENT RACES WERE NOT PROSECUTED

■ **INSTANT FACTS** Armstrong (D) and others were indicted on several charges involving possession and intent to distribute crack cocaine, as well as using a firearm. Armstrong (D) moved for discovery to show that he was singled out for prosecution because of his race.

■ **BLACK LETTER RULE** To go forward on a claim of selective prosecution based on race, the claimant must produce evidence that similarly situated offenders of a different race could have been prosecuted but were not.

■ PROCEDURAL BASIS

Certiorari to review a decision of the Ninth Circuit Court of Appeals affirming the dismissal of the charges against the defendants.

■ FACTS

Armstrong (D) and others were indicted on charges involving conspiring to possess crack cocaine with intent to distribute, conspiring to distribute crack cocaine, and federal firearms offenses. Armstrong (D) moved the court for discovery, claiming that he was singled out for prosecution because he is black. The prosecution argued that Armstrong (D) did not produce enough evidence to entitle him to discovery on a claim of selective prosecution. The court granted the motion and ordered the Government (P) to provide information relating to all cocaine and firearm offenses for the previous three years, indicating the race of each defendant. The Government (P) moved for reconsideration and filed a detailed affidavit explaining why the defendants were charged. After reconsideration was denied, the court dismissed the case when the Government (P) indicated it would not comply with the discovery order. The Ninth Circuit Court of Appeals ultimately affirmed the dismissal.

■ ISSUE

In order to obtain discovery on a claim of selective prosecution, must a defendant produce evidence that other similarly situated offenders could have been prosecuted, but were not?

■ DECISION AND RATIONALE

(Rehnquist, C.J.) Yes. Pretrial discovery is governed by Federal Rule of Criminal Procedure 16, which requires the government to produce upon request such information in the government's possession that is "material to the preparation of the defendants' defense or [is] intended for use by the government as evidence in chief at the trial." The context of the rule, however, limits information material to the defendant's defense to that information useful to defend against the government's evidence. It applies only to evidence that may be used as a shield, not a sword, against the government. The rule elsewhere exempts government work product, such as documents related to the investigation or prosecution of the crime, from disclosure. To maintain symmetry between these two provisions, evidence of the government's motives for prosecution does not fall within the rule.

A selective-prosecution claim is not a defense on the merits. Instead, it is an affirmative claim challenging the constitutionality of the government's actions and asks the judiciary to exercise its authority over the Executive Branch. While the government is bound to prosecute within the limits of the Constitution, there is a strong presumption that its prosecution is valid. To overcome this presumption, the defendant must present "clear evidence to the contrary." Drawing on equal protection principles, a defendant must establish that the government's prosecutorial policy "had a discriminatory effect and that it was motivated by a discriminatory purpose," with evidence that similarly situated individuals of a different race were not prosecuted. Here, the evidence relied upon the defendants in their motion for discovery failed to identify individuals who were not black and who could have been prosecuted for the offenses charged but were not. Without such a showing, pretrial discovery is unavailable. Reversed and remanded.

■ DISSENT

(Stevens, J.) While the defendants did not establish the facts necessary to establish a selective prosecution defense, the facts were sufficient to require some disclosure. Under the federal sentencing guidelines, the penalties for possession and distribution of crack cocaine are severe, especially in comparison to the penalties for possession and distribution of powder cocaine. The statistics reflect that although sixty-five percent of crack users are white, eighty-five percent of those charged with its possession and distribution are black, and the sentences imposed on black defendants are over forty percent longer than those imposed on white defendants. These objective facts warrant consideration of the motives underlying the government's prosecutorial policy to uncover any discriminatory intent. The court should take judicial notice of these facts and compel the government to justify its decisions to prosecute.

Analysis:

Note that a claim of selective prosecution is not a defense to the merits of the criminal charge itself, but an independent claim that a prosecutor exceeded the bounds of his or her discretion by bringing a criminal charge for constitutionally impermissible reasons. Generally, selective-prosecution claims are not likely to succeed because of the heavy burden defendants bear to prove them. Also, federal courts are reluctant to review the decisions of federal prosecutors because federal prosecutors are members of the executive branch of government, whose duty to assist the President in executing federal laws originates in the Constitution.

■ CASE VOCABULARY

DISCOVERY: Compulsory disclosure, at a party's request, of information that relates to the litigation.

SELECTIVE PROSECUTION: The practice or an instance of a criminal prosecution brought at the discretion of a prosecutor rather than as a matter of course in the normal functioning of the prosecuting authority's office.

United States v. Batchelder

(*Prosecuting Government*) v. (*Convicted Felon*)
442 U.S. 114, 99 S. Ct. 2198, 60 L. Ed. 2d 755 (1979)

PROSECUTORS HAVE DISCRETION TO DETERMINE WHICH OFFENSES TO CHARGE

■ **INSTANT FACTS** After Batchelder (D) was convicted and sentenced for receiving a firearm in violation of a federal statute, the court of appeals remanded the case for resentencing.

■ **BLACK LETTER RULE** Identical substantive criminal statutes do not offend due process by establishing different sentencing provisions available upon conviction.

■ PROCEDURAL BASIS

Certiorari to review a decision of a federal court of appeals that remanded the case for resentencing.

■ FACTS

Batchelder (D), a previously convicted felon, was convicted of receiving a firearm that had traveled through interstate commerce, in violation of 18 U.S.C. § 922(h). He was sentenced to the maximum five-year prison term. On appeal, the federal court of appeals affirmed the conviction, but remanded the case for resentencing because the substantive elements of § 922(h) are identical with 18 U.S.C. § 1202(a), which carries a maximum two-year prison sentence.

■ ISSUE

Must a defendant convicted under one of two substantively identical statutes, which has a higher maximum sentence than the other, be sentenced only under the less punitive statutory provision when his conduct violates both statutes?

■ DECISION AND RATIONALE

(Marshall, J.) No. The two statutes and their sentencing provisions act independently of one another and due process is not offended by holding the defendant to the standard established by the statute providing the higher sentence. Due process requires that "[n]o one may be required at peril of life, liberty, or property to speculate as to the meaning of penal statutes." The statutes at issue unambiguously define the prohibited conduct and the sentences available upon conviction. The fact that the two statutes carry different sentencing provisions does not detract from the notice given to the defendant of the elements of the offense and the possible penalty upon conviction. Similarly, the different sentencing provisions do not grant the prosecutor unfettered discretion as to which charge to bring against a defendant; rather, they merely afford the sentencing judge options when considering the appropriate penalty to impose. Reversed.

Analysis:

The extent of the prosecutor's discretion is broad and includes what charges may be brought against a defendant, what penalty to seek within the sentencing guidelines, whether or not to negotiate a plea, and whether to forego charges altogether. So long as the prosecutor's discretion is not abused and his or her acts fall within the permissible limits of the Constitution, the prosecutor's decisions will go largely unchallenged.

■ CASE VOCABULARY

DUE PROCESS: The conduct of legal proceedings according to established rules and principles for the protection and enforcement of private rights, including notice and the right to a fair hearing before a tribunal with the power to decide the case.

SENTENCE: The judgment that a court formally pronounces after finding a criminal defendant guilty; the punishment imposed on a criminal wrongdoer.

United States v. Goodwin

(*Prosecuting Authority*) v. (*Criminal Defendant*)
457 U.S. 368, 102 S. Ct. 2485, 73 L. Ed. 2d 74 (1982)

PRETRIAL ADDITIONS TO THE CHARGES AGAINST A DEFENDANT ARE NOT NECESSARILY VINDICTIVE

■ **INSTANT FACTS** After Goodwin (D) invoked his right to a jury trial on misdemeanor charges against him, the charges were changed to felonies and he was convicted.

■ **BLACK LETTER RULE** Due process does not prohibit a prosecutor from adding more severe or additional charges against a defendant after the defendant requests a trial by jury.

■ PROCEDURAL BASIS

Certiorari to review a decision of the federal court of appeals reversing the defendant's conviction.

■ FACTS

After Goodwin (D) was stopped for speeding in Maryland, the officer noticed a clear plastic bag underneath the armrest of the vehicle. When the officer asked Goodwin (D) to lift the armrest, Goodwin (D) accelerated and struck the officer, knocking him into the highway. The officer gave chase, but Goodwin (D) eluded him. The next day, the officer filed charges against Goodwin (D) for, among other things, assault. Goodwin (D) was arrested and a trial date was set. Goodwin (D) fled the jurisdiction. Three years later, Goodwin (D) was arrested in Virginia and returned to Maryland to stand trial. The case was assigned to an attorney for the Justice Department with authority to try petty crimes and misdemeanors before a U.S. Magistrate. Although initially agreeable to plea negotiations, Goodwin (D) later informed the Government (P) that he did not wish to plead guilty and requested a jury trial. The case was transferred to a United States Attorney, who decided to prosecute Goodwin (D) in district court on felony charges. Goodwin (D) was convicted on a felony count and a misdemeanor count. Goodwin (D) moved to set aside the conviction because the felony conviction appeared to be a product of prosecutorial retaliation for his refusal to plead guilty to the misdemeanor charges. The motion was denied. The court of appeals reversed, finding that although there was no actual vindictiveness, the Due Process Clause prohibited a prosecutor from bringing more serious charges after a jury trial has been requested.

■ ISSUE

May the Government raise new additional felony charges against a defendant who has asserted his right to a jury trial on misdemeanor charges against him?

■ DECISION AND RATIONALE

(Stevens, J.) Yes. When a defendant successfully appeals an initial conviction against him, the Due Process Clause requires that the Government cannot thereafter impose a heavier sentence than was imposed by the initial conviction. To so permit would discourage defendants from pursuing their legal rights of appeal. When a heavier sentence is imposed on retrial, a presumption of prosecutorial vindictiveness arises, rebuttable by objective, affirmative evidence of the defendant's conduct after the initial sentencing proceeding to justify the increased sentence. Unlike a heavier sentence after trial, however, this case involves a prosecutor's decision to charge the defendant with a felony *before* trial. A pretrial change in position, either by dismissing charges identified in an indictment or adding additional charges, lies within the prosecutor's discretion and is proper conduct during the plea negotiation process. In such situations, no presumption of vindictiveness arises. Before trial, a prosecutor continues to collect evidence, evaluate the Government's (D) position, and determine the appropriate charges to be brought. After trial, however, the Government's position is reasonably established by the evidence and any decision on the charges has been made. The prosecutor's discretion is unaffected by a request for a jury trial. By refusing to apply a presumption of vindictiveness, the door still remains open to a defendant to prove actual vindictiveness through objective evidence demonstrating a punitive motive.

■ CONCURRENCE

(Blackmun, J.) There is no distinction between pretrial and post-trial vindictiveness. However, when a prosecutor adds charges after a defendant refuses to plead guilty, he does so on the basis of objective evidence supporting the charges. The explanation derived from this evidence satisfies the Government's burden to rebut any appearance of vindictiveness such that due process is not offended.

■ DISSENT

(Brennan, J.) The difference between a request for a jury trial and a waiver of that right in lieu of a bench trial is significant. A jury trial puts a heavier burden on the prosecution and requires much more effort to obtain a conviction and avoid a mistrial based on errors made. As such, a prosecutor may frequently desire that the defendant waive his right to a jury trial. If the defendant doesn't and the prosecutor thereafter increases the charges against him, a realistic suggestion of vindictiveness arises.

Analysis:

How likely is it in this case that the prosecutor uncovered additional evidence three years after the incident took place that would justify an additional felony charge? Consider the position the defendant was in: three years after committing the acts charged, he faced misdemeanor charges and decided not to plead guilty. Had he accepted a plea or waived his right to a jury trial, his conviction would have been considerably less severe. On the other hand, the defendant's counsel should have been aware of the possibility of additional felony charges upon a jury trial demand and counseled his client accordingly.

■ CASE VOCABULARY

MAGISTRATE: A judicial officer with strictly limited jurisdiction and authority, often on the local level and often restricted to criminal cases.

FELONY: A serious crime usually punishable by imprisonment for more than one year or by death.

MISDEMEANOR: A crime that is less serious than a felony and is usually punishable by fine, penalty, forfeiture, or confinement (usually for a brief time) in a place other than prison (such as a county jail).

CHAPTER ELEVEN

Screening the Prosecutor's Decision to Charge

Coleman v. Alabama

Instant Facts: Coleman (D) was convicted of assault with intent to murder in Alabama after he was not provided with appointed counsel at the preliminary hearing.

Black Letter Rule: Because preliminary hearings are a critical stage of prosecution, defendants are entitled to the assistance of counsel.

Vasquez v. Hillery

Instant Facts: Hillery (D) was convicted of murder on an indictment delivered by a grand jury from which African-Americans were excluded.

Black Letter Rule: Racial discrimination in the selection of the grand jury requires dismissal of the defendant's conviction.

Costello v. United States

Instant Facts: Costello (D) moved to dismiss an indictment as improperly based on hearsay testimony.

Black Letter Rule: Grand jury indictments may be issued based solely on hearsay evidence.

Coleman v. Alabama

(Convicted Criminal) v. *(Prosecuting State)*
399 U.S. 1, 90 S. Ct. 1999, 26 L. Ed. 2d 387 (1970)

DEFENDANTS ARE ENTITLED TO COUNSEL AT PRELIMINARY HEARINGS

■ **INSTANT FACTS** Coleman (D) was convicted of assault with intent to murder in Alabama after he was not provided with appointed counsel at the preliminary hearing.

■ **BLACK LETTER RULE** Because preliminary hearings are a critical stage of prosecution, defendants are entitled to the assistance of counsel.

■ PROCEDURAL BASIS

Certiorari to review a decision by the Alabama Court of Appeals affirming the trial court.

■ FACTS

Coleman (D) was convicted of assault with intent to murder for shooting Reynolds, who had parked his car on the side of the road to change a flat tire. Coleman (D) did not have appointed counsel to represent him at the preliminary hearing. Coleman (D) argued that the failure to provide him with counsel at this stage violated his constitutional right to the assistance of counsel.

■ ISSUE

Is a criminal defendant entitled to counsel at a preliminary hearing?

■ DECISION AND RATIONALE

(Brennan, J.) Yes. Even though it is not necessarily a required step, a preliminary hearing is a "critical stage" in a criminal proceeding that requires the assistance of counsel because there is a potential for substantial prejudice to the defendant's rights that counsel may help to avoid. Counsel is necessary at the preliminary hearing to protect an indigent accused from an erroneous or improper prosecution by exposing weaknesses in the State's case, developing testimony for impeachment purposes at trial, obtaining discovery vital to preparing a defense, and arguing on issues such as psychiatric examinations and bail.

State law prohibits the use of any information obtained at the preliminary hearing at the defendant's trial. Although no such information was introduced, the question remains for the Alabama courts to determine whether the denial of counsel was harmless error. Accordingly, the decision of the court of appeals is vacated and remanded to determine whether the failure to provide counsel was harmless error.

■ CONCURRENCE

(Black, J.) Under Alabama law, the purpose of the preliminary hearing is to determine whether an offense has been committed and whether there is probable cause for charging the defendant with that offense. Because this hearing is a definite part or stage of prosecution, a defendant is entitled to counsel under the Sixth Amendment. Counsel must be present at the preliminary hearing to protect the rights of the accused. However, the focus of the decision should be on the defendant's right to counsel under the Sixth and Fourteenth Amendments, not the right to a fair trial, which is found nowhere in the Constitution.

■ CONCURRENCE

(Douglas, J.) A strict construction of the Sixth Amendment requires the assistance of counsel at the preliminary hearing stage. The Sixth Amendment provides, "In all criminal prosecutions, the accused shall enjoy the right . . . to have the assistance of Counsel for his defence." A criminal prosecution does not begin at the trial, but at its earlier stages. Defense counsel needs time to prepare the defendant's defense and the right to counsel attaches at the earliest point of the criminal prosecution, including the preliminary hearing.

■ CONCURRENCE

(White, J.) While the right to counsel exists at the preliminary hearing, such a right threatens the elimination of preliminary hearings by the prosecutorial decision to take the case directly to the grand jury. Moreover, the harmless error standard is unlikely to result in error, particularly after the prosecution has presented its evidence to the jury and obtained a conviction beyond a reasonable doubt. Only when "important testimony of witnesses unavailable at the trial could have been preserved had counsel been present to cross-examine opposing witnesses or to examine witnesses for the defense" may a new trial be appropriate.

■ CONCURRENCE IN PART

(Harlan, J.) While the majority correctly determined that the defendant's constitutional rights had been violated, its mandate on remand is too broad. Reversal of the conviction should not be based on the speculative position that the defendant's defense may have been strengthened with the assistance of counsel at the preliminary hearing. Instead, the defendant on remand should be called to illustrate particular testimony irretrievably lost by the early denial of counsel.

■ DISSENT

(Stewart, J.) If the assistance of counsel is necessary to ensure that the defendant receives a fair trial, then the majority should have vacated the convictions and required a new preliminary hearing to determine whether there was sufficient evidence to take the case to the grand jury. If, as the majority argues, the role of counsel is so crucial, the case should not be remanded for a determination of whether the denial of counsel was harmless error.

■ DISSENT

(Burger, C.J.) The majority inexplicably translates the constitutional phrase "criminal prosecution" to mean every "critical event" in a criminal case. Nowhere in the Constitution is such a translation suggested and the majority's analysis is misplaced. The constitutional focus should be whether a preliminary hearing is a "criminal prosecution," not whether it is a "critical event." By conferring the right of counsel at the preliminary hearing stage, the Court creates a situation where counsel must be present at a hearing to determine whether a case should go to the grand jury, while there is no right to counsel at the more critical grand jury proceeding itself. Defendants are already protected from government abuse by the exclusion of all information obtained at the preliminary hearing. There is no need to strain the intent of the Constitution to afford additional protections.

Analysis:

The purpose of the preliminary hearing is to allow a magistrate or judge to determine whether there is sufficient evidence to allow the prosecutor to go forward with the case against the defendant. However, in 1913, the Supreme Court ruled in *Lem Woon v. Oregon*, 229 U.S. 586 (1913), that a preliminary hearing is not constitutionally required for defendants in state courts. In federal courts, a defendant who is charged with a felony but is not yet indicted is entitled to a preliminary hearing under Fed. R. Crim. P. 5.1. During this hearing, the magistrate or judge may consider hearsay evidence, and the defendant has the right to introduce evidence and cross-examine the Government's witnesses.

■ CASE VOCABULARY

BIND OVER: To hold (a person) for trial; to turn (a defendant) over to a sheriff or warden for imprisonment pending further judicial action.

GRAND JURY: A body of (often 12) people who are chosen to sit permanently for at least a month—and sometimes a year—and who, in ex parte proceedings, decide whether to issue indictments.

HARMLESS ERROR: An error that does not affect a party's substantive rights or the case's outcome.

PRELIMINARY HEARING: A criminal hearing (usually conducted by a magistrate) to determine whether there is sufficient evidence to prosecute an accused person. If sufficient evidence exists, the case will be set for trial or bound over for grand-jury review, or an information will be filed in the trial court.

RIGHT TO COUNSEL: A criminal defendant's constitutional right, guaranteed by the Sixth Amendment, to representation by a court-appointed lawyer if the defendant cannot afford to hire one.

Vasquez v. Hillery

(*Prison Warden*) v. (*Murder Defendant*)
474 U.S. 254, 106 S. Ct. 617, 88 L. Ed. 2d 598 (1986)

RACIAL DISCRIMINATION IN GRAND JURY SELECTION VIOLATES THE EQUAL PROTECTION CLAUSE

■ **INSTANT FACTS** Hillery (D) was convicted of murder on an indictment delivered by a grand jury from which African-Americans were excluded.

■ **BLACK LETTER RULE** Racial discrimination in the selection of the grand jury requires dismissal of the defendant's conviction.

■ PROCEDURAL BASIS

Certiorari to review a decision of the Ninth Circuit Court of Appeals affirming a grant of a writ of habeas corpus.

■ FACTS

Hillery (D) was indicted for murder by a California grand jury. Before trial, Hillery (D) moved to quash the indictment because it was issued by a grand jury from which blacks were systematically excluded. The judge refused to quash the indictment. Hillery (D) was convicted of murder. Hillery (D) spent the next sixteen years appealing his conviction in the state court system, before filing a petition for a writ of habeas corpus in federal court. The federal court granted the writ upon finding that the grand jury was a product of discrimination. The Ninth Circuit Court of Appeals affirmed.

■ ISSUE

Must a conviction be dismissed when it is based on an indictment issued by a grand jury from which African-Americans were excluded?

■ DECISION AND RATIONALE

(Marshall, J.) Yes. Since 1880, an indictment from a grand jury from which blacks have been excluded has required reversal of the subsequent conviction. Racial discrimination in the selection of a grand jury "strikes at the fundamental values of our judicial system and our society as a whole," and the defendant's equal protection rights are violated when he has been indicted by a grand jury from which a particular racial group has been excluded. The taint placed on the indictment by such discrimination cannot be ameliorated because the defendant's conviction was supported by the evidence at trial. Harmless error is not a defense to the violations, for the discrimination threatens the integrity of the judicial process and potentially impacts the decisions of the grand jury.

■ DISSENT

(Powell, J.) The Court reverses the defendant's conviction because blacks were purposely excluded from the grand jury twenty-three years earlier, although the jury found him guilty beyond a reasonable doubt in a fair trial. The reversal is wrong because any error in the grand jury selection is harmless error and, even if the harmless-error rule does not apply, reversal is the improper remedy for the wrong.

Although there is outdated authority requiring reversal of the conviction for errors in the grand jury selection, more recent Court authority demonstrates that harmless constitutional errors are not grounds for reversing the conviction. Grand jury discrimination, while threatening the "appearance of justice" and the "integrity of the judicial process," is no more important than other constitutional errors on which actual prejudice has been required to set aside a conviction.

Even assuming the harmless-error rule does not apply, the reversal of the defendant's conviction is not the proper remedy for the constitutional violation. The grand jury plays a comparatively unimportant part in the criminal process. Grand jury discrimination does not call the correctness of the jury's conviction into doubt. Nor did the race of the grand jurors cause any cognizable injury. When the period between conviction and reversal is long, as it is here, the cost on the state to resurrect its case, locate necessary witnesses, and undertake a retrial of the defendant is significant. The burden on the state at this late time is too substantial to warrant reversal.

Analysis:

While the grand jury is not a legal formality, application of the harmless error rule would seem to be justified in situations in which trying the defendant a second time would present significant obstacles to the prosecution. Grand jurors are empowered to increase or reduce the number and severity of the offense charged, but do not determine the defendant's guilt or innocence on the charges. Thus, even when an indictment may be a product of discrimination, the conviction must ultimately be determined beyond a reasonable doubt at trial. This protective measure seems to reduce the effect on the constitutional violation, especially when retrial would be impracticable.

■ CASE VOCABULARY

DISCRIMINATION: The effect of a law or established practice that confers privileges on a certain class or that denies privileges to a certain class because of race, age, sex, nationality, religion, or handicap.

EQUAL PROTECTION: The constitutional guarantee under the 14th Amendment that the government must treat a person or class of persons the same as it treats other persons or classes in like circumstances.

HABEAS CORPUS: A writ employed to bring a person before a court, most frequently to ensure that the party's imprisonment or detention is not illegal.

HARMLESS ERROR: An error that does not affect a party's substantive rights or the case's outcome.

STARE DECISIS: The doctrine of precedent, under which it is necessary for a court to follow earlier judicial decisions when the same points arise again in litigation.

Costello v. United States

(*Tax Evader*) v. (*Prosecuting Authority*)
350 U.S. 359, 76 S. Ct. 406, 100 L. Ed. 397 (1956)

GRAND JURIES ARE NOT BOUND BY FORMAL PROCEDURAL OR EVIDENTIARY RULES

■ **INSTANT FACTS** Costello (D) moved to dismiss an indictment as improperly based on hearsay testimony.

■ **BLACK LETTER RULE** Grand jury indictments may be issued based solely on hearsay evidence.

■ PROCEDURAL BASIS

Certiorari to review an undisclosed decision of a federal court of appeals affirming the defendant's conviction.

■ FACTS

Costello (D) was indicted on charges of federal income tax evasion for falsely reporting less income than he and his wife received. Costello (D) filed a motion for inspection of the grand jury minutes and dismissal of the indictment, based on an affidavit that he believed there was no legal and competent evidence to sustain the indictment since he correctly reported all income and paid all taxes due. The motion was denied. At trial, the Government (P) examined many witnesses concerning Costello's (D) business transactions and expenditures. Additionally, three government agents were called to summarize the evidence against Costello (D) and demonstrate computations of his net worth. On cross-examination, it was revealed that the government agents were the only witnesses who had testified before the grand jury. Costello (D) again moved to dismiss the indictment as based on hearsay testimony, since the agents had no first-hand knowledge of the transactions supporting their computations. The motion was denied and Costello (D) was convicted. The federal court of appeals affirmed the conviction.

■ ISSUE

Can hearsay evidence alone support a grand jury indictment, which leads to a subsequent trial and conviction?

■ DECISION AND RATIONALE

(Black, J.) Yes. Although the Fifth Amendment requires that all criminal defendants stand trial only after a grand jury indictment, the Amendment does not indicate what type of evidence may properly support an indictment. Historically, the grand jury has not been encumbered by strict procedural or evidentiary standards, but has been free to use common judgment to determine whether evidence supports a criminal charge. A grand jury indictment may not be disturbed because it is based on incompetent evidence. If an indictment could be challenged on the merits because of the sufficiency of the evidence, a defendant would have a preliminary right to evaluate the evidence presented to the grand jury, although such a right exists at trial. The result would be great delay in the grand jury process. No such challenge is constitutionally required.

■ CONCURRENCE

(Burton, J.) While the indictment should not have been quashed, examination of the evidence before a grand jury may be permissible in some instances, such as for potential bias or prejudice. A defendant need not stand trial on an empty indictment based on no rationally competent evidence.

Analysis:

Under the Court's decision, grand jury indictments are essentially unreviewable. It matters not whether the evidence supports the charges or whether the grand jury gave careful consideration to all the evidence presented. Instead, so long as the indictment is valid on its face, the indictment will suffice.

■ CASE VOCABULARY

HEARSAY: Traditionally, testimony that is given by a witness who relates not what he or she knows personally, but what others have said, and that is therefore dependent on the credibility of someone other than the witness.

INDICTMENT: The formal written accusation of a crime, made by a grand jury and presented to a court for prosecution against the accused person.

Barker v. Wingo

(*Convicted Murderer*) v. (*Prison Official*)

407 U.S. 514, 92 S. Ct. 2182, 33 L. Ed. 2d 101 (1972)

THE DEFENDANT'S ASSERTION OF HIS RIGHTS IS ONE CONSIDERATION IN A SPEEDY-TRIAL CASE

■ **INSTANT FACTS** Barker (D) was not brought to trial for murder until more than five years after he was arrested, during which time the prosecution obtained numerous continuances. He ultimately filed a motion to dismiss the indictment asserting that his right to a speedy trial had been violated.

■ **BLACK LETTER RULE** When addressing speedy trial claims, courts must apply a balancing test in which the conduct of both the prosecution and the defendant are weighed, including a consideration of the length of delay, the reason for delay, the defendant's assertion of his right, and prejudice to the defendant.

■ PROCEDURAL BASIS

Certiorari to review the defendant's conviction.

■ FACTS

On July 20, 1958, an elderly couple was beaten to death by intruders wielding an iron tire tool. Two suspects, Manning and Barker (D), were indicted. The Commonwealth had a stronger case against Manning and believed that Barker (D) could not be convicted unless Manning testified against him. Manning was unwilling to incriminate himself. By first convicting Manning, the Commonwealth would remove the possible problems of self-incrimination and would be able to assure his testimony against Barker (D). Barker (D) was not brought to trial for murder until more than five years after he had been arrested, during which time the prosecution obtained sixteen continuances. Before Manning was finally convicted, he was tried six times. Barker (D) made no objection to the continuances until three-and-one-half years after he was arrested. He ultimately filed a motion to dismiss the indictment, asserting that his right to a speedy trial had been violated. The motion was denied and trial commenced with Manning as the chief prosecution witness. Barker (D) was convicted and given a life sentence.

■ ISSUE

Is a defendant deprived of his due process right to a speedy trial if he does not complain about the ensuing delay and is not prejudiced thereby?

■ DECISION AND RATIONALE

(Powell, J.) No. The right to a speedy trial involves both the accused's rights and societal interests in avoiding judicial backlogs, prison congestion, and the release of suspected criminals into the public where additional crimes may be committed. Witnesses may become unavailable after significant delay and their testimony becomes less reliable with time. However, the right to a speedy trial is not measured by a rigid timeline within which the defendant must stand trial. Nor is the right dependent upon a defendant's demand for a speedy trial, for it is the State's burden to bring a defendant to trial, not the defendant's. Accordingly, when addressing speedy trial claims, courts must apply a balancing test in which the conduct of both the prosecution and the defendant are weighed. Factors to consider include the length of delay, the reason for delay, the defendant's assertion of his right, and prejudice to the defendant.

Barker (D) was not seriously prejudiced by the more than five-year delay between his arrest and trial. His Sixth Amendment right to a speedy trial was not violated even though more than four years of the period were attributable to the prosecution's failure or inability to try Manning in order to use Manning's testimony at Barker's (D) trial. The lack of any serious prejudice and the fact, as disclosed by the record, that Barker (D) did not want a speedy trial outweigh opposing considerations and compel the conclusion that Barker (D) was not deprived of his due process right to a speedy trial.

Analysis:

It is impossible to determine with precision when the right to speedy trial has been denied. A defendant's constitutional right to a speedy trial cannot be established by an inflexible rule, but must be determined only on a case-by-case basis pursuant to which the conduct of the prosecution and the defendant are weighed.

■ CASE VOCABULARY

HABEAS CORPUS: A form of collateral attack. An independent proceeding initiated to determine whether a defendant is being unlawfully deprived of his or her liberty.

SIXTH AMENDMENT: The constitutional amendment guaranteeing in criminal cases the right to a speedy and public trial by jury, the right to be informed of the nature of the accusation, the right to confront witnesses, the right to counsel, and the right to compulsory process for obtaining favorable witnesses.

SPEEDY TRIAL: A trial that the prosecution, with reasonable diligence, begins promptly and conducts expeditiously. The Sixth Amendment secures the right to a speedy trial. In deciding whether an accused has been deprived of that right, courts generally consider the length of delay, the reason for the delay, and the prejudice to the accused.

Doggett v. United States

(Drug Smuggler) v. *(Prosecuting Authority)*

505 U.S. 647, 112 S. Ct. 2686, 120 L. Ed. 2d 520 (1992)

THE FAILURE TO WORK DILIGENTLY TO LOCATE A DEFENDANT FOR TRIAL VIOLATES THE SIXTH AMENDMENT

■ **INSTANT FACTS** Doggett (D) was arrested more than eight years after an indictment for conspiracy to import cocaine was issued.

■ **BLACK LETTER RULE** Lengthy delays between indictment and trial caused by the Government's negligence violate the Sixth Amendment right to a speedy trial.

■ PROCEDURAL BASIS

Certiorari to review a decision of a federal court of appeals affirming the defendant's conviction.

■ FACTS

In February 1980, Doggett (D) was indicted for conspiracy to import and distribute cocaine. In March 1980, two police officers set out to arrest Doggett (D) in North Carolina under the instructions of Driver, a federal Drug Enforcement Administration agent. When they arrived, they learned that Doggett (D) had left for Colombia four days earlier. Driver then informed U.S. Customs of the outstanding arrest warrant, directed them to catch Doggett (D) on his return, and entered his name in federal computer systems designed to assist Customs officials in screening people entering the country. Doggett's (D) listing expired in September 1980. In September 1981, Driver learned that Doggett (D) had been arrested in Panama and requested his extradition. Rather than return Doggett (D) to the United States, however, Doggett (D) was allowed to return to Colombia following the Panamanian proceedings. Doggett (D) returned to the United States undetected in September 1982 and resided in Virginia. It was not until 1985 that Driver discovered that Doggett (D) was no longer in Panama, though he had made no effort to locate him prior to that time. In 1988, the United States Marshal's Service discovered Doggett (D) living in Virginia when it ran credit checks on many outstanding arrest warrants. Doggett (D) was arrested in September 1988, over eight years after the indictment issued. Doggett (D) moved to dismiss the indictment for failure to provide him with a speedy trial. A magistrate recommended denial of the motion, contending that Doggett (D) had failed to demonstrate that the delay prevented him from asserting a successful defense. The district court denied the motion and the court of appeals affirmed.

■ ISSUE

When a lengthy delay between indictment and trial is caused by the Government's negligence in locating the defendant, is the defendant entitled to dismissal of the indictment?

■ DECISION AND RATIONALE

(Souter, J.) Yes. While, literally speaking, the Sixth Amendment forbids the government to delay an accused's trial for any reason, the right to a speedy trial has been tempered by four factors, including whether the delay was unreasonably long, whether the government or the defendant is more responsible for the delay, whether the defendant properly asserted his right to a speedy trial, and whether the defendant suffered prejudice from the delay.

To trigger a speedy trial analysis, the defendant must first demonstrate that the length of time between accusation and trial is substantial enough to be "presumptively prejudicial." If so, the court must then consider the length of the delay to determine the strength of the presumption. Here, given the eight-and-a-half-year delay in bringing Doggett (D) to trial, the inquiry is triggered. The delay is undoubtedly caused by the Government's (P) six-year failure to determine Doggett's (D) whereabouts. Although Doggett (D) may have been relatively unimportant in the world of drug trafficking, had the Government (P) made a simple inquiry of the Panamanian government, he could have been easily located. Similarly, there is no evidence that suggests that Doggett (D) knew of the indictment at the time it was issued, for witnesses with such knowledge all denied informing him of the indictment. Doggett (D) cannot be faulted for his failure to invoke his right to a speedy trial. Finally, in considering Doggett's (D) burden of proving that the delay resulted in prejudice, he need not affirmatively produce proof of particularized delay, but rather may rest on a presumption that, with time, the loss of exculpatory evidence and testimony is likely, though incapable of affirmative proof. The strength of this presumption, then, depends on the determination of the other factors. Because some delay in bringing a defendant to trial is necessary for the Government to collect evidence and prepare its case, minor delays are not strongly prejudicial. When the Government intentionally delays the trial, however, the strength of the presumption of prejudice heightens. Delays caused by the Government's negligence, as here, fall somewhere in the middle, but are closer to intentional delays. When the negligence results in a lengthy delay and the presumption of prejudice is not rebutted, the defendant is entitled to relief. Reversed.

■ DISSENT

(Thomas, J.) The Sixth Amendment does not protect a defendant from prejudice to his defense or the disruption of his life. The right to a speedy trial does not attach until the defendant has been accused of a crime. Yet, prejudice to an accused's defense is not created by the span between accusation and trial, but rather the span between the crime itself and trial. A trial occurring ten years after the commission of a crime carries the same prejudice to the defense whether the indictment was one week after the crime or one week before the trial. Yet, the Sixth Amendment is implicated only in the latter. Doggett (D) is not entitled to relief because the Government (P) was negligent and the resulting delay *may* have prejudiced his defense. Likewise, the Sixth Amendment does not serve to protect a defendant who has committed a crime from disruption of his life years later. The Sixth Amendment is not a statute of repose placing strict time limits on the Government's prosecution of an offense.

Analysis:

While the Court did not establish a definitive rule on what length of delay is presumptively prejudicial, it is generally accepted that a delay of eight months or longer suffices to presume prejudice, thereby triggering a speedy trial analysis. On the other hand, delays of less than five months are generally presumed not to be prejudicial. As a result, courts rarely engage in a speedy trial analysis under such circumstances.

■ CASE VOCABULARY

PREJUDICE: Damage or detriment to one's legal rights or claims.

PRESUMPTION: A legal inference or assumption that a fact exists, based on the known or proven existence of some other fact or group of facts. A presumption shifts the burden of production or persuasion to the opposing party, who can then attempt to overcome the presumption.

STATUTE OF REPOSE: A statute that bars a suit a fixed number of years after the defendant acts in some way (as by designing or manufacturing a product), even if this period ends before the plaintiff has suffered any injury.

United States v. Lovasco

(*Prosecuting Authority*) v. (*Indicted Defendant*)

431 U.S. 783, 97 S. Ct. 2044, 52 L. Ed. 2d 752 (1977)

DUE PROCESS DOES NOT REQUIRE AN IMMEDIATE INDICTMENT

■ **INSTANT FACTS** The district court dismissed an indictment of Lovasco (D) brought an allegedly prejudicial seventeen months after the Government (D) collected the evidence necessary to indict him.

■ **BLACK LETTER RULE** To prosecute a defendant following investigative delay does not deprive him of due process, even if his defense might have been somewhat prejudiced by the lapse of time.

■ PROCEDURAL BASIS

Certiorari to review a decision of the Eighth Circuit Court of Appeals affirming the dismissal of the indictment.

■ FACTS

In March 1975, Lovasco (D) was indicted for possessing firearms stolen from the U.S. mail and dealing in firearms without a license. The offenses were alleged to have occurred in the summer of 1973. Because of the delay, Lovasco (D) moved to dismiss the indictment because his defense had allegedly been prejudiced. At the hearing, the court considered a Postal Inspector's report submitted by Lovasco (D) indicating that the Government (P) had known of his offenses one month after its investigation commenced, but that the Government (P) was unable to refute his claim that he found the firearms in his car without knowing from where they came. Lovasco (D) contended that because of the delay, he lost testimony due to the death of two material witnesses. The Government (P) made no effort to explain the delay in bringing the indictment. Based on the evidence, the court dismissed the indictment because the Government (D) had all the information needed to indict the defendant from the Postal Inspector's report and failed to justify the unreasonable delay, prejudicing Lovasco's (D) defense. The Eight Circuit Court of Appeals affirmed.

■ ISSUE

Does an unjustified preindictment delay violate the Sixth Amendment when the delay prejudices the defendant's defense?

■ DECISION AND RATIONALE

(Marshall, J.) No. The Sixth Amendment right to a speedy trial does not attach until an indictment is brought. Instead, criminal statutes of limitations provide a defendant protection from stale criminal charges. The Sixth Amendment notwithstanding, however, unjustified preindictment delays may invoke due process concerns. While proof of actual prejudice is necessary for such a due process claim, such proof does not establish a violation per se, since the reasons for delay are relevant. Here, the Government (P) claimed that the delay was a result of a prosecutorial decision to withhold the indictment in hopes of discovering others who may have been involved in the offense. Prosecutors are under a duty to reasonably determine that probable cause exists to bring an indictment, but need not bring an indictment as soon as probable cause arises. Requiring a prosecutor to bring an indictment as soon as probable cause is determined, although the investigation into other potentially culpable defendants continues, would result in multiple trials against defendants charged with the same offense.

It would also compel prosecutors to bring charges on evidence that may establish probable cause, but not necessarily support a conviction. Likewise, continued investigation helps the prosecutor decide whether an apparently culpable defendant in fact acted with sufficient criminal culpability to justify prosecution. By satisfying herself that the charges are warranted, the prosecutor does not deviate from "fundamental conceptions of justice" as required by the Due Process Clause, but rather enforces them. "[T]o prosecute a defendant following investigative delay does not deprive him of due process, even if his defense might have been somewhat prejudiced by the lapse of time." Here, the Government's (P) delay was caused by its efforts to identify others who may have participated in the offenses. Such a delay is not fundamentally unfair. Reversed.

Analysis:

A successful due process challenge to preindictment delay requires an examination of the prosecutor's subjective motives. Because of the extreme deference afforded prosecutorial discretion, it is often found that a prosecutor has reasonable law enforcement justifications for any delay, even if he or she was subjectively acting in bad faith. This is especially true when the evidence demonstrates that a crime was committed, but doesn't definitively establish a suspect's guilt. In such circumstances, delay to discover the true offender will likely be found reasonable.

■ CASE VOCABULARY

DUE PROCESS: The conduct of legal proceedings according to established rules and principles for the protection and enforcement of private rights, including notice and the right to a fair hearing before a tribunal with the power to decide the case.

INDICTMENT: The formal written accusation of a crime, made by a grand jury and presented to a court for prosecution against the accused person.

Williams v. Florida

(*Convicted Robber*) v. (*Prosecuting State*)
399 U.S. 78, 90 S. Ct. 1893, 26 L. Ed. 2d 446 (1970)

A DEFENDANT MUST GIVE NOTICE OF AN ALIBI DEFENSE

■ **INSTANT FACTS** Prior to his trial for robbery, Williams (D) objected to the requirement that he provide notice of his intention to claim an alibi and furnish details regarding the alibi.

■ **BLACK LETTER RULE** The Fifth Amendment privilege against self-incrimination is not violated by a requirement that a defendant provide notice of an alibi defense and disclose his alibi witnesses to the prosecution prior to trial.

■ PROCEDURAL BASIS

Certiorari to review the defendant's conviction.

■ FACTS

Prior to his trial for robbery in Florida, Williams (D) filed a motion for a protective order, seeking to be excused from the requirements of Rule 1.200 of the Florida Rules of Criminal Procedure requiring a defendant, on written demand from the prosecuting attorney, to give notice in advance of trial of his intention to claim an alibi and to furnish information as to the place he claims to have been and the names and addresses of the alibi witnesses he intends to use. Williams openly declared his intent to claim an alibi, but objected to the further disclosure requirements on the ground that the rule "compels the Defendant in a criminal case to be a witness against himself" in violation of his Fifth and Fourteenth Amendment rights. The motion for a protective order was denied.

■ ISSUE

Did application of the Florida notice-of-alibi rule deprive Williams of due process or a fair trial or otherwise compel him to be a witness against himself?

■ DECISION AND RATIONALE

(White, J.) No. The notice-of-alibi rule is a form of limited pretrial discovery whereby the defendant must disclose to the prosecution the evidence on which he intends to rely at trial. In exchange, the prosecution is obligated to disclose all evidence it intends to use to rebut the alibi. Because an alibi can be easily fabricated, liberal discovery is necessary to enable the prosecution to properly carry its burden in the case. The rule does not compel the defendant to be a witness against himself in violation of the Fifth Amendment because the rule does not compel the defendant to testify at all. Instead, the rule requires that once the defendant chooses to testify as to an alibi defense, he must disclose the nature of the defense and all witnesses who may corroborate his alibi. While the choice between testifying and remaining silent may be difficult, the choice remains with the defendant.

■ CONCURRENCE

(Burger, C.J.) The notice-of-alibi rule not only places the prosecution on equal footing with the defendant concerning an alibi defense, but it also has the added benefit of allowing the prosecution to measure the merit of its case by the reliability of the alibi after collecting evidence and deposing witnesses. If the prosecution deems the defense credible, it may dismiss the charges and relieve the court of the burden of conducting a meaningless trial.

■ DISSENT

(Black, J.) Aside from practical considerations that distinguish the pretrial disclosure of an alibi from an in-trial disclosure, the Fifth Amendment clearly states that a criminal defendant cannot be required to give evidence, testimony, or any other assistance to the State to aid it in convicting him or her of a crime. The notice-of-alibi rule violates this constitutional provision by requiring a defendant to disclose information that the State can use against him. The defendant has a constitutional right to remain silent at all times, not just at trial, and cannot be compelled to provide evidence that will help the prosecution prove his guilt beyond a reasonable doubt.

Analysis:

The reciprocal duties of both the State and the defense under the Florida notice-of-alibi rule are key to the Court's conclusion in this case. Disclosure of an alibi defense and evidence relating thereto is not "compelled" testimony within the meaning of the Fifth and Fourteenth Amendments, even when it proves to be testimonial or incriminating.

■ CASE VOCABULARY

ALIBI: A defense based on the physical impossibility of a defendant's guilt by placing the defendant in a location other than the scene of the crime at the relevant time.

PROTECTIVE ORDER: Any order or decree of a court whose purpose is to protect a person from further harassment or abusive service of process or discovery.

SELF–INCRIMINATION: The act of indicating one's own involvement in a crime or exposing oneself to prosecution, especially by making a statement.

United States v. Bagley

(*Prosecuting Government*) v. (*Convicted Criminal*)

473 U.S. 667, 105 S. Ct. 3375, 87 L. Ed. 2d 481 (1985)

CONVICTIONS MAY BE OVERTURNED IF MATERIAL EVIDENCE WAS WITHHELD

■ **INSTANT FACTS** Bagley (D) was convicted of federal narcotics and firearms crimes. The prosecutor failed to disclose evidence that the defense may have used to impeach the Government's witnesses by showing bias or interest.

■ **BLACK LETTER RULE** The Government's failure to assist the defense by disclosing impeachment evidence that might have been helpful in conducting cross-examination of Government witnesses amounts to a constitutional violation only if it deprived the defendant of a fair trial, and a conviction must be reversed only if the evidence is material in the sense that its suppression undermines confidence in the outcome of the trial.

■ PROCEDURAL BASIS

Certiorari to review the court of appeals' decision reversing the district court's denial of the defendant's motion to vacate, set aside, or correct the sentence received for narcotics convictions.

■ FACTS

Bagley (D) was indicted on charges of violating federal narcotics and firearms statutes. Before trial, he filed a discovery motion requesting information on any deals, promises, or inducements made to Government witnesses in exchange for their testimony. The Government's discovery response did not disclose that any deals, promises, or inducements had been made to its two principal witnesses. The Government did produce signed affidavits by these witnesses recounting their undercover dealings with Bagley (D) and concluding with the statement that the affidavits were made without any threats or rewards or promises of reward. Bagley (B) waived his right to a jury trial and was tried before the District Court. He was found guilty of the narcotics charges but not guilty on the firearms charges.

Bagley (D) subsequently learned of the existence of the contracts signed by the principal Government witnesses during the undercover investigation, which stated that the Government would pay money to the witnesses commensurate with the information they furnished. Bagley (D) moved to vacate his sentence, alleging that the Government's failure to disclose these contracts, which he could have used to impeach the witnesses, violated his right to due process. The district court denied the motion, finding beyond a reasonable doubt that had the existence of the contracts been disclosed during trial, the disclosure would not have affected the outcome, because the principal Government witnesses' testimony was primarily devoted to the firearms charges on which the respondent was acquitted, and was exculpatory on the narcotics charges. The court of appeals reversed, holding that the Government's failure to disclose the requested impeachment evidence that Bagley (D) could have used to conduct an effective cross-examination of the Government's principal witnesses required automatic reversal. The court of appeals disagreed with the district court's conclusion that the nondisclosure was harmless beyond a reasonable doubt, noting that the witnesses' testimony was in fact inculpatory on the narcotics charges.

■ ISSUE

Was the evidence relating to any deals, promises, or inducements of the witnesses that the Government failed to disclose in discovery "material" in the sense that it would require a reconsideration of Bagley's (D) conviction?

■ DECISION AND RATIONALE

(Blackmun, J.) Yes. "[T]he suppression by the prosecution of evidence favorable to an accused upon request violates due process where the evidence is material either to guilt or punishment." Evidence withheld by the Government is "material" only if there is a reasonable probability that, had the evidence been disclosed, the result of the proceeding would have been different.

The standard of materiality of evidence, discovered after trial, that was useful to the defense and known but not disclosed by the prosecution falls into three situations. First, when the prosecution knowingly uses perjured testimony or knowingly fails to disclose that testimony used to convict the defendant was false, the conviction is fundamentally unfair and must be set aside if there is a reasonable likelihood that the testimony could have affected the outcome. Second, even when the defendant fails to request pretrial discovery and the prosecution fails to disclose evidence favorable to the defense, the nondisclosure is per se fundamentally unfair and is not subject to a harmless-error analysis. Finally, when the defense makes a specific request and the prosecution fails to disclose the requested evidence, the nondisclosure is "seldom, if ever, excusable." These three standards have been harmonized by one rule, requiring "that a new trial must be granted when evidence is not introduced because of the incompetence of counsel only if there is a reasonable probability that, but for counsel's unprofessional errors, the result of the proceeding would have been different."

Here, there is a significant likelihood that the Government's (P) response to the discovery motion misled the defense to believe that the witnesses could not be impeached. The judgment of the court of appeals must be reversed and the case remanded for a determination as to whether there was a reasonable probability, that, had the inducements offered by the Government to its two principal witnesses been disclosed to the defense, the result of the trial would have been different. Reversed and remanded.

■ CONCURRENCE

(White, J.) Bagley (D) is not entitled to have his conviction overturned unless he can show that the evidence withheld by the Government (P) was "material." Evidence is material only if there is a reasonable probability that, had the evidence been disclosed to the defense, the result of the proceeding would have been different. However, because the standard for materiality is flexible, there is no need to discuss the specificity required of the defendant's discovery motion to satisfy the standard.

■ DISSENT

(Marshall, J.) When the Government withholds evidence that might impeach the prosecution's only witnesses, that failure to disclose cannot be deemed harmless error. Because of the secrecy of jury deliberations, there is no meaningful way of determining which piece of evidence may create a reasonable doubt in the minds of the jurors. The disclosure of all material evidence to the defendant is at the heart of a fair trial. Similarly, the prosecutor, under the dual duty to advocate for conviction and pursue truth and justice, must not only zealously advocate the State's position, but must also ensure that the defendant's constitutional rights are protected through full disclosure of all material evidence. Any rule that treats nondisclosure as harmless error threatens this pursuit of justice and must not be endorsed. When the government fails to disclose material evidence, the conviction should be set aside automatically.

Analysis:

The "*Brady* Rule," derived from a 1963 Supreme Court ruling, set the standard for what prosecutors must do to help a defendant. It requires prosecutors to turn over to defendants any evidence that might help prove them innocent or show the biases and criminal records of witnesses against them. To guard against discovery violations, some federal prosecutors, as recently as fifteen years ago, opened all of their files on a case to the defendant's attorney. Over the past decade, however, prosecutors have intentionally withheld discovery evidence in hundreds of cases, but only in extreme cases have verdicts been overturned.

■ CASE VOCABULARY

EXCULPATORY EVIDENCE: Evidence that clears or tends to clear an accused person from alleged guilt.

HARMLESS ERROR: An error that does not affect a party's substantive rights or the case's outcome.

Pennsylvania v. Ritchie

(Prosecuting Authority) v. *(Convicted Defendant)*
480 U.S. 39, 107 S. Ct. 989, 94 L. Ed. 2d 40 (1987)

STATUTORY PRIVILEGES YIELD TO THE DEFENDANT'S RIGHT TO EXCULPATORY EVIDENCE

■ **INSTANT FACTS** Ritchie (D) was convicted after his request to review the State's (D) investigative file was denied.

■ **BLACK LETTER RULE** The nondisclosure of even privileged records violates due process and threatens fundamental fairness in the trial process.

■ PROCEDURAL BASIS

Certiorari to review a decision of the Pennsylvania Supreme Court remanding the case.

■ FACTS

Ritchie's (D) thirteen-year-old daughter reported that Ritchie (D) had continuously sexually assaulted her over the previous four years. After an investigation by a state agency, Ritchie (D) was charged with rape, involuntary deviate sexual intercourse, incest, and corruption of a minor. During pretrial discovery, Ritchie (D) served the Government (P) with a subpoena requesting access to all agency records relating to the charges as well as an earlier investigation of child abuse, arguing that the records may reveal favorable witnesses and other exculpatory evidence. Although a state statute declared the records privileged, an exception permitted disclosure pursuant to an order from a court of competent jurisdiction. The court refused to order the disclosure. At trial, defense counsel cross-examined the daughter at length, but Ritchie (D) was convicted. On appeal, the Pennsylvania Superior Court held that the denial of the disclosure violated Ritchie's (D) constitutional rights by depriving him meaningful cross-examination based on information potentially contained in the records. The matter was remanded to the trial court to determine whether the nondisclosure constituted harmless error. The State (P) appealed to the Pennsylvania Supreme Court, which affirmed the remand, holding that Ritchie (D) was entitled to review the State's (P) entire file for useful evidence.

■ ISSUE

Does the State's (D) nondisclosure of potentially material, but privileged, records violate the defendant's constitutional rights?

■ DECISION AND RATIONALE

(Powell, J.) Yes. The Sixth Amendment's Confrontation Clause entitles a defendant the right to effectively confront witnesses against him. The Pennsylvania Supreme Court construed Court precedent to mean that a statutory privilege must yield to a defendant's pretrial need for protected information that might be used at trial to impeach a witness' testimony. The Confrontation Clause, however, confers a *trial* right and does not encompass a pretrial claim for information that may assist in cross-examination at trial. Because the defendant had the opportunity to cross-examine the witness, the failure to order the pretrial disclosure of the State's (P) records does not violate the Confrontation Clause. Neither does the nondisclosure violate the Sixth Amendment's guarantee of compulsory process. The Compulsory

Process Clause does not include the right to have the State's assistance in discovering potentially useful evidence.

Instead, the Due Process Clause governs this issue to ensure fundamental fairness in the trial process. To ensure fairness, the State (P) must disclose evidence that is both favorable to the defendant and material to his guilt or innocence. Because disclosure is excepted from the statutory privilege by court order, the materiality of the records must be determined to assess whether disclosure is required. However, the agency records have not been disclosed to the defense nor seen by the prosecution to appropriately determine whether they are material. Upon remand, the defendant is not entitled to a full review of the agency records to discover any potentially useful evidence, but rather the records shall be inspected *in camera* to protect the State's interest in the confidentiality of the records and satisfy the defendant's need for disclosure. Affirmed in part, reversed in part, and remanded.

■ CONCURRENCE IN PART

(Blackmun, J.) While the nondisclosure violates the defendant's due process rights, it also violates the Confrontation Clause. There can be no distinction for Confrontation Clause purposes between the opportunity to cross-examine a witness and an opportunity to *effectively* cross-examine a witness. A state may not give the defendant an opportunity to cross-examine while withholding the information necessary to make it meaningful. To do so would leave the right of confrontation empty.

■ DISSENT

(Brennan, J.) By depriving the defendant access to material information crucial to prepare for cross-examination, the State (D) violated the Confrontation Clause. The use of a due process analysis does not remedy this violation in every case, for the information must be material to find a due process violation. This determination, however, is made by a trial judge, not defense counsel. But, only defense counsel is in a position to determine the effectiveness of the information against the Government's case. The Confrontation Clause operates independently of the Due Process Clause.

Analysis:

The Court's resort to a due process analysis is interesting. While the Confrontation Clause and Compulsory Process Clause provide specific protections to criminal defendants, the Court pays them cursory attention and falls back to the over-arching theme of fundamental fairness in the trial process. One may reasonably surmise, however, that the right to cross-examination and the right to compulsory process, as well as the right to trial by jury, right to counsel, and many other enumerated constitutional rights, stem from the over-arching theme of fundamental fairness. From this perspective, the Due Process Clause could be invoked for any alleged constitutional violation affecting a defendant's trial-related rights.

■ CASE VOCABULARY

COMPULSORY PROCESS CLAUSE: The clause of the Sixth Amendment to the U.S. Constitution giving criminal defendants the subpoena power for obtaining witnesses in their favor.

CONFRONTATION CLAUSE: The Sixth Amendment provision guaranteeing a criminal defendant's right to directly confront an accusing witness and to cross-examine that witness.

DUE PROCESS: The conduct of legal proceedings according to established rules and principles for the protection and enforcement of private rights, including notice and the right to a fair hearing before a tribunal with the power to decide the case.

IN CAMERA: In the judge's private chambers.

Bordenkircher v. Hayes

(*Prison Superintendent*) v. (*Repeat Offender*)
434 U.S. 357, 98 S. Ct. 663, 54 L. Ed. 2d 604 (1978)

A DEFENDANT MAY BE REINDICTED ON MORE SERIOUS CHARGES IF HE REFUSES TO PLEAD GUILTY TO A LESSER OFFENSE

■ **INSTANT FACTS** A state prosecutor carried out a threat to reindict Hayes (D) under the state's Habitual Criminal Act if Hayes (D) did not plead guilty to the offense with which he was originally charged.

■ **BLACK LETTER RULE** It is not a vindictive exercise of a prosecutor's discretion, and therefore not a violation of due process, to carry out a threat to reindict a defendant on more serious charges if the defendant does not plead guilty to the original offense charged.

■ PROCEDURAL BASIS

Certiorari to review a decision of the Sixth Circuit Court of Appeals reversing the district court's dismissal of the defendant's habeas corpus petition.

■ FACTS

After being indicted on a charge of uttering a false instrument, Hayes (D) was told by the prosecutor that if he didn't plead guilty to that charge the prosecutor would reindict Hayes (D) under the state's Habitual Criminal Act and, if convicted, he would be sentenced to life in prison. Hayes (D) did not plead guilty and the prosecutor reindicted him on the more serious charge. Hayes (D) was found guilty and, as required by the Act, sentenced to life in prison. After the Kentucky Court of Appeals affirmed the sentence, Hayes (D) petitioned the federal court for a writ of habeas corpus. The federal court denied the writ, but the Sixth Circuit Court of Appeals reversed, holding that the prosecutor's conduct was a vindictive exercise of the prosecutor's discretion.

■ ISSUE

Is it a vindictive exercise of the prosecutor's discretion and a violation of the Due Process Clause to carry out a threat made during plea negotiations to reindict a criminal defendant on more serious charges if the defendant does not plead guilty to the offense with which he or she was originally charged?

■ DECISION AND RATIONALE

(Stewart, J.) No. A prosecutor does not vindictively exercise his or her discretion, and therefore does not violate due process, by carrying out a threat to reindict a defendant on more serious charges if the defendant does not plead guilty to the originally charged offense. Hayes (D) was fully informed of the terms of the plea offer and understood that he risked being reindicted under the Habitual Criminal Act if he did not plead guilty. As a practical matter, the case was no different than if Hayes (D) had initially been indicted as a recidivist and the prosecutor had offered to drop that charge as part of a plea agreement. While it is a violation of the Due Process Clause to punish a person for legally attacking a conviction, there is no such element of punishment or retaliation in plea bargaining so long as the defendant is free to accept or reject the prosecution's offer. Reversed.

■ DISSENT

(Blackmun, J.) It was a vindictive exercise of the prosecutor's discretion, and, therefore, violative of the Due Process Clause, to reindict Hayes (D) under the Habitual Criminal Act because the sole reason for the new indictment was to discourage Hayes (D) from exercising his right to a trial.

■ DISSENT

(Powell, J.) Given that Hayes's (D) two prior felony convictions did not result in any imprisonment and the third charge involved less than $100, the prosecutor was not justified in seeking a reindictment under the Habitual Criminal Act when a conviction would result in Hayes (D) receiving a mandatory sentence of life in prison. The prosecutor's actions denied Hayes (D) due process because the admitted purpose was to discourage Hayes (D) from exercising his constitutional rights by threatening him with a potential penalty that was extreme considering Hayes's (D) criminal history.

Analysis:

There is a distinction between reindicting a convicted misdemeanant on a felony charge after the defendant invoked an appellate remedy and carrying out a threat to reindict a defendant on more serious charges if the defendant does not plead guilty to the original charge. The former action violates due process because it is retaliation against the defendant for legally attacking a conviction while the latter does not violate due process because there is no such element of punishment or retaliation so long as the defendant is free to accept or reject the prosecution's offer.

■ CASE VOCABULARY

DUE PROCESS: The constitutional guarantee of notice and the opportunity to be heard and to defend in an orderly proceeding adapted to the nature of case; the guarantee of due process requires that every person have the protection of a day in court and the benefit of general law.

RECIDIVIST: Habitual criminal; a criminal repeater.

Santobello v. New York

(*Criminal Defendant*) v. (*Prosecuting State*)

404 U.S. 257, 92 S. Ct. 495, 30 L. Ed. 2d 427 (1971)

PROSECUTORS MUST KEEP THEIR PROMISES TO GUILTY–PLEADING DEFENDANTS

■ **INSTANT FACTS** After Santobello (D) pleaded guilty to a lesser-included offense as part of a plea agreement whereby a prosecutor agreed to dismiss the more serious charge and not make a recommendation as to the sentence, a different prosecutor appeared at the sentencing hearing and recommended that Santobello (D) receive the maximum prison sentence.

■ **BLACK LETTER RULE** When a plea of guilty has been entered in consideration of a promise made by a prosecutor, the prosecutor must fulfill that promise.

■ PROCEDURAL BASIS

Certiorari to review a decision of a state appellate court affirming the defendant's conviction.

■ FACTS

Santobello (D) agreed to plead guilty to a lesser-included offense in exchange for the prosecutor's promises that he would dismiss the more serious charge and that he would not make a recommendation at the sentencing hearing. At the sentencing hearing, the original prosecutor was replaced by a new prosecutor who recommended that Santobello (D) receive the maximum prison sentence, which the judge imposed. Santobello (D) sought to withdraw his guilty plea, but his request was denied. His conviction was affirmed on appeal.

■ ISSUE

Is the prosecutor's office bound by a promise not to make a sentencing recommendation when that promise was the consideration for a plea of guilty?

■ DECISION AND RATIONALE

(Burger, C.J.) Yes. Plea agreements presuppose a fairness in securing the agreement between the defendant and the prosecutor. When a promise or agreement of the prosecutor is the inducement for the defendant to plead guilty, that promise must be fulfilled. Here, the state failed to keep a commitment concerning a sentencing recommendation on the defendant's guilty plea, so the case must be remanded to the state court to decide whether the circumstances require only that there be specific performance of the agreement on the guilty plea, or whether the circumstances require that the petitioner be granted the opportunity to withdraw his plea of guilty. Vacated and remanded.

■ CONCURRENCE

(Douglas, J.) When a prosecutor fails to follow through with a plea bargain, the sentence must be vacated and the state court must decide, in light of the circumstances of each case, whether due process requires (1) that there be specific performance of the plea bargain or (2) that the defendant be given the option to go to trial on the original charges.

■ CONCURRENCE IN PART

(Marshall, J.) Because the constitutional waiver of the right to trial accompanying a guilty plea is conditioned on the prosecutor's agreement, a defendant must be allowed to rescind that waiver when the prosecutor does not carry out his or her end of the bargain.

Analysis:

The disposition of charges pursuant to plea agreements plays an essential part in the efficiency of judicial administration. However, the value of plea agreements presupposes fairness in the securing the agreement. Consequently, if a defendant enters a plea of guilty in reliance on a promise or agreement by the prosecutor, the prosecutor must fulfill that promise or agreement.

■ CASE VOCABULARY

PLEA BARGAIN: A negotiated agreement between a prosecutor and a criminal defendant whereby the defendant pleads guilty to a lesser offense or to one of multiple charges in exchange for some concession by the prosecutor, usually a more lenient sentence or a dismissal of the other charges.

Mabry v. Johnson

(*Prison Official*) v. (*Criminal Defendant*)
467 U.S. 504, 104 S. Ct. 2543, 81 L. Ed. 2d 437 (1984)

A SUBSEQUENT PLEA MAY BE VOLUNTARY EVEN IF THE PROSECUTOR REFUSED TO HONOR AN EARLIER PLEA AGREEMENT

■ **INSTANT FACTS** Johnson (D) agreed to a less favorable plea after the prosecutor refused to honor an initial plea bargain that Johnson (D) had accepted.

■ **BLACK LETTER RULE** A voluntary and intelligent plea of guilty made by an accused person, who has been advised by competent counsel, may not be collaterally attacked.

■ PROCEDURAL BASIS

Certiorari to review a decision of a federal court of appeals reversing the defendant's sentence.

■ FACTS

Johnson (D) was convicted of burglary, assault, and murder, but the Arkansas Supreme Court set aside the murder conviction. As a result, Johnson (D) began serving concurrent twenty-one-and twelve-year sentences for burglary and assault. During the retrial of the murder charges, the prosecutor proposed to recommend a concurrent twenty-one-year sentence to the judge if Johnson (D) would plead guilty to a charge of accessory to felony murder. When Johnson (D) accepted the plea bargain the next day, however, the prosecutor claimed the offer was a mistake and that the recommendation would be a twenty-one-year consecutive sentence in exchange for the guilty plea. Johnson (D) declined the offer and went to trial. After a mistrial was declared, the prosecutor made a second offer, which Johnson (D) accepted, and Johnson (D) was sentenced to another twenty-one-year sentence to be served consecutively. On habeas review, a federal court of appeals reversed the conviction, holding that the defendant's acceptance of the plea proposal prevented the prosecutor from withdrawing it.

■ ISSUE

Does a defendant's acceptance of a prosecutor's proposed plea bargain create a constitutional right to specific enforcement of the bargain?

■ DECISION AND RATIONALE

(Stevens, J.) No. "[A] voluntary and intelligent plea of guilty made by an accused person, who has been advised by competent counsel, may not be collaterally attacked." The validity of a plea is called into question only when its voluntariness may be in debate. Here, Johnson (D) freely pleaded guilty knowing that the prosecutor would recommend a consecutive sentence. His inability to enforce the prosecutor's earlier mistaken offer has no constitutional significance, for it does not affect the voluntariness of his acceptance of the second plea. Johnson (D) was not denied a liberty interest in a fundamentally unfair way. Reversed.

Analysis:

The Court's focus in this case is confusingly on the validity of the second plea rather than the appropriateness of the initial plea. The Court determined that the conviction was not fundamentally unfair because Johnson (D) fully knew the consequences of the second plea at the time of his acceptance. If Johnson (D) had not pleaded guilty and instead was convicted and sentenced to a consecutive sentence after trial, would the Court's reasoning apply? In such circumstances, one may argue that the prosecutor's refusal to honor the initial plea bargain is fundamentally unfair, for the element of voluntariness is lacking.

■ CASE VOCABULARY

CONCURRENT SENTENCE: Two or more sentences of jail time to be served simultaneously. For example, it a defendant receives concurrent sentences of 5 years and 15 years, the total amount of jail time is 15 years.

CONSECUTIVE SENTENCE: Two or more sentences of jail time to be served in sequence. For example, if a defendant receives consecutive sentences of 20 years and 5 years, the total amount of jail time is 25 years.

SPECIFIC PERFORMANCE: A court-ordered remedy that requires precise fulfillment of a legal or contractual obligation when monetary damages are inappropriate or inadequate, as when the sale of real estate or a rare article is involved.

United States v. Benchimol

(*Prosecuting Authority*) v. (*Juvenile Defendant*)

471 U.S. 453, 105 S. Ct. 2103, 85 L. Ed. 2d 462 (1985)

THE PROSECUTOR NEED NOT RECOMMEND AN AGREED–UPON SENTENCE WITH ENTHUSIASM

■ **INSTANT FACTS** Benchimol (D) was sentenced to juvenile treatment after the Government (D) merely concurred with the defendant's recommended probation sentence rather than affirmatively recommending such a sentence under a plea agreement.

■ **BLACK LETTER RULE** Each party must comply with the precise terms of a plea agreement.

■ PROCEDURAL BASIS

Certiorari to review a decision of a federal court of appeals reversing the defendant's sentence.

■ FACTS

Benchimol (D) pleaded guilty to mail fraud in exchange for the Government's (P) recommendation of probation conditioned on restitution. The court disregarded the recommendation and sentenced Benchimol (D) to six years of juvenile treatment and supervision. He moved to withdraw his plea or vacate the sentence, claiming the Government (P) did not comply with the plea bargain. The court denied the motion. On appeal, the court of appeals reversed because the Government (P) did not in fact recommend probation to the court, but merely concurred in the defendant's counsel's recommendation.

■ ISSUE

Must the Government (P) explain the reasons underlying a sentencing recommendation to comply with a plea bargain?

■ DECISION AND RATIONALE

(Per curiam.) No. Under Rule 11(e) of the Federal Rules of Criminal Procedure, the Government (P) may agree to recommend a particular sentence or to not oppose a defendant's recommended sentence as part of a plea bargain. The rule, however, does not define the degree of enthusiasm with which the Government (P) must act. The Government (P) may, as part of the plea bargain, agree to explain to the court its reasoning for its recommendation, but the evidence here does not suggest it made such an agreement. The court of appeals erred in implying such an agreement. Reversed.

■ CONCURRENCE

(Stevens, J.) If the defendant wished to object to the Government's (P) actions, he should have done so at the time of sentencing or on direct appeal.

■ DISSENT

(Brennan, J.) "The Court today continues its unsettling practice of summarily reversing decisions rendered in favor of criminal defendants, based not on broad principle but on idiosyncratic facts and without full briefing or oral argument."

Analysis:

The Court's decision in this case was an attempt to short-circuit potential debate over not what the prosecution did, but with what degree of enthusiasm it acted. With so many Court decisions pondering about the effect of criminal procedure on effective law enforcement and prosecution techniques, would litigation over a prosecutor's enthusiasm serve any useful purpose?

United States v. Ruiz

(*Prosecuting Government*) v. (*Drug Possessor*)
536 U.S. 622, 122 S. Ct. 2450, 153 L. Ed. 2d 586 (2002)

THE PROSECUTION NEED NOT DISCLOSE IMPEACHMENT INFORMATION BEFORE A DEFENDANT PLEADS GUILTY

■ **INSTANT FACTS** Ruiz (D) declined a plea offer that would have given her a lighter sentence in exchange for a waiver of the right to receive impeaching information about witnesses.

■ **BLACK LETTER RULE** The Constitution does not require disclosure of impeaching information about witness testimony before entry of a guilty plea.

■ PROCEDURAL BASIS

Certiorari to review a decision of the Ninth Circuit Court of Appeals vacating the defendant's sentence.

■ FACTS

Ruiz (D) was offered a "fast track" plea bargain on charges of drug possession. The bargain required Ruiz (D) to waive indictment, trial, and appeal. In return, the U.S. (P) would recommend a downward departure from the sentence that would otherwise have been imposed on Ruiz (D). The agreement also contained a statement that the U.S. (P) had turned over any known information regarding the factual innocence of Ruiz (D) and acknowledged the continuing duty of the U.S. (P) to provide such information, but required Ruiz (D) to waive her right to receive impeachment information regarding any informants or witnesses, as well as the right to receive information supporting any affirmative defense. Ruiz (D) refused to agree to the waiver of the right to receive impeachment information, and the plea bargain was withdrawn. Ruiz (D) pleaded guilty without an agreement, and her request for a downward departure in her sentence was denied. The Ninth Circuit vacated her sentence, holding that the obligation to provide impeachment information is the same prior to a plea agreement as it is at trial. The court held that the right to receive this information could not be waived.

■ ISSUE

Do the Fifth and Sixth Amendments require federal prosecutors, before entering into a binding plea agreement with a criminal defendant, to disclose impeachment information relating to any informants or other witnesses?

■ DECISION AND RATIONALE

(Breyer, J.) No. The Constitution does not require disclosure of impeaching information before entry of a guilty plea. Impeachment information relates to the fairness of a trial, not whether a plea was voluntary. "[T]he law ordinarily considers a waiver knowing, intelligent, and sufficiently aware if the defendant fully understands the nature of the right and how it would likely apply *in general* in the circumstances—even though the defendant may not know the *specific detailed* consequences of invoking it." The usefulness of impeachment information is not critical information required to ensure a fair trial because it largely depends upon the defendant's independent knowledge of the prosecution's case. Likewise, a guilty plea may be accepted despite a defendant's misapprehension about various factors, including the penalties, the quality of the prosecution's case, and constitutional flaws in the prosecution. Nor do due process considerations support any right to receive impeachment information. Whether a process is constitutionally required involves a consideration of the nature of the private interest at stake, the value of the additional safeguard, and the adverse impact of the requirement on the interests of the government. As stated, the value of any pre-plea right to impeachment information would depend on the independent knowledge of the defendant about the government's case, and, in any event, even without such a safeguard the government is still required to provide information about the factual innocence of the defendant. At the same time, a constitutional obligation could interfere with the government's interest in securing factually justified plea agreements and disrupt ongoing criminal investigations. Reversed.

■ CONCURRENCE

(Thomas, J.) The majority's focus on the degree of help impeachment information will have at the plea stage is unnecessary, for the only constitutional protection is that of a fair trial. The fairness of trial is not a concern at the plea stage.

Analysis:

Ruiz (D) was arrested in possession of marijuana, so impeachment information may have related more to possible constitutional challenges to her arrest and search than to the accuracy of trial testimony. The line between "factual innocence" information and "impeachment" information may not always be as clear as the Court suggests. For example, suppose the government's case is built on the testimony of witnesses, rather than on physical evidence. Does information that casts doubt on the reliability of those witnesses or their testimony fall on the "impeachment" or "factual innocence" side of the line?

■ CASE VOCABULARY

DOWNWARD DEPARTURE: In the federal sentencing guidelines, a court's imposition of a sentence more lenient than the standard guidelines propose, as when the court concludes that a criminal's history is less serious than it appears.

SENTENCING GUIDELINES: A set of standards for determining the punishment that a convicted criminal should receive, based on the nature of the crime and the offender's criminal history. The federal government and several states have adopted sentencing guidelines in an effort to make judicial sentencing more consistent.

Boykin v. Alabama

(Robber) v. *(Prosecuting Authority)*

395 U.S. 238, 89 S. Ct. 1709, 23 L. Ed. 2d 274 (1969)

THE DEFENDANT'S SILENCE DOES NOT EQUAL A WAIVER OF RIGHTS

■ **INSTANT FACTS** Boykin (D) was sentenced to death by a jury after pleading guilty to five robbery indictments.

■ **BLACK LETTER RULE** A waiver of constitutional rights through a guilty plea must be voluntarily and willingly made.

■ PROCEDURAL BASIS

Certiorari to review the defendant's conviction and sentence.

■ FACTS

Boykin (D) was arrested and indicted for five counts of common-law robbery, an offense punishable by death under state law. Because Boykin (D) was indigent, counsel was appointed. At his arraignment, Boykin (D) pleaded guilty to all five indictments. A sentencing trial was thereafter conducted to hear evidence on the character of the offenses. After trial, the jury sentenced Boykin (D) to death on all five indictments. At no time did the petitioner speak to the court or the jury, nor did the judge question Boykin (D) concerning his plea.

■ ISSUE

Did Boykin (D) voluntarily and knowingly waive his constitutional right to a trial by jury by his guilty plea?

■ DECISION AND RATIONALE

(Douglas, J.) No. A guilty plea involves the loss of several constitutional rights, including the right to trial by jury, the right against self-incrimination, and the right to confront one's accusers. Before a court accepts a guilty plea as a waiver of those rights, it must be satisfied that the waiver is voluntary and willful. A waiver may not be presumed from the defendant's silence. Instead, it must be established on the record in order to evaluate the validity of the waiver on review and to avoid collateral attacks. Because the court failed to question Boykin (D) concerning his plea, his constitutional rights may not be presumed to have been waived. Reversed.

■ DISSENT

(Harlan, J.) A guilty plea has been upheld as voluntary under the Fifth Amendment Due Process Clause when collateral proceedings have so indicated despite the silence of the record. The Fourteenth Amendment Due Process Clause can provide no different protections than the Fifth Amendment. Boykin's (D) relief, if any, should be through collateral proceedings challenging the voluntariness of his waiver, not through a rigid rule concerning the silence of the record.

Analysis:

The Court places the burden of ensuring the plea is voluntary on the trial court rather than on defendant's counsel. While ideally perhaps both should maintain such a duty, when a defendant is represented by counsel and no ineffective assistance of counsel has been claimed, why shouldn't a voluntary waiver be presumed from the waiver itself?

■ CASE VOCABULARY

PLEA: An accused person's formal response of "guilty," "not guilty," or "no contest" to a criminal charge.

WAIVER: The voluntary relinquishment or abandonment—express or implied—of a legal right or advantage.

Henderson v. Morgan

(*Prison Superintendent*) v. (*Developmentally Disabled Convicted Criminal*)
426 U.S. 637, 96 S. Ct. 2253, 49 L. Ed. 2d 108 (1976)

DEFENDANTS MUST HAVE FULL NOTICE OF THEIR CHARGES BEFORE PLEADING GUILTY

■ **INSTANT FACTS** Morgan (D), who was developmentally disabled, pleaded guilty to a charge of second-degree murder without being informed by either his attorney or the court that the intent to cause the death of his victim was an element of the offense.

■ **BLACK LETTER RULE** A guilty plea is not knowingly and intelligently made, and therefore not voluntarily made, if the defendant did not receive adequate notice of the offense to which he pleaded guilty.

■ PROCEDURAL BASIS

Certiorari to review a decision of a federal court of appeals affirming a decision vacating the defendant's conviction.

■ FACTS

Morgan (D), who was mentally challenged, was charged with first-degree murder. His attorneys advised Morgan (D) to accept the prosecution's offer to plead guilty to the lesser charge of second-degree murder. His attorneys did not, however, advise Morgan (D) that the intent to cause the death of his victim was an element of that offense. When Morgan (D) appeared in court to enter his guilty plea, there was no discussion of the elements of the offense of second-degree murder, no indication that the nature of the offense had ever been discussed with him, and no reference of any kind to the requirement of intent to cause the death of his victim. Morgan (D) petitioned for a writ of habeas corpus in federal court, and the court granted the writ because the failure to explain the elements of the pleaded offense rendered the plea involuntary. The court of appeals affirmed.

■ ISSUE

Is a guilty plea voluntarily made if the defendant was not informed of the elements of the offense?

■ DECISION AND RATIONALE

(Stevens, J.) No. A plea of guilty cannot support a judgment of guilt unless it is voluntary in a constitutional sense. A plea cannot be voluntary in the sense that it constituted an intelligent admission of an offense unless the defendant received real notice of the true nature of the charge against him or her. Morgan's (D) plea of guilty to second-degree murder was not voluntary because he was not advised by either his attorneys or the court that intent to cause the death of his victim was an element of the offense to which he pleaded guilty. His plea was not voluntary and cannot support his conviction. Affirmed.

■ CONCURRENCE

(White, J.) The defendant's guilt has been established neither by a jury beyond a reasonable doubt nor by his own admission. The "long-accepted principle that a guilty plea must provide a trustworthy basis for believing that the defendant is in fact guilty'' applies here, prohibiting a conviction on the basis of a plea in which the defendant was not informed of the elements of the offense.

■ DISSENT

(Rehnquist, J.) Because the plea was voluntarily made with full knowledge of the consequences of the plea, the only question is whether the defendant was properly advised of the substance of the plea. The defendant was initially charged with first-degree murder, and the intent elements of that offense were made known to the defendant. The evidence in this case clearly suggests that the intent to kill is not seriously in dispute. The defendant was advised by experienced counsel whose tactical decision to avoid the more severe penalties of first-degree murder should suffice.

Analysis:

Even when, as here, there is overwhelming evidence of guilt and the defendant otherwise received competent counsel, a plea of guilty is only voluntary when it constitutes an intelligent admission that the accused committed the offense. If, as in *Morgan*, a defendant is not made aware of the elements of the offense to which he is pleading, the plea is not knowingly and intelligently made and, therefore, not voluntary. Although the Court noted that Morgan (D) was mentally challenged, it did not articulate a different standard for adequate notice in such cases, but it did note that the defendant's mental capacity could have impacted his ability to form the requisite intent and thus the error was not harmless.

■ CASE VOCABULARY

COLLATERAL ATTACK: An attack made by or in an action or proceeding that has an independent purpose other than impeaching or overturning the judgment.

KNOWINGLY: With knowledge; consciously, intelligently; willfully; intentionally.

VOLUNTARY: Unconstrained by interference, not impelled by another's influence; done by design or intention; proceeding from the free will and unrestrained will of the person.

North Carolina v. Alford

(*Prosecuting State*) v. (*Confessed Murderer*)
400 U.S. 25, 91 S. Ct. 160, 27 L. Ed. 2d 162 (1970)

A DEFENDANT CAN PLEAD GUILTY AND STILL PROFESS HIS INNOCENCE

■ **INSTANT FACTS** Alford (D) maintained that he was innocent of the murder for which he had been charged, but, after considering the evidence against him, pleaded guilty to second-degree murder to avoid being sentenced to death if he was found guilty of the charge.

■ **BLACK LETTER RULE** A court may not enter a judgment upon a plea of guilty unless it is satisfied that there is a factual basis for the plea.

■ PROCEDURAL BASIS

Certiorari to review a decision of a federal court of appeals reversing a denial of a writ of habeas corpus.

■ FACTS

Alford (D) was indicted for first-degree murder, a crime punishable by death upon conviction by a jury or life imprisonment upon a guilty plea. Alford (D), after hearing the evidence against him, decided to plead guilty to a lesser charge of second-degree murder. At the time Alford (D) entered his plea, he maintained to the court that he was innocent of the charge. The judge accepted Alford's (D) plea and sentenced him to prison. Alford (D) argued in a federal habeas proceeding that, because he continued to maintain that he did not commit the murder, the judge should not have accepted his guilty plea. The court denied the writ of habeas corpus, but the court of appeals reversed, finding that the plea was involuntary and motivated by fear of the death penalty.

■ ISSUE

Should the court accept a plea of guilty when the defendant continues to profess his innocence at the time the plea is entered?

■ DECISION AND RATIONALE

(White, J.) Yes. Although a defendant professes innocence, a guilty plea may be accepted when there is a factual basis supporting the charge against the defendant. Here, though Alford's (D) plea included a disclaimer of guilt, the evidence demonstrates a sufficient factual basis to support the plea. The State's (P) evidence shows that Alford (D) took a gun from his house, stated his intention to kill the victim, and returned home declaring that he had killed the victim. An express admission of guilt is not a constitutional prerequisite to the imposition of a criminal penalty, and an individual accused of a crime may voluntarily, knowingly, and understandingly consent to the imposition of a prison sentence even if he is unwilling (or unable) to admit participation in the crime. There is also no "material difference between a plea that refuses to admit commission of the criminal act and a plea containing a protestation of innocence when . . . a defendant intelligently concludes that his interests require entry of a guilty plea and that the record before the judge contains strong evidence of actual guilt." Vacated and remanded.

■ DISSENT

(Brennan, J.) "[I]t is sufficient in my view to state that the facts set out in the majority opinion demonstrate that Alford was 'so gripped by fear of the death penalty' that his decision to plead guilty was not voluntary but was 'the product of duress as much so as choice reflecting physical constraint.' "

Analysis:

Ordinarily, a judgment of conviction based on a plea of guilty is justified by (1) the admission that the defendant committed the crime and (2) the consent that judgment be entered without a trial. When a guilty plea does not include an admission of guilt but rests on a protestation of innocence, state and lower courts are divided as to whether the plea can be accepted. The Court here noted that there was no constitutional distinction between (1) neither admitting nor denying charges in plea of *nolo contendere* and (2) expressly denying the charges. Thus, a plea of guilty does not need to include an express admission of guilt in order for the plea to be accepted and a criminal penalty imposed, as long as the evidence points to the defendant's guilt.

■ CASE VOCABULARY

ALFORD PLEA: A guilty plea that a defendant enters as part of a plea bargain, without actually admitting guilt.

NOLO CONTENDERE: "I will not contest it"; a plea in a criminal case that has a similar legal effect to pleading guilty; a type of plea that may be entered with leave of court to a criminal complaint or indictment by which the defendant neither admits nor denies the charges, though a fine or sentence may be imposed pursuant to it.

Duncan v. Louisiana

(*Convicted Assailant*) v. (*Prosecuting Government*)
391 U.S. 145, 88 S. Ct. 1444, 20 L. Ed. 2d 491 (1968)

THE FOURTEENTH AMENDMENT INCORPORATES THE SIXTH AMENDMENT RIGHT TO A JURY TRIAL

■ **INSTANT FACTS** Duncan (D) was denied his request for a jury trial on an assault charge because the Louisiana Constitution provided a right to jury trial only in felony cases.

■ **BLACK LETTER RULE** Under the Sixth Amendment, all criminal defendants have a constitutional right to trial by jury.

■ PROCEDURAL BASIS

Certiorari to review the defendant's conviction.

■ FACTS

Duncan (D) was charged with simple assault in Louisiana state court. Duncan (D) requested a jury trial, which was denied because the Louisiana Constitution provided for jury trials only in felony cases. Duncan (D) was convicted and sentenced to sixty days in a local prison and a fine.

■ ISSUE

Is the Sixth Amendment's right to trial by jury incorporated in the Fourteenth Amendment?

■ DECISION AND RATIONALE

(White, J.) Yes. The Sixth Amendment guarantees all criminal defendants the constitutional right to a jury trial. The right to a trial by jury has long been considered "fundamental to the American scheme of justice." In the years leading up to the drafting of the Constitution, trial by jury had been a prominent right in England and was carried forward to the state constitutions of the original thirteen colonies as a protection against oppression by the government. In light of this historical perspective, the right to trial by jury is afforded to all state court criminal defendants if such a right would be afforded in a federal court. Reversed.

■ CONCURRENCE

(Black, J.) Not only is the Sixth Amendment incorporated in the Fourteenth Amendment, but all provisions of the Bill of Rights are applicable to the states. The Fourteenth Amendment forbids a state from enacting or enforcing "any law which shall abridge the privileges and immunities of the citizens of the United States." The right to claim the protections afforded by the Bill of Rights is a fundamental privilege of American citizens. The dissent's view that the Due Process Clause provides no "permanent meaning" and is left to the subjective interpretation of the Court on a case-by-case basis strips the Fourteenth Amendment of the protections established to limit governmental power by empowering judges to selectively determine from time to time which protections remain implicit in the concept of ordered liberty.

■ CONCURRENCE

(Fortas, J.) While states are bound by the Sixth Amendment's right to a jury trial, the states need not follow federal procedures governing the operation of trial by jury. Federal notions of due process do not infringe upon the construction of that term by the states. Principles of federalism require that states be free to determine for themselves how due process can be achieved, because federal practices like unanimous verdicts and twelve-member juries, for example, should not be thrust upon the states as long as the states otherwise maintain practices furthering the fundamental fairness required by the Fourteenth Amendment.

■ DISSENT

(Harlan, J.) The majority's decision to incorporate the Sixth Amendment is without logical reason. If the goal of the Fourteenth Amendment is to achieve fundamental fairness in the judicial system, there is no justifiable reason to hold that the requirements of the Sixth Amendment are necessary in every case considered by a state court, as not every case presents such unfairness. The Court offers no reason to declare the rights afforded by the Sixth Amendment to be fundamental, while other rights in the Bill of Rights are not. While the Fourteenth Amendment was never intended to incorporate any of the rights afforded in the Bill of Rights, *total* incorporation would at least provide a logical reason to support the Court's conclusion. The concepts of due process and liberty are evolving principles, not confined to any specific rights or protections that may change through time as society progresses. The Due Process Clause requires only that criminal trials in the states be fundamentally fair, and trial by jury is not necessarily a requirement for fairness. Without evidence of unfairness in the trial below, due process has not been offended and the conviction should be sustained.

Analysis:

Justice Black's concurring opinion argues for "total incorporation" of the Bill of Rights by the Fourteenth Amendment. Under this approach, the Due Process Clause extends each right protected by the Bill of Rights to the states, but creates no other rights. Refusing to apply total incorporation, the majority employed "selective incorporation," the process of selecting those rights deemed fundamentally fair to the administration of justice. While the "total incorporation" approach never gained support in the Supreme Court, many of the rights espoused in the Bill of Rights have been selectively incorporated over time.

■ CASE VOCABULARY

INCORPORATION: The process of applying the provisions of the Bill of Rights to the states by interpreting the Fourteenth Amendment's Due Process Clause as encompassing those provisions.

JURY TRIAL: A trial in which the facts are determined by a jury, not by the judge.

Blanton v. City of North Las Vegas

(*Drunk Driver*) v. (*Prosecuting Government*)
489 U.S. 538, 109 S. Ct. 1289, 103 L. Ed. 2d 550 (1989)

DUI CHARGES UNDER NEVADA LAW DO NOT REQUIRE A JURY TRIAL

■ INSTANT FACTS The casebook excerpt includes no facts.

■ BLACK LETTER RULE The right to trial by jury attaches when a crime carries a maximum jail term of six months or more or the legislature otherwise classifies the offense as serious.

■ PROCEDURAL BASIS

Certiorari to review an undisclosed state court decision.

■ FACTS

The casebook excerpt includes no facts.

■ ISSUE

Is there a constitutional right to a trial by jury for persons charged with driving under the influence of alcohol under state law?

■ DECISION AND RATIONALE

(Marshall, J.) No. The Sixth Amendment does not require a trial by jury for petty crimes and offenses. A petty offense can objectively be determined by the severity of the maximum penalty authorized by the legislature. Particular attention is paid to the maximum period of incarceration, for probation and fines do not involve the loss of freedom that a prison term entails. Accordingly, the right to trial by jury always exists for crimes involving a maximum jail term of six months or more. For those charges authorizing a lesser jail sentence, a defendant is entitled to a trial by jury only by demonstrating that additional penalties, in conjunction with the jail sentence, indicate a legislative determination that the crime charged is a "serious" one. The state DUI law authorizes a maximum jail term of less than six months and involves insufficient additional penalties to merit a trial by jury.

Analysis:

Although the Supreme Court determined that the U.S. Constitution does not require a trial by jury for petty crimes and offenses for which the maximum sentence does not exceed six months, states often impose such a requirement. And although the U.S. Constitution mandates a trial by jury for serious crimes, the requirement is federal and merely prescribes minimum protections. States are free to provide more protection than the Constitutional minimum.

■ CASE VOCABULARY

PETTY OFFENSE: A minor or insignificant crime.

PROBATION: A court-imposed criminal sentence that, subject to stated conditions, releases a convicted person into the community instead of sending the criminal to jail or prison.

Burch v. Louisiana

(*Pornographer*) v. (*Prosecuting Authority*)
441 U.S. 130, 99 S. Ct. 1623, 60 L. Ed. 2d 96 (1979)

NONUNANIMOUS VERDICTS THREATEN THE RIGHT TO TRIAL BY JURY

■ **INSTANT FACTS** Burch (D) was convicted of a criminal offense by a five-to-one vote of a six-member jury.

■ **BLACK LETTER RULE** When a jury consists of six members, its verdict must be unanimous.

■ **PROCEDURAL BASIS**

Certiorari to review a decision of the Supreme Court of Louisiana affirming the defendant's conviction.

■ **FACTS**

Burch (D) was charged with the exhibition of obscene motion pictures. He was tried before a six-person jury, which voted five-to-one to convict him. Burch (D) was sentenced to two consecutive seven-month prison terms, which were suspended, and fined $1000. On appeal to the Supreme Court of Louisiana, Burch (D) claimed that conviction by a nonunanimous jury on nonpetty offenses violated the Sixth and Fourteenth Amendments. The court affirmed the conviction.

■ **ISSUE**

Does a conviction by a nonunanimous six-person jury in a state criminal trial for a nonpetty offense violate the right to trial by jury under the Sixth and Fourteenth Amendments?

■ **DECISION AND RATIONALE**

(Rehnquist, J.) Yes. Under the Louisiana Constitution and Code of Criminal Procedure, criminal cases in which the punishment that may be imposed exceeds a six-month jail term must be tried before a jury of six members, five of whom must concur to render a verdict. Although state law may provide for six-member juries in criminal cases, the five-member verdict provision cannot stand; unanimity is required to render a verdict. While unanimity may not necessarily be required from a twelve-member jury, when the jury size is reduced to six, fairness of the judicial process and preservation of the right to a jury trial require a unanimous verdict.

Analysis:

Due process in a state trial does not require a unanimous verdict by a twelve-person jury. Thus, in *Johnson v. Louisiana*, 406 U.S. 356 (1972), the Supreme Court approved provisions of Louisiana law sustaining a conviction for an offense punishable by hard labor in which nine of twelve empanelled jurors voted to convict. The Court reasoned that the three dissenting votes did not demonstrate that the prosecution failed to prove the defendant's guilt beyond a reasonable doubt.

■ CASE VOCABULARY

UNANIMOUS: Agreeing in opinion; being in complete accord.

Singer v. United States

(Mail Fraud Defendant) v. *(Prosecuting Government)*
380 U.S. 24, 85 S. Ct. 783, 13 L. Ed. 2d 630 (1965)

A CRIMINAL DEFENDANT DOES NOT HAVE A CONSTITUTIONAL RIGHT TO A BENCH TRIAL

■ **INSTANT FACTS** Singer (D) sought to waive his right to a jury trial, but the Government (D) would not consent.

■ **BLACK LETTER RULE** The Sixth Amendment does not give a defendant the absolute right to waive a jury trial.

■ PROCEDURAL BASIS

Certiorari to review the defendant's conviction.

■ FACTS

Singer (D) was charged with thirty counts of mail fraud. At trial, Singer (D) waived his right to a jury trial to shorten the trial. Although the court was willing to approve the waiver, the Government (P) refused to consent under Federal Rule of Criminal Procedure 23(a). Singer (D) was convicted on all but one of the counts.

■ ISSUE

Does a criminal defendant have the unconditional right to waive a jury trial?

■ DECISION AND RATIONALE

(Warren, C.J.) No. Federal Rule of Criminal Procedure 23(a) provides that a defendant may waive his right to a jury trial "in writing with the approval of the court and the consent of the government." While the Sixth Amendment provides the defendant the absolute right to have his criminal case tried to a jury, there is no historical precedent for an absolute right to waive that right and have a case tried by a judge. The Government (P) also has an interest in litigating its case before the appropriate forum and, while it may not demand a trial by a judge, it may insist on a trial by jury.

Analysis:

Like many constitutional rights, the right to trial by jury affords a criminal defendant protection from government oppression. Unlike other constitutional rights, however, the defendant does not have the absolute right to waive his right to a jury trial. When the criminal defendant has reason to believe that his chances of acquittal are better in the hands of the government than his peers, why should he be denied that decision? One may surmise that a rule requiring the government's consent to such a waiver places the defendant at greater risk of oppression than the bench trial itself.

■ CASE VOCABULARY

BENCH TRIAL: A trial before a judge without a jury. The judge decides questions of fact as well as questions of law.

WAIVER: The voluntary relinquishment or abandonment—express or implied—of a legal right or advantage.

Carter v. Jury Commission

(*African–American Citizen*) v. (*Governmental Body*)

396 U.S. 320, 90 S. Ct. 518, 24 L. Ed. 2d 549 (1970)

THE DISCRIMINATORY ENFORCEMENT OF A JURY–SELECTION STATUTE DOES NOT RENDER THE STATUTE UNCONSTITUTIONAL

■ **INSTANT FACTS** African–American citizens filed a class action lawsuit challenging the constitutionality of a state jury-selection statute systematically excluding blacks from jury service.

■ **BLACK LETTER RULE** The Constitution does not forbid states to prescribe relevant qualifications for their jurors.

■ PROCEDURAL BASIS

Certiorari to review a decision of a federal district court upholding the constitutionality of a state jury-selection statute.

■ FACTS

African–American citizens of Greene County, Alabama, filed a class action lawsuit challenging the constitutionality of a state jury-selection statute and the county's enforcement thereof. By statute, the Governor selected a three-member Jury Commission for each county to obtain the names of every eligible voter in the county. From the information the Jury Commission (P) prepared a jury roll of all qualified citizens who maintained "good character and sound judgment." The plaintiffs alleged that the system excluded black citizens from jury service and that the state statute was unconstitutional on its face. The district court determined that the county's enforcement of the statute departed from the statutory scheme by failing to fully include all eligible voters on the jury roll, especially rural blacks whose reputation was largely unknown to the Jury Commission (D). The result was a jury roll continuously including those who had served in prior years, who were primarily white. Black citizens were therefore largely unrepresented on county juries. The court, however, declined to enjoin the enforcement of the challenged state statute.

■ ISSUE

Is a state jury-selection statute prescribing juror qualifications unconstitutional because it results in racial discrimination as applied?

■ DECISION AND RATIONALE

(Stewart, J.) No. A statute requiring prospective jurors to maintain a good standing in the community is not unconstitutional merely because it vests discretion for such a determination in jury officials. "The Constitution does not forbid States to prescribe relevant qualifications for their jurors." Instead, the Constitution minimally requires that a jury comprise a fair cross-section of the community. Despite the apparent discrimination committed by the Jury Commission (P), the statute is not unconstitutional on its face. It does not mention race and is entirely capable of constitutional enforcement when done so appropriately.

Analysis:

While the Court reinforces the states' authority to establish qualifications for its jurors, states are clearly not free to establish them arbitrarily. Such exclusionary qualifications as prior felony convictions reasonably relate to the juror's ability to render an impartial verdict under the law. States may not, however, use discriminatory bases such as race, ethnicity, or gender as a disqualifying characteristic.

■ CASE VOCABULARY

FAIR-CROSS-SECTION REQUIREMENT: The principle that a person's right to an impartial jury, guaranteed by the Sixth Amendment, includes a requirement that the pool of potential jurors fairly represent the composition of the jurisdiction's population.

JURY: A group of persons selected according to the law and given the power to decide questions of fact and return a verdict in the case submitted to them.

Taylor v. Louisiana

(*Convicted Kidnapper*) v. (*Prosecuting State*)
419 U.S. 522, 95 S. Ct. 692, 42 L. Ed. 2d 690 (1975)

SYSTEMATIC EXCLUSION OF WOMEN FROM PETIT JURIES VIOLATES THE SIXTH AMENDMENT

■ **INSTANT FACTS** Taylor (D) was tried and convicted by an all-male jury because Louisiana law systematically excluded women from jury service.

■ **BLACK LETTER RULE** A petit jury must represent a fair cross-section of the community to ensure a defendant's right to trial by an impartial jury under the Sixth Amendment.

■ PROCEDURAL BASIS

Certiorari to review the defendant's conviction.

■ FACTS

The Louisiana Constitution and the Code of Criminal Procedure excluded women from jury service unless they previously declared their desire to participate.

■ ISSUE

Does the system of excluding women from jury service unless they previously file a written declaration of their desire to participate violate the Sixth and Fourteenth Amendments by denying defendants a jury consisting of a fair cross-section of the community?

■ DECISION AND RATIONALE

(White, J.) Yes. While the state jury-selection system impacts the rights of women, Taylor (D) does not lack standing to challenge a violation of his constitutional rights though he is not a member of the excluded class. The selection of a petit jury from a representative cross-section of the community is an essential element of the right to a trial by an impartial jury. The purpose of a jury is to expose the arbitrary power of the courts to the common-sense judgment of the community as a whole, which is destroyed if large segments of the population are systematically excluded from the jury pool. A jury selection procedure that systematically excludes women, who actually constitute a majority in the jurisdiction, violates the fair-cross-section rule essential to the Sixth Amendment. While the Court has held that a system excluding women from jury selection does not violate women's due process or equal protection rights because a rational basis for their exclusion was demonstrated, that issue is quite different from whether such a system violates the defendant's Sixth Amendment rights. A state may exempt individuals from jury duty on the basis of special hardship or incapacity, but it is untenable to conclude that all women, as a class, would suffer such hardship. A system that presumes that women fall under this exemption, without a case-by-case evaluation, does not result in a fair cross-section of the community. While the states are free to fashion the qualifications and exemptions applicable to jury selection in their courts, those requirements must be designed to ensure that jury panels represent a fair cross-section. The rule established by the Court does not, however, require that every jury consist of any particular composition. A jury resulting from a state procedure that does not systematically favor one section of the population over another meets the requirements of the Sixth Amendment. Reversed and remanded.

■ DISSENT

(Rehnquist, J.) The Court's decision provides no reason why the purpose of the jury system is undermined by the exclusion of one sex over the other. While women may offer perspectives distinct from those of their male counterparts, so too do doctors, lawyers, and other groups, whose exclusion has been endorsed by the majority. The Court offers no reason why the prophylactic purpose of the jury system is destroyed absent the female perspective.

Analysis:

The Court's decision does not go so far as to guarantee that a defendant's jury, or even the venire from which it is chosen, constitutes a fair cross-section of the community. Instead, the Court merely condemns the systematic exclusion of large, distinct groups, such as women, from the venire. While fifty-three percent of the jurisdiction's population eligible for jury service was female, the actual female representation on the venire may be much less. Indeed, the jury may continue to be predominantly male without violating the Sixth Amendment.

■ CASE VOCABULARY

JURY WHEEL: A physical device or electronic system used for storing and randomly selecting names of potential jurors.

PETIT JURY: A jury, usually consisting of six or twelve persons, summoned and empanelled in the trial of a specific case.

VENIRE: A panel of persons selected for jury duty and from among whom the jurors are to be chosen.

Turner v. Murray

(*Murderer*) v. (*Prison Official*)

476 U.S. 28, 106 S. Ct. 1683, 90 L. Ed. 2d 27 (1986)

POTENTIAL RACIAL PREJUDICE AMONG JURORS DOES NOT INVALIDATE A GUILTY VERDICT

■ **INSTANT FACTS** Turner (D) was convicted of murder by a jury after his request to question prospective jurors on racial prejudice was denied.

■ **BLACK LETTER RULE** A capital defendant accused of an interracial crime is entitled to have prospective jurors informed of the race of the victim and questioned on the issue of racial bias.

■ PROCEDURAL BASIS

Certiorari to review a decision of the Fourth Circuit Court of Appeals affirming the defendant's conviction.

■ FACTS

Turner (D) was a black man indicted for murder for shooting a white store proprietor during a robbery. During voir dire, Turner (D) was denied a request to question the prospective jurors on racial prejudice. The jury convicted Turner (D) and sentenced him to death. The Virginia Supreme Court upheld the sentence, ruling that Turner (D) received a fair trial. Turner (D) petitioned for a writ of habeas corpus, which was denied. The Fourth Circuit Court of Appeals affirmed.

■ ISSUE

Is a capital sentence constitutionally permissible in an interracial crime case when the defendant was not afforded an opportunity to question prospective jurors on the issue of racial prejudice?

■ DECISION AND RATIONALE

(White, J.) Yes. When the jury is charged with choosing the sentence for a capital crime, it must make an individualized judgment regarding the punishment the defendant deserves. The state statute requires the jury to consider the severity of the crime committed and the likelihood of future violent offenses and weigh it against any mitigating circumstances relevant to minimizing the sentence imposed. Because of the extreme discretion vested in the jury and the extreme consequences of capital sentencing, the potential of racial prejudice particularly threatens the judicial system and the defendant's rights. The judge must take all reasonable precautions to avoid the infusion of racial prejudice in the jury's verdict. Accordingly, "a capital defendant accused of an interracial crime is entitled to have prospective jurors informed of the race of the victim and questioned on the issue of racial bias." Because no such inquiry was permitted, the defendant's sentence must be vacated. On remand, however, the defendant is not entitled to a new trial on his guilt, but rather a new sentencing hearing must be held with protections against racial prejudice. Vacated in part and remanded.

■ CONCURRENCE IN PART

(Brennan, J.) A conviction tainted by racial bias violates the same values as a racially tainted death sentence. If a jury is racially motivated to sentence a defendant to death, certainly it is racially motivated to find him guilty of the capital crime. The requirement of an impartial jury applies as much to the trial itself as to the sentencing phase.

■ CONCURRENCE IN PART

(Marshall, J.) Whenever a case involves an interracial violent crime, the defendant should be allowed to inquire about potential racial bias regardless of the potential sentence. The risk of a racially motivated verdict outweighs the slight cost of the defendant's voir dire.

■ DISSENT

(Powell, J.) Capital sentencing, like criminal guilt, requires the State to prove the required elements beyond a reasonable doubt. These limitations on the prosecution are sufficient to safeguard a defendant from an inappropriate sentence, making the Court's per se rule inappropriate. There is no more reason to presume that a jury will unduly sentence a defendant to death than there is to presume a racially motivated guilty verdict.

Analysis:

The Court's tolerance of racial prejudice in determining a criminal defendant's guilt while abhorring it in capital sentencing is curious. In fact, if the underlying guilty verdict was racially tainted, any similar effect on the sentence is a secondary if not moot issue. It seems that the real issue here should be avoiding racial prejudice at each step of the proceedings, capital case or otherwise.

■ CASE VOCABULARY

CAPITAL OFFENSE: A crime for which the death penalty may be imposed.

DEATH PENALTY: A sentence imposing death as punishment for a serious crime.

DEATH SENTENCE: A sentence that imposes the death penalty.

VOIR DIRE: A preliminary examination of a prospective juror by a judge or lawyer to decide whether the prospect is qualified and suitable to serve on a jury.

Lockhart v. McCree

(Prison Official) v. *(Convicted Murderer)*

476 U.S. 162, 106 S. Ct. 1758, 90 L. Ed. 2d 137 (1986)

DEATH PENALTY OBJECTORS ARE NOT A CONSTITUTIONALLY DISTINCTIVE GROUP

■ **INSTANT FACTS** McCree (D) was convicted of murder after the trial court removed for cause those jurors opposed to the death penalty.

■ **BLACK LETTER RULE** The Constitution does not prohibit the removal for cause in a capital case of prospective jurors opposed to the death penalty and unable to impose it if necessary.

■ PROCEDURAL BASIS

Certiorari to review a decision of the Eighth Circuit Court of Appeals affirming a decision reversing the defendant's conviction.

■ FACTS

McCree (D) was charged with capital murder. During voir dire, the judge removed for cause eight prospective jurors who stated they could not under any circumstances impose the death penalty. The jury convicted McCree (D), but sentenced him to life imprisonment rather than death. His conviction was affirmed on appeal. McCree (D) then petitioned for a writ of habeas corpus, claiming that the removal of the prospective jurors violated his right to an impartial jury including a cross-section of the community. The district court considered several social studies on the effect on a jury of the exclusion of prospective jurors opposed to the death penalty, ultimately ruling that any resulting jury was more prone to convict and therefore did not comprise a fair cross-section of the community. The Eighth Circuit Court of Appeals affirmed.

■ ISSUE

Does the Constitution prohibit the removal for cause, prior to the guilt phase of a bifurcated capital trial, of prospective jurors whose opposition to the death penalty is so strong that it would prevent or substantially impair the performance of their duties as jurors at the sentencing phase of the trial?

■ DECISION AND RATIONALE

(Rehnquist, J.) No. Even if the social studies considered by the district court are sufficient to demonstrate that a jury empanelled after those objecting to the death penalty are removed is more prone to conviction, the Constitution does not prohibit the removal of such prospective jurors. The fair-cross-section requirement has never been applied to a petit jury, as opposed to jury panels or venires, to require a representative petit jury. Even if it were to apply, the fair-cross-section requirement strikes at the systematic exclusion of distinctive groups in the community, such as by race, ethnicity, or gender. Those sharing common beliefs that prevent them from carrying out their duties as jurors do not form a distinctive group. One's attitude, unlike race or gender, is an attribute particularly within his or her control, and may be suppressed in order to discharge his or her functions if desired. It is not one's opposition to the death penalty that requires removal, but the admission that the opposition precludes the prospective juror from upholding the law. Furthermore, the prospective juror is not entirely excluded from jury service by his removal, for he remains eligible to serve in future noncapital cases. Nor can it be presumed that by empanelling a jury without opposition to the death penalty, the jury was predisposed to conviction.

■ DISSENT

(Marshall, J.) Prospective jurors not opposed to issuing the death penalty possess different perspectives than those who are. They are more likely to hold a defendant's silence against him and generally hold pro-prosecution biases. The result is a fundamentally unfair and partial jury. While it is likely proper to exclude those who cannot impose the death sentence from the penalty phase, there is no reason to exclude them from the guilt phase. There is no justifiable reason why a capital defendant cannot be tried before one jury and sentenced by another.

Analysis:

Were the death penalty a mandatory sentence for capital crimes, the exclusion of jurors incapable of imposing the death penalty would certainly seem necessary at the guilt phase. Faced with sentencing the defendant to death or setting him free despite his guilt, such objectors would presumably choose the latter. Even with discretionary sentencing, however, a juror at the guilt phase who objects to the death penalty may be predisposed to acquittal if he or she knows that the ultimate sentence will be determined by other jurors who are not fundamentally unwilling to impose death. Arguably, it is the objecting juror's participation in the sentencing phase that ensures impartiality at the guilt phase.

■ CASE VOCABULARY

BIFURCATED TRIAL: A trial that is divided into two stages, such as for guilt and punishment or for liability and damages.

Batson v. Kentucky

(*Convicted Burglar*) v. (*Prosecuting State*)
476 U.S. 79, 106 S. Ct. 1712, 90 L. Ed. 2d 69 (1986)

THE USE OF PEREMPTORY CHALLENGES TO STRIKE ALL BLACK JURORS IS *PRIMA FACIE* DISCRIMINATORY

■ **INSTANT FACTS** Batson (D), a black man, was convicted of burglary by an all-white jury after the government used its peremptory challenges to remove all black persons from the jury.

■ **BLACK LETTER RULE** The exercise of a peremptory challenge by the State to strike black jurors from a black defendant's jury violates the Equal Protection Clause of the Fourteenth Amendment absent a race-neutral explanation for the challenge.

■ PROCEDURAL BASIS

Certiorari to review the defendant's conviction.

■ FACTS

Batson (D), a black man, was indicted in Kentucky state court for second-degree burglary and receipt of stolen goods. During jury selection, the prosecutor used his peremptory challenges to strike all four black persons on the venire, resulting in an all-white jury. Defense counsel moved to discharge the jury because the striking of the black potential jurors violated the fair-cross-section requirements of the Sixth Amendment and the Equal Protection Clause of the Fourteenth Amendment. The judge denied the motion, ruling that the parties were free to exercise their peremptory challenges for any reason they chose and that the fair-cross-section requirement applied only to the selection of the venire, not selection of the jury. Batson (D) was convicted. The Supreme Court of Kentucky affirmed.

■ ISSUE

Does a race-based exercise of peremptory challenges violate the Equal Protection Clause of the Fourteenth Amendment?

■ DECISION AND RATIONALE

(Powell, J.) Yes. Although a peremptory challenge generally may be exercised for any reason, the Equal Protection Clause prohibits a prosecutor from excluding a black juror based on a presumption that he will be unable to impartially serve on the jury on account of his race. Although the Court's jurisprudence has held that a peremptory challenge is subject to the constraints of the Equal Protection Clause, many courts have construed this directive as requiring a defendant to prove that the prosecutor has engaged in the systematic exclusion of black jurors over an extended period of time. The result of this near impossible burden has left prosecutors' peremptory challenges virtually immune from constitutional scrutiny. To establish a prima facie constitutional violation, however, a defendant need not look at the past conduct of the prosecutor, but only demonstrate the systematic use of peremptory challenges on the basis of race in the defendant's trial. The defendant must establish that he is a member of a cognizable racial group, that the prosecutor has used peremptory challenges to exclude members of his racial group from the venire, and that the facts and other circumstances create an inference that the prosecutor has used peremptory challenges on the basis of race. The trial judge supervising voir dire must consider the circumstances presented, including any pattern of striking black jurors and any statements or questions posed by the prosecution, to determine whether a prima facie case of purposeful discrimination is established. The burden then shifts to the State to establish a race-neutral explanation for each peremptory challenge. While the prosecutor's explanation need not rise to the level of a challenge for cause, it must not rest on the assumption that blacks as a group will be partial because they share the same race as the defendant. The court must determine whether the proffered explanation sufficiently rebuts the presumption of discrimination. While the peremptory challenge serves an important function in our system of justice, the limitations placed upon them are necessary to further equal protection and the interests of justice. Here, the defendant made a timely objection to the prosecutor's peremptory challenges and the court failed to require a race-neutral explanation for the challenges. The matter is remanded for such a determination and, if no proper explanation is offered, the conviction must be reversed. Remanded.

■ CONCURRENCE

(Marshall, J.) The Court's decision takes a giant leap toward eliminating racial discrimination through the use of peremptory challenges, but the only certain cure is the elimination of peremptory challenges completely. The Court's holding addresses only those flagrant demonstrations of racial discrimination that rise to a prima facie case, allowing more subtle discrimination to survive. Even for those flagrant violations, a prosecutor can easily fashion a race-neutral explanation for the challenge, such as the juror's demeanor during voir dire, without the court's exacting scrutiny. The inherent dangers of race-based peremptory challenges can only be eradicated through the abolition of the peremptory challenge.

■ DISSENT

(Burger, C.J.) The peremptory challenge is essential to ensuring that an impartial jury is selected. The Court's opinion ignores the fact that individuals develop predispositions through common human experiences, including one's race, and that peremptory challenges account for these experiences without the necessity of expressing the truth prevalent in most common stereotypes. Further, while the Court professes to limit its decision to prosecutors only, it can hardly be expected that defendants are free to use race-based peremptory challenges while their adversaries are not. Defendants are left then with choosing a jury composed of members feared by the defendant, correctly or not, to be biased and partial against his position. The result threatens the confidence in the entire jury system.

■ DISSENT

(Rehnquist, J.) The use of a peremptory challenge to exclude a black juror from the jury of a black defendant does not violate the Equal Protection Clause so long as a peremptory challenge can be used to exclude a white juror from a white defendant's jury, Hispanics from a Hispanic defendant's jury, and Asians from an Asian defendant's jury. The peremptory challenge is race neutral, not singling out a specific race for discriminatory treatment. While it may be exercised based on stereotype in a given case, it does not violate the Equal Protection Clause if applied to all races.

Analysis:

While *Batson* marks an important development in criminal procedure, its holding is limited. Notice that in order to challenge race-based peremptory challenges, the Court requires the jury to share the same race as the defendant. If the State uses peremptory challenges to strike black jurors in a murder trial of a white defendant accused of killing a white man because the victim had beaten and tortured blacks, the literal language of *Batson* would not apply. The Court has since relaxed the standing requirement to permit a challenge in this circumstance, though a prima facie showing of purposeful discrimination becomes more difficult.

■ CASE VOCABULARY

BATSON CHALLENGE: A defendant's objection that the prosecution has used peremptory challenges to exclude potential jurors on the basis of race, ethnicity, or gender.

PEREMPTORY CHALLENGE: One of a party's limited number of challenges that need not be supported by any reason, although a party may not use such a challenge in a way that discriminates on the basis of race, ethnicity, or gender.

PRIMA FACIE: Sufficient to establish a fact or raise a presumption unless disproved or rebutted.

STRIKE: The removal of a prospective juror from the jury panel.

J.E.B. v. Alabama ex rel. T.B.

(*Putative Father*) v. (*State Seeking Child Support*)
511 U.S. 127, 114 S. Ct. 1419, 128 L. Ed. 2d 89 (1994)

GENDER–BASED PEREMPTORY CHALLENGES VIOLATE THE FOURTEENTH AMENDMENT

■ **INSTANT FACTS** In a paternity and child support suit brought by the State of Alabama (P) against J.E.B. (D), the alleged father, the State (P) exercised its peremptory challenges to remove male jurors from the jury panel, leaving an all-female jury.

■ **BLACK LETTER RULE** Peremptory challenges on the basis of gender violate the Equal Protection Clause.

■ PROCEDURAL BASIS

Certiorari to review a decision of an Alabama appeals court affirming a trial court judgment.

■ FACTS

The State of Alabama (P) filed suit for paternity and child support against J.E.B. (D) on behalf of the mother of a minor child. Twelve of the thirty-six potential jurors were male. After two male jurors were removed for cause, the State (P) exercised peremptory challenges to remove nine additional male jurors, believing a predominantly female jury would better sympathize with its case. Consequently, an all-female jury was selected. After J.E.B. (D) objected to the State's (P) peremptory challenges as unconstitutional under the Equal Protection Clause, the jury was empanelled. The jury found against J.E.B. (D) and judgment was entered. J.E.B. (D) renewed his objection that the jury was improperly selected, which objection was again overruled by the court.

■ ISSUE

Does the Equal Protection Clause of the Fourteenth Amendment forbid intentional discrimination on the basis of gender in the exercise of a peremptory challenge?

■ DECISION AND RATIONALE

(Blackmun, J.) Yes. In *Batson v. Kentucky*, the Supreme Court ruled that the use of peremptory challenges to exclude jurors on the basis of race violates the Equal Protection Clause. Under the same reasoning, peremptory challenges may not be exercised on the basis of gender or other classifications, such as race, that are subject to heightened constitutional scrutiny. "Intentional discrimination by state actors violates the Equal Protection Clause, particularly where, as here, the discrimination serves to ratify and perpetuate invidious, archaic, and overbroad stereotypes about the relative abilities of men and women." While the exclusion of women from jury service has not persisted to the same extent as the exclusion of African–Americans, both groups share a long history of exclusion from juries. Because of such historical treatment, any gender-based classification must be subjected to heightened scrutiny under the Equal Protection Clause, requiring an "exceedingly persuasive justification" that substantially furthers an important government objective to pass constitutional muster.

The State (P) argues that men are more likely to be sympathetic to J.E.B.'s (D) position, while women would sympathize more with the arguments it sets forth. Such a justification is not exceedingly persuasive, as it plays on "the very stereotype the law condemns." Gender-based discrimination relying on stereotype or bias ratifies and reinforces the prejudicial views of the relative abilities of men and women, threatening the confidence the public places on the judicial system. The Equal Protection Clause prohibits discrimination in jury selection on the basis of gender, or on the assumption that an individual will be biased in a particular case for no reason other than the person's gender. Reversed and remanded.

■ CONCURRENCE

(O'Connor, J.) The effect of the Court's decision may be to erode away the peremptory challenge. Since a peremptory challenge generally permits a party to remove a juror for any reason without justification, the Court's holding opens the door to objections to such challenges, requiring the party asserting the challenge to justify his or her reasons. To preserve the peremptory challenge as a vital tool, the decision should be limited to the government's use of a peremptory challenge, as opposed to criminal defendants' and private civil litigants', since individual litigants are not state actors and the Equal Protection Clause pertains only to state actors.

■ DISSENT

(Rehnquist, C.J.) The fundamental differences between men and women, both biologically and by experience, create different views and perspectives that cannot be passed off as mere stereotyping. Measured against the heightened scrutiny standard, gender-based peremptory challenges substantially further an important government objective, passing equal protection muster.

■ DISSENT

(Scalia, J.) The practice of peremptory challenges by gender does not violate the Equal Protection Clause because the adversarial system is even handed. Also, the majority's decision destroys the essential characteristic of a peremptory challenge by requiring reasons for its use when challenged, and damages the justice system by creating additional litigation to challenge jury-selection processes.

Analysis:

Just as *Batson v. Kentucky*, 476 U.S. 79 (1986), prohibits race-based peremptory challenges and this case prohibits gender-based peremptory challenges, the Supreme Court has similarly prohibited peremptory challenges based on other prejudices or biases, such as ethnic origin, but not because a juror was unable to speak the English language. Other classifications, such as religion, have been prohibited under various state laws, though not addressed by the Supreme Court.

CHAPTER SIXTEEN

Fair Trial/Free Press

Murphy v. Florida

Instant Facts: Murphy (D) was convicted of breaking and entering by a jury who had learned of his prior criminal reputation through the media.

Black Letter Rule: In order for media coverage to infect a trial with unfairness, a juror's preconceived notions of guilt or innocence must prevent him or her from rendering a verdict based on the evidence presented in court.

Gentile v. State Bar of Nevada

Instant Facts: Gentile (D) was sanctioned for violating a state ethical rule prohibiting public comment that is substantially likely to materially prejudice a court proceeding.

Black Letter Rule: Pure political speech is protected under the First Amendment absent a legitimate government interest in its suppression.

Chandler v. Florida

Instant Facts: Chandler (D) and others were convicted after the jury was potentially exposed to televised footage of trial testimony.

Black Letter Rule: Publicized trials are not per se a due process violation.

Press-Enterprise Co. v. Superior Court [Press Enterprise II]

Instant Facts: Press–Enterprise Co. (D) sought access to a closed preliminary hearing transcript.

Black Letter Rule: The qualified First Amendment right of access to criminal proceedings applies to preliminary hearings that function similarly to criminal trials.

Murphy v. Florida

(*Robber*) v. (*Prosecuting Government*)

421 U.S. 794, 95 S. Ct. 2031, 44 L. Ed. 2d 589 (1975)

JURORS NEED NOT BE UNAWARE OF MEDIA COVERAGE TO BE IMPARTIAL

■ **INSTANT FACTS** Murphy (D) was convicted of breaking and entering by a jury who had learned of his prior criminal reputation through the media.

■ **BLACK LETTER RULE** In order for media coverage to infect a trial with unfairness, a juror's preconceived notions of guilt or innocence must prevent him or her from rendering a verdict based on the evidence presented in court.

■ PROCEDURAL BASIS

Certiorari to review the defendant's conviction.

■ FACTS

Murphy (D) was charged with breaking and entering, while armed, with intent to commit robbery and of assault with intent to commit robbery. Murphy's (D) arrest received considerable media attention because he had been in the news before regarding his role in the theft of the Star of India sapphire from a New York museum. He had also been the subject of news stories concerning several other indictments and convictions. When eight jurors and two alternates were chosen to serve on the jury for his breaking and entering trial, Murphy (D) moved to dismiss them because they were aware of his museum heist and a murder. The motions were denied, as was a motion for change of venue. In protest, the defendant did not testify or cross-examine the State's (P) witnesses. He was convicted. After the conviction was affirmed on appeal, he sought habeas corpus relief in federal court, which was denied.

■ ISSUE

Is a defendant denied a fair trial because members of the jury had learned from a news account about a prior felony conviction or certain facts about the crime with which he was charged?

■ DECISION AND RATIONALE

(Marshall, J.) No. The right to a fair trial requires an impartial jury, but jurors need not be totally ignorant of the facts and issues involved. In order to establish that media coverage has infected a trial with unfairness, a defendant must show that a juror's preconceived notions of guilt or innocence prevent him or her from rendering a verdict based on the evidence presented in court. Here, there has been no such showing. Some of the jurors have a bare recollection of the news accounts, but none sufficiently indicated that he or she would be unable to set aside the recollection in considering the evidence. Even if juror impartiality is not questioned, a trial may be unfair when the media coverage leaves the courtroom atmosphere inflammatory. But such was not the case here, as the media reports were published months before the trial. Affirmed.

■ CONCURRENCE

(Burger, C.J.) Although the trial judge did not do enough to insulate the prospective jurors from the media attention the case garnered or to limit discussion among the prospective jurors, the trial, being in a state court, did not violate the Fourteenth Amendment.

■ DISSENT

(Brennan, J.) The trial court did not sufficiently prohibit discussion of the case or prevent pretrial publicity from infecting the trial. One juror openly admitted to a predisposition to convict the defendant, establishing his bias. Others stated some prejudice against the defendant because of his prior criminal activities. These prejudices were compounded by the court's failure to instruct the prospective jurors not to discuss the media reports among themselves. As a consequence, the publicity given to the defendant's prior acts resulted in an unfair trial. The motion for a change of venue should have been granted.

Analysis:

Actual prejudice can often be very difficult to prove. For instance, a well-intentioned juror who is aware of facts presented by the media may very well state during voir dire that she is capable of separating the media sensationalism from the evidence at trial. Yet, such a juror may fail to consider the potential for subconscious recollection of the media accounts while hearing and considering the evidence. Especially in long, complicated criminal trials, the juror may honestly believe certain evidence was presented in court, when in fact it came from the media. Likewise, media accounts may create the possibility of inferences being drawn from the evidence that otherwise would not have been.

■ CASE VOCABULARY

IMPARTIAL JURY: A jury that has no opinion about the case at the start of the trial and that bases its verdict on competent legal evidence.

Gentile v. State Bar of Nevada

(*Lawyer*) v. (*Ethics Committee*)

501 U.S. 1030, 111 S. Ct. 2720, 115 L. Ed. 2d 888 (1991)

PUBLIC COMMENTS ABOUT A CASE BY DEFENSE COUNSEL MAY BE PROTECTED BY THE FIRST AMENDMENT

■ **INSTANT FACTS** Gentile (D) was sanctioned for violating a state ethical rule prohibiting public comment that is substantially likely to materially prejudice a court proceeding.

■ **BLACK LETTER RULE** Pure political speech is protected under the First Amendment absent a legitimate government interest in its suppression.

■ PROCEDURAL BASIS

Certiorari to review a decision of the Nevada Supreme Court affirming the defendant's ethical sanction.

■ FACTS

Drugs and money stored by the Las Vegas police in a safety deposit box at Western Vault for an undercover operation were stolen. The police investigation focused on Sanders, the owner of Western Vault. After a year of media coverage, other owners of safety deposit boxes reported various other items as stolen. Sanders was indicted on theft charges and arraigned. Sanders's attorney, Gentile (D), held a press conference on the day of arraignment, claiming that the evidence against two police officers was stronger than against his client and accusing law enforcement officers of a cover-up. Gentile (D) also questioned the credibility of others reporting items missing, characterizing them as known drug dealers and money launderers who intimidated the police into falsely accusing Sanders. In response to a question, Gentile (D) claimed that an officer could be witnessed on videotape suffering from cocaine use, but he declined to elaborate further because of ethical obligations. The prosecution responded in the media that the indictment was legitimate and the officers had been exonerated. Six months later, Sanders was acquitted by a jury. The State Bar of Nevada (P) then brought ethics charges against Gentile (D) and concluded that he had violated an ethical rule barring extrajudicial statements that would reasonably be expected to be disseminated in the media if the lawyer knew or should have known that the statements were substantially likely to materially prejudice the criminal proceedings. The State Bar (P) issued a private reprimand, and the state supreme court affirmed.

■ ISSUE

Does a state ethics rule banning pure political speech critical of the government and its officials violate the First Amendment?

■ DECISION AND RATIONALE

(Kennedy, J.) Yes. Public opinion is the most powerful check on the potential abuse of power by government officials. The American criminal justice system bestows upon law enforcement and elected prosecutors tremendous authority, and public opinion on the manner in which that authority is exercised is vitally important. Viewed narrowly, the state ethics rule is capable of serving legitimate government interests and is capable of application without infringing upon First Amendment rights. However, on the record, the evidence is insufficient to demonstrate that Gentile (D) knew or should have known that his remarks created a "substantial likelihood of material prejudice." Gentile (D) explained that his comments were motivated out of fear that unless the weakness of the prosecution's evidence was exposed, persistent media accounts of the case would poison potential jurors with allegedly erroneous information released by the prosecutor and the police. He had no intention to attempt to sway potential jurors to form an opinion in advance of trial, but rather sought to ensure that potential jurors did not form opinions based solely on the prosecutor's released information. Furthermore, Gentile (D) sought by his comments to protect his client's interests as any lawyer must. His client's health and financial wellbeing had adversely suffered from the negative publicity, and Gentile (D) used the public forum to minimize the public scrutiny his client had endured. He carefully researched the ethics rule and calculated, based on prior precedent, that his statements, which were made six months before a jury would be selected, would not prejudice potential jurors' views of the case given the size of the jury pool and the length of time before trial. Also, the content of Gentile's (D) statements had been previously published and the remainder was available to any journalist willing to investigate. Finally, during voir dire, not one of the empanelled jurors admitted any recollection of Gentile (D) or his statements, indicating no actual prejudice.

In any event, the rule as applied is void for vagueness because of its safe harbor provision reasonably misleading Gentile (D) into believing his statement was permissible. The rule's safe harbor provision allows a lawyer to state the general nature of his client's defense without elaboration, even if he knew or reasonably should have known of the substantial likelihood of material prejudice. Gentile (D) testified that he believed his statements were permitted under the rule. Vague restrictions on speech are capable of discriminatory enforcement and are strictly prohibited. Thus, at times, political speech by attorneys is required to protect their clients' interests and uncover abuses of power. While such statements may not be made to frustrate the criminal process, they are otherwise protected under the First Amendment.

■ CONCURRENCE

(O'Connor, J.) Lawyers engaged in the practice of law do not enjoy the same First Amendment rights as those afforded to the press. As officers of the court, they do not lose their First Amendment rights, but are subject to less demanding standards than otherwise applicable. The "substantial likelihood of material prejudice" standard is an appropriate balance between the First Amendment and disciplinary regulation.

Separate Opinion (Dissent in part): (Rehnquist, C.J.) The courts have long regulated the legal profession and exercised the authority to discipline lawyers in violation of ethical regulations. Of vital importance to the states is the limitation of the dissemination of trial information to the public through the media. Over time, a majority of states have adopted ethical rules prohibiting extrajudicial comments by lawyers when the comments present a "reasonable likelihood of prejudice" on the court proceeding. The Court has held, however, that before a person could be punished for exercising his First Amendment freedom of speech, the State must make a higher showing of clear and present danger of prejudice.

Because of the unique potential for extrajudicial comments by an attorney to affect a defendant's right to a fair trial, the attorney may be properly disciplined upon a lesser showing than applicable to the press. Lawyers are officers of the court and owe a fiduciary duty to uphold the fair administration of justice. They have special access to court information not generally available to the press. The "substantial likelihood of material prejudice" standard is an appropriate balance between ethical regulation and an attorney's First Amendment rights.

Any restraint on free speech in an ethical rule is narrowly tailored to meet the legitimate government interests of avoiding a taint on the outcome of a trial and prejudicing potential jurors. The Nevada rule illustrates a non-exhaustive list of statements that are likely to cause material prejudice. It does not apply to all extrajudicial statements and applies only to lawyers involved in a pending case. The rule is not unconstitutional on its face. Neither is the rule void for vagueness. The rule clearly sets forth the conduct that is prohibited and, despite the safe harbor provision, no reasonable person would believe the comments made were general statements of his client's defense. Gentile (D) received fair notice of the rule's requirements, and he violated it. Although the statements were made well in advance of trial, they were calculated to be delivered at a time where public interest in the case was at its highest and the influence on potential jurors was maximized. Indeed, Gentile (D) called the press conference for the admitted purpose of influencing the venire.

Gentile (D) was admitted to practice law in Nevada, and the Court should not disturb the State's enforcement of its ethical requirements merely because the First Amendment is involved. The decision of the Nevada Supreme Court should be affirmed.

Analysis:

If the extrajudicial comment rule is designed to meet its narrowly tailored objective of ensuring a fair trial, is there any real need for the rule at all? After all, if extrajudicial comments tainted an individual juror, surely he would be stricken for cause during voir dire, relieving the risk of an unfair trial. The rule appears in this sense to be one more of judicial convenience than attorney discipline, for eliminating the potential for juror prejudice expedites jury selection and reduces the number of motions for a change of venue.

■ CASE VOCABULARY

FIRST AMENDMENT: The constitutional amendment, ratified with the Bill of Rights or 1791, guaranteeing the freedoms of speech, religion, press, assembly, and petition.

Chandler v. Florida

(*Burglar*) v. (*Prosecuting Government*)

449 U.S. 560, 101 S. Ct. 802, 66 L. Ed. 2d 740 (1981)

ACTUAL PREJUDICE IS REQUIRED TO ESTABLISH A DUE PROCESS VIOLATION BASED ON CAMERAS IN THE COURTROOM

■ **INSTANT FACTS** Chandler (D) and others were convicted after the jury was potentially exposed to televised footage of trial testimony.

■ **BLACK LETTER RULE** Publicized trials are not per se a due process violation.

■ PROCEDURAL BASIS

Certiorari to review the defendant's conviction.

■ FACTS

In 1975, the Florida Supreme Court approved a one-year pilot program allowing electronic media coverage of judicial proceedings. After the pilot program expired, the court collected various reports and surveys of the program and concluded that televised proceedings promoted public confidence in the judicial process. As a result, the court revised Canon 3A(7) to permit electronic media and still photography in appellate and trial proceedings, subject to judicial discretion. In 1977, Chandler (D) was charged with conspiracy to commit burglary, grand larceny, and possession of burglary tools. Because Chandler (D) and his coconspirators were Miami Beach police officers who were overheard planning a robbery over their police radios, the incident received considerable media attention. Counsel moved to declare Rule 3A(7) unconstitutional, but the court denied relief. During voir dire, each juror stated that he or she would be able to be fair and impartial despite the presence of cameras in the courtroom. After the jury was empanelled, the judge declined to order sequestration, but ordered the jurors to avoid watching the local news. The judge did not, however, order the jurors to avoid watching footage of testimony presented at trial. Throughout the trial, cameras were present only during the prosecution's case in chief and closing arguments, resulting in less than three minutes of televised footage. After the evidence had been presented, the jury convicted the defendants. The defendants moved for a new trial, arguing the television coverage made the trial unfair and partial, but no evidence of prejudice was offered.

■ ISSUE

May a state allow radio, television, and still photographic coverage of a criminal trial for public broadcast, notwithstanding the defendant's objection?

■ DECISION AND RATIONALE

(Burger, C.J.) Yes. In *Estes v. Texas*, 381 U.S. 532 (1965), a plurality of the Court considered the limitations due process places on televising criminal trials. Justice Harlan, writing for the plurality, acknowledged that the right to access to the courtroom includes no constitutional right to have live testimony recorded or broadcast. Justice Harlan further explained that in the "notorious" criminal case presented, "the considerations against allowing television in the courtroom so outweigh the countervailing factors advanced in its support as to require a holding that what was done in [that] case infringed the fundamental right to a fair trial." He explained that televised trials intimidate reluctant witnesses, bolster the testimony of boisterous witnesses, and otherwise change the character of the trial, thus threatening its fairness. On the other hand, televised trials expose the courtroom to the public for its educational and informational benefit. But *Estes* was limited to its facts and did not establish a per se constitutional rule barring photographic, radio, or television coverage of criminal trials as a due process violation. Although broadcast coverage of the trial has the potential to influence jurors, the potential risk of prejudice is insufficient to create a constitutional ban of publicized trials. A defendant may, however, demonstrate actual prejudice resulting from his or her publicized trial by showing that the publicity compromised the jury's ability to impartially consider the evidence presented.

Any inherent psychological prejudice arising from recording equipment in the courtroom has been diminished since the *Estes* holding by technological advances and expanded safeguards built into states' experimental rules to protect vulnerable witness such as children, victims of sex crimes, and some informants. The Florida Canon requires the trial judge to vigilantly oversee broadcast coverage to ensure the right of a fair trial. It provides that objections to trial coverage must be heard and considered seriously by the judge, to determine whether the trial will be tainted. Appellate review of that decision is available to an aggrieved defendant. Experimentation with state procedures benefits society's social and economic interests and must not be suppressed for fear of prejudice. Thus, proof of actual prejudice is required. Here, Chandler (D) failed to provide any evidence that the presence of cameras precluded the jurors from carrying out their duty to impartially consider the evidence in rendering a verdict. Absent a constitutional violation, the Court has no authority to regulate a state's experimentation with state criminal procedures. Affirmed.

■ CONCURRENCE

(Stewart, J.) *Estes v. Texas* established a per se ban on the presence of television cameras in a criminal trial. Rather than unsuccessfully attempting to distinguish *Estes* from the instant case, *Estes* should be overruled.

■ CONCURRENCE

(White, J.) *Estes* should be overruled, but the Court's decision effectively "eviscerates" that decision. There is nothing inherently prejudicial about the presence of television cameras in the courtroom, and the Florida Canon places no limitation on the type of case in which television cameras are permitted absent specific prejudice. Thus, even under the facts of *Estes*, the Florida Canon overrides a defendant's objections.

Analysis:

Expanded media coverage of court proceedings has developed into a lucrative commercial business and captured the public's attention. Beginning long ago with *The People's Court* and expanding into modern-day programs such as *Judge Judy*, the public's interest in the courtroom has grown exponentially. Today, entire cable networks are devoted to televising and analyzing courtroom scenarios and trial tactics. The extensive coverage of the O.J. Simpson and the mock Michael Jackson trial illustrate the high-level of public fascination with criminal trials, especially those involving recognized defendants.

■ CASE VOCABULARY

DUE PROCESS: The conduct of legal proceedings according to established rules and principles for the protection and enforcement of private rights, including notice and the right to a fair hearing before a tribunal with the power to decide the case.

PREJUDICE: Damage or detriment to one's legal rights or claims.

SEQUESTRATION: Custodial isolation of a trial jury to prevent tampering and exposure to publicity, or of witnesses to prevent them from hearing the testimony of others.

Press-Enterprise Co. v. Superior Court [Press Enterprise II]

(*Media*) v. (*State Court*)
478 U.S. 1, 106 S. Ct. 2735, 92 L. Ed. 2d 1 (1986)

A REQUEST TO CLOSE A PRELIMINARY HEARING MUST YIELD TO THE FIRST AMENDMENT, ABSENT PREJUDICE

■ **INSTANT FACTS** Press–Enterprise Co. (D) sought access to a closed preliminary hearing transcript.

■ **BLACK LETTER RULE** The qualified First Amendment right of access to criminal proceedings applies to preliminary hearings that function similarly to criminal trials.

■ PROCEDURAL BASIS

Certiorari to review a decision of the California Supreme Court denying a writ of mandate.

■ FACTS

The State of California filed a criminal complaint against Diaz, a nurse, for allegedly murdering twelve patients by injecting them with lethal doses of a heart medication. Diaz moved to close the proceedings to the public. The magistrate granted the motion because of national publicity surrounding the case. The preliminary hearing spanned forty-one days and involved considerable medical and scientific evidence, as well as witness testimony. After the hearing, Press–Enterprise Co. (P) asked that the transcript of the proceeding be released. The magistrate refused and sealed the record. When the State, joined by Press–Enterprise (P), moved to have the transcript released, the superior court denied the motion because there was a "reasonable likelihood that release of all or any part of the transcript might prejudice [Diaz's] right to a fair and impartial trial." Press–Enterprise (P) sought a writ of mandate in the California Supreme Court to compel the transcript's release. Although Diaz had then waived his right to a jury trial and the transcript had already been released, the California Supreme Court held that the proceedings should remain closed because the public right to access must give way to the defendant's right to a fair trial, but only after a determination that the open proceeding will have a "reasonable likelihood of substantial prejudice."

■ ISSUE

Does the qualified First Amendment right of access to criminal proceedings apply to preliminary hearings functioning similarly to criminal trials?

■ DECISION AND RATIONALE

(Burger, C.J.) Yes. The right to a public trial belongs to the accused and the public, both of whom seek fairness in the trial proceeding. While most often the accused objects to a closed proceeding in order to expose the trial to the public, Diaz here sought to close the proceeding in the face of a competing First Amendment claim for public access. First Amendment claims such as this generally must consider whether the place and process have historically been open to the press and the importance of public access to the particular proceeding. While some government processes clearly require secrecy, the openness of a criminal trial enhances fairness to the accused and the appearance of fairness to further public confidence in the justice system.

Even when public access is supported by this test, however, the right is not absolute. An accused's interest in restricting public access in some criminal trials may overcome the First Amendment. This is equally true at the preliminary hearing phase. Although preliminary hearings have traditionally been open to the public, preliminary hearings function similarly to criminal trials. "[T]he qualified First Amendment right of access to criminal proceedings applies to preliminary hearings as they are conducted in California." Therefore, to overcome the right of access, the accused must demonstrate a substantial probability that trial publicity will prejudice his right to a fair trial and that no less restrictive alternatives to closure of the proceedings exist. Because the California Supreme Court required a "reasonable likelihood of substantial prejudice" rather than a "substantial probability" of prejudice and failed to consider any lesser alternatives to closure, its decision was incorrect. The First Amendment right to access cannot be overcome by the mere potential for prejudice to the accused's rights. Reversed.

■ DISSENT

(Stevens, J.) The right sought to be enforced is not the right to publish or disseminate information, but rather the right to access information not already in the media's possession. While the First Amendment generally requires the free flow of information, nothing protects the right to gain access to information that the government has a legitimate interest in concealing. Here, the accused, the prosecutor, and the judge agreed that closure of the proceedings served a legitimate government objective and protected the risk to the defendant, which was significant. There is nothing to suggest otherwise.

Furthermore, at the adoption of the First Amendment, there was no right of access to preliminary hearing proceedings, and the Framers could not have intended that the First Amendment encompass such a right. By opening the preliminary hearing to the public, the Court threatens to open grand jury proceedings to the public as well, although such proceedings have likewise been closed. The logic of the Court's decision is hard to decipher. There is no harm in delaying the public access to the preliminary hearing for at least a short time before trial.

Analysis:

While the preliminary hearing is similar to a criminal trial, important differences suggest that the right to access in the former should be restricted. First, at the preliminary hearing stage, no formal charges have yet been brought against the defendant. Trial publicity of the preliminary hearing has the potential to destroy the presumption of innocence, not perhaps in a legal sense, but in the eyes of the public. Second, the rules of evidence are relaxed at a preliminary hearing, permitting hearsay and other inadmissible evidence, which can be broadcast by the media without distinguishing their probative value. Finally, the preliminary hearing, which is open, is the precursor to a grand jury proceeding, which is closed. Is there any justification for access to a preliminary hearing transcript, but not to the subsequent grand jury transcript?

■ CASE VOCABULARY

PRELIMINARY HEARING: A criminal hearing (usually conducted by a magistrate) to determine whether there is sufficient evidence to prosecute an accused person. If sufficient evidence exists, the case will be set for trial or bound over for grand-jury review, or an information will be filed in the trial court.

CHAPTER SEVENTEEN

The Role of Counsel

Strickland v. Washington

Instant Facts: Washington (D) was tried and convicted of several felony charges, including capital murder; in preparation for and during Washington's (D) sentencing hearing, counsel made decisions that Washington (D) later alleged rendered the lawyer's assistance ineffective.

Black Letter Rule: To show entitlement to reversal of a conviction or sentence based on the ineffective assistance of counsel, a defendant must show that counsel's performance was deficient and that this deficiency was prejudicial to the defense.

Rompilla v. Beard

Instant Facts: Rompilla (D) was sentenced to death after trial counsel failed to investigate court files and other evidence in mitigation of the sentence.

Black Letter Rule: Even when a capital defendant's family members and the defendant himself have suggested that no mitigating evidence is available, his lawyer is bound to make reasonable efforts to obtain and review material that counsel knows the prosecution will probably rely on as evidence of aggravation at the sentencing phase of trial.

Florida v. Nixon

Instant Facts: Nixon (D) was convicted of murder and sentenced to death after defense counsel conceded guilt when Nixon (D) refused to approve or reject such a strategy.

Black Letter Rule: Counsel's failure to obtain the defendant's express consent to a strategy of conceding guilt in a capital trial does not render counsel's assistance ineffective when it is reasonable under the circumstances.

Wheat v. United States

Instant Facts: Wheat (D) was convicted of drug charges after his request to substitute counsel was denied.

Black Letter Rule: The Sixth Amendment does not afford a defendant the right to chosen counsel when a conflict of interest may arise.

Mickens v. Taylor

Instant Facts: Mickens (P) alleged ineffective assistance of counsel because his attorney briefly represented the victim of Mickens's (P) crime.

Black Letter Rule: When counsel represents successive defendants with a potential conflict of interest, a defendant must demonstrate that a conflict existed that affected the outcome of his case.

Faretta v. California

Instant Facts: Faretta (D) was charged with grand theft and requested permission to represent himself, but the trial court denied his request.

Black Letter Rule: Under the Sixth Amendment, a defendant has the right to represent himself at trial, as long as his decision to do so is voluntary and intelligent.

Strickland v. Washington

(*State Official*) v. (*Convicted Felon*)

466 U.S. 668, 104 S. Ct. 2052, 80 L. Ed. 2d 674 (1984)

UNREASONABLE AND PREJUDICIAL REPRESENTATION CONSTITUTES INEFFECTIVE ASSISTANCE OF COUNSEL

■ **INSTANT FACTS** Washington (D) was tried and convicted of several felony charges, including capital murder; in preparation for and during Washington's (D) sentencing hearing, counsel made decisions that Washington (D) later alleged rendered the lawyer's assistance ineffective.

■ **BLACK LETTER RULE** To show entitlement to reversal of a conviction or sentence based on the ineffective assistance of counsel, a defendant must show that counsel's performance was deficient and that this deficiency was prejudicial to the defense.

■ PROCEDURAL BASIS

Certiorari to review a decision of a federal court of appeals reversing and remanding the defendant's sentence.

■ FACTS

Washington (D) was indicted in Florida for kidnapping and murder and was appointed counsel. Against the advice of his counsel, Washington (D) confessed to two murders, waived his right to a jury trial, and pleaded guilty to capital murder. Washington (D) stated that he was under extreme stress when he committed the crimes. In preparation for the sentencing hearing, counsel did not seek out character witnesses or request a psychiatric examination. He also did not request a pre-sentence report, believing that the report would be more detrimental than beneficial. After a hearing, Washington (D) was sentenced to death. The Florida Supreme Court affirmed both the conviction and sentence.

In a collateral state proceeding, Washington (D) challenged his sentence on the ground that he was provided ineffective assistance of counsel. Washington (D) claimed his counsel's representation was ineffective because he failed to request a continuance to prepare for sentencing, request a psychiatric evaluation, investigate and present character witnesses, seek a pre-sentence report, present meaningful arguments to the sentencing judge, investigate the medical examiner's reports, and cross-examine the prosecution's medical experts. The court denied Washington (D) relief. The Florida Supreme Court again affirmed. Washington (D) then sought a writ of habeas corpus in federal court, which was denied for lack of prejudice. The court of appeals reversed and remanded after fashioning its own framework for ineffective assistance of counsel claims, requiring counsel to investigate all reasonably substantial lines of defense before selecting a strategy.

■ ISSUE

In order to obtain a reversal of a conviction or sentence based on ineffective assistance of counsel, must a defendant show that his counsel's performance was deficient and that this deficiency actually prejudiced his defense?

■ DECISION AND RATIONALE

(O'Connor, J.) Yes. The Sixth Amendment right to counsel encompasses the right to the effective assistance of counsel; when counsel's representation is ineffective, the defendant's constitutional rights are violated. The crux of assessing whether counsel's performance was ineffective is determining whether his or her conduct so undermined the functioning of the adversarial process that the trial did not yield a fair result. A defendant must show that counsel's performance was not objectively reasonable. In assessing counsel's performance, courts must be highly deferential and adhere to a strong presumption that counsel's conduct falls within the range of reasonable professional assistance. Likewise, courts must view the conduct not from a hindsight perspective, but from counsel's perspective at the time of the conduct.

Even if counsel's performance was professionally unreasonable, a conviction or sentence will not be set aside unless this conduct actually prejudiced the defense. While there is a presumption of prejudice in cases involving conflicts of interest, in most cases the defendant must affirmatively demonstrate prejudice. To demonstrate actual prejudice, the defendant must show, based on the totality of the evidence, that there is a reasonable probability that, but for counsel's deficient professional conduct, the result of the proceeding would have been different. "Reasonable probability" is a probability sufficient to undermine confidence in the outcome. In this case, Washington's (D) counsel's performance was neither professionally deficient nor prejudicial to Washington (D). Reversed.

■ DISSENT IN PART

(Brennan, J.) The majority correctly sets forth the appropriate standards for claims of ineffective assistance of counsel, especially at the sentencing phase. While retrial of the merits can present substantial burden to the state, the burden of resentencing is minimal compared to the extent of liberty interests at stake for the defendant.

■ DISSENT

(Marshall, J.) The majority's standards for adjudicating claims of ineffective assistance of counsel are meaningless and will not provide appropriate guidance for lower courts. Although defense attorneys' decision-making should be accorded a certain amount of deference in assessing the reasonableness of their performance, there are certain aspects of a criminal attorney's job that are more conducive to judicial oversight and thus more precise standards. The majority's standard for prejudice is also problematic because it is difficult to tell, from a cold record, whether a better result would have been achieved by competent counsel. Moreover, there is the possibility that evidence of prejudice may be missing from the record because of the incompetence of counsel. Finally, despite the strength of evidence of guilt, due process requires that all criminal defendants obtain a fair trial with the effective assistance of counsel. Whether prejudice exists or not, due process requires a new trial when counsel has been ineffective.

Analysis:

In the vast majority of cases in which a defendant claims ineffective assistance of counsel, courts have concluded that counsel's performance fell within the range of reasonable professional conduct. Counsel's performance is not deficient simply because a different attorney may have made different tactical or strategic decisions. In addition, even though certain conduct has been found to be deficient in one case, the same conduct may be found sufficient in another case.

■ CASE VOCABULARY

AGGRAVATING CIRCUMSTANCE: A fact or situation that relates to a criminal offense or defendant and that is considered by the court in imposing punishment (especially a death sentence).

INEFFECTIVE ASSISTANCE OF COUNSEL: Representation in which the defendant is deprived of a fair trial because the lawyer handles the case unreasonably, usually either by performing incompetently or by not devoting full effort to the defendant, especially because of a conflict of interest. In determining whether a criminal defendant received ineffective assistance of counsel, courts generally consider several factors: (1) whether the lawyer had previously handled criminal cases; (2) whether strategic trial tactics were involved in the allegedly incompetent action; (3) whether, and to what extent, the defendant was prejudiced as a result of the lawyer's alleged ineffectiveness; and (4) whether the ineffectiveness was due to matters beyond the lawyer's control.

MITIGATING CIRCUMSTANCE: A fact or situation that does not bear on the question of a defendant's guilt but that is considered by the court in imposing punishment and especially in lessening the severity of a sentence.

Rompilla v. Beard

(*Convicted Murder*) v. (*Prison Official*)

545 U.S. 374, 125 S. Ct. 2456, 162 L. Ed. 2d 360 (2005)

REASONABLE LAWYERS DO NOT RELY SOLELY ON THEIR CLIENT'S UNDERSTANDING OF THE EVIDENCE

■ **INSTANT FACTS** Rompilla (D) was sentenced to death after trial counsel failed to investigate court files and other evidence in mitigation of the sentence.

■ **BLACK LETTER RULE** Even when a capital defendant's family members and the defendant himself have suggested that no mitigating evidence is available, his lawyer is bound to make reasonable efforts to obtain and review material that counsel knows the prosecution will probably rely on as evidence of aggravation at the sentencing phase of trial.

■ PROCEDURAL BASIS

Certiorari to review a decision of the Third Circuit Court of Appeals reversing a district court's grant of habeas corpus.

■ FACTS

Rompilla (D) was indicted for murder and other offenses and faced the death penalty. Two public defenders were appointed to defend him. After trial, the jury convicted Rompilla (D) on all charges. During the sentencing phase, the prosecutor demonstrated that the murder occurred in the course of committing another felony and involved torture, and that Rompilla (D) had a history of felony convictions. Rompilla (D) offered as mitigating factors a plea of mercy from his young son and the potential for rehabilitation. The jury sentenced him to death. The Supreme Court of Pennsylvania affirmed both the conviction and the sentence. With new lawyers, Rompilla (D) sought post-conviction relief, claiming ineffective assistance of counsel in failing to present mitigating evidence about Rompilla's (D) childhood, mental capacity, and alcoholism. The court denied relief, and the Supreme Court of Pennsylvania affirmed. Rompilla (D) then sought a writ of habeas corpus in federal court, again alleging ineffective assistance of counsel. The court granted the writ, but the Third Circuit Court of Appeals reversed, ruling that counsel had adequately investigated the relevant evidence.

■ ISSUE

Does counsel act unreasonably when he relies on statements of the defendant and his family as mitigating evidence at the sentencing stage rather than conduct an independent investigation of the evidence?

■ DECISION AND RATIONALE

(Souter, J.) Yes. To establish his ineffective assistance claim, Rompilla (D) must demonstrate that he was prejudiced by his counsel's objectively unreasonable investigation. This is not a case, however, where counsel ignored his obligation to discover mitigating evidence, for counsel interviewed Rompilla (D) and his family and considered reports of three mental health experts, all of which were unhelpful. New counsel, however, looked to school records, juvenile and adult conviction records, and further evidence of his alcoholism unexplored by trial counsel. Trial counsel's failure to investigate these sources was clearly unreasonable. Counsel knew that the Commonwealth sought the death penalty in part because of Rompilla's (D) history of violent crime. Aware that the conviction records were claimed as aggravating factors, a reasonable attorney would have reviewed those files and discovered the potentially mitigating evidence. Without reviewing those files, trial counsel could not have adequately understood the extent of the prosecution's aggravating evidence nor discovered portions of the file downplayed in advocating its position. It is incumbent upon counsel to obtain and review all evidence the prosecution will use against his client in furtherance of his investigative duties. No reasonable lawyer would forgo review of the court file in lieu of asking his client and relatives what information it contains. Such questioning does not relieve his duty to investigate further into other sources for mitigating evidence.

Counsel's unreasonableness clearly prejudiced Rompilla's (D) position during sentencing. A review of the court file would not only have uncovered mitigating evidence of Rompilla's (D) childhood difficulties, but reasonably prompted additional investigation to discover the evidence found by postconviction counsel, including the effects of alcoholism and mistreatment on his upbringing. In turn, this evidence would have been useful to the mental health experts evaluating Rompilla (D) and likely changed their conclusions. In all, the undiscovered evidence would have mounted a much different case for mitigation than the pleas for mercy made to the jury. There is a strong likelihood that the jury's decision would have been different. Reversed and remanded for resentencing.

■ CONCURRENCE

(O'Connor, J.) To effectively represent a client, counsel need not always review the case file of a prior conviction, but only must do so when reasonable under the circumstances. Because trial counsel knew that the prosecution was relying on information in the case file as part of its case, reasonableness required counsel to review the file. Likewise, counsel did not make an informed tactical decision to look at other evidentiary sources rather than the case file, but rather inattentively neglected to consider any evidentiary sources to corroborate or refute his client's statements.

■ DISSENT

(Kennedy, J.) The Court effectively requires all counsel to review the contents of old case files in hopes of stumbling across relevant evidence. But here trial counsel represented Rompilla (D) reasonably. The lawyers exhaustively interviewed Rompilla (D) regarding the details of his childhood and upbringing. They questioned family members for any mitigating information that might spare Rompilla (D) the death penalty. And they consulted three highly respected mental health experts to fashion a mitigating profile to present to the jury. Counsel was aware that mitigating evidence was crucial to avoid the death penalty and reasonably sought it out. The Court's per se rule requiring counsel in every case to review case files of prior convictions ignores the case-by-case review required by *Strickland v. Washington* and affords no deference to counsel's strategic decisions.

Even assuming counsel acted unreasonably, Rompilla (D) has failed to show prejudice. The Court finds prejudice by chance. However, it has not been proven that had counsel reviewed the court file, it would have discovered mitigating information that would have led to the review of the chain of evidence the Court suggests.

Analysis:

The interesting problem with *Rompilla* is not that defense counsel failed to offer sufficient mitigating evidence, but that he failed to look for it in the first place. Assume, for instance, that counsel did review the prior court file and determined tactically that there was little mitigating value to the information obtained. The Court's decision seems to afford considerable discretion to that tactical decision. Yet, because counsel failed to even investigate the material (perhaps strategically), the exclusion of the evidence was ineffective assistance of counsel.

■ CASE VOCABULARY

PREJUDICE: Damage or detriment to one's legal rights or claims.

Florida v. Nixon

(*Prosecuting Government*) v. (*Murder Defendant*)
543 U.S. 175, 125 S. Ct. 551, 160 L. Ed. 2d 565 (2004)

COUNSEL MAY MAKE CERTAIN STRATEGIC DECISIONS WITHOUT THE CLIENT'S CONSENT

■ **INSTANT FACTS** Nixon (D) was convicted of murder and sentenced to death after defense counsel conceded guilt when Nixon (D) refused to approve or reject such a strategy.

■ **BLACK LETTER RULE** Counsel's failure to obtain the defendant's express consent to a strategy of conceding guilt in a capital trial does not render counsel's assistance ineffective when it is reasonable under the circumstances.

■ PROCEDURAL BASIS

Certiorari to review a decision of the Florida Supreme Court reversing the defendant's conviction.

■ FACTS

Nixon (D) was arrested after his brother informed police that Nixon (D) had confessed to a gruesome murder. Nixon (D) confessed to police, describing in detail the events that occurred. The state then corroborated the confession through independent investigation. Nixon (D) was indicted for murder, among other charges, and represented by a public defender. Defense counsel pleaded not guilty and deposed the State's (P) witnesses, whereupon he initiated plea negotiations because of the strength of the evidence against Nixon (D). No plea agreement was reached. Faced with going to trial, counsel believed that the only way to avoid the death penalty would be to concede the defendant's guilt, hoping to persuad the jury to spare Nixon's (D) life. Counsel attempted to explain the strategy to Nixon (D) several times, but Nixon (D) never verbally approved nor protested the strategy. Counsel therefore exercised professional judgment and conceded Nixon's (D) guilt at trial. The trial proceeded with the prosecution's evidence which, along with Nixon's (D) counsel's concession, brought a guilty verdict. At the penalty phase, counsel emphasized many factors mitigating against the death penalty, but the jury sentenced Nixon (D) to death. On appeal, the Florida Supreme Court found the evidence inconclusive to establish an ineffective assistance of counsel claim. Nixon (D) then sough postconviction relief, raising again his claim of ineffective assistance of counsel. The trial court denied the relief, but the Florida Supreme Court reversed and remanded the matter for a new trial, finding that conceding guilt without the affirmative consent of the defendant is equivalent to an unauthorized guilty plea, which constitutes ineffective assistance of counsel and presumed prejudice.

■ ISSUE

Does counsel's failure to obtain the defendant's express consent to a strategy of conceding guilt in a capital trial automatically render counsel's assistance ineffective?

■ DECISION AND RATIONALE

(Ginsburg, J.) No. Counsel need not obtain the client's consent for every tactical decision made. Some decisions, however, bear such importance to a defendant's basic rights that their exercise or waiver may not be made by the attorney, including whether to plead guilty, whether to waive a jury, whether to testify on his or her own behalf, and whether to appeal. By pleading guilty, a defendant waives important constitutional rights. Therefore, anything less than affirmative approval of a guilty plea is insufficient. A concession of guilt, however, is not the same as a guilty plea. With a concession of guilt, the basic rights waived by a guilty plea are preserved. The defendant enjoys the right to a jury trial, to confront witnesses against him, to put the prosecution to its burden of proof, and to pursue an appeal of any trial errors. Counsel had a duty to inform Nixon (D) of his trial strategy, which he did, and Nixon's (D) failure to respond does not render the strategy unreasonable.

Because the Florida Supreme Court considered counsel's strategy as ineffective, it presumed prejudice under *United States v. Cronic*, 466 U.S. 648 (1984), for failing to meaningfully advocate the defendant's position. The court therefore did not require the defendant to prove that counsel's actions in failing to meaningfully advocate his innocence was unreasonable. When the evidence strongly supports a defendant's guilt, it is not unreasonable to focus on the penalty phase to minimize the criminal consequences of the evidence. "[I]n a capital case, counsel must consider in conjunction both the guilt and penalty phases in determining how best to proceed. When counsel informs the defendant of the strategy counsel believes to be in the defendant's best interest and the defendant is unresponsive, counsel's strategic choice is not impeded by any blanket rule demanding the defendant's explicit consent." If the strategic choice is objectively reasonable, no claim of ineffective assistance of counsel may be maintained. Reversed and remanded.

Analysis:

In concluding that the decision to concede guilt is a "tactical decision" of which counsel need only inform the defendant, the Court points to all the constitutional rights the defendant embraces at trail, including the right to a jury and the right to confront witnesses. Yet, what of the defendant's more important right to a presumption of innocence and conviction only upon proof beyond a reasonable doubt? While the prosecution at trial continues to have the burden, how easily is that burden met when the defense concedes to guilt? Clearly the prosecution will not contradict its own testimony to create such doubt. The focus on the rights preserved rather than the rights lost is curious.

Wheat v. United States

(Drug Conspirator) v. *(Prosecuting Government)*
486 U.S. 153, 108 S. Ct. 1692, 100 L. Ed. 2d 140 (1988)

COURTS HAVE CONSIDERABLE LATITUDE TO DENY A REQUEST FOR SUBSTITUTION OF COUNSEL

■ INSTANT FACTS Wheat (D) was convicted of drug charges after his request to substitute counsel was denied.

■ BLACK LETTER RULE The Sixth Amendment does not afford a defendant the right to chosen counsel when a conflict of interest may arise.

■ PROCEDURAL BASIS

Certiorari to review a decision of the Ninth Circuit Court of Appeals affirming the defendant's conviction.

■ FACTS

Wheat (D), along with Gomez–Barajas and Bravo, was charged with drug conspiracy. Gomez–Barajas and Bravo were represented by an attorney named Iredale. Gomez–Barajas was tried first and acquitted of drug charges overlapping those against Wheat (D). Gomez–Barajas then pleaded guilty to tax evasion and illegal importation to avoid a second trial on other drug charges. At the time of Wheat's (D) trial, however, the plea had not been accepted such that it could be rejected by the court or withdrawn by Gomez–Barajas. Also before Wheat's (D) trial, Bravo pleaded guilty to the charges against him. At the conclusion of Bravo's plea hearing, Wheat (D) moved for substitution of Iredale. The Government (P) objected, reasoning that Iredale's representation of Wheat (D) created a conflict of interest should Gomez–Barajas's plea be rejected, necessitating Wheat's (D) testimony at that trial, and should Bravo be called to testify against Wheat (D), counsel would be conflicted on cross-examination. Wheat (D) responded that he would waive any conflict of interest, and that such a conflict was potential at best. The court denied the request to substitute counsel because of an irreconcilable conflict of interest. Wheat (D) was convicted with Iredale as his counsel, and the Ninth Circuit Court of Appeals affirmed.

■ ISSUE

Does the Sixth Amendment afford a defendant the absolute right to counsel of his choice?

■ DECISION AND RATIONALE

(Rehnquist, C.J.) No. While the Sixth Amendment affords a defendant the right to counsel of his choosing, the purpose of the right is to ensure the defendant has a competent advocate, not that he have the advocate he prefers. The right is tempered by requirements that the advocate be a licensed attorney, that the advocate may decline to represent a defendant, and that the advocate may not present a conflict of interest. Federal courts have an obligation to protect the institutional interest in just verdicts and further professional ethical standards. The court must carefully inquire into cases of joint representation to advise each defendant of his right to the effective assistance of counsel and take appropriate measures to protect clients from conflicts of interest.

A waiver of any conflict of interest does not adequately protect the court's judgment from a later ineffective assistance of counsel claim. Thus, when a conflict of interest is perceived, the court may justifiably deny a joint defendant's waiver. Because a court must determine the effects of a conflict of interest early, without the benefit of hindsight to determine whether prejudice will result, its decisions must be afforded considerable latitude. Here, there was reason to believe that had Iredale been substituted, a conflict of interest would have existed during his cross-examination of Bravo, whom the Government (D) had indicated would testify at Wheat's (D) trial. Likewise, if Gomez–Barajas's plea were rejected, Wheat (D) would have been called to testify at his trial, presenting the same conflict of interest. The trial court's decision to deny the substitution was reasonably within its discretion and did not violate Wheat's (D) Sixth Amendment rights.

■ DISSENT

(Marshall, J.) The right to counsel involves a presumption in favor of a defendant's chosen counsel. Although a court need not endorse counsel when a conflict of interest in fact exists, the mere potential for a conflict of interest is insufficient to deprive the defendant of his right to chosen counsel. When a conflict is merely potential, there is no assurance that chosen counsel will infuse unfairness into the trial. Appellate courts, however, should not defer to trial court discretion in determining when the potential for conflict arises to a serious threat to fairness, for more than fairness to the court is involved. A decision denying chosen counsel results in unfairness to the defendant and threatens his Sixth Amendment rights. Such a decision should be made on the basis of the facts and supported by the court's detailed rationale to assist appellate review. Here, the decision to deny the substitution of counsel was based on the mere speculation that Gomez–Barajas's plea could have been rejected and that the substance of Bravo's testimony at Wheat's (D) trial could have resulted in a conflict. Such considerations are too speculative to justify the violation of Wheat's (D) Sixth Amendment rights.

Analysis:

Many constitutional rights are subject to a defendant's voluntary and knowing waiver. The Court's decision appears to indicate that the effective assistance of counsel is not one of them. If a defendant, fully informed of the potential consequences of conflicts of interests, voluntarily agrees to forgo his rights, why should he not be allowed to do so? Certainly the waiver would not prejudice the government, for a valid waiver should not limit counsel's role on cross-examination at all. Likewise, the defendant would not have grounds for appeal based on the conflict of interest, ensuring that the court's decision would stand.

■ CASE VOCABULARY

CONFLICT OF INTEREST: A real or seeming incompatibility between the interests of two of a lawyer's clients, such that the lawyer is disqualified from representing both clients if the dual representation adversely affects either client or if the clients do not consent. *See* Model Rules of Professional Conduct 1.7(a).

WAIVER: The voluntary relinquishment or abandonment—express or implied—of a legal right or advantage.

Mickens v. Taylor

(*Convicted Murderer*) v. (*Warden*)

535 U.S. 162, 122 S. Ct. 1237, 152 L. Ed. 2d 291 (2002)

A COURT NEED NOT INQUIRE INTO A POTENTIAL CONFLICT OF INTEREST UNLESS IT KNEW OR SHOULD HAVE KNOWN ABOUT IT

■ **INSTANT FACTS** Mickens (P) alleged ineffective assistance of counsel because his attorney briefly represented the victim of Mickens's (P) crime.

■ **BLACK LETTER RULE** When counsel represents successive defendants with a potential conflict of interest, a defendant must demonstrate that a conflict existed that affected the outcome of his case.

■ PROCEDURAL BASIS

Certiorari to review a decision of the Fourth Circuit Court of Appeals affirming the denial of a petition for habeas corpus.

■ FACTS

Mickens (P) was convicted of the murder of Hall and was sentenced to death. After trial, Mickens's (P) counsel in a federal habeas corpus action learned that the judge had earlier appointed Mickens's (P) trial counsel to represent Hall in relation to other charges. The attorney did not disclose to the court, co-counsel, or Mickens (P) that he had previously represented Hall. The trial court denied the petition for habeas corpus relief and the Fourth Circuit Court of Appeals affirmed. The court held that Mickens (P) had not demonstrated that he suffered any adverse effect from his attorney's conflict of interest.

■ ISSUE

Is a murder defendant denied the effective assistance of counsel if his appointed counsel once represented the victim of the crime?

■ DECISION AND RATIONALE

(Scalia, J.) No. Generally, a Sixth Amendment violation requires a showing of "a reasonable probability that, but for counsel's unprofessional errors, the result of the proceeding would have been different." When a defendant is denied counsel entirely or at a critical stage of the proceeding, such an effect may be presumed because of the high probability that the verdict is unreliable. Likewise, when counsel actively represents conflicting interests, a presumption may arise that the assistance of counsel was ineffective. When defense counsel is compelled to represent codefendants over his objection, reversal of a conviction is required unless the court determined that no actual conflict exists. However, when counsel fails to object to his representation of multiple defendants, automatic reversal is not appropriate, and the defendant must show that a conflict of interest affected the outcome of the case. Under such circumstances, the court need not inquire into a potential conflict unless it knew or should have known that a conflict affecting the adequacy of representation existed.

Here, counsel did not object to his representation of Mickens (P), and the court's failure to make a conflict inquiry does not lessen Mickens' (P) burden to demonstrate a conflict affected the outcome of his trial. Because Mickens (P) has made no such showing, his conviction must stand. Affirmed.

■ CONCURRENCE

(Kennedy, J.) Mickens's (P) attorney worked under the belief that he owed no further duty to Hall, and counsel's trial strategies were not affected by any confidential information obtained while representing Hall. Even if the judge should have known of a conflict, the conflict did not influence the choices the attorney made during the trial or affect its outcome.

■ DISSENT

(Stevens, J.) Counsel's failure to disclose his prior representation of Hall resulted in an indefensible conflict of interest. Upon conviction of his client, counsel must offer evidence in the best light to the defendant to reduce the impact of the crime in the eyes of the jury. Yet, his continuing ethical duty to Hall required him to protect the reputation and confidences of his former client. Moreover, when the court appoints counsel, it must do so in a manner that preserves the defendant's constitutional right to the assistance of counsel. Without an inquiry into potential conflicts of interest, the court places the defendant in an attorney-client relationship in which the defendant cannot possibly serve his undivided interests. His conviction should be set aside to maintain public confidence in the legal system and ensure that Mickens (P) receives his constitutional right to the effective assistance of counsel.

■ DISSENT

(Souter, J.) It should be immaterial whether Mickens's (P) counsel objected to his appointment, for the court was aware of a potential conflict of interest and failed to inquire about it. When the judge knows of a potential conflict, his or her duty to investigate the nature of the conflict to ensure the effective assistance of counsel does not depend on whether counsel insists the judge act. The judge is under a constitutional duty to uphold the Sixth Amendment. The defendant should not be held to a burden of proving actual prejudice from such a violation when the judge blatantly breaches his or her constitutional duty.

■ DISSENT

(Breyer, J.) Because of the egregious conflict at issue, Court precedent addressing the issue of the duty to inquire does not govern. This is a capital murder case in which the defendant's lawyer represented the murder victim only days before his appointment. The victim's character in such cases is often a key piece of evidence to exonerate or mitigate criminal liability. When defense counsel has divided loyalties, the risk of actual prejudice is easily surmised. Likewise, the conflict was not merely overlooked by the court, but actually created by it. This is not a situation in which a court was required to consider the potential for conflict upon meeting defense counsel for the first time, but rather knew of the conflict before it arose. In such unique situations, prejudice is so likely to occur that it should be presumed as a matter of law.

Analysis:

It is difficult to imagine the kind of prejudice that would justify overturning a conviction under the standard enunciated by the Court. Cases that discuss the adequacy of representation afford counsel a wide range of discretion on how to proceed and find adequate representation in most cases in which a particular course of action or inaction could have some tactical justification. Even if a conflict of interest leads an attorney to make consistently bad, but justifiable, tactical decisions, a defendant may have a difficult time proving actual prejudice.

■ CASE VOCABULARY

HABEAS CORPUS: A writ employed to bring a person before a court, most frequently to ensure that the party's imprisonment or detention is not illegal.

Faretta v. California

(*Convicted Felon*) v. (*Prosecuting State*)

422 U.S. 806, 95 S. Ct. 2525, 45 L. Ed. 2d 562 (1975)

CRIMINAL DEFENDANTS HAVE A CONSTITUTIONAL RIGHT TO REPRESENT THEMSELVES AT TRIAL

■ **INSTANT FACTS** Faretta (D) was charged with grand theft and requested permission to represent himself, but the trial court denied his request.

■ **BLACK LETTER RULE** Under the Sixth Amendment, a defendant has the right to represent himself at trial, as long as his decision to do so is voluntary and intelligent.

■ PROCEDURAL BASIS

Certiorari to review the decisions of a state appellate court affirming the defendant's conviction.

■ FACTS

Faretta (D) was charged with grand theft under California law. A public defender was assigned to represent him. Faretta (D) requested that he be permitted to represent himself. The trial judge advised Faretta (D) that he thought he was making a mistake, but initially allowed him to proceed *pro se*. Later, however, after questioning Faretta about the extent of his legal research, the trial judge ruled that Faretta had not knowingly and intelligently waived his right to counsel and that he had no constitutional right to represent himself. The judge re-appointed the public defender to represent Faretta (D) and required that Faretta's (D) defense be conducted only through the lawyer. The jury convicted Faretta (D) and he was sentenced to imprisonment. The conviction was affirmed on appeal.

■ ISSUE

Does a defendant have a constitutional right to represent himself in a criminal prosecution?

■ DECISION AND RATIONALE

(Stewart, J.) Yes. The Sixth Amendment requires that a criminal defendant be permitted to represent himself or herself, as long as the waiver of counsel is voluntary and intelligent. The right of self-representation is implied in the language and spirit of the Sixth Amendment, the provisions of which accord the accused the right to make a defense. This right is personal to the defendant because it is he or she who suffers the consequences if the defense fails. The implied right to self-representation is well supported in history. Self-representation was required practice in felony prosecutions in England, and was guaranteed in various colonial charters and declarations of rights. Historically, the right to counsel was considered supplemental to the right of self-representation. In addition, when a defendant does not want representation, a lawyer's skill and experience are less valuable to the process.

However, before waiving the right to counsel, a defendant must be advised of the dangers and disadvantages of doing so. The record must establish that the defendant's election to represent himself or herself is made with full understanding and free will. Here, the record demonstrates that Faretta (D) was competent enough to understand the consequences of proceeding without counsel and unequivocally and voluntarily waived the assistance of counsel. Reversed.

■ DISSENT

(Burger, C.J.) The right to self-representation is not included in either the express language or history of the Sixth Amendment. The Sixth Amendment guarantees that defendants receive the fullest possible defense, which is usually realized through the express guarantee of the right to counsel. The majority also improperly relies on history to support its decision by taking English and early American history out of context. Moreover, because the Sixth Amendment was proposed and adopted after Congress signed legislation guaranteeing the right to self-representation, the omission of this right from the Sixth Amendment must be construed as intentional. Thus, the issue of whether to allow defendants to proceed *pro se* must be left to the decision of legislatures.

■ DISSENT

(Blackmun, J.) The majority's holding presents a host of procedural problems for trial courts. For example, it is not clear whether or when a defendant must be advised of the right to proceed *pro se*. Likewise, the standards for measuring whether the defendant's waiver of counsel is "voluntary" and "intelligent" are not clear. If a defendant proceeds *pro se*, is he or she constitutionally entitled to "standby" counsel or to be treated differently at trial?

Analysis:

In *Martinez v. Court of Appeal of California*, 528 U.S. 152 (2000), the Supreme Court declined to extend the holding in *Faretta* to appellate proceedings. The Court found that neither history nor constitutional structure require that a defendant be guaranteed the right of self-representation in pursuing an appeal. The decision in *Martinez* deals only with constitutional requirements; a state may nonetheless legislate a defendant's right of self-representation in appellate proceedings.

■ CASE VOCABULARY

PRO SE: For oneself; on one's own behalf; without a lawyer.

Illinois v. Allen

(*Prosecuting Government*) v. (*Convicted Robber*)

397 U.S. 337, 90 S. Ct. 1057, 25 L. Ed. 2d 353 (1970)

AN UNRULY DEFENDANT DOES NOT HAVE THE RIGHT TO DISRUPT HIS OWN TRIAL

■ **INSTANT FACTS** Allen (D) was ordered removed from his criminal trial because of his disruptive behavior.

■ **BLACK LETTER RULE** A defendant can lose his right to be present at trial if, after he has been warned by the judge that he will be removed if he continues his disruptive behavior, he nevertheless insists on conducting himself in a manner so disorderly, disruptive, and disrespectful of the court that his trial cannot be carried on with him in the courtroom.

■ PROCEDURAL BASIS

Certiorari to review a decision of a federal court of appeals reversing the defendant's conviction.

■ FACTS

Allen (D) was on trial for armed robbery. Before trial, the judge granted Allen's (D) request to represent himself, although counsel was appointed to preserve the record. When the judge admonished Allen (D) during voir dire to keep his questions related to the prospective jurors' qualifications, Allen (D) became unruly and threatened the judge. The judge had Allen (D) removed and the appointed counsel completed voir dire. At trial, Allen (D) continued to act inappropriately and he was again removed during the State's (P) case in chief. Allen (D) was allowed to return for his defense, which was conducted by appointed counsel. The jury convicted Allen (D). The Supreme Court of Illinois affirmed the conviction, and Allen's (D) later petition for habeas corpus was denied by a federal court. The federal court of appeals reversed, holding that Allen (D) had an absolute right under the Sixth Amendment to be present at his criminal trial.

■ ISSUE

Does a criminal defendant have an absolute right to be present at his trial, regardless of unruly behavior?

■ DECISION AND RATIONALE

(Black, J.) No. While the Sixth Amendment affords a defendant the right to confront witnesses against him, the right may be lost by consent or misconduct. "[A] defendant can lose his right to be present at trial, if, after he has been warned by the judge that he will be removed if he continues his disruptive behavior, he nevertheless insists on conducting himself in a manner so disorderly, disruptive, and disrespectful of the court that his trial cannot be carried on with him in the courtroom." The right can be reclaimed, however, by displaying conduct consistent with orderly courtroom decorum.

In dealing with a disruptive defendant, the court has three options: (1) bind and gag him while keeping him present in the courtroom; (2) cite him for contempt; or (3) remove him from the courtroom until he agrees to cooperate. While the first option affords the defendant his right to confront witnesses, the sight of a bound defendant will cause significant prejudice to the defendant in the eyes of the jury and constitute an affront to his personal dignity. A contempt citation is not likely to remedy the problem, for it requires an additional trial that the defendant may disrupt. Removal of the defendant while his counsel represents his interests ensures that the court properly functions, trial proceeds, and the defendant's interests are represented. While the court should choose the remedy least infringing on the defendant's rights, the court must further its interests in justice as well. Here, the court properly warned Allen (D) that further disruptive behavior would result in his removal, which action it carried out when Allen (D) refused to acquiesce. Allen (D) lost his right to be present at trial.

■ CONCURRENCE

(Brennan, J.) To ensure that the infringement on a removed defendant's rights is minimized, the defendant should be afforded ample opportunity to confer with counsel during the trial.

■ CONCURRENCE

(Douglas, J.) In the classic criminal case, the Court's reasoning is sufficient. However, removal of a disruptive defendant must be carefully evaluated in political trials and challenges against repressive Constitutional standards, where passion often inspires heated debate.

Analysis:

The competing interests at stake here create an interesting Constitutional dilemma. While the court maintains an interest in conducting a trial, the defendant's presence in the courtroom to face his accusers and effectively consult with counsel is also pivotal. These rights exist to prevent judicial oppression and ensure the defendant receives a fair trial. Yet, the Court's decision hints at no limits on the court's discretion to remove an unruly defendant. What level of disruption is required before the court may order him removed? While such a determination must necessarily be made on a case-by-case basis, appellate courts face a difficult task in determining whether a defendant's behavior warranted removal without the benefit of personal observation.

■ CASE VOCABULARY

CONFRONTATION CLAUSE: The Sixth Amendment provision guaranteeing a criminal defendant's right to directly confront an accusing witness and to cross-examine that witness.

Crawford v. Washington

(*Convicted Defendant*) v. (*Prosecuting Government*)
541 U.S. 36, 124 S. Ct. 1354, 158 L. Ed. 2d 177 (2004)

AN OUT–OF–COURT STATEMENT IS INADMISSIBLE IF THE DEFENDANT HAS NO OPPORTUNITY TO CROSS–EXAMINE THE DECLARANT

■ **INSTANT FACTS** Crawford (D) was convicted of assault and attempted murder after his nontestifying wife's tape-recorded statement was admitted into evidence against him.

■ **BLACK LETTER RULE** The Sixth Amendment Confrontation Clause demands that, in order for an out-of-court statement to be admitted into evidence, the witness must be unavailable and the defendant must have had a prior opportunity to cross-examine the declarant.

■ PROCEDURAL BASIS

Certiorari to review a decision of the Washington Supreme Court reinstating the defendant's conviction.

■ FACTS

Crawford (D) stabbed a man who allegedly tried to rape his wife. After giving Crawford (D) and his wife *Miranda* warnings, Crawford (D) confessed to police that he and his wife went to the man's apartment, where a fight ensued; the man was stabbed in the torso and the wife's hand was cut. In a tape-recorded statement, the wife stated that she did not know how she was cut and that she sometimes remembers things wrong "when things like this happen." Her statement corroborated the events leading up to the fight, but she gave an inconsistent account of the fight, suggesting the stabbing was not in self-defense. Crawford (D) was charged with assault and attempted murder, to which Crawford (D) claimed self-defense. Because of the state marital privilege, the wife did not testify at trial, but her tape-recorded statement was introduced into evidence without an opportunity for Crawford (D) to cross-examine her. Crawford (D) was convicted. On appeal, the Washington Court of Appeals reversed, reasoning that the statement was untrustworthy and did not satisfy the hearsay exception. The Washington Supreme Court reversed and reinstated the conviction, finding that the statements were sufficiently reliable and trustworthy.

■ ISSUE

Does the Confrontation Clause prohibit the admission into evidence of an out-of-court testimonial statement from an unavailable witness when the defendant has no opportunity for cross-examination?

■ DECISION AND RATIONALE

(Scalia, J.) Yes. The Confrontation Clause provides that every defendant shall have the right to confront witnesses against him. Nonetheless, in *Ohio v. Roberts*, 448 U.S. 56 (1980), the Court allowed the admission of an unavailable witness's out-of-court statement as long as sufficient indicia of reliability exist. The Confrontation Clause is not restricted to witnesses who physically testify in court against a defendant, but extends broadly to any statement made against the defendant, whether in court or out. History demonstrates that the Clause requires the right to confront an adverse witness, subject not to court-created exceptions, but only to those that existed at common law. At common law, out-of-court statements against an accused were inadmissible unless the witness was subjected to cross-examination at trial or at the time the statement was made. In practice, the Court has applied these principles in criminal cases without resort to indicia of reliability. "Testimonial statements of witnesses absent from trial have been admitted only where the declarant is unavailable, and only where the defendant has had a prior opportunity to cross-examine."

The rationale for such a practice, however, has been inconsistent. *Ohio v. Roberts* allows hearsay testimony at trial if the statement falls under a "firmly rooted hearsay exception" or bears "particularized guarantees of trustworthiness." This test is too broad, for it establishes the admissibility of out-of-court statements for which no right of cross-examination has been afforded. Moreover, it admits all testimony merely because it is deemed reliable, without application of the rules of evidence. Although reliability is a goal of the Confrontation Clause, reliability is not to be determined by the findings of a trial judge, but rather through the right of cross-examination by the defendant. "Dispensing with confrontation because testimony is obviously reliable is akin to dispensing with jury trial because the defendant is obviously guilty." Despite the strength of the assumption, the Constitution prescribes various rights to reach the obvious result. The Confrontation Clause plainly intended to exclude certain statements not subjected to cross-examination, and a judicial determination based on various factors indicating reliability is improper. "Where nontestimonial hearsay is at issue, it is wholly consistent with the Framers' design to afford the States flexibility in their development of hearsay law.... Where testimonial evidence is at issue, however, the Sixth Amendment demands what the common law required: unavailability and a prior opportunity for cross-examination."

■ CONCURRENCE

(Rehnquist, C.J.) It is unnecessary to overrule *Ohio v. Roberts* to reach the Court's conclusion. Its distinction between nontestimonial and testimonial statements is no more deeply rooted in tradition than the *Roberts* approach. There is no indication that the Framers were more concerned with testimonial statements than nontestimonial statements. Furthermore, the Confrontation Clause does not categorically exclude testimonial evidence. At the time the Sixth Amendment was adopted, various exceptions to the hearsay rule existed, and there is no indication that the Framers intended that list to be exclusive at the time. Exceptions are formulated because of the inherent reliability of certain out-of-court statements, and while cross-examination is a valuable means of testing reliability, it is not the only means required by the Sixth Amendment. Rather than fashion a new rule and overrule longstanding Court doctrine, it would suffice to apply other Court precedent that has established that "an out-of-court statement [is] not admissible simply because the truthfulness of that statement was corroborated by other evidence at trial."

Analysis:

Crawford marks a dramatic shift in the Court's Confrontation Clause jurisprudence. Prior to *Crawford*, the Court consistently emphasized that the purpose of confrontation is to ensure the reliability of the testimony against the defendant. Yet, in *Crawford*, the Court refused to settle on this key aim, requiring cross-examination as the means of ensuring reliability. In so doing, the Court changes its view not only of the admissibility of hearsay statements, but also its analysis of the underlying purpose of the Confrontation Clause.

■ CASE VOCABULARY

CONFRONTATION CLAUSE: The Sixth Amendment provision guaranteeing a criminal defendant's right to directly confront an accusing witness and to cross-examine that witness.

CROSS-EXAMINATION: The questioning of a witness at a trial or hearing by a party opposed to the party who called the witness to testify.

HEARSAY: In federal law, a statement (either a verbal assertion or nonverbal assertive conduct), other than one made by the declarant while testifying at the trial or hearing, offered in evidence to prove the truth of the matter asserted.

Richardson v. Marsh

(*Prison Official*) v. (*Convicted Murderer*)

481 U.S. 200, 107 S. Ct. 1702, 95 L. Ed. 2d 176 (1987)

A CODEFENDANT'S REDACTED CONFESSION IS ADMISSIBLE

■ INSTANT FACTS In a joint trial for assault and murder, a nontestifying codefendant's redacted confession was admitted with a limiting instruction not to consider it as evidence against codefendant Marsh (D).

■ BLACK LETTER RULE The Confrontation Clause is not violated by the admission of a nontestifying codefendant's confession, with a proper limiting instruction, when, as here, the confession is redacted to eliminate not only the defendant's name, but any reference to her existence.

■ PROCEDURAL BASIS

Certiorari to review a decision of a federal court of appeals reversing the defendant's conviction.

■ FACTS

Marsh (D), Williams, and Martin were charged with assault and murder. Marsh (D) and Williams were tried together. At trial, the sole survivor of the assault testified that Marsh (D), Martin, and Williams carried out a plan to rob her and the other victims, forcibly restraining them and shooting her, her son, and her boyfriend in the process. The State also offered as corroborating evidence Williams's confession made shortly after his arrest. The confession was redacted to omit all references to any other person other than Williams and Martin as having been involved in the robbery. Williams did not testify, and the jury was instructed not to use the confession against Marsh (D) in any way. Marsh (D) testified after the State rested, stating that she accompanied Williams and Martin to the victim's house but had no prior knowledge of their plan to rob the victim and did not intend to rob or kill them. During closing argument, the prosecutor reminded the jury not to consider Williams's confession against Marsh (D), but linked Marsh (D) to Williams's confession through her direct testimony. The jury convicted Marsh (D) of two counts of felony murder and one count of aggravated assault. After the Michigan Court of Appeals affirmed, the Michigan Supreme Court denied the appeal. Marsh (D) sought a writ of habeas corpus, alleging that the admission of the confession violated her Sixth Amendment rights. The petition was denied but the federal court of appeals reversed, finding that the relative lack of direct evidence of Marsh's (D) knowledge and involvement in the crime was insufficient to overcome the incriminating effect of the confession.

■ ISSUE

Does the admission into evidence of a nontestifying codefendant's confession at a joint trial violate the Sixth Amendment's Confrontation Clause, when the confession is redacted to omit any reference to the defendant but the defendant is nonetheless linked to the confession by evidence properly admitted at trial?

■ DECISION AND RATIONALE

(Scalia, J.) No. Under the Confrontation Clause, a criminal defendant has a right to cross-examine witnesses against her at trial. Ordinarily, where the jury is instructed to consider a codefendant's confession against the codefendant only, the codefendant is not considered a witness against the defendant. However, when the circumstances make it likely that a jury will not or cannot follow the limiting instruction, a confession incriminating on its face must not be offered in a joint trial. When the confession is redacted to omit any reference to the defendant or other unnamed third persons, the confession is not incriminating on its face and the risk that the jury will not obey instructions is reduced. Any inference created by the confession is too speculative to presume that the jury has not obeyed its orders not to consider the evidence against the defendant.

While all conflict with the Confrontation Clause may be avoided by trying defendants separately, the burden created on the government and the court system by doing so outweighs the burden on joint defendants' rights after limiting instructions are issued and confessions are appropriately redacted. Separate trials would dramatically increase the criminal caseload and risk inconsistent verdicts. "[T]he Confrontation Clause is not violated by the admission of a nontestifying codefendant's confession with a proper limiting instruction, when, as here, the confession is redacted to eliminate not only the defendant's name, but any reference to her existence." However, by linking Marsh's (D) direct testimony to Williams's confession in closing argument, the prosecutor sought to undo the protective effect of the limiting instruction. The case is therefore remanded to determine the effect of the prosecutor's comments.

■ DISSENT

(Stevens, J.) The Court's decision to admit a codefendant's redacted confession against a defendant disregards the power of an inference linking the two together in a criminal plan. Even when a codefendant's confession expressly names the defendant, it need not be excluded if the impact on the defendant's guilt is minimal. On the other hand, if it is presumed that jurors carefully consider all the evidence presented at trial, the damage to a defendant's defense can be as significant though her connection to the defendant is by inference as it is by direct implication. Just as joint trials further the interests in justice in many respects, so too does the Sixth Amendment. Although separate trials undoubtedly burden the government and the court system, the cost to the defendants' rights is more significant.

Analysis:

The confession in this case was carefully redacted to omit any reference to the defendant or any other third person from which the jury could infer the defendant's involvement. But In *Gray v. Maryland*, a confession redacted with the use of blank spaces, ellipses, or other clear indications of redaction was held inadmissible. Thus, in order for the confession to be admissible, there must be no indication on the face of the confession that the defendant or any third party was involved. Such indications create the unavoidable risk that the jury will attribute the redacted portions of the confession to the defendant.

■ CASE VOCABULARY

CONFESSION: A criminal suspect's acknowledgement of guilt, usually in writing and often including details about the crime.

REDACTION: The careful editing of a document, especially to remove confidential references or offensive material.

Davis v. Alaska

(*Robber*) v. (*Prosecuting Government*)
415 U.S. 308, 94 S. Ct. 1105, 39 L. Ed. 2d 347 (1974)

A STATE'S INTEREST IN PROTECTING JUVENILE DELINQUENTS MUST YIELD TO A DEFENDANT'S SIXTH AMENDMENT RIGHTS

■ **INSTANT FACTS** Davis (D) was not allowed to cross-examine a prosecution witness regarding his juvenile record to establish bias or prejudice.

■ **BLACK LETTER RULE** The Confrontation Clause requires that a defendant be afforded a meaningful opportunity to cross-examine a witness against him concerning potential bias or motive.

■ PROCEDURAL BASIS

Certiorari to review a decision of the Alaska Supreme Court affirming the defendant's conviction.

■ FACTS

Police located a safe, with its contents removed, that had been reported stolen from a local bar near the home of Jess Straight. Straight's stepson, Richard Green, informed police that he had spoken with two black men driving a metallic-blue late-model Chevrolet sedan near the area where the safe was recovered. Green later identified Davis (D) in a photo lineup. Davis (D) was arrested, and Green again identified him in a lineup of seven African American men. At trial, police introduced evidence of paint chips found in the trunk of Davis's (D) rented blue Chevrolet that could have come from the stolen safe. Green testified for the prosecution that he had spoken with Davis (D) near the place where the safe was recovered and that Davis (D) was holding a crowbar during the conversation.

Before the testimony, the prosecution sought a protective order to prevent any cross-examination regarding Green's juvenile record and his adjudication as a juvenile delinquent for a prior burglary. Defense counsel argued that Green's juvenile record was necessary to establish bias and prejudice, i.e., his testimony was given out of fear of his being named a suspect in the burglary case. The trial court granted the protective order. On cross-examination, defense counsel generally established Green's state of mind at the time he spoke with the police, including his fear and concern that he may be suspected of the crime, but he denied that police had ever questioned him "like that" before. The defense, however, was prohibited from challenging Green's assertion on police questioning. Davis (D) was convicted, and the conviction was affirmed by the Alaska Supreme Court.

■ ISSUE

Does the Confrontation Clause require that a criminal defendant be allowed to impeach the credibility of a prosecution witness by cross-examination directed at possible bias deriving from the witness's status as a juvenile delinquent, when the impeachment would conflict with the State's interest in preserving the confidentiality of juvenile adjudications?

■ DECISION AND RATIONALE

(Burger, C.J.) Yes. Confrontation means more than a physical encounter with a witness and requires the opportunity to meaningfully cross-examine the witness. Cross-examination is the means by which the truth of the witness's testimony is tested and any ulterior motive or bias is discovered. Without such impeachment, the right of cross-examination is seriously undermined. Whether or not defense counsel would have persuaded the jury that Green's prior burglary conviction established a motive to identify Davis (D) as the culprit to spare himself from police suspicion, the Confrontation Clause gives Davis (D) the opportunity to present his defense to the jury for consideration. It is insufficient to enable counsel to ask the witness if he his biased, without permitting the facts underlying the line of questioning to establish the reasons for counsel's questioning. While the State (P) maintains a strong interest in preserving the confidentiality of juvenile offenders, any resulting embarrassment in this matter from disclosing Green's criminal history cannot overcome the deprivation of Davis's (D) constitutional rights. Reversed and remanded.

■ CONCURRENCE

(Stewart, J.) While the Sixth Amendment does not afford an absolute right to question a prosecution witness on past juvenile or criminal convictions, such cross-examination is appropriate under the facts of this case.

■ DISSENT

(White, J.) The extent of cross-examination in a state criminal proceeding is properly within the discretion of the trial judge and should not be questioned by federal courts imposing their views on matters of state procedure.

Analysis:

The balancing of the interests in this case swayed in favor of the defendant's Sixth Amendment rights. But how does a court balance a defendant's rights in a rape case when the alleged victim takes the stand? Many states have enacted rape shield laws prohibiting the defendant from raising issues related to an alleged rape victim's past sexual history. Yet, if the victim's sexual history establishes a motive or bias that undermines the credibility of her accusations, is not the defendant's Sixth Amendment right of confrontation equally as strong? Many courts have recognized the dichotomy here and allow cross-examination regarding the victim's sexual history.

■ CASE VOCABULARY

BIAS: Inclination; prejudice.

JUVENILE DELINQUENT: A minor who is guilty of criminal behavior, usually punishable by special laws not pertaining to adults.

MOTIVE: Something, especially willful desire, that leads one to act.

Griffin v. California

(*Convicted Murderer*) v. (*Prosecuting Government*)
380 U.S. 609, 85 S. Ct. 1229, 14 L. Ed. 2d 106 (1965)

COMMENTS ON A DEFENDANT'S REFUSAL TO TESTIFY ARE NOT ALLOWED

■ **INSTANT FACTS** Griffin (D) was convicted of murder after the prosecutor commented on his failure to testify on his own behalf.

■ **BLACK LETTER RULE** Under the Fifth Amendment, a prosecutor may not comment on a defendant's decision not to testify at his trial and the court may not instruct the jury that the defendant's silence is evidence of his guilt.

■ PROCEDURAL BASIS

Certiorari to review the decision of the California Supreme Court affirming the defendant's conviction.

■ FACTS

Griffin's (D) California murder trial was bifurcated on the issues of guilt and penalty. While the defendant did not testify during the guilt phase, the judge instructed the jury, in accordance with the California Constitution, that the failure of the defendant to explain or deny facts or evidence against him of which the defendant could be reasonably assumed to have knowledge justifies an inference of the truth of those facts. The court warned, however, that no such inference can be drawn if it is determined that the defendant had no knowledge of the facts. The evidence at trial indicated that on the night of the murder, Griffin (D) was with the victim in the alley where her body was found. As permitted by the state constitution, the Government made numerous comments to the jury regarding Griffin's (D) failure to testify and rebut the evidence against him. The jury convicted the defendant of murder and the death penalty was imposed. The California Supreme Court affirmed the conviction.

■ ISSUE

Does commenting on a defendant's failure to testify on his own behalf to rebut evidence offered against him violate the Fifth Amendment right against self-incrimination as applied to the states?

■ DECISION AND RATIONALE

(Douglas, J.) Yes. In federal court, it is well established that a prosecutor's comment on a defendant's failure to testify constitutes reversible error as a violation of a federal statute. The same reasoning underlying the federal statute applies to the Fifth Amendment. Both preserve the presumption of innocence and recognize that the reasons for a defendant's refusal to take the stand may vary, including nervousness, timidity, and the desire to avoid impeachment on cross-examination. An evidentiary rule, such as that within the California Constitution, that penalizes a defendant for asserting his constitutional rights cannot be applied by the courts. Even if a jury reaches an inference of guilt from the defendant's silence, the court must not solemnize such an inference by highlighting the defendant's refusal to testify. The Fifth Amendment, as applied to the federal courts directly and to the state courts by the Fourteenth Amendment, forbids comment on the accused's silence or instructions from the court that the accused's silence is evidence of his guilt.

■ DISSENT

(Stewart, J.) At issue is whether prosecutorial comments concerning a defendant's failure to testify on his own behalf compel him to be a witness against himself in violation of the Fifth and Fourteenth Amendments. The compulsion that gave rise to the Fifth Amendment concerned forcing one tried for a crime to answer questions favorable to the Government for fear of incarceration, banishment, or mutilation. The state practice of allowing comment on the failure to testify and permitting an inference of the truth of uncontested evidence stretches the limits of the meaning of "compulsion." A comment concerning a defendant's refusal to provide rebuttal testimony does not compel his testimony, as the comment does nothing more than demonstrate the obvious fact that the defendant has not testified and, therefore, has offered no evidence to rebut that which the State has offered against him. States must be free to establish the rules governing their courts. The California procedure does nothing more than bring forward a fact obvious from the proceedings with instructions to the jury to limit any impermissible inferences it may draw. The procedure does not compel the defendant to testify, as he did not in fact testify at his trial, and there is no Fifth Amendment violation.

Analysis:

While comment by the court on the defendant's failure to testify violates the Fifth Amendment, the Court here reserved the question of whether the defendant can request the court to comment and instruct the jury on the reasonable inferences it may draw from his refusal to testify. Later, in *Carter v. Kentucky*, the Court addressed this issue, concluding that a defendant has a right to request an instruction that the jury may draw no inference from the defendant's refusal to testify. The Court has also held that a judge's decision to provide a "no-inference" instruction, as opposed to the "negative-inference" instruction given in *Griffin*, does not violate the Fifth Amendment.

■ CASE VOCABULARY

BIFURCATED TRIAL: A trial that is divided into two stages, such as for guilt and punishment or for liability and damages.

SELF-INCRIMINATION CLAUSE: The clause of the Fifth Amendment to the U.S. Constitution barring the government from compelling criminal defendants to testify against themselves.

Rock v. Arkansas

(*Convicted Defendant*) v. (*Prosecuting Government*)
483 U.S. 44, 107 S. Ct. 2704, 97 L. Ed. 2d 37 (1987)

THE RIGHT TO TESTIFY INCLUDES THE ADMISSION OF RELIABLE HYPNOTICALLY REFRESHED TESTIMONY

■ **INSTANT FACTS** Rock (D) was convicted after her hypnotically refreshed testimony was excluded from her trial.

■ **BLACK LETTER RULE** The per se exclusion of all hypnotically refreshed testimony without regard to its reliability in a particular case is arbitrary and does not further a legitimate state interest.

■ PROCEDURAL BASIS

Certiorari to review a decision of the Supreme Court of Arkansas affirming the defendant's conviction.

■ FACTS

Rock (D) was charged with manslaughter in the death of her husband. Rock (D) told police that after a domestic dispute, her husband prevented her from leaving the house. She confessed that as she got up to leave, her husband grabbed her by her throat and began choking her. She walked away, grabbed a gun, and pointed it at the floor. When her husband hit her again, she shot him. Unable to recall the exact details of the encounter, Rock (D) submitted to hypnosis to refresh her memory. During two hypnosis sessions, Rock (D) did not reveal any new information. After one of the sessions, however, Rock (D) recalled that she did not have her finger on the trigger and that the gun discharged when her husband grabbed her. A firearm expert confirmed that the handgun was defective and prone to discharge without pulling the trigger. The prosecutor moved to exclude the testimony, which motion was granted. Rock (D) was convicted of manslaughter. The Supreme Court of Arkansas affirmed, ruling that Rock's (D) right to present a defense was not violated by the exclusion of her hypnotically refreshed testimony.

■ ISSUE

Does the Arkansas evidentiary rule prohibiting the admission of hypnotically refreshed testimony violate a defendant's right to testify on her own behalf at trial?

■ DECISION AND RATIONALE

(Blackmun, J.) Yes. A defendant's constitutional right to assert a defense includes the right to take the witness stand and testify in her own behalf. Criminal defendants are generally presumed competent to testify at trial, and the right to do so is grounded in several constitutional provisions. The Due Process Clause of the Fourteenth Amendment requires the right to be heard in protection of one's liberty interests. Similarly, the Compulsory Process Clause of the Sixth Amendment affords the right to call witnesses favorable to a defendant's defense, including herself, for a defendant's untruthfulness can be detected on cross-examination just as with any witness. Finally, the right to testify is a corollary to the Fifth Amendment right against compelled testimony since the defendant may waive her right to remain silent.

The right to testify, however, may be limited by state rules. Legitimate interests of the criminal process may require the right to yield to important state interests, but the limitations must not be arbitrary or disproportionate to the interest at stake. Here, the Arkansas rule excluding hypnotically refreshed testimony is a per se exclusion, leaving no discretion to the court in determining whether the testimony offered is proportionate to the state interest asserted. The testimony offered deprived Rock (D) of testifying as to the events of the shooting, although the testimony was corroborated by other evidence. While such a per se rule may be justified when applied to witnesses in a criminal proceeding, the infringement of such a rule on the defendant's constitutional rights requires judicial consideration of the testimony's reliability. Hypnosis is a scientifically recognized practice that has proven useful in many areas of law enforcement and can be carefully controlled through procedural safeguards, such as requiring specially trained professionals to administer hypnosis, the use of corroborating evidence, and well-crafted jury instructions. The exclusion of all hypnotically refreshed testimony without regard to its reliability in a particular case is arbitrary and does not further a legitimate state interest. The per se rule violates the defendant's right to testify at her trial. Vacated and remanded.

■ DISSENT

(Rehnquist, C.J.) Having found that hypnosis produces several influences that render one's testimony unreliable, the Court calls upon state court judges to make their own scientific assessment of the testimony's reliability before deciding whether to exclude it. The exclusion of the unreliable testimony is designed to foster the truth-seeking function of the court—the same goal the exclusionary rule furthers—and recognizes that the defendant's enhanced sense of confidence in the truth of her hypnotic recollection cannot be discredited on cross-examination. Hypnotism has not garnered the scientific consensus necessary to impose such a practice upon the state courts.

Analysis:

Because the use of hypnotically refreshed testimony requires a case-by-case determination of the reliability of the testimony, expert testimony will undoubtedly be required. As most states have adopted in some form the Court's approach to the admissibility of expert testimony set forth in *Daubert v. Merrell Dow Pharmaceuticals*, a framework generally exists to guide state courts in determining the reliability of the statements. Under *Daubert*, the court must generally find that the method used has been or can be tested, that the method has been subjected to peer review, that the potential rate of error has been established, that standards and controls over the method have been stated and maintained, and that the method is generally accepted in the scientific community.

■ CASE VOCABULARY

PER SE: Of, in, or by itself; standing alone, without reference to additional facts.

Holmes v. South Carolina

(*Convicted Criminal*) v. (*Prosecuting State*)
547 U.S. 319, 126 S.Ct. 1727, 164 L.Ed.2d 503 (2006)

THE DEFENDANT MAY INTRODUCE EVIDENCE OF A THIRD PARTY'S GUILT

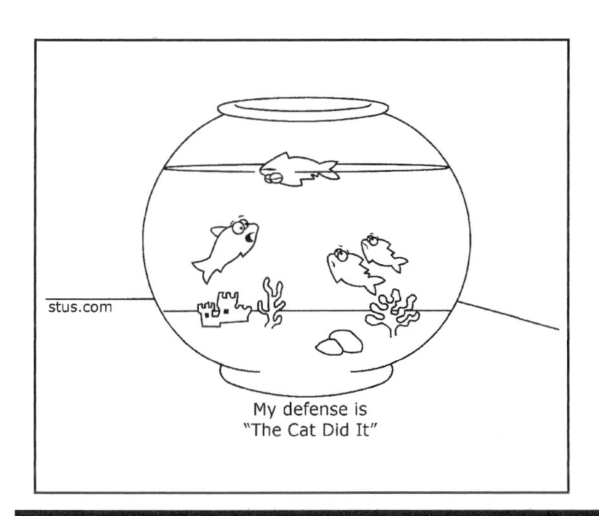

■ **INSTANT FACTS** Holmes (D) was tried and convicted in the death of an elderly woman without being permitted to introduce evidence of a third party's responsibility for the crime.

■ **BLACK LETTER RULE** Rules of evidence in criminal trials may not be arbitrary, must be focused on the central issues in the case, and must be applied in such a manner as to afford the defendant a meaningful opportunity to present a complete defense.

■ PROCEDURAL BASIS

Certiorari to review the defendant's conviction in state court.

■ FACTS

On December 31, 1989, an eighty-six-year-old woman was sexually assaulted and murdered. Holmes (D) was tried and convicted of the crimes and sentenced to death. He sought certiorari in the United States Supreme Court but was denied review. Pursuant to state post-conviction relief, however, he was granted a new trial. At that trial, the prosecutor presented scientific evidence, including DNA evidence, supporting the prosecution's case for Holmes's (D) involvement in the crime. Holmes (D) attempted to defend himself by introducing evidence that another man, White, was actually the murderer. The trial court refused to allow this evidence, however, based on the South Carolina case of *State v. Gregory*, which held that evidence of a third party's guilt is only admissible in a criminal trial if it goes to the defendant's own innocence, rather than casting suspicion on another. Where there is strong evidence of the defendant's guilt, a third party's alleged guilt does not raise a sufficient inference of the defendant's innocence. Because Holmes (D) could not overcome the forensic evidence against him to raise a reasonable inference as to his own innocence, the evidence of White's involvement in the crime was not allowed and Holmes's (D) conviction was upheld. After the second trial, the Supreme Court granted certiorari.

■ ISSUE

Is a criminal defendant denied a fair trial if he is not permitted to introduce reliable evidence of a third party's guilt?

■ DECISION AND RATIONALE

(Alito, J.) Yes. Although state and federal rulemakers have latitude in crafting rules of evidence, that latitude is not without limits. Rules of evidence in criminal trials may not be arbitrary, must be focused on the central issues in the case, and must be applied in such a manner as to afford the defendant a meaningful opportunity to present a complete defense. When a rule interferes with that opportunity, it must be stricken. Thus, in *Washington v. Texas*, the Court struck down a rule that prevented one who had been charged as a participant in a crime from testifying in defense of another alleged participant, even if the witness had not been acquitted. And in *Chambers v. Mississippi*, the Court invalidated a rule that precluded a criminal defendant from cross-examining another who had previously confessed to the crime but recanted while on the witness stand. Similarly, the exclusion of the circumstances surrounding the defendant's confession was ruled unconstitutional in *Crane v. Kentucky*, and in *Rock v. Arkansas* the same result was reached with regard to the wholesale exclusion of hypnotically refreshed testimony.

Federal Rule of Evidence 403 allows trial court judges to exclude any evidence if its probative value is outweighed by the possibility of unfair prejudice, confusion of the issues, or misleading the jury. Apparently the South Carolina court thought it was acting consistently with this concept, but it went too far. The South Carolina approach does not focus on the probative value of the evidence of third-party guilt; rather, the emphasis is on the strength of the prosecution's case, regardless of the strength of the evidence proffered by the defendant. Nor did the court even take into consideration the defendant's challenges to the prosecution's evidence (which, by the way, arose from a deliberate plot to frame Holmes (D)).

The rule applied by the South Carolina Supreme Court loses sight of the need to focus a criminal trial on the central issues by excluding evidence that has only a weak connection thereto. The strength of the prosecution's case simply cannot be evaluated without considering challenges to the prosecution's evidence. And even if the prosecution has a strong case, it does not necessarily follow that evidence of a third party's guilt is weak. Moreover, the resolution of the critical factual issues should be left to the trier of fact—in this case, the jury—and not taken out of its hands by a court's evidentiary ruling. Because the rule applied by the South Carolina court in this case was arbitrary and did not serve any legitimate end, it violates a criminal defendant's right to have a meaningful opportunity to present a complete defense. Judgment vacated and case remanded.

Analysis:

Holmes was one of five death penalty cases for which the Supreme Court granted review during the 2005–2006 term. This case was the only one, however, whose core issue was third-party guilt. On May 1, 2006, the Court issued its opinion, unanimously siding with Holmes. In Justice Alito's first opinion as a Supreme Court Justice, he concluded that Holmes's constitutional rights were violated by an evidence rule that prevented him from countering forensic evidence that, if believed, strongly supported a guilty verdict. By evaluating the strength of only one party's evidence, Justice Alito reasoned, no logical conclusion can be reached regarding the strength of contrary evidence. That defect renders the rule arbitrary and violates a defendant's right to have a meaningful opportunity to present a complete defense.

■ CASE VOCABULARY

INFERENCE: A conclusion reached by considering other facts and deducing a logical consequence from them.

Taylor v. Kentucky

(Convicted Robber) v. *(Prosecuting Government)*
436 U.S. 478, 98 S. Ct. 1930, 56 L. Ed. 2d 468 (1978)

A DEFENDANT'S RIGHT TO A FAIR TRIAL REQUIRES APPROPRIATE JURY INSTRUCTIONS

■ **INSTANT FACTS** Taylor (D) was convicted of robbery after the trial judge denied his request to instruct the jury on the presumption of evidence and evidentiary value of the indictment.

■ **BLACK LETTER RULE** When a jury is likely to consider extrajudicial factors in determining a defendant's guilt, the trial court must properly instruct the jury on the presumption of innocence and the lack of evidentiary value of an indictment.

■ PROCEDURAL BASIS

Certiorari to review a decision of the Kentucky Supreme Court denying an appeal of the defendant's conviction.

■ FACTS

Taylor (D) was charged with robbery. During voir dire, defense counsel questioned the prospective jurors on their understanding of the presumption of innocence, the government's burden of proof, and the evidentiary value of the indictment. After the prosecution offered testimony from the alleged victim, which was contradicted by the defendant's testimony, the defense requested that the court instruct the jury on the presumption of innocence and the indictment's lack of evidentiary value. The court denied the request, but instructed the jury on the State's (P) burden of proof beyond a reasonable doubt. Taylor (D) was convicted and the Kentucky Court of Appeals affirmed. The Kentucky Supreme Court denied review.

■ ISSUE

Does the Fourteenth Amendment's Due Process Clause require a trial court to give a requested instruction on the presumption of innocence and an indictment's lack of evidentiary value?

■ DECISION AND RATIONALE

(Powell, J.) Yes. The presumption of innocence "is the undoubted law, axiomatic and elementary, and its enforcement lies at the foundation of the administration of our criminal law." While the reasonable doubt standard and the presumption of innocence are related principles, the presumption of innocence carries a special message to juries to remove from their mind any preconceived notions of the defendant's guilt and rely solely on the State's (P) evidence in deciding whether the prosecution has met its burden. Here, the trial judge's instructions on the burden of proof did little to stress upon the jury the importance of determining Taylor's (D) guilt solely on the basis of the evidence, and these shortcomings were compounded by the prosecutor's remarks during opening and closing arguments. There, the prosecutor stressed the facts of the indictment and linked the defendant to "every other defendant" who has been convicted. These comments, together with the court's narrow definition of reasonable doubt, invited the jury to consider factors other than the evidence in reaching its verdict. When such a threat exists, the court must take extra measures to ensure that the jury properly understands that the defendant is presumed innocent unless the government establishes his guilt beyond a reasonable doubt, without resort to the indictment. The failure to properly instruct the jury in this case deprived Taylor (D) of his right to a fair trial under the Due Process Clause. Reversed and remanded.

■ CONCURRENCE

(Brennan, J.) Although not explicit in the Constitution, the presumption of innocence is necessary to ensure a defendant's right to a fair trial. Accordingly, trial judges should instruct the jury on the presumption in all cases in which it is requested.

■ DISSENT

(Stevens, J.) Although it is reversible error to deny a request for an appropriate instruction on the presumption of innocence, it is not constitutionally required. A reasonable doubt instruction accomplishes the goal of informing the jury of the government's burden to establish the defendant's guilt. Here, there was no constitutional violation, for the jurors were informed of the government's burden and adequately questioned on the presumption of innocence during voir dire.

Analysis:

As seen in other cases, the concept of due process is not static and must be viewed in the context of the facts of a particular case. Indeed, the Court does not establish an absolute right to an instruction on the presumption of innocence, but rather considers the overall effect of the prosecutor's comments and the extent of the actual jury instructions to determine that additional instructions were necessary. In limiting its decision to the facts of this case, the Court suggests that a defendant may receive a fair trial in other cases although the jury has not been instructed on the presumption of innocence.

■ CASE VOCABULARY

PRESUMPTION OF INNOCENCE: The fundamental criminal-law principle that a person may not be convicted of a crime unless the government proves guilt beyond a reasonable doubt, without any burden placed on the accused to prove innocence.

REASONABLE DOUBT: The doubt that prevents one from being firmly convinced of a defendant's guilt, or the belief that there is a real possibility that a defendant is not guilty.

VOIR DIRE: A preliminary examination of a prospective juror by a judge or lawyer to decide whether the prospect is qualified and suitable to serve on a jury.

Darden v. Wainwright

(*Convicted Murderer*) v. (*Prison Official*)

477 U.S. 168, 106 S. Ct. 2464, 91 L. Ed. 2d 144 (1986)

IMPROPER COMMENTS IN RESPONSE TO DEFENSE COUNSEL'S SUMMATION ARE NOT FUNDAMENTALLY UNFAIR

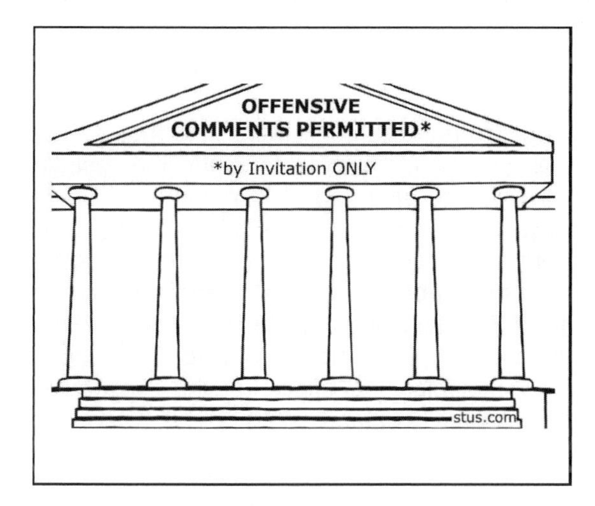

■ **INSTANT FACTS** Darden (D) was convicted of murder after the prosecutor made inappropriate comments during closing arguments.

■ **BLACK LETTER RULE** Improper prosecutorial comments do not require reversal of a conviction unless they so infected the trial with unfairness as to make the resulting conviction a denial of due process.

■ PROCEDURAL BASIS

certiorari to review a decision of the Eleventh Circuit Court of Appeals affirming the defendant's conviction.

■ FACTS

An African American man entered a furniture store owned and operated by Mr. and Mrs. Turman, who lived in a house behind the store. At the time, only Mrs. Turman was present in the store. The man looked around at some furniture with Mrs. Turman's assistance and told her he would return with his wife before purchasing. The man returned a few minutes later with a gun and ordered Mrs. Turman to open the cash register. After the thief took the money, Mr. Turman entered the store from the back door. Mrs. Turman screamed and the man shot Mr. Turman between the eyes. Mr. Turman fell out the back door, with one leg remaining inside.

Learning that something had happened to Mr. Turman, a neighbor ordered her sixteen-year-old son, Phillip Arnold, to help him. Phillip approached Mr. Turman and entered the back door. As Mrs. Turman yelled for Phillip to leave, the man pulled the trigger, but the gun misfired. He pulled the trigger again and shot Phillip in the mouth. As Phillip ran away, he was shot twice more before making his way to a neighbor's house for assistance. The neighbor called the ambulance and saw a late-model green Chevrolet leave on a highway toward Tampa.

Minutes later, Darden (D), who had recently been furloughed from prison, was driving a late-model green Chevrolet along the highway toward Tampa when he went off the road due to his excessive speed and struck a telephone pole. Darden (D) left the scene before police arrived. Recognizing that the car matched the neighbor's description, the police searched the area. They found a pistol near the crash site, from which one shot had been fired, followed by one misfire and two more subsequent shots. The bullet that killed Mr. Turman was matched to the gun.

Darden (D) was arrested and charged with murder, robbery, and assault with intent to kill. During closing argument, defense counsel gave the initial summation, referring to a lack of evidence, referring to the perpetrator of the crimes as an "animal," and giving his personal view of the strength of the evidence. In response, the prosecutor made several inappropriate comments, including putting blame on the Department of Corrections for granting Darden's (D) furlough, implying that the death penalty was the only punishment certain to prevent such a crime from reoccurring, incorporating defense counsel's use of the word "animal," and making other offensive comments. The jury convicted Darden

(D) and recommended the death sentence, which recommendation was accepted by the trial judge. On appeal, the Florida Supreme Court affirmed, reasoning that although the prosecutor's comments were inappropriate they did not render the trial unfair. Darden (D) then sought a writ of habeas corpus in federal court. After the writ was denied, the Eleventh Circuit Court of Appeals affirmed.

■ ISSUE

Do improper comments during closing argument require reversal of a conviction resulting from an otherwise fair trial?

■ DECISION AND RATIONALE

(Powell, J.) No. Although the prosecutor's comments during closing arguments were improper, Darden (D) is entitled to relief only if they "so infected the trial with unfairness as to make the resulting conviction a denial of due process." Here, due process was not offended. The comments did not misstate or manipulate the evidence presented or infringe upon any of Darden's (D) constitutional rights. They were an invited response to defense counsel's summation. While the "invited response" doctrine does not excuse the prosecutor's comments, it gives them perspective in determining whether they rendered the trial unfair. The evidence against Darden (D) was strong and the jury was instructed to consider only the evidence, rather than closing arguments, in deciding on a verdict. Moreover, defense counsel used his rebuttal argument to effectively minimize the effects of the prosecutor's comments on the jury's determination. The trial was not fundamentally unfair.

■ DISSENT

(Blackmun, J.) Standards of professional conduct establish that a prosecutor may not offer opinions as to the credibility of a witness or a defendant's guilt, and should not distract the jury's attention away from its duty to decide the case by injecting broader issues for consideration or use arguments calculated to inflame the passions of the jury. The prosecutor's closing argument clearly violates these standards, yet the Court condemns them as merely improper because no other constitutional rights were violated. The fact that the comments followed the defense's closing argument does not make them any less improper, especially since the prosecutor's invited response exceeded any necessary comments to rebut the defense argument. The case ultimately was decided on the jury's determination of the credibility of three witnesses at trial, including the defendant. The jury cannot be expected to ignore the prosecutor's comments, despite curative comments and an opportunity for rebuttal, in deciding whose testimony is more credible.

Analysis:

The invited response doctrine is actually a tool designed to keep defense counsel in check rather than to justify prosecutorial comments during closing argument. In theory, the doctrine affords prosecutors the ability to respond to improper comments made by defense counsel without risk that his or her own comments will result in an unfair trial. Preventing abuse by defense counsel minimizes the risk of a new trial and ineffective assistance of counsel claims.

■ CASE VOCABULARY

CLOSING ARGUMENT: In a trial, a lawyer's final statement to the judge or jury before deliberation begins, in which the lawyer requests the judge or jury to consider the evidence and to apply the law in his or her client's favor.

Herrera v. Collins

(*Murderer*) v. (*Prison Official*)

506 U.S. 390, 113 S. Ct. 853, 122 L. Ed. 2d 203 (1993)

NEW EVIDENCE JUSTIFYING A NEW TRIAL MUST BE DISCOVERED WITHIN THE TIME PERIOD PRESCRIBED BY STATE STATUTE OR RULE

■ **INSTANT FACTS** Herrera (D) sought post-conviction relief based on new evidence demonstrating his "actual innocence."

■ **BLACK LETTER RULE** A defendant's actual innocence based on newly discovered evidence is an insufficient basis for challenging a conviction on habeas review unless an independent constitutional violation exists.

■ PROCEDURAL BASIS

Certiorari to review a decision of a federal court of appeals vacating a stay of execution.

■ FACTS

A police officer was found shot in the head next to his patrol car along a Texas highway. At approximately the same time, another officer stopped a speeding vehicle traveling away from the site of the first crime, and the driver shot and killed that officer. A few days later, Herrera (D) was arrested and charged with both murders. At the trial, a witness recounted the shooting of the second officer, provided the number for a license plate registered to Herrera's (D) live-in girlfriend, and identified the vehicle that was stopped. Herrera's (D) Social Security card was found on the scene of the first murder and blood found in the car and on Herrera's (D) pants and wallet matched the slain officer's blood type. Herrera (D) also possessed a handwritten letter implicating him in the shooting. Herrera (D) was convicted of murdering the second officer and later pleaded guilty to killing the first officer. Herrera (D) was sentenced to death. On appeal the Texas Criminal Court of Appeals affirmed. After the U.S. Supreme Court denied certiorari, Herrera (D) sought a writ of habeas corpus in state court, which was denied. Herrera (D) then turned to the federal court, seeking a similar writ. The federal court, too, denied habeas corpus relief, and the Supreme Court again denied certiorari. Herrera (D) then returned to the state court, filing a second petition for a writ of habeas corpus, producing evidence that his brother had confessed to the murders before his death. The writ was denied, and the Texas Court of Criminal Appeals affirmed. The Supreme Court denied certiorari. Relentless, Herrera (D) then sought a second writ of habeas corpus in federal court, seeking a stay of execution based on the new evidence of his innocence and claiming that his execution constituted cruel and unusual punishment under the Eighth Amendment. The federal court granted the stay of execution so that he could present his evidence in state court. The federal court of appeals vacated the stay, concluding that his "actual innocence" claim was not cognizable.

■ ISSUE

Is a convicted defendant entitled to a new trial based on newly discovered evidence of his actual innocence years after his conviction?

■ DECISION AND RATIONALE

(Rehnquist, C.J.) No. Due process requires that every criminal defendant have a fair trial at which his or her guilt is established beyond a reasonable doubt. Important constitutional rights, including the right to counsel, the right to confront witnesses, and the right to a jury trial, help to ensure that an innocent defendant is not wrongfully punished. Until his guilt is established, the defendant is presumed to be innocent. After a fair trial, however, the presumption of innocence is lost. Here, the defendant was convicted at a fair trial, but proclaims his innocence based on affidavits presenting evidence not available at trial. In Texas, absent a motion for a new trial within thirty days of sentencing, a conviction may not be challenged based on newly discovered evidence that establishes actual innocence. Neither is actual innocence grounds for habeas relief unless an independent constitutional violation has occurred. In such cases, newly discovered evidence must supplement the constitutional violation, but is no grounds for habeas relief on its own footing.

Herrera's (D) claimed Eighth Amendment violation does not establish the necessary constitutional violation, for it is not his sentence he challenges, but rather his underlying guilt based on newly discovered evidence. The death sentence is not cruel and unusual punishment for a capital crime, and the defendant cannot create a constitutional violation relating to his sentence in order to challenge the underlying conviction. Likewise, the Fourteenth Amendment Due Process Clause does not support a new trial based on Herrera's (D) actual innocence claim. The Constitution itself does not mention new trials, and the Court affords state legislators considerable deference in fashioning state criminal procedure. While new trials were historically limited, they were extended over time to criminal cases upon certain grounds, including newly discovered evidence. However, federal courts have long adhered to the common-law rule that new trials were available only within the period established by the state. While the time permitted varies among the states, it cannot be said that the state court's refusal to grant a new trial based on newly discovered evidence eight years after conviction is fundamentally unfair in violation of the Due Process Clause. Herrera (D) may, of course, petition for executive clemency, but clemency is a discretionary act of the state, and nothing constitutionally requires that it be entertained or granted.

Assuming that actual innocence is a valid reason for a new trial, the burden on the state to retry convicted defendants years later on stale evidence requires a high showing to invoke the new trial. Here, Herrera (D) would not meet such a burden. Herrera (D) offers as newly discovered evidence certain affidavits containing hearsay statements and various inconsistencies that call their reliability into question. There is no explanation for the affiant's eight-year delay in coming forward with the statements, and their inherent reliability is insufficient to overcome the highly probative evidence of his guilt presented at trial. Affirmed.

■ CONCURRENCE

(O'Connor, J.) It is unnecessary for the Court's decision to assume that actual innocence is a cognizable basis for postconviction relief, and it should not be suggested that such a claim is available upon a sufficiently high showing. Nonetheless, on the record here, there is no basis to overturn Herrera's (D) conviction on the newly discovered evidence provided.

■ CONCURRENCE

(Scalia, J.) Because the issue presented relates to the right to a new trial based on newly discovered evidence, which was allegedly denied in violation of the Due Process Clause and constituted cruel and unusual punishment, the Court need only demonstrate that nothing in the text, tradition, or contemporary practice of the Constitution supports such a right. Because of the high burden the Court establishes should such a right arguably exist, there will unlikely be a future occasion to consider this issue again, for such evidence would appear to be sufficient for an executive pardon. Nonetheless, the Court's *arguendo* discussion should not be construed as an endorsement of a right to a new trial on sufficiently probative newly discovered evidence, for no such right exists.

■ CONCURRENCE

(White, J.) If a defendant's newly discovered evidence is sufficiently persuasive to call his initial conviction into serious doubt, it would be unconstitutional to carry out his sentence. To invoke such a right, however, a petitioner must demonstrate on the basis of both the newly discovered evidence and the evidence presented at trial that no rational trier of fact would declare his guilt. The evidence presented here fails to meet this burden.

■ DISSENT

(Blackmun, J.) A death sentence of an innocent person shocks the conscience and should not be carried out. Whether the defendant's constitutional rights were violated in the underlying criminal trial is irrelevant, for when his innocence is established, he should not be convicted and sentenced even when no constitutional violation has occurred. Cruel and unusual punishment is a flexible concept and must be viewed in terms of "contemporary standards of fairness and decency." The guarantees of the Eighth Amendment do not end upon a defendant's conviction and sentencing, but extend throughout the period before and during enforcement of his sentence. Likewise, due process applies as much to substantive defects in the criminal case as procedural problems. The execution of an innocent person does not frustrate mere timelines established for seeking a new trial, but also the fundamental interest in one's life.

Because both the Eighth Amendment and Fourteenth Amendment present sufficient challenges to an allegedly erroneous conviction based on newly discovered evidence, actual innocence is itself a constitutional claim. To sufficiently support such a claim, a defendant must show by the evidence that "he probably is innocent." Because the presumption of innocence has been stripped away upon his valid conviction, the defendant bears the burden not to create reasonable doubt as to his guilt, but to affirmatively prove his innocence. The reliability of the evidence must be considered on a case-by-case basis to determine whether the defendant's burden has been met. Because Herrera (D) has produced evidence suggesting his innocence, both the newly discovered evidence and the evidence on the trial record should be considered by the district court to determine whether the defendant has satisfied his burden of proving his innocence.

Analysis:

Actual innocence differs from legal innocence. With legal innocence, a guilty defendant may nonetheless be acquitted because the government's evidence is insufficient to establish his guilt beyond a reasonable doubt. Actual innocence, however, is just that—the defendant is in fact *actually* innocent, despite the apparent strength of the government's proof. Much debate has circulated concerning which is the lesser of two evils—setting a guilty defendant free or sentencing an innocent defendant to death. The American criminal justice system is not perfect, but the constitutional and procedural protections put in place strive for the best criminal results, attempting to err on the side of letting criminals go free rather than executing the innocent.

■ CASE VOCABULARY

CLEMENCY: Mercy or leniency; especially, the power of the President or a governor to pardon a criminal or commute a criminal sentence.

NEWLY DISCOVERED EVIDENCE: Evidence existing at the time of a motion or trial but then unknown to a party, who, upon later discovering it, may assert it as grounds for reconsideration or new trial.

NEW TRIAL: A postjudgment retrial or reexamination of some or all of the issues determined in an earlier judgment.

STAY: An order to suspend all or part of a judicial proceeding or a judgment resulting from that proceeding.

CHAPTER NINETEEN

Retrials

Ashe v. Swenson

Instant Facts: Ashe (P) was acquitted on charges that he robbed one of six men, and then was tried and convicted on charges that he robbed another of the six.

Black Letter Rule: The Fifth Amendment protection against double jeopardy bars trial of an acquitted defendant on another charge unless the prior acquittal was based on evidence other than that involved in the second prosecution.

United States v. Dixon

Instant Facts: Dixon (D) was held in contempt for violating an order that he not commit any crimes while free on bail, and he claimed that the Double Jeopardy Clause barred his prosecution for the underlying criminal offense.

Black Letter Rule: A person who has been held in criminal contempt for committing a criminal offense may not be criminally prosecuted for committing the underlying offense if prosecution for the criminal offense does not require proof of different facts.

Heath v. Alabama

Instant Facts: Heath (D) pleaded guilty in Georgia to the murder of his wife and was later convicted in Alabama for her murder.

Black Letter Rule: Under the dual sovereignty doctrine, the Double Jeopardy Clause does not bar successive prosecutions for the same conduct by two states.

Hudson v. United States

Instant Facts: Hudson (D) paid a penalty to the Office of the Comptroller of the Currency for banking law violations and was later criminally prosecuted for the same offenses.

Black Letter Rule: A penalty will implicate the Double Jeopardy Clause only if there was a legislative intent that the penalty be criminal in nature and if the statutory scheme is so punitive as to make the remedy criminal.

Arizona v. Washington

Instant Facts: The trial judge declared a mistrial in Washington's (D) second trial for murder because of his defense counsel's opening remarks, and the federal court granted Washington's (D) habeas corpus petition on double jeopardy grounds.

Black Letter Rule: Granting a mistrial over a defendant's objection when the prosecutor proves that there was a manifest necessity for the mistrial does not violate the Double Jeopardy Clause.

Oregon v. Kennedy

Instant Facts: Kennedy (D) moved for a mistrial after the prosecutor made improper remarks, and then claimed that the Double Jeopardy Clause barred his retrial.

Black Letter Rule: If a defendant's request for a mistrial is granted, retrial is barred only if the mistrial was due to prosecutorial conduct that was intended to provoke a mistrial.

United States v. Scott

Instant Facts: Two counts of an indictment against Scott (D) were dismissed due to delay and the Government (P) appealed the dismissal.

Black Letter Rule: Retrial after the dismissal of a prosecution is barred only when the case was dismissed because the evidence was legally insufficient to support a conviction.

Burks v. United States

Instant Facts: Burks's (D) conviction for bank robbery was overturned due to insufficient evidence and the appellate court allowed the trial court to determine whether a new trial should be ordered.

Black Letter Rule: The Double Jeopardy Clause bars retrial of a defendant whose conviction was reversed on appeal based on insufficient evidence to sustain a conviction.

Ashe v. Swenson

(*Convicted of Robbery*) v. (*Prison Warden*)
397 U.S. 436, 90 S. Ct. 1189, 25 L. Ed. 2d 469 (1970)

DOUBLE JEOPARDY BARS A PROSECUTION BASED ON THE SAME EVIDENCE USED TO ACQUIT

■ **INSTANT FACTS** Ashe (P) was acquitted on charges that he robbed one of six men, and then was tried and convicted on charges that he robbed another of the six.

■ **BLACK LETTER RULE** The Fifth Amendment protection against double jeopardy bars trial of an acquitted defendant on another charge unless the prior acquittal was based on evidence other than that involved in the second prosecution.

■ PROCEDURAL BASIS

Appeal from an order affirming a denial of habeas corpus relief.

■ FACTS

Three or four armed, masked men broke into a house and robbed the six participants in a poker game. Ashe (D) was arrested and charged with being one of the robbers. He went on trial for robbing Knight, one of the participants in the poker game. Four of the six participants in the poker game were called to testify. There was no question that the robbery had taken place, or that the four players had each been robbed of property. The identification of Ashe (D) as one of the robbers was weak, however, and the cross-examination of the witnesses by Ashe's (D) attorney focused on the weakness of the identification. The jury was instructed that a conviction would be sustained if Ashe (D) was one of the robbers and if any money had been taken from Knight. The jury was also instructed that Ashe (D) was guilty if he was one of the robbers, even if he had not personally robbed Knight. The jury found Ashe (D) not guilty, noting that the acquittal was "due to insufficient evidence."

Six weeks later, Ashe (D) was tried for the robbery of Roberts, one of the other participants in the poker game. A motion to dismiss based on the earlier acquittal was denied. The identification testimony of the witnesses was stronger at the second trial, and one of the participants in the poker game who did not identify Ashe (D) as one of the robbers was not presented. The jury was given instructions that were virtually identical to the instructions in the first trial, but in the second trial Ashe (D) was convicted of armed robbery.

■ ISSUE

Was the second prosecution barred by the constitutional protection against double jeopardy?

■ DECISION AND RATIONALE

(Stewart, J.) Yes. The Fifth Amendment protection against double jeopardy bars trial of an acquitted defendant on another charge unless the prior acquittal was based on evidence other than that involved in the second prosecution. Collateral estoppel is an established part of federal criminal law, and that rule is a part of the protection against double jeopardy. The rule of collateral estoppel is not to be applied mechanically, but upon consideration of the pleadings, the charges, the evidence, and other relevant matter. The question when an acquittal is based on a general verdict is whether a rational jury could have arrived at its verdict on an issue other than the one the defendant seeks to foreclose from consideration.

The question here, then, is not whether Ashe (D) could be prosecuted or punished for six separate offenses, but simply whether Ashe (D) may be called upon to relitigate the issue of whether he was one of the robbers. The State (P) may not treat the first prosecution as a dry run for the second prosecution, which the Sate (P) conceded that it did. Reversed and remanded.

■ CONCURRENCE

(Brennan, J.) The "same evidence" test is not mandated by the Constitution. The Double Jeopardy Clause requires prosecutors, except in limited circumstances, to bring one prosecution for all of the charges against a defendant that arise out of a single act or occurrence. This rule not only prevents multiple prosecutions, but also promotes judicial economy and convenience.

■ DISSENT

(Burger, J.) The collateral estoppel rule enunciated by the majority is not constitutionally required. Collateral estoppel is a product of civil litigation and does not fit well into criminal proceedings. This case does not remotely suggest harassment of Ashe (D), and the harassment aspect does not rise to constitutional levels.

In this case there were six charges of armed robbery, committed against six separate victims. It demeans the dignity of human personality to think of six separate assaults against six separate victims as a "single transaction." To the victims, the incident was not single, but was readily divisible and intensely personal.

Analysis:

It is significant here that the jury was instructed that Ashe (D) would be guilty if he were one of the robbers, even if he personally did not rob the victim whose robbery was at issue in that trial. Based on that instruction, and based on the evidence presented, acquittal in the first trial was an implicit acquittal for all of the robberies: the jury found that Ashe (D) wasn't responsible. Justice Burger's dissent emphasizes the fact that there were six victims, but the jury instruction put the robberies of all six victims at issue in both trials.

■ CASE VOCABULARY

DOUBLE JEOPARDY CLAUSE: The Fifth Amendment provision stating, "nor shall any person be subject for the same offense to be twice put in jeopardy of life or limb."

United States v. Dixon

(*Prosecuting Authority*) v. (*Possessor of Cocaine*)
509 U.S. 688, 113 S. Ct. 2849, 125 L. Ed. 2d 556 (1993)

CRIMINAL CONTEMPT PROSECUTIONS BAR PROSECUTION FOR THE UNDERLYING ACT

You want to prosecute the guy, but I want to hold him in criminal contempt.... I say we flip for it.

■ **INSTANT FACTS** Dixon (D) was held in contempt for violating an order that he not commit any crimes while free on bail, and he claimed that the Double Jeopardy Clause barred his prosecution for the underlying criminal offense.

■ **BLACK LETTER RULE** A person who has been held in criminal contempt for committing a criminal offense may not be criminally prosecuted for committing the underlying offense if prosecution for the criminal offense does not require proof of different facts.

■ PROCEDURAL BASIS

Appeal from orders of the court of appeals holding that the Double Jeopardy Clause barred prosecutions.

■ FACTS

Dixon (D) was charged with second-degree murder and released on bail. One of the conditions of his release was that he not commit any criminal offense. While he was on bail, Dixon was arrested and indicted for possession of cocaine with intent to distribute. After a hearing, the trial court found Dixon (D) guilty of criminal contempt for violating the conditions of his release. Dixon (D) moved to dismiss the cocaine indictment on double jeopardy grounds, and his motion was granted.

In a separate case, Foster's (D) wife obtained a civil protection order (CPO) against Foster (D). Foster (D) consented to the order, which required that he not assault, threaten, or physically abuse his wife. Foster's (D) wife made three motions to have Foster (D) held in contempt for various actions, including threats made on November 12, 1987, March 26, 1988, and May 17, 1988, as well as assaults on November 6, 1987 and May 21, 1988. The contempt motions were prosecuted by counsel for Foster's (D) wife and mother-in-law. The Government (P) knew of the action, but did not participate. The court required Foster's (D) wife to prove that there was a CPO, and then that an assault, as defined by the criminal code, occurred. Foster was acquitted on some of the counts, including making threats on November 12 and May 17, but was found guilty beyond a reasonable doubt on the other counts, including the November 6 and May 21 assaults. The Government (P) later obtained an indictment charging Foster (D) with simple assault, threatening to injure, and assault with intent to kill. The simple assault and assault with intent to kill counts were based on the assaults for which Foster (D) was acquitted at his contempt trial, and the threats were the threats for which he was found in criminal contempt. Foster (D) moved to dismiss the indictment on double jeopardy grounds, and on collateral estoppel grounds with regard to the charges of making threats. The court denied his double jeopardy motion and did not rule on his collateral estoppel claim.

The District of Columbia Court of Appeals consolidated Dixon's (D) and Foster's (D) cases and ruled that the Double Jeopardy Clause barred the prosecutions in both cases.

■ ISSUE

Can the Double Jeopardy Clause bar prosecution for an offense that underlies a criminal contempt holding?

■ DECISION AND RATIONALE

(Scalia, J.) Yes. In this case, the prosecution of Dixon (D) and the simple assault count against Foster (D) are barred on account of double jeopardy, but the assault with intent to kill and threat charges are not. A person who has been held in criminal contempt for committing a criminal offense may not be criminally prosecuted for committing the underlying offense if prosecution for the criminal offense does not require proof of different facts. Criminal contempt, at least non-summary contempt, is a criminal prosecution in every fundamental sense. The test, as set out in *Blockburger v. United States,* 284 U.S. 299 (1932), is whether the contempt action and the criminal prosecution make use of the same elements. If one offense contains an element not found in the other, they are not the same offense and the subsequent prosecution is not barred. Dixon's (D) violation of his release order did not become an offense until he violated a criminal statute. The offense of possession of cocaine with intent to sell was a type of lesser-included offense of the contempt charge. The distinction between a contempt charge and any other criminal charge is not important in this context.

The prosecution of Foster (D) for simple assault is likewise barred by the Double Jeopardy Clause, in that his prior contempt prosecution alleged that his contemptuous act was violation of the same statute. The charge of assault with intent to kill, however, required a specific intent not present in a prosecution for simple assault. And the other contempt charges required proof that Foster (D) knew about the CPO when he committed the violations. Each contempt offense thus contained an element not present in the later prosecutions.

The case of *Grady v. Corbin*, 495 U.S. 508 (1990), is not controlling here. *Grady* defined the "same offense" for double jeopardy purposes as crimes that involved the same conduct. The "same conduct" test is contrary to earlier precedent and to the common-law understanding of double jeopardy. Cases relied upon to support the contention that *Grady* has constitutional or historical antecedents do not support that conclusion. In addition, *Grady* has proven to be unstable, as exceptions to its rule for prosecutions for conspiracy have already been made. *Grady* was a mistake, and should be overruled. The court of appeals is affirmed in Dixon's (D) case and reversed regarding the assault with intent to kill and threat prosecutions in Foster's (D) case.

■ CONCURRENCE IN PART

(Rehnquist, C.J.) The same-element test does not bar the prosecutions in either case. Contempt of court requires a court order made known to the defendant and a willful violation of that order. Neither element is necessarily satisfied by proof of the substantive offense, and no element of the substantive offenses is necessarily satisfied by proof that a defendant has been found guilty of contempt. It defies common sense to say that the underlying offense is a lesser-included offense of contempt.

■ CONCURRENCE IN PART

(White, J.) The prosecutions of both defendants should be barred by the Double Jeopardy Clause. In double jeopardy cases, the interest of the defendant is paramount to the interests of the government. The CPO should not be considered, but the substantive offenses should be compared. Focusing on the statutory elements of an offense makes sense when the question involves cumulative punishments, since there the aim is to uncover legislative intent. However, legislative intent is less important when the question is successive prosecutions. The same-elements test is an inadequate safeguard against multiple prosecutions, because it leaves legislatures the option of making modifications to the statutory definitions of offenses.

The decision in this case does not limit the power of courts to punish those who flout their orders. The urgency of punishing those who violate court orders is no more, and is no less, than the interest in punishing those who violate the criminal laws.

■ CONCURRENCE IN PART

(Blackmun, J.) The purpose of contempt of court is to punish the specific offense of violating a court order, not to punish an offense against the community at large. The interests served are fundamentally different. Neither prosecution at issue in this case should be barred by the Double Jeopardy Clause.

■ CONCURRENCE IN PART

(Souter, J.) *Grady v. Corbin* was decided correctly, and even if it were not, there is no reason to overrule it now. The interests at stake in avoiding successive prosecution are different from those involved in avoiding successive punishments. Successive prosecutions should be barred if the second prosecution requires the relitigation of factual issues resolved by the first prosecution. *Blockburger* does not provide sufficient protection against subsequent prosecutions.

Analysis:

The majority's analysis has had a reach beyond the relatively narrow question of contempt at issue here. Civil or administrative actions brought by the government because of criminal activity, such as forfeitures or debarment proceedings, have been held not to violate the Double Jeopardy Clause based on this case. Note that Foster's (D) collateral estoppel claim is not an issue here, since the trial court never ruled on that claim.

■ CASE VOCABULARY

CRIMINAL CONTEMPT: An act that obstructs justice or attacks the integrity of the court. A criminal contempt proceeding is punitive in nature.

Heath v. Alabama

(*Hired Murderers*) v. (*Prosecuting Authority*)
474 U.S. 82, 106 S. Ct. 433, 88 L. Ed. 2d 387 (1985)

PROSECUTION FOR THE SAME OFFENSE BY DIFFERENT STATES IS NOT DOUBLE JEOPARDY

■ **INSTANT FACTS** Heath (D) pleaded guilty in Georgia to the murder of his wife and was later convicted in Alabama for her murder.

■ **BLACK LETTER RULE** Under the dual sovereignty doctrine, the Double Jeopardy Clause does not bar successive prosecutions for the same conduct by two states.

■ PROCEDURAL BASIS

Appeal on a writ of certiorari to the Supreme Court of Alabama.

■ FACTS

Heath (D), who lived in Alabama, hired two men to kill his wife. He met with the two men in Georgia, and the men later went to Heath's (D) home in Alabama and kidnapped his wife. Her body was found in a car in Georgia, however, and the evidence was consistent with the theory that the murder took place in Georgia.

Heath (D) was indicted in Georgia for "malice murder." He pleaded guilty and was sentenced to life imprisonment, with the understanding that he would be eligible for release in seven years. A grand jury in Alabama also indicted Heath (D) for the murder. He pleaded *autrefois convict* and double jeopardy to that charge, but both pleas were rejected. Heath (D) was convicted by a jury of murder during a kidnapping in the first degree and was sentenced to death. The court found that the sole aggravating factor—that the murder was committed during a kidnapping—outweighed the sole mitigating factor—that Heath (D) had been sentenced to life for the offense in Georgia. The state appellate courts affirmed the verdict and the sentence.

■ ISSUE

Does the Double Jeopardy Clause bar the prosecution of a defendant by more than one state for the same criminal offense?

■ DECISION AND RATIONALE

(O'Connor, J.) No. Under the dual sovereignty doctrine, the Double Jeopardy Clause does not bar successive prosecutions for the same conduct by two states. A crime is an offense against the sovereignty of the government. If a defendant commits a single act that violates the "peace and dignity" of two sovereigns, that defendant has committed two distinct offenses.

The crucial determination is whether the two entities that seek to prosecute a defendant are in fact separate sovereigns. States have been held to be separate sovereigns from the federal government. They are no less sovereign with respect to each other. The power of a state to prosecute crimes derives from separate and independent sources of authority. In cases in which the doctrine has been held not to apply, the powers to prosecute were not derived from independent sources of authority.

The Court will not create a test in which the interests of both sovereigns are balanced. A balancing of interests approach cannot be reconciled with dual sovereignty. Affirmed.

■ DISSENT

(Marshall, J.) There is no double jeopardy issue when a state and the federal government prosecute a defendant for the same crime, because different interests are at stake. When two states seek to prosecute the same defendant for the same crime in different proceedings, the justifications in the federal-state context for an exemption from double jeopardy do not hold. The sovereign concerns to be vindicated are the same for both states. The burden of successive prosecutions by different states cannot be justified as a *quid pro quo* of dual citizenship.

Analysis:

The Court's holding does not completely remove prosecutions of the same act by different authorities from double jeopardy questions. It is important that the two states here have authority that derives from independent sources of power. Thus, a city or county may have the authority to make violations of some of its ordinances crimes, and many of those offenses may overlap crimes created by state statute. But the authority of the city or county to prosecute derives from the state, so the dual sovereignty doctrine would not apply.

■ CASE VOCABULARY

AUTREFOIS CONVICT: A plea in bar of arraignment that the defendant has been convicted of the offense.

DUAL–SOVEREIGNTY DOCTRINE: The rule that the federal and state governments may both prosecute someone for a crime, without violating the constitutional protection against double jeopardy, if the person's act violated both jurisdictions' laws.

Hudson v. United States

(Banker) v. *(Prosecuting Authority)*

522 U.S. 93, 118 S. Ct. 488, 139 L. Ed. 2d 450 (1997)

DOUBLE JEOPARDY DOES NOT APPLY TO CIVIL PENALTIES

■ **INSTANT FACTS** Hudson (D) paid a penalty to the Office of the Comptroller of the Currency for banking law violations and was later criminally prosecuted for the same offenses.

■ **BLACK LETTER RULE** A penalty will implicate the Double Jeopardy Clause only if there was a legislative intent that the penalty be criminal in nature and if the statutory scheme is so punitive as to make the remedy criminal.

■ PROCEDURAL BASIS

Appeal from an order of the court of appeals reversing an order dismissing charges.

■ FACTS

The Office of the Comptroller of the Currency (OCC) accused Hudson (D) of banking law violations. Hudson (D) agreed to pay a monetary penalty and to refrain from participating in the affairs of any bank without OCC authorization. A few years later, Hudson (D) was indicted on criminal charges arising out of the same transactions. He moved to dismiss the charges on double jeopardy grounds, and the district court granted his motion. The court of appeals reversed.

■ ISSUE

Does the Double Jeopardy Clause bar the prosecution of a defendant who has been held civilly liable for the same conduct?

■ DECISION AND RATIONALE

(Rehnquist, C.J.) No. A penalty will implicate the Double Jeopardy Clause only if there was a legislative intent that the punishment be a criminal penalty and if the statutory scheme is so punitive as to make the remedy criminal. The second factor involves a consideration of whether the sanction involves an affirmative disability or restraint; whether it has traditionally been regarded as a punishment; whether it requires a finding of scienter; whether it will promote the traditional aims of punishment, retribution, and deterrence; whether the behavior it applies to is already a crime; whether an alternate purpose may be assigned to it; and whether it appears excessive in relation to the alternate purpose. These factors will be considered only in regard to the statute on its face, and only the clearest proof will suffice to overcome legislative intent and transform a civil remedy into a criminal penalty.

In this case, double jeopardy does not apply. Congress intended the penalties imposed by the OCC to be civil, not criminal. There is also little evidence to suggest that the penalties are criminal. Neither monetary penalties nor debarment have historically been viewed as punishment. There is no disability or restraint that approaches imprisonment. The sanctions do not require scienter, but are imposed without regard to a violator's state of mind. Although the conduct for which the penalties were imposed may be criminal, that is not sufficient to make the monetary penalties or debarment criminal penalties. There is always some deterrent effect to civil penalties, but the mere presence of deterrence is not enough to make a penalty criminal, since deterrence may serve civil as well as criminal purposes.

United States v. Halper, 490 U.S. 435 (1989), was ill-considered. In that case, the Court focused solely on whether the penalty was disproportionate to the injury caused and did not consider the statute on its face. *Halper* deviated from traditional double jeopardy analysis in both regards. Affirmed.

■ CONCURRENCE

(Scalia, J.) The Double Jeopardy Clause prohibits successive prosecution, not successive punishment. Multiple punishments are prohibited only when there have been multiple prosecutions.

■ CONCURRENCE

(Stevens, J.) It was not necessary to re-examine the holding in *Halper.* It is extremely important to acknowledge that civil penalties may implicate double jeopardy concerns.

■ CONCURRENCE

(Souter, J.) The "clearest proof" necessary to find that a civil statute is actually criminal depends upon the context. "Clearest proof" is indicative of the strength of the indications of the civil nature of a statute. It does not necessarily mean that a finding that a civil statute is in fact criminal will be a rare occurrence in the future.

■ CONCURRENCE

(Breyer, J.) The "clearest proof" language is misleading. The proof will not "transform" a civil penalty into a criminal penalty. A statute should not be evaluated only on its face, but the actual character of the sanctions imposed should be considered. There is nothing in the majority's opinion to show why *Halper* should be abandoned.

Analysis:

Although the Court was unanimous in its result, at least four of the Justices (Justice Ginsburg concurred with Justice Breyer) were less than pleased with the majority's reasoning. In portions of his concurrence not reproduced in the excerpt, Justice Steven noted that this was an inappropriate case to use to re-examine the double jeopardy implications of civil penalties. He noted that, even under the *Halper* test, the penalty imposed on Hudson (D) was not so disproportionate as to raise double jeopardy concerns. In fact, the court of appeals based its ruling that denied relief on *Halper.* Justice Stevens also noted that the Court could not show one successful double jeopardy challenge to a civil penalty since *Halper* was decided.

■ CASE VOCABULARY

CIVIL PENALTY: A fine assessed for a violation of a statute or regulation.

PENALTY: Punishment imposed on a wrongdoer, usually in the form of imprisonment or fine; especially, a sum of money exacted as punishment for either a wrong to the state or a civil wrong (as distinguished from compensation for the injured party's loss). Though usually for crimes, penalties are also sometimes imposed for civil wrongs.

Arizona v. Washington

(*Prosecuting Authority*) v. (*Accused Murderer*)

434 U.S. 497, 98 S. Ct. 824, 54 L. Ed. 2d 717 (1978)

GRANTING A MISTRIAL MAY NOT BE DOUBLE JEOPARDY

■ **INSTANT FACTS** The trial judge declared a mistrial in Washington's (D) second trial for murder because of his defense counsel's opening remarks, and the federal court granted Washington's (D) habeas corpus petition on double jeopardy grounds.

■ **BLACK LETTER RULE** Granting a mistrial over a defendant's objection when the prosecutor proves that there was a manifest necessity for the mistrial does not violate the Double Jeopardy Clause.

■ PROCEDURAL BASIS

Appeal from a decision of the court of appeals affirming a grant of habeas corpus relief.

■ FACTS

Washington (D) was tried and convicted of murder. His conviction was reversed, and a new trial granted, because the prosecutor withheld exculpatory evidence from the defense. At his second trial, the prosecutor (P) stated in his opening statement that some of the witnesses had testified in earlier proceedings. In his opening, Washington's (D) attorney told the jury that evidence was hidden from Washington (D) at the first trial. He also told that jury that Washington (D) had been granted a new trial because the evidence had been withheld. The prosecutor (P) moved for a mistrial and the motion was granted. The trial judge did not make an express finding that there was a "manifest necessity" for a mistrial. The judge also did not make findings that alternative solutions had been considered and that none would be adequate. Washington (D) petitioned the federal district court for habeas corpus relief, and the petition was granted because of the lack of findings. The court of appeals affirmed.

■ ISSUE

Did the granting of the motion for a mistrial violate Washington's (D) protection against double jeopardy?

■ DECISION AND RATIONALE

(Stevens, J.) No. Granting a mistrial over a defendant's objection when the prosecutor proves that there was a manifest necessity for the mistrial does not violate the Double Jeopardy Clause. There are varying degrees of necessity for declaring a mistrial. At one extreme are mistrials used to buttress weaknesses in a prosecutor's case. Such mistrials require the highest level of scrutiny. At the other extreme are mistrials granted because a jury is unable to reach a verdict. Courts have held, without exception, that judges may order a retrial in those circumstances. The prosecution is given one complete opportunity to secure a conviction. The defendant also avoids the possibility that a verdict may result from pressures on the jurors rather than their considered judgment. A judge is granted a great deal of discretion in deciding whether to grant a motion for a mistrial in these circumstances. The trial judge's determination will not be reversed absent an abuse of discretion.

It is appropriate to defer to the trial court's judgment in this case as well. Washington's (D) lawyer made improper remarks during his opening statement. The trial judge was in the best position to determine the effect the inappropriate remarks had on the jury. There were other alternatives for the judge, but it was up to the judge to determine the appropriate actions. This is not a case in which the judge acted irrationally or irresponsibly.

The trial judge was not required to make an explicit finding of "manifest necessity." The record supplies sufficient justification for the trial court's ruling. Reversed

■ DISSENT

(White, J.) It was not appropriate for the Court to examine the record in the first instance. The case should be remanded to the court of appeals to make the initial judgment, under the correct legal standard, as to whether the writ should issue.

■ DISSENT

(Marshall, J.) There is nothing in the record on which to base a conclusion that the prejudicial impact of defense counsel's remarks was sufficient to support the granting of a mistrial. The prejudicial remarks were only a small part of a lengthy opening statement, and no objection was made at the time of the remarks, even though the prosecutor interrupted at other times to object. These circumstances suggest that the prejudicial impact was minimal and probably could have been cured by a cautionary instruction to the jury.

Explicit findings of a manifest necessity are not required, but would have made this a different case. The record as it stands is ambiguous.

Analysis:

The Court avoids the problem of a close analysis of "manifest necessity" by seeming to give broad deference to the decision of the trial judge. Nevertheless, the majority necessarily must engage in some factual analysis in order to find that there was no abuse of discretion. Justice Marshall undertakes an analysis of the misconduct and reaches an opposite conclusion, based on the factual record of the case. The majority's decision may have been made easier by the fact that defense counsel seemingly provoked the mistrial.

■ CASE VOCABULARY

MISTRIAL: A trial that the judge brings to an end, without a determination on the merits, because of a procedural error or serious misconduct occurring during the proceedings; a trial that ends inconclusively because the jury cannot agree on a verdict.

Oregon v. Kennedy

(*Prosecuting Authority*) v. (*Alleged Thief*)
456 U.S. 667, 102 S. Ct. 2083, 72 L. Ed. 2d 416 (1982)

MISTRIALS CAUSED BY INTENTIONAL PROSECUTORIAL MISCONDUCT WILL BAR RETRIAL

■ **INSTANT FACTS** Kennedy (D) moved for a mistrial after the prosecutor made improper remarks, and then claimed that the Double Jeopardy Clause barred his retrial.

■ **BLACK LETTER RULE** If a defendant's request for a mistrial is granted, retrial is barred only if the mistrial was due to prosecutorial conduct that was intended to provoke a mistrial.

■ PROCEDURAL BASIS

Appeal from an order of the Oregon Court of Appeals that held that retrial was barred on double jeopardy grounds.

■ FACTS

Kennedy (D) was charged with the theft of a rug. The prosecution (P) called an expert witness to testify regarding the value of the rug. The expert was asked about a criminal complaint he had filed against Kennedy (D) in another matter. The prosecutor (P) asked about the reasons for the complaint, and objections to that line of questioning were sustained. The prosecutor (P) then asked if the reason the witness had never done business with Kennedy (D) was because he was a crook. Kennedy's (D) motion for a mistrial was granted.

When the State (P) moved to try Kennedy (D) again, he moved to dismiss the charges on grounds of double jeopardy. The trial court found that the prosecutor (D) had not intended to cause a mistrial and denied the motion to dismiss. Kennedy (D) was retried and convicted. The court of appeals sustained Kennedy's (D) double jeopardy claim, however, and held that retrial was barred because the prosecutor's (P) conduct was "overreaching."

■ ISSUE

Was the retrial of Kennedy (D) after a mistrial barred on double jeopardy grounds?

■ DECISION AND RATIONALE

(Rehnquist, J.) No. If a defendant's request for a mistrial is granted, retrial is barred only if the mistrial was due to prosecutorial conduct that was intended to provoke a mistrial. Under most circumstances, a defendant who moves for a mistrial is held to have waived his or her right to have a trial completed by the first jury impaneled to hear the case. It is difficult to apply that rule, however, when a prosecutor goads the defendant into requesting a mistrial.

The question is one of what standard will be used. Standards that are more general than intent offer no guidance for their application. Everything a prosecutor does is meant to "prejudice" a defendant, and it will be a rare trial in which a prosecutor does not offer objectionable evidence. But the most serious type of conduct may necessitate a mistrial. A standard that requires a showing of intent before charges will be dismissed is manageable, requiring only that the trial court make a finding of fact. Prosecutorial conduct that might justify granting a motion for a mistrial will not bar retrial unless the trial court finds that there was an intent to subvert the protections of the Double Jeopardy Clause. Any other standard might not benefit criminal defendants, as trial judges might be less willing to grant motions for mistrial if a defendant could not be retried.

In this case, the trial court made a finding that the prosecutor (P) did not intend to provoke a mistrial. Kennedy's (D) retrial thus did not violate the Double Jeopardy Clause. Reversed.

■ CONCURRENCE

(Brennan, J.) The state courts are free, on remand, to conclude that Kennedy's (D) retrial violates the double jeopardy prohibition in the Oregon Constitution.

■ CONCURRENCE

(Powell, J.) Because a prosecutor's subjective intent may be unknowable, a court should rely primarily on the objective facts and circumstances of a case in deciding a double jeopardy motion. In this case, a review of the entire record supports the conclusion that the prosecutor's (P) actions were unintentional. There was no prior sequence of overreaching, the prosecutor (P) seemed surprised by the motion, and she testified that there was no intention to cause a mistrial.

■ CONCURRENCE

(Stevens, J.) The subjective intent standard announced by the majority eviscerates the exception to the rule that retrial after a mistrial does not violate the Double Jeopardy Clause. It will be almost impossible to prove what a prosecutor's subjective intent may have been. A prosecutor may engage in willful misconduct for many reasons, other than merely to provoke a mistrial. The overreaching standard used by the Oregon court does not require a court to divine the exact motive for prosecutorial misconduct. It is sufficient that the court is satisfied that egregious prosecutorial misconduct has made a defendant's choice to abort or continue the proceedings unmeaningful. A finding of deliberate misconduct would normally be necessary to bar reprosecution. In addition, there would normally be a finding that the prosecutorial error virtually eliminated, or substantially reduced, the chances of acquittal in a case that was going badly for the government. In this case, however, the error was minor and occurred at an early stage of the trial. It does not come within the exceptions to the rules on retrial.

Analysis:

Determining a prosecutor's subjective intent is difficult, even though similar questions are often before the courts. Clearly, a court should not give too much weight to a prosecutor's testimony, as it is hard to imagine why a prosecutor would admit to provoking a mistrial, knowing that the defendant then could not be retried. As Justice Powell suggests, the court will have to consider the totality of the circumstances surrounding the grant of the mistrial, including conduct by the prosecutor other than the specific incident that led to the mistrial motion.

United States v. Scott

(*Prosecuting Authority*) v. (*Police Officer*)
437 U.S. 82, 98 S. Ct. 2187, 57 L. Ed. 2d 65 (1978)

RETRIAL AFTER DISMISSAL UNRELATED TO GUILT DOES NOT VIOLATE DOUBLE JEOPARDY

Wearing black trunks is the prosecution, magically resurrected by the Supreme Court for a second round after an apparent knockout by the defense in the first.

■ **INSTANT FACTS** Two counts of an indictment against Scott (D) were dismissed due to delay and the Government (P) appealed the dismissal.

■ **BLACK LETTER RULE** Retrial after the dismissal of a prosecution is barred only when the case was dismissed because the evidence was legally insufficient to support a conviction.

■ PROCEDURAL BASIS

Appeal from an order of the court of appeals barring further prosecution.

■ FACTS

Scott (D) was charged with distribution of narcotics. He moved to dismiss two counts of the indictment on the grounds of prejudicial delay. Scott (D) made his motions both before trial and twice during trial. The court granted his motion at the close of all the evidence. The Government (P) appealed the dismissal of the two counts, but the court of appeals held that the Double Jeopardy Clause barred further prosecution of Scott (D). The court's decision relied on *United States v. Jenkins,* 420 U.S. 358 (1975).

■ ISSUE

Was further prosecution of Scott (D) after dismissal on the ground of delay barred by the Double Jeopardy Clause?

■ DECISION AND RATIONALE

(Rehnquist, J.) No. Retrial after the dismissal of a prosecution is barred only when the case was dismissed because the government's evidence was legally insufficient to support a conviction. The two principles of double jeopardy jurisprudence are that a defendant who has been acquitted may not be tried again, but a defendant whose conviction has been overturned on appeal for a reason other than a lack of evidence may be retried. Retrial, even after an appeal, will be barred only when it is plain that the trial court evaluated the evidence against the defendant and concluded that it was legally insufficient to support a conviction. *Jenkins v. United States* was wrongly decided and is overruled.

In this case, Scott (D) sought to have the proceedings against him terminated for reasons unrelated to his guilt or innocence. The government (P) is not relentlessly pursuing a defendant who has been found not guilty or who has at least insisted on having the issue of guilt submitted to the first trier of fact. Scott (D) has chosen to avoid conviction and imprisonment because of a legal claim that the government's case must fail even though it may show beyond a reasonable doubt that he was guilty. He has not been deprived of his right to have his case heard by the first jury. Reversed.

■ DISSENT

(Brennan, J.) The purpose of the Double Jeopardy Clause is to protect defendants from having to endure multiple prosecutions. The Government (P) should be afforded only one complete opportunity to convict an accused. Acquittals may be based on many things other than a finding of innocence. A defendant whose conviction is overturned for reasons other than insufficient evidence should not stand on different constitutional footing than the defendant who has been found not guilty. The Government's (P) interest in retrying a defendant cannot vary according to the ground of final termination in the defendant's favor.

Analysis:

The indictment against Scott (D) contained three counts, two of which were dismissed. Scott (D) was acquitted on the count that was submitted to the jury. The dismissal of the two counts against Scott (D) is unlike the usual reversal of a conviction or termination of a prosecution. Here, the trial court made an implicit finding, after the evidence had been submitted, that those two counts should not have been sent to the jury in the first place.

■ CASE VOCABULARY

DISMISS: To send (something) away; specifically, to terminate (an action or claim) without further hearing, especially before the trial of the issues involved.

RETRIAL: A new trial of an action that has already been tried.

Burks v. United States

(*Accused Bank Robber*) v. (*Prosecuting Authority*)
437 U.S. 1, 98 S. Ct. 2141, 57 L. Ed. 2d 1 (1978)

REVERSAL FOR INSUFFICIENT EVIDENCE BARS SUBSEQUENT PROSECUTION

■ **INSTANT FACTS** Burks's (D) conviction for bank robbery was overturned due to insufficient evidence and the appellate court allowed the trial court to determine whether a new trial should be ordered.

■ **BLACK LETTER RULE** The Double Jeopardy Clause bars retrial of a defendant whose conviction was reversed on appeal based on insufficient evidence to sustain a conviction.

■ PROCEDURAL BASIS

Appeal by Burks (D) form an order of the court of appeals reversing his conviction but allowing a retrial.

■ FACTS

Burks (D) was tried and convicted of bank robbery. His defense was insanity, and he produced expert witnesses to substantiate his claim. The prosecution (P) offered testimony to rebut the contention that he was insane. One expert testified that Burks (D) had a character disorder but was not mentally ill. Another acknowledged the character disorder, but gave an ambiguous answer on the question of whether Burks (D) was capable of conforming his conduct to the law. Lay witnesses also testified that Burks (D) appeared sane.

On appeal, Burks (D) claimed only that the evidence was insufficient to support his conviction. The court of appeals agreed, holding that the prosecution (P) had not effectively rebutted Burks's (D) evidence with respect to insanity and criminal responsibility. The court of appeals remanded the case to the district court for a determination of whether a new trial or a directed verdict of acquittal should be ordered.

■ ISSUE

Does retrial of a criminal defendant after reversal of his conviction for insufficient evidence violate the prohibition against double jeopardy?

■ DECISION AND RATIONALE

(Burger, C.J.) Yes. The Double Jeopardy Clause bars retrial of a defendant whose conviction was reversed on appeal due to insufficient evidence to sustain a conviction. By contrast, the prohibition against double jeopardy is not violated when a defendant is retried after a conviction is reversed because of a trial error. A reversal for trial error does not constitute a decision that the government has failed to prove its case against the defendant, and nothing is implied with respect to the guilt or innocence of the defendant. But the situation is different when a conviction is overturned due to a failure of proof at trial. The government had an opportunity to present its evidence. An appellate reversal means that the case should not even have been submitted to the jury. Given the high threshold for the granting of a motion for a judgment of acquittal, the purposes of the Double Jeopardy Clause would be negated by allowing the government a second chance to prove guilt. It does not matter that the defendant may have moved for a new trial. Moving for a new trial is not a waiver of the right to a judgment of acquittal. Reversed.

Analysis:

Reversal of a conviction on appeal is usually only a partial victory. In most cases, all the defendant has won is the "right" to be tried all over again. In the very rare event that the conviction is overturned due to a complete failure of proof, the reviewing court has, in effect, held that the case should not have been submitted to the jury in the first place. In those cases, the defendant does not have to go through the process all over again. The first trial is not a practice run.

■ CASE VOCABULARY

INSANITY DEFENSE: An affirmative defense alleging that a mental disorder caused the accused to commit the crime. Unlike other defenses, a successful insanity defense may not result in an acquittal but instead in a special verdict ("not guilty by reason of insanity") that usually leads to the defendant's commitment to a mental institution.

CHAPTER TWENTY

Sentencing Procedures

United States v. Grayson

Instant Facts: The judge who sentenced Grayson (D) for unlawful escape considered Grayson's (D) false testimony in setting his sentence.

Black Letter Rule: A judge may consider a defendant's false trial testimony when setting a sentence, as long as the sentence falls within the statutory limits.

Mitchell v. United States

Instant Facts: Mitchell (D) pleaded guilty to drug conspiracy charges and did not testify or present evidence at her sentencing hearing.

Black Letter Rule: A plea of guilty is not a waiver of the privilege against self-incrimination at sentencing, and a sentencing judge may not draw an adverse inference from a defendant's silence.

Blakely v. Washington

Instant Facts: Due to the deliberate cruelty of his crime, Blakely (D) received an exceptional sentence after he pleaded guilty to kidnapping, but he claimed that the facts necessary for such a sentence were not proven.

Black Letter Rule: A judge may not increase a sentence beyond the maximum allowed for an offense based on facts not proven at trial or admitted as a part of the guilty plea.

McCleskey v. Kemp

Instant Facts: McCleskey (D) was sentenced to death and introduced a statistical study in support of a claim that the death penalty was imposed in a racially discriminatory manner.

Black Letter Rule: In order to challenge a death sentence on the basis of racial discrimination, a defendant must show either a discriminatory purpose in his case or a discriminatory purpose in enacting or maintaining the death penalty.

Roper v. Simmons

Instant Facts: Simmons (D) was sentenced to death for a murder he committed before he turned eighteen.

Black Letter Rule: The Eighth Amendment prohibits imposing the death penalty for crimes committed by a minor.

United States v. Grayson

(*Prosecuting Authority*) v. (*Escapee*)
438 U.S. 41, 98 S. Ct. 2610, 57 L. Ed. 2d 582 (1978)

SENTENCING JUDGES MAY CONSIDER THE DEFENDANT'S FALSE TESTIMONY

I'm grounding you two weeks for sneaking out of the house, and another two weeks for lying about it.

■ INSTANT FACTS The judge who sentenced Grayson (D) for unlawful escape considered Grayson's (D) false testimony in setting his sentence.

■ BLACK LETTER RULE A judge may consider a defendant's false trial testimony when setting a sentence, as long as the sentence falls within the statutory limits.

■ PROCEDURAL BASIS

Appeal from an order of the court of appeals vacating a sentence.

■ FACTS

Grayson (D) escaped from a prison in which he was serving a sentence for distributing a controlled substance. At trial, he claimed that he escaped because another inmate threatened him. Grayson (D) called one inmate who testified that he heard an argument, but denied hearing any threats or seeing any fighting. The government (P) introduced evidence that contradicted Grayson's (D) testimony. Grayson (D) also changed his version of the facts surrounding his escape on cross-examination.

The jury returned a verdict of guilty. At sentencing, the judge told Grayson (D) that he could sentence him to five years in prison without any explanation, but he wanted to explain his reasons for imposing the sentence that he did. His reasons were, first, that he wanted to deter Grayson (D) and others from escaping from prison, and second, that he thought Grayson's (D) defense was a complete fabrication and that it did not have the slightest merit. Grayson (D) was sentenced to two years in prison, consecutive to his unexpired sentence. The court of appeals vacated the sentence and remanded for resentencing without consideration of the false testimony.

■ ISSUE

Is it permissible for a sentencing judge to consider that the defendant falsely testified?

■ DECISION AND RATIONALE

(Burger, C.J.) Yes. A judge may consider a defendant's false trial testimony when setting a sentence, as long as the sentence falls within the statutory limits. The prevailing philosophy of penology is that punishment should be tailored to the particular offender. In order to achieve that objective, it is important that the sentencing judge know as much as possible about a defendant's character and propensities. Congress has reaffirmed this practice by enacting statutes that allow a judge to consider any information about a defendant for the purpose of imposing an appropriate sentence. It is for this reason that pre-sentence investigations are prepared, to give the court pertinent information so the punishment given may be individualized. The sentencing judge may legitimately consider not only the information contained in a pre-sentence report, but also the evidence heard during the trial and the demeanor of the accused.

A defendant's truth or falsity in testifying on his or her own behalf has been deemed probative of the defendant's attitude toward society and prospects for rehabilitation, and is thus relevant to sentencing. The Sixth Circuit is the only federal circuit that has rejected consideration of false testimony in sentencing, stating that the pressures on a defendant who wishes to remain out of jail will lead even guilty defendants to protest their innocence. Although these psychological pressures are real, the foundation of the criminal justice system is that normal individuals have the ability and duty to choose between good and evil. A defendant's readiness to lie under oath is probative of his or her prospects for rehabilitation.

Grayson (D) argued that his sentence was punishment for perjury, a crime for which he was never indicted, tried, or convicted. It is impermissible for the court to use a sentence for one crime as a way to avoid the burden on the government (P) of prosecuting another crime, and it is impossible to separate this impermissible purpose from the permissible purpose of evaluating a defendant's prospects. Neither reason is sufficient justification for prohibiting the practice. It is proper, and even necessary, to consider a defendant's whole person and personality when imposing a sentence. Furthermore, the Court has long permitted consideration of a defendant's conduct at trial. No rule can be created to prevent the improper use of firsthand observations of perjury. There is also no merit to Grayson's (D) argument that allowing consideration of false testimony will have a chilling effect on a defendant's right to testify on his or her own behalf. There is no right to testify falsely. Reversed.

■ DISSENT

(Stewart, J.) There has been no determination that Grayson's (D) trial testimony was false. The majority's opinion essentially holds that, whenever a defendant testifies on his or her own behalf and is later found guilty, there is a possibility that the defendant's sentence will be enhanced. There are no safeguards to minimize a defendant's rational fears that truthful testimony will be perceived as false.

Analysis:

The sentence meted out to Grayson (D) was well within the statutory limits for the offense of escape. The trial judge noted that it would have been in his power to give Grayson (D) a sentence more than twice as long. In many jurisdictions, including the federal system, sentencing guidelines limit the discretion of the judge when imposing a sentence. Sentencing guidelines typically consider only two factors: the offense committed and the criminal history of the defendant. The limitation of a judge's discretion is meant to promote uniformity in sentencing and to eliminate racial, social, or economic disparities in sentences handed down for the same crime.

■ CASE VOCABULARY

SENTENCING GUIDELINES: A set of standards for determining the punishment that a convicted criminal should receive, based on the nature of the crime and the offender's criminal history. The federal government and several states have adopted sentencing guidelines in an effort to make judicial sentencing more consistent.

Mitchell v. United States

(*Convicted Conspirator*) v. (*Prosecuting Authority*)
526 U.S. 314, 119 S. Ct. 1307, 143 L. Ed. 2d 424 (1999)

A GUILTY PLEA IS NOT A FIFTH-AMENDMENT WAIVER

■ **INSTANT FACTS** Mitchell (D) pleaded guilty to drug conspiracy charges and did not testify or present evidence at her sentencing hearing.

■ **BLACK LETTER RULE** A plea of guilty is not a waiver of the privilege against self-incrimination at sentencing, and a sentencing judge may not draw an adverse inference from a defendant's silence.

■ PROCEDURAL BASIS

Appeal from an order of the court of appeals affirming a sentence.

■ FACTS

Mitchell (D) was charged with conspiring to distribute five or more kilograms of cocaine and with three counts of distributing cocaine within 1,000 feet of a school or playground. She pleaded guilty to all four counts but reserved the right to contest the amount of cocaine attributable to her under the conspiracy count. Before the court accepted her plea, the judge told Mitchell (D) that the exact sentence imposed on her would depend on the amount of cocaine she distributed. Mitchell (D) was placed under oath and asked if she had committed the offenses with which she was charged. She replied that she had done "[s]ome of that," and stated that, although she was present for one of the transactions, she was not the one who delivered the cocaine to the purchaser. When Mitchell (D) was told that she would still be liable as an aider and abettor, she reaffirmed her intention to plead guilty.

Nine codefendants, who had been indicted along with Mitchell (D), went to trial. One of them testified that Mitchell (D) was a regular seller of drugs for the leader of the conspiracy. At Mitchell's (D) sentencing, one of the codefendants provided additional information regarding the amount of drugs sold by Mitchell (D), but conceded on cross-examination that he had not seen Mitchell (D) regularly during that time. Mitchell (D) did not testify at her sentencing hearing and offered no evidence. Her attorney made an argument regarding the reliability of the evidence presented. The court sentenced Mitchell (D) to ten years in prison and six years of supervised release. The judge told her that one of the factors that influenced his decision was the fact that Mitchell (D) did not testify at the sentencing hearing, and that he held against her the fact that she did not come forward and say that she only sold drugs "a couple of times."

■ ISSUE

Does a defendant waive her Fifth Amendment protection against self-incrimination at the sentencing hearing by pleading guilty?

■ DECISION AND RATIONALE

(Kennedy, J.) No. A plea of guilty is not a waiver of the privilege against self-incrimination at sentencing, and a sentencing judge may not draw an adverse inference from a defendant's silence. If Mitchell (D) had pleaded not guilty and testified at her own trial, her testimony would have operated as a complete waiver of her Fifth Amendment privilege. A witness may not pick and choose the testimony he or she will offer. The concerns that justify this rule when a defendant has pleaded not guilty are not present at a plea colloquy, however. The purpose of the plea colloquy is to make sure that a defendant is not entering an unintelligent or involuntary plea. There is no reason why such a narrow inquiry should entail an extensive waiver of the privilege. The defendant who pleads guilty does not put the essentials of the offense in dispute, but instead takes those essentials out of dispute. The Federal Rules of Criminal Procedure do not contemplate such a broad waiver. The court is allowed to make an inquiry of the defendant on a plea of guilty, but there is little danger that the court will be misled by a defendant's selective disclosure. A defendant who withholds information at a plea colloquy runs the risk that the court will find the factual basis for the guilty plea inadequate.

Treating the plea as a waiver of privilege would encroach on the rights of defendants. The government (P) stated, at oral argument in this case, that a defendant's plea of guilty could be used as a way to prove unknown facts in an indictment, such as, in this case, the amount of drugs sold. If the government's (P) position were accepted, prosecutors could indict without specifying the quantity of drugs involved, obtain a guilty plea, and then require the defendant to testify at sentencing to fill in the blank. Such a practice would enlist the defendant as an instrument of his or her own condemnation.

The protection against self-incrimination is not extinguished by a guilty plea. When the sentence has not yet been imposed, incrimination is not complete. There is no further possibility of incrimination until there are no more adverse consequences that can happen due to a defendant's testimony. And the normal rule is that negative inferences may not be drawn from a defendant's failure to testify. The Court will not adopt an exception for the sentencing phase of a prosecution. Although such adverse inferences are permissible in civil actions, sentencing is not a civil action. The concerns that mandate the rule against negative inferences from a failure to testify at trial apply with equal force at sentencing. The rule against negative inferences is a reminder that the question in a criminal case is not whether the defendant committed the acts of which he or she is accused, but whether the government can prove its allegations while respecting the rights of the defendant. Reversed.

■ DISSENT

(Scalia, J.) Mitchell (D) had the right to remain silent at her sentencing hearing. The court should be free to draw adverse inferences from her failure to testify, however. Adverse inferences are not the same as compelling testimony. Although the cases that prohibit such an inference should not be overruled, they lack support in logic and history and should not be extended into other areas. It is normal to draw negative inferences when a person is asked a question and fails to give an answer. In addition, historically, the maxim *nemo tenetur seipsum prodere* (no one is bound to proceed against himself) was thought to apply only to testimony compelled by compulsory oath or physical torture. Defendants were expected to testify directly to juries throughout the seventeenth and eighteenth centuries, and there is no indication that the drafters of the U.S. Constitution intended a change in criminal procedure when they ratified the Fifth Amendment. Defendants continued to speak directly in court until representation by counsel became more common. The issue of negative inferences did not arise until states began enacting statutes that allowed defendants to testify on their own behalves. There is no reason to believe that a negative inference was considered the type of compulsion that the Fifth Amendment was intended to prohibit. And the case of *Griffin v. California,* 380 U.S. 609 (1965), was not rooted in the Fifth Amendment, but instead was based on a statutory mandate.

There is a longstanding dichotomy between the trial phase of a prosecution and the sentencing phase. Various trial rights are inapplicable at sentencing, and consistency points to a conclusion that negative inferences should be allowed, just as they are in other types of proceedings. The rule announced by the majority goes against the notion that a sentencing judge should be allowed to use whatever information is available in order to craft an appropriate sentence.

■ DISSENT

(Thomas, J.) *Griffin v. California,* 380 U.S. 609 (1965), lacks foundation in the Constitution's text, history, and logic. That case, and its progeny, should be re-examined.

Analysis:

The range of discretion given to the sentencing judge in Mitchell's (D) case was considerable. Mitchell (D) could have received as little as one year in prison, as opposed to the ten-year maximum sentence she received. It is perhaps only natural, as Justice Scalia points out, to draw negative inferences from silence, but it seems as though the sentencing judge drew the worst possible inferences in this case.

■ CASE VOCABULARY

COLLOQUY: Any formal discussion, such as an oral exchange between a judge, the prosecutor, the defense counsel, and a criminal defendant in which the judge ascertains the defendant's understanding of the proceedings and of the defendant's rights.

Blakely v. Washington

(*Kidnapper*) v. (*Prosecuting Authority*)
542 U.S. 296, 124 S. Ct. 2531, 159 L. Ed. 2d 403 (2004)

FACTS THAT INCREASE A SENTENCE BEYOND THE MAXIMUM MUST BE PROVEN BEYOND A REASONABLE DOUBT

■ **INSTANT FACTS** Due to the deliberate cruelty of his crime, Blakely (D) received an exceptional sentence after he pleaded guilty to kidnapping, but he claimed that the facts necessary for such a sentence were not proven.

■ **BLACK LETTER RULE** A judge may not increase a sentence beyond the maximum allowed for an offense based on facts not proven at trial or admitted as a part of the guilty plea.

■ PROCEDURAL BASIS

Appeal from an order of the Washington Court of Appeals affirming a sentence.

■ FACTS

Blakely (D) was charged with first-degree kidnapping for abducting his estranged wife. He pleaded guilty to second-degree kidnapping involving domestic violence and use of a firearm. His plea admitted only the kidnapping, domestic violence, and firearm violations, but nothing else. Second-degree kidnapping was a class B felony with a maximum penalty of ten years in prison, but the law limited the penalty for Blakely's (D) offense to a sentence in the range of forty-nine to fifty-three months. Any departure from that sentence had to be justified by substantial and compelling reasons, and a judge who imposed such an exceptional sentence was required to set forth findings of fact and conclusions of law in support of the sentence. The judge sentenced Blakely (D) to ninety months in prison. He made findings that Blakely (D) had acted with deliberate cruelty when he abducted his wife, which was one of the factors listed as justifying a departure. Blakely (D) objected, claiming that the sentencing violated his right to have all of the facts legally essential to his sentence determined by a jury beyond a reasonable doubt.

■ ISSUE

Did Blakely's (D) sentencing violate his right to a trial by jury?

■ DECISION AND RATIONALE

(Scalia, J.) Yes. A judge may not increase a sentence beyond the maximum allowed for an offense based on facts not proven at trial or admitted as a part of the guilty plea. This case involves application of the rule of *Apprendi v. New Jersey,* 530 U.S. 466 (2000), which provides that any fact that increases the penalty for a crime, other than the fact of a prior conviction, must be submitted to a jury and proved beyond a reasonable doubt. Here, the fact that Blakely (D) acted with deliberate cruelty was neither admitted by Blakely (D) nor found by a jury. Although the state (P) claims that *Apprendi* was not violated because the statutory maximum sentence was ten years, the actual maximum sentence to be considered is the one that the judge could have imposed without any additional findings of fact. When a judge inflicts a punishment not allowed by the jury's verdict alone, the jury has not found all of the facts necessary for the punishment.

Apprendi sets out a rule that gives credence to the right of trial by jury. The authority of a judge to impose a sentence derives entirely from a jury's verdict. Without that restriction, the jury would not have the control intended by the framers of the Constitution. Rejection of *Apprendi* leaves open two possibilities. One is that juries will be left to find only that a defendant committed some offense, and that the elements of that offense will be labeled sentencing factors to be found by the judge. This alternative clearly would be unconstitutional. The other alternative is that legislatures may establish sentencing factors within limits. Such a procedure would leave too much discretion with the sentencing judge.

Determinate sentencing is not unconstitutional. The issue before the Court is the manner in which determinate sentencing works in practice. Determinate sentencing schemes are unconstitutional only if they infringe upon the role of the jury. The Sixth Amendment is not a limitation on judicial power, but a reservation of the jury's power. Indeterminate sentencing, in which a judge has great discretion in setting a sentence, is not unconstitutional, because the facts found by a judge to support a sentence have no bearing on whether the defendant is entitled to a lesser sentence. The traditional function of a jury of finding facts necessary to punishment is not limited.

Defendants are free to waive their *Apprendi* rights and argue sentencing factors to a judge. Similarly, if the defendant so stipulates, the state is free to argue for an increased sentence if a defendant who pleads guilty either stipulates to judicial fact-finding or stipulates to the relevant facts. *Apprendi* also does not limit the right of defendants to plea bargain over relevant sentencing factors. If there is any difference between bargaining over sentencing factors and bargaining over elements of an offense, bargaining over the elements of an offense probably favors the defendant. Evaluation of the fairness of *Apprendi* must be viewed in light of the regime it replaced, in which a defendant's sentence could be increased with no warning in either the indictment or the plea. It does not matter that *Apprendi* may encourage plea-bargaining. Even if that were true, the Sixth Amendment guarantees the right to a jury trial, but does not say that the right may not be waived.

The decision in this case does not depend on the efficiency or fairness of the criminal justice system. Many countries dispense with juries and have facts found by professionals. But that is not the system envisioned by the drafters of the Constitution. Reversed and remanded.

■ DISSENT

(O'Connor, J.) The decision in this case casts doubt over all determinate sentencing laws, both state and federal. Unguided discretion in sentencing led to severe disparities in sentences received and served by defendants committing the same offense and having the same criminal history. Determinate sentencing was enacted to correct those disparities. The change to determinate sentencing served principles of due process and the right to a jury trial. Criminal defendants were better able to predict the real consequences of their actions. Equal protection considerations have also been served, as the racial disparities in sentencing have also been reduced. Applying *Apprendi* to this case imposes significant costs on a legislature's determination that a particular fact, not historically an element, merits a higher sentence. Some facts relevant to sentencing—such as the character of the accused—may not be presented to the jury. Other facts may not be known until sentencing.

The Washington Sentencing Reform Act did not alter the ten-year maximum to which Blakely (D) was exposed. The majority's opinion seems like doctrinaire formalism. A few state decisions and an old criminal procedure treatise have little relevance in determining the original intent of the drafters of the Constitution.

■ DISSENT

(Kennedy, J.) The majority ignores the fundamental principle that different branches of the government must converse with one another on matters of vital common interest. Sentencing guidelines were a prime example of this process. Legislatures acted to respond to problems of disparities in criminal sentencing by enacting measures to correct the problems. The majority's mistrust of judges leads to a shutdown of a legislatively created scheme that arose from alternate nonjudicial sources of ideas and experience.

■ DISSENT

(Breyer, J.) The majority ignores the probable consequences of its decision. Sentencing must now take one of three forms. One is a purely determinate scheme, in which all defendants convicted of a certain charge receive the same sentence. Different cases would not be treated differently. The second option is indeterminate sentencing, in which sentences are left to the discretion of the judge or parole board. Sentences would produce unfair disparities, including race-based differences. The third option would be a scheme that would allow judges to depart downward from a presumptive sentence upon a finding of mitigating factors, but could not depart upward unless aggravating factors were charged and proved beyond a reasonable doubt.

The third option would be implemented in one of two ways. The legislature could subdivide each crime into a list of complex offenses, each of which would be defined to include sentencing factors. Such a system would be merely a form of the "pure charge" system and have all the deficiencies of that system. The other method would be to have two juries, one to determine guilt and one to determine disputed facts that would aggravate the sentence. That type of system would be costly, in terms of both time and resources.

Legislatures could simply write laws that impose lengthy sentences for all crime, and then include a long list of mitigating factors. These factors would mostly be an absence of aggravating factors. The political impediments to such a rewrite of the criminal laws would be great, however, and it is difficult to see why the Sixth Amendment would require it.

The historical analysis relied upon by the majority does not support the conclusion it reaches. Judges have historically had the discretion to impose a sentence that fell within a range. Determinate sentencing seeks only to limit that discretion. The majority also overlooks considerations of legislative authority to make a fact a sentencing factor or an element of the offense. The fairness and effectiveness of the sentencing system require that the legislature be allowed to make that determination.

Analysis:

Determinate sentencing schemes typically set out a non-exclusive list of factors to be considered both to mitigate and to increase a sentence. Lists of impermissible factors—such as race, economic status, and whether a defendant pleaded guilty or went to trial—also were set out. Courts often seemed confused about the distinction between an element of an uncharged offense and an aggravating factor. For example, a common aggravating factor was the "age and vulnerability" of the victim. In a prosecution for a crime against a child that could have been charged as a form of child abuse, was the age of the victim a legitimate aggravating factor, or an element of the offense?

■ CASE VOCABULARY

DETERMINATE SENTENCE: A sentence for a fixed length of time rather than for an unspecified duration.

INDETERMINATE SENTENCING: The practice of not imposing a definite term of confinement, but instead prescribing a range for the minimum and maximum term, leaving the precise term to be fixed in some other way, usually based on the prisoner's conduct and apparent rehabilitation while incarcerated.

McCleskey v. Kemp

(*Death Sentence Recipient*) v. (*Prison Superintendent*)

481 U.S. 279, 107 S. Ct. 1756, 95 L. Ed. 2d 262 (1987)

STATISTICAL STUDIES DO NOT DEMONSTRATE RACE–BASED DEATH SENTENCING

■ **INSTANT FACTS** McCleskey (D) was sentenced to death and introduced a statistical study in support of a claim that the death penalty was imposed in a racially discriminatory manner.

■ **BLACK LETTER RULE** In order to challenge a death sentence on the basis of racial discrimination, a defendant must show either a discriminatory purpose in his case or a discriminatory purpose in enacting or maintaining the death penalty.

■ PROCEDURAL BASIS

Appeal from an order of the court of appeals affirming denial of a petition for habeas corpus.

■ FACTS

McCleskey (D), who was African American, was convicted in Georgia of murder for killing a police officer during an armed robbery. The police officer was white. The jury found the existence of two aggravating factors beyond a reasonable doubt: the murder was committed during an armed robbery, and the victim was a peace officer engaged in the performance of official duties. The jury recommended the death penalty, and McCleskey (D) was sentenced to death.

McCleskey (D) then brought a petition for a writ of habeas corpus. One of his claims was that the Georgia death sentencing law was administered in a racially discriminatory manner, in violation of the Eighth and Fourteenth Amendments. In support of his claim, McCleskey (D) introduced a statistical study that showed racial discrepancies in the imposition of death sentences. The study concluded that defendants who killed white victims were 4.3 times more likely to receive the death penalty than defendants who killed African American victims. The study also concluded that African Americans were 1.1 times as likely to receive the death penalty as other defendants. The study thus concluded that African American defendants who killed white victims had the greatest likelihood of being sentenced to death. The district court denied relief, finding that the methodology of the study was flawed. The court of appeals assumed that the study was valid but denied relief, stating that McCleskey (D) had not shown discriminatory intent or that the sentence he received was irrational, arbitrary, or capricious.

■ ISSUE

Did the statistical evidence show that the imposition of the death sentence results in unconstitutional racial disparities?

■ DECISION AND RATIONALE

(Powell, J.) No. In order to challenge a death sentence on the basis of racial discrimination, a defendant must show either a discriminatory purpose in his case or a discriminatory purpose in enacting or maintaining the death penalty. McCleskey (D) did not show proof of a racial motive in his case. His petition asked the court to infer from the statistics that there was a racial motive in his sentencing. However, each jury that imposes a death sentence is unique and deals with a unique set of circumstances. Statistical evidence has been allowed in other types of racial discrimination cases, such as challenges to a jury venire panel and employment discrimination claims. Those types of cases, however, typically relate to fewer entities, and there are fewer variables relevant to the challenged decision. In addition, in venire selection and employment discrimination cases, the decision maker has an opportunity to explain the challenged decision. In this case, the state (P) has no practical opportunity to rebut the statistical study, even though here there is an unchallenged explanation for the imposition of the sentence, namely, McCleskey's (D) conviction of a crime for which the death penalty may be imposed. Finally, McCleskey's (D) claim strikes at the heart of the criminal justice system. Implementation of the criminal law necessitates discretionary judgments. The unique nature of the decisions made in this case means that statistical studies cannot support an inference of discrimination.

In order for McCleskey (D) to prevail on his claim that the Georgia death penalty statute constitutes racial discrimination, he must show that the statute was enacted or maintained because of an anticipated racially discriminatory effect. In the case of *Gregg v. Georgia,* 428 U.S. 153 (1976), the Court found that the Georgia death penalty statute could operate in a fair and neutral manner. There was no evidence then of a discriminatory motive in enacting the statute, and no such evidence has been shown in this case. There is also no evidence that the statute is maintained because of a discriminatory effect.

The statistical study does not show an Eighth Amendment violation. There is a constitutionally permissible range of discretion in imposing the death penalty. The state must establish rational criteria that narrow the decision maker's judgment as to whether the circumstances of a particular defendant's case meet the minimum threshold for the application of the death penalty. The state must also allow the consideration of any relevant circumstance that could lead to the penalty not being imposed. McCleskey (D) does not argue that his sentence was disproportionate to the crime he committed. Instead, he argues that his sentence is disproportionate to the sentences imposed in other murder cases. McCleskey's (D) claim must fail. His sentence has been found to be not disproportionate to other death sentences imposed in Georgia. Furthermore, unless he can make a claim that the Georgia capital punishment system operates in an arbitrary and capricious manner, McCleskey (D) cannot show a constitutional violation by showing that other similarly situated defendants did not receive the death penalty.

McCleskey (D) makes the argument that the Georgia capital punishment system is arbitrary and capricious because racial considerations may influence capital sentencing considerations. The statistical evidence does not support his claim. At most, the study shows that racial factors may have entered into some decisions. There are risks that racial prejudice, as well as other kinds of prejudice, may influence criminal trials. The question is when that risk becomes constitutionally unacceptable. Having a jury that is representative of a defendant's community assures a diffused impartiality, so that the jury can express the community's conscience on the ultimate question of life and death.

The discretion afforded to a jury in capital cases is not unconstitutional. Discretion offers substantial benefits to a defendant. Juries may decline to convict, may convict of a lesser charge, or may decline to impose the death penalty. Such exercises of leniency are not reviewable on appeal. Apparent disparities in sentencing are an inevitable part of the criminal justice system. Discrepancies, even those that appear to correlate with race, are a far cry from major systematic defects. There can be no perfect procedure, and constitutional guarantees are met when the system has been surrounded by safeguards to make it as fair as possible.

McCleskey's (D) claim, if taken to its logical conclusion, throws into serious question the principles that underlie the entire criminal justice system. If the Court accepted the claim that racial bias had impermissibly tainted capital sentencing decisions, all other criminal sentences would be in doubt. Other types of prejudice or discrimination could be raised to challenge sentences. In addition, McCleskey's (D) claim is one that is best addressed by the legislature. It is not the place of the Court to determine the appropriate penalty for crimes. The function of the courts is to decide individual cases. In McCleskey's (D) case, the law was properly applied. Affirmed.

■ DISSENT

(Brennan, J.) The death penalty is a *per se* violation of the Eighth Amendment prohibition against cruel and unusual punishment. Even if it were not, McCleskey (D) has demonstrated that his sentence was unconstitutional. The risk of the imposition of an arbitrary sentence is the crucial question. The emphasis on risk acknowledges the difficulty in divining a jury's motivation in a particular case. The statistical evidence documents the risk that McCleskey's (D) sentence was influenced by racial considerations. There was a better than even chance in Georgia that race would influence the decision to impose the death penalty. The conclusion suggested by the numbers is also consonant with an understanding of history and human experience. Georgia has had a history of racial discrimination in its criminal justice system. It is unrealistic to ignore the influence of that history in assessing the plausible implications of McCleskey's (D) evidence. The Georgia capital sentencing system grants great discretion to prosecutors and jurors and creates many opportunities for racial considerations to influence the proceedings.

The majority cites four reasons for not accepting McCleskey's (D) challenge: the desirability for discretion in the criminal justice system, the existence of statutory safeguards, the consequences for broader challenges to sentencing, and the limits of the judicial role. Discretion, however, is a means to an end, not an end in itself. *Gregg v. Georgia* only assumed that the statutory safeguards were sufficient. That case did not bestow permanent approval on the Georgia system. The prospect of broader challenges to sentencing may be dismaying, but does not justify complete abdication of the judicial role. Recognizing the possibility of further challenges is nothing more than a recognition that the system is imperfect. Race is a factor that has been recognized as unconstitutional, based not only on statistics, but on history and experience. Finally, the judiciary must be able to exercise close scrutiny over the government's power to extinguish life.

■ DISSENT

(Blackmun, J.) The majority recognizes the complexity of McCleskey's (D) claim, but then proceeds to ignore a significant element of that claim. If McCleskey's (D) claim is considered in its entirety, it fits within the framework of other racial discrimination cases. Under the rules established in other cases, McCleskey (D) must show that he is a member of a group that is singled out for different treatment. He must show a substantial degree of different treatment. Finally, he must establish that the allegedly discriminatory procedure is susceptible to abuse or is not racially neutral. McCleskey (D) has introduced evidence showing that African Americans in Georgia are singled out for different treatment. McCleskey (D) also produced evidence showing the role of racial factors at the various stages of the process and that the race of the victim was an especially significant factor in a prosecutor's decision to pursue a death sentence. He also introduced evidence to demonstrate the potential for abuse in the decision to pursue the death penalty. Individual prosecutors were given complete discretion as to when they would seek the death penalty. The evidence gives rise to an inference of a discriminatory purpose.

The majority's reasons for not applying these factors are not persuasive. There are not fewer variables or decisionmakers at work in employment or venire discrimination cases. It is not the jury that must explain its actions, but instead it is the prosecutor who should explain the decisions that led to the request for the death penalty. The fact that granting McCleskey (D) relief could lead to additional challenges to sentences is no reason to deny relief. Acceptance of McCleskey's (D) claim will not eliminate capital punishment in Georgia, but will narrow the range of defendants eligible for the death penalty.

Analysis:

The majority seems to foreclose any possibility that statistical evidence of racial disparities could ever defeat a death sentence. The statistical study relied upon by McCleskey (D) showed only that an African American who murdered a white person was more likely to receive the death penalty than a white person who killed an African American, or a murderer who was of the same race as the victim. The study thus considered only the penalty, and not whether white defendants were charged with capital crimes for comparable offenses.

■ CASE VOCABULARY

VENIRE: A panel of persons selected for jury duty and from among whom the jurors are to be chosen.

Roper v. Simmons

(*Prison Superintendent*) v. (*Juvenile Murderer*)
543 U.S. 551, 125 S. Ct. 1183, 161 L. Ed. 2d 1 (2005)

THERE IS NO DEATH PENALTY FOR JUVENILES

■ **INSTANT FACTS** Simmons (D) was sentenced to death for a murder he committed before he turned eighteen.

■ **BLACK LETTER RULE** The Eighth Amendment prohibits imposing the death penalty for crimes committed by a minor.

■ PROCEDURAL BASIS

Appeal from an order of the Missouri Supreme Court that set aside Simmons's (D) death sentence.

■ FACTS

Simmons (D) was convicted of a murder he committed while he was seventeen years old. He confessed to committing the murder, and there was evidence that he planned the killing and that he later bragged about it. Simmons (D) urged two friends to assist him, saying that they could "get away with it" because they were minors. Simmons (D) was tried as an adult and sentenced to death. Simmons (D) filed a petition for postconviction relief, based on the reasoning of *Atkins v. Virginia,* 536 U.S. 304 (2002), which barred the execution of mentally retarded defendants. The Missouri Supreme Court agreed with Simmons's (D) reasoning and set aside his death sentence.

■ ISSUE

Is the execution of juveniles unconstitutional?

■ DECISION AND RATIONALE

(Kennedy, J.) Yes. The Eighth Amendment prohibits imposing the death penalty for crimes committed by a minor. Implementation of the prohibition against cruel and unusual punishment looks to the necessity of referring to the evolving standards of decency that mark the progress of a maturing society. Those evolving standards will determine which punishments are so disproportionate as to be cruel and unusual. In *Thompson v. Oklahoma,* 487 U.S. 815 (1988), the Court determined that those evolving standards prohibited the execution of an offender who was under sixteen at the time of the crime. The Court noted that no state that set a minimum age for executions had set it at an age lower than sixteen, and that respected professional organizations, the other countries that share the Anglo–American legal heritage, and leading members of the western European community all agreed that executing such young offenders offended civilized standards of decency. The Court also noted that the last execution of an offender under sixteen had been carried out in 1948.

The next year, in two separate decisions handed down on the same day, the Court held that contemporary standards of decency did not prohibit the execution of juvenile offenders over fifteen but under eighteen, or the execution of mentally retarded offenders. There was no national consensus that either punishment was cruel and unusual. Since those decisions, a consensus has developed that the execution of mentally retarded offenders was cruel and unusual. The Court reconsidered the acceptability of executing the mentally retarded and held that the practice was unconstitutional.

The evidence for a national consensus regarding the death penalty for juveniles is similar. Thirty states prohibit the death penalty for juveniles, including the twelve states that have abandoned the death penalty altogether. The practice is infrequent even in the states where such executions are allowed. Although the pace of the change has been slow, it has been consistent. No state that previously prohibited the execution of juveniles has changed its law to allow juvenile executions. When the United States ratified the International Covenant on Civil and Political Rights, it did so subject to a reservation of the clause prohibiting the execution of juveniles, but that does not show a national consensus in favor of juvenile executions. Since the reservation was passed, five states outlawed the execution of juveniles. In addition, when Congress enacted the Federal Death Penalty Act, 18 U.S.C. § 3591, it declined to extend the death penalty to juveniles.

The death penalty is reserved for a narrow range of offenses and offenders. There are three general differences between juveniles under eighteen and adults that require that juveniles not be classified among the worst offenders. First, juveniles more often have a lack of maturity and an underdeveloped sense of responsibility that can lead to reckless, ill-considered behavior. Second, juveniles are more susceptible to negative influences and outside pressures, including peer pressure. The third difference is that the character of a juvenile is not as well formed as that of an adult, but is more transitory. These differences render suspect any conclusion that a juvenile falls within the category of the worst offenders. The penological justifications for the death penalty apply with lesser force to juveniles than to adults. Retribution is not served for offenders of lesser culpability, such as juveniles, and the deterrent effect of the death penalty on juveniles is questionable.

There are juveniles who commit particularly heinous crimes, and there may be juveniles who demonstrate sufficient emotional maturity to merit a sentence of death. But the differences between juveniles and adults are too marked and well-understood to risk allowing a young person of insufficient culpability to receive the death penalty. It is difficult enough for expert psychologists to differentiate between immaturity and irreparable corruption. Juries should not be asked to make such a decision. Drawing the line for executions at eighteen is subject to the objections raised by all categorical rules. There are immature adults, and mature juveniles. Nevertheless, eighteen is the age at which society draws the line between childhood and adulthood, and that is where the line will be drawn in this case.

The decision that the death penalty is disproportionate for offenders under eighteen finds confirmation in the fact that the United States is the only country in the world that allows the execution of juveniles. Although that fact is not controlling, it does inform the decision on whether the death penalty for juveniles is "cruel and unusual." Only seven countries other than the United States have executed juvenile offenders since 1990, and since then, each of those countries has either abolished capital punishment for juveniles or has publicly disavowed the practice. It is proper to acknowledge the overwhelming weight of world opinion against the death penalty for juveniles. Affirmed.

■ CONCURRENCE

(Stevens, J.) The importance of the majority's decision is in the Court's reaffirmation of the principles of the Eighth Amendment. If the meaning of the Amendment had become frozen when it was adopted, there would be no impediment to the execution of seven-year olds. The pace of the evolution of the Amendment may be open to debate, but the understanding that the Constitution will evolve has long been settled.

■ DISSENT

(O'Connor, J.) The Court must determine for itself whether a penalty comports with contemporary standards of decency. The most reliable indicator of contemporary values is the action of the state legislatures. Although legislatures have moved away from allowing the imposition of the death penalty on juveniles, the halting pace of the change gives reason for pause. Such evidence of legislative intent cannot be dispositive, but is entitled to independent weight. The decisive inquiry is the proportionality of the sentence. There is no evidence that the death penalty is always disproportionate for young offenders. The fact that juvenile offenders generally are less culpable than adult offenders does not necessarily mean that they are never as culpable. An especially depraved juvenile offender may be just as culpable as an adult. Similarly, the fact that the death penalty may be less likely to deter a juvenile does not mean that it cannot deter some juveniles. The majority relies on difference in the aggregate between juveniles and adults, which frequently are not true when individuals are compared.

The analogy between mentally retarded offenders and juvenile offenders is flawed. A mentally retarded offender is so highly unlikely to be culpable enough to merit the death penalty, or is so highly unlikely to be deterred, that execution is not a defensible punishment. Juveniles have no such inherent limitation. The proportionality concerns raised by the majority implicate Eighth Amendment concerns. Those concerns should not be addressed by an arbitrary, age-based rule. There is no showing that individual juries are unable to weigh the mitigating circumstances of a juvenile or to evaluate an offender's maturity.

There is no clear national consensus that juvenile offenders should not be subject to execution. The Court should not substitute its own subjective judgment for that of the state legislatures.

■ DISSENT

(Scalia, J.) The meaning of the Eighth Amendment should not be determined by the subjective views of five members of the Court and like-minded foreigners. Previous cases have required a showing of an overwhelming opposition to a challenged practice, generally over a long period of time. The infrequency of executions of those under eighteen is explained both by the smaller percentage of capital crimes committed by those under eighteen and by the fact that juries must consider an offender's young age as a mitigating factor.

If the Eighth Amendment is an ever-changing reflection of evolving standards of decency, it is inappropriate for the Court to prescribe those standards. Instead, those standards should be considered as they are reflected in the judgments of the legislature. The facts and studies relied upon by the majority are flawed and have been contradicted. Courts are ill equipped to determine which science is correct; that judgment should be left to the legislatures. The evidence cited by the majority shows, at best, that most persons under eighteen are unable to take moral responsibility for their actions. It does not show that all are incapable. The criminal justice system provides for individualized consideration of each defendant. In other contexts, such as obtaining an abortion without parental consent, the Court has recognized that at least some minors will be mature enough to make difficult decisions that involve moral considerations. It is hard to see why this context should be different. Deciding whether to have an abortion is surely a more complex decision than whether to kill an innocent person in cold blood. The death penalty is not always disproportionate for juveniles, and there is no evidence that the death penalty will not deter teenage offenders. The facts of this case show the latter proposition to be false.

Although the views of U.S. citizens are irrelevant to the majority, the views of other countries and the so-called international community take center stage. The failure of the Senate and President to sign and ratify a treaty prohibiting the execution of juveniles can only suggest that the United States has not reached a national consensus. The premise that American law should conform to the laws of the rest of the world should be rejected out of hand. Many rules of U.S. law—both those found explicitly in the Constitution and those that are interpretations of the Constitution—are unique to America. It is particularly indefensible to look at the laws of the United Kingdom, which have developed since the American Revolution into a system quite different from our own. To invoke alien law only when it agrees with one's own thinking, and ignore it otherwise, is sophistry. Foreign sources are cited by the majority not to underscore the centrality of our rights and freedoms, but to set aside a long-standing legal practice. Acknowledgment of foreign approval has no place in the legal opinion of this Court unless it is a part of the basis of the Court's judgment.

Analysis:

Justice Stevens's concurrence seems to chide Justice Scalia for his adherence to what he believes to be the original intent of the drafters of the Constitution. For his part, Justice Scalia disapproves—strongly and unambiguously—of the majority's citation of foreign law as persuasive authority. The tones of the different opinions in this case clearly suggest that there is more at play here than this one case, or even more than a disagreement on the proper interpretation of the Constitution.
